Colkitto

Colkitto!

A CELEBRATION OF
CLAN DONALD
OF
COLONSAY
(1570–1647)

KEVIN BYRNE

First published 1997 by
House of Lochar
Isle of Colonsay
Argyll PA61 7YR

ISBN 1 899863 19 2

Typeset by XL Publishing Services, Lurley, Tiverton
Printed in Great Britain
by SRP, Exeter
for House of Lochar
Isle of Colonsay, Argyll PA61 7YR

PREFACE

This book has been written with a somewhat specialised readership in mind, which may be broadly divided into two categories.

The first category consists of people who live, work or travel in the area which was once the territory of Clan Donald of the South, or who have roots in the area, people who will have detailed knowledge of certain events and locations but will be interested in other traditions as well. For their convenience I have tried to include some general historical background in order to keep the more local detail in context, and it is for their interest that I have identified minor sites of historic interest. I hope that yachtsmen and ramblers will enjoy references to places that they know well.

The second category of people addressed is somewhat wider, and includes those who have a specific interest in *Colla Ciotach* himself, or in the events with which he and his family were associated. We all know that a number of stories have been put about over the years which discredit Coll and his family – examples include the "piracy" episode of 1615, when Coll is said to have behaved "aimlessly"; the alleged "betrayal" of MacDuffie later in that year; the supposed "murder" of MacDuffie a few years later; and in the case of *Alasdair*, his "betrayal" of Montrose, his incontinent "flight" before Leslie, his "abandonment" of his troops in Kintyre. All these allegations are based on real events, but any sort of review of contemporary sources shows that the facts of the case were open to interpretation; it is because they have been so universally interpreted to the discomfiture of the Highlanders that it has seemed worthwhile to return to the contemporary sources, whether in the text or in the appendices.

Kevin Byrne, March 1997

CONTENTS

List of Maps and Genealogical Tables 8

1. THE ORIGINS OF CLAN DONALD OF COLONSAY 11
   Colla Ciotach; Clann Iain Mhóir; Threats to Clann Iain Mhóir; Dunivaig and the Glens

2. HEBRIDEAN STRUGGLES 21
   Clan Donald of Colonsay; MacDonalds and MacLeans; MacLean raids on Colonsay; Strategic importance of Colonsay; Cattle Raid at Inbhir Cnoc Bhreach; The Feast at Mulindry

3. THE GROWTH OF ROYAL AUTHORITY 33
   The Forfeiture of Angus of Dunivaig; The Fire at Askomel; The Battle of Traigh Ghruineart; The Submission of Dunivaig;

4. FAMILY LIFE IN COLONSAY 44
   Colla Ciotach's Marriage; Colla Ciotach's Children; Social, Domestic and Agricultural Conditions

5. RANALD OG'S RISING – 1614 55
   The Rising at Dunivaig; Ranald Og Ejected; George Graham's Intrigue; The Bombardment and Surrender of Dunivaig

6. A TOUR OF THE HEBRIDES 65
   Colla Ciotach's Escape to Ireland; The Irish Dimension; Robert Williamson's Testimony; Sir Rory McLeod's version; Colla Ciotach in St. Kilda; Sir James MacDonald breaks ward

7. SIR JAMES MACDONALD'S RISING – 1615 77
   Interlude in Colonsay; Dunivaig Seized Again; Sir James Pledges his Fealty; Argyll's military campaign; Colla Ciotach's treaty with Argyll

8. THE WIDER WORLD 89
   A brief resume of the context of these events

9. *COLLA CIOTACH'S* FEUD WITH MACDUFFIE 95
   The aftermath of 1615; MacDonald tenure of Colonsay; Malcolm MacDuffie's return from Edinburgh; Death of Malcolm MacDuffie

10. COLONSAY YEARS 102
    Colla Ciotach and his neighbours; The Fiar's term in Islay (1626-39); The Counter-Reformation; The Franciscan Mission (1619-1629); Coll's Tenancy under Threat

11. THE PRELUDE TO WAR 115
The National Covenant; Antrim to the aid of his King; Colonsay laid waste; Irish Rebellion 1641; The Portnaw Massacre; Alasdair's Ulster campaign; "Black Friday"; Argyll's Intervention; Alasdair's treaty with Leven

12. ANTRIM MOVES AGAINST THE REBELS 132
Alasdair's Royal Commission; Major-General Alastair MacDonald; Journal of Rev. John Weir

13. THE YEAR OF GLORY – 1645 143
"Fear Tollaidh nan Tighean"; The Battle of Inbhir Lochaidh; Release of the hostages; The Battle of Auldearn; The Battle of Kilsyth; Sir Alastair MacDonald, Knight; Defeat of Montrose at Philiphaugh

14. THE REARGUARD – 1646 154
After Philiphaugh; Angus MacCholla and the Factor; Conquest of Argyll's estates; Sabhal nan Cnàimh; Colla Ciotach in Islay; Antrim redoubles his efforts; the Spanish contract; Antrim returns to Scotland

15. LESLIE THWARTED – 1647 167
The sale of the King; The "New Model" army; Leslie marches north; Evacuation from Kintyre; Colla Ciotach appointed Commander-in-Chief; Leslie moves west; Evacuation to Islay; Leslie's revenge at Dunaverty

16. THE END OF THE STRUGGLE 179
Alasdair needed in Ireland; Surrender of Dunivaig; Colla Ciotach kidnapped; "Trial" and execution; Alasdair fights on, in Ireland; Alasdair is murdered; Coll's epitaph?

EPILOGUE 192
King Charles; Huntly; Montrose; Argyll; Antrim; Alasdair's family; The rivals of Knocknanoss; Clan Donald adherents; Clan Donald of Colonsay

APPENDICES
1. Details of Trial of Angus *Og* following his surrender of Dunivaig Castle 203
2. Statements concerning the defeat of Sir James MacDonald, 1615 204
3. A comparison of the varying treatments accorded to *Colla Ciotach*'s negotiated surrender in 1615 and the associated "capture" of MacDuffie 215
4. List of Colonsay inhabitants "converted to the True Faith" by Patrick Hegarty O.F.M., 1625 217
5. Latin translation of a testimonial provided to the missionaries by *Colla Ciotach* 224
6. Journal of Rev. John Weir 225
7. Civil War Chronology 231
Selected Bibliography 238

MAPS AND GENEALOGICAL TABLES

MAPS

1. Colonsay   20

2. Colonsay and Islay   32

3. The Western Isles of Scotland   67

4. Ireland   116

5. Scotland   142

6. Kintyre and Lorn   166

TABLES

I   Pedigree of Clan Donald of Colonsay   199

II Clan Donald of Colonsay   200

III Descendants of Alasdair MacCholla   201

IV Descendants of Alasdair MacCholla   202

AUTHOR'S FOREWORD

This is a simple salutation of *Colla Ciotach* MacDonald, a very remarkable man who was an undoubted hero in his world, the Gaelic world. In his own lifetime he became a legend and the songs and stories that grew up around him and his family were to be the inspiration of generations. His demise, in 1647, signalled an end to the way of life that had been established some 1500 years ago, when *Fergus Mór* and his fellow Scots first came over from Ireland and settled at *Dùn Add*.

I came to live in Colonsay in 1978 and it was from *Para Mór* (Peter McAllister), a gifted local historian and story-teller, that I first heard of *Colla Ciotach* ("ambidextrous Coll") and his mighty son, Sir Alexander MacDonald of Colonsay, Knight of the Field. As the years went by, other people heard that I was interested and added to the tale, nearly always telling the best bits with great relish in the vernacular, and then translating into English with the explanation that "it sounds *better* in Gaelic".

When I came to examine *Colla Ciotach*'s position in the published histories, I was surprised to find that he had been marginalised or, rather worse, he appeared as a base, rather ignorant sort of a chap. Eventually, he actually came to be described as a "renegade MacDonald" on a plaque, erected in Colonsay, by persons who must, in their hearts, know better. Although it is easy to understand how this came about, such a reputation is clearly completely at odds with the traditions of the Highlands and Islands and, in all honesty, with the known facts.

So it was that I was encouraged to try my hand at a brief and accessible biography, one which would be a little bit sympathetic to the legend; I have probably been somewhat selective, but to my mind it is the colour and the detail and the perspective that is the fun – "Glory be to God for dappled things!"

I have leaned heavily on contemporary or traditional accounts; no doubt these are distorted, but they have the merit of immediacy and, perhaps more importantly, they tell us something about the people involved, and those that followed them. In many cases, the bald facts are less interesting than the way in which they were perceived or presented. There is an unfortunate lack of consistency in both names and spellings of persons and places, and in many cases this lack of consistency is still current usage, but for purposes of clarity I have tried to stick to a standard form.

Having said that I was encouraged in this project, I can blame nobody but myself for this, the result; all errors and omissions, all opinions and suggestions are completely mine. I do sincerely thank all who have helped me, especially Lady Kingarth who read the manuscript, G.P. Sell of RCAHMS who parted me from a red herring, John Kington of University of East Anglia for information on weather patterns, Dr. Louise Yeoman of National Library of Scotland who unravelled Rev. Weir's diary, and Caroline Taylor for most helpful criticism and advice. I also thank my family and good friends, especially Georgina Hobhouse, Alastair Scouller and Frank Nicholson, for bearing with me in this project, and, not least, Liz McNichol for a very extended loan of her Latin dictionary.

SOURCES

Although an attempt has been made to avoid copious footnotes and extensive references, sources are normally acknowledged in the text. For further details, readers are
asked to refer to the Bibliography

1

THE ORIGINS OF CLAN DONALD OF COLONSAY

Colla Ciotach ("ambidextrous Coll")

Born of noble parentage in 1570 on an island in Antrim, Coll *Ciotach* MacDonald was taken as an infant to the island of Colonsay in Argyll where he grew to adulthood, raised his own family and based himself throughout a long and turbulent life. Both in time and space, his life bridged the difficult gap between two cultures. Coll was born a Catholic and a Gael; he was a man of valour, honour and nobility, and it was his tragedy to live at a period when old values were being abandoned and when deceit and treachery came to be rewarded by high office and enhanced estates.

His name itself is witness to the enigma, reflecting the old order; and it is as well to consider it now, however briefly, because it has been the cause of a great deal of confusion. For their own reasons, some modern writers have sought to revile Coll; they have called him a renegade and have even twisted his name, to suggest that the word "*ciotach*" in this context meant "sinister" or "untrustworthy". The simple fact is that surnames were not in daily use in normal Highland circles; indeed, they are redundant still in many cases, where title or rank are sufficient to identify the individual. People were named as individuals, and further identified by their characteristics, by their family or by their locality. Coll was his name, *ciotach* was his characteristic – it commonly means 'left-handed' and can be taken simply to mean that he was proficient with that hand or, more probably, that he was ambidextrous; it also has connotations such as 'cute', in the sense of 'sharp'.

It so happens that many people are more proficient with their left-hand, in the modern English sense of 'left-handed', so in that sense '*ciotach*' would make a fairly pointless sobriquet. No doubt there could be circumstances in which a left-handed swordsman could have had an advantage, but the ambidextrous one would be surely more remarkable. There is also actuarial evidence which in itself would make it improbable that *Colla Ciotach* was simply left-handed: research has shown that even today, when longevity has greatly increased, 'left-handed' males die at an average age of 62 years and three months, compared with 'right-handed' males who can expect to reach an average age of 72 years and four months; yet Coll died prematurely when he was almost eighty, and not of an illness.

If his longevity suggests that he was not 'left-handed' in the modern sense, the supposition that he was ambidextrous is supported by the fact that his mighty son, *Alasdair* ("Alexander"), was famous for that characteristic, one of the many qualities that he shared with his father. George Hill, writing in 1873, states categorically that *ciotach* "does not imply merely the dexterous use of the left hand, as generally supposed; in his case at least, it meant that he could wield his ponderous sword in whatever hand the peculiar circumstances of each encounter with his foes required that it should be grasped."

Although it is a fact that the word *ciotach* can also be taken as meaning crafty or cunning, as in 'sinister', it is noticeable that this has only been suggested in reference to *Colla Ciotach* by modern writers (1920 and later) and by people who are, perhaps, unwilling to recognise the characteristics of Coll himself. A less devious man would be hard to imagine; the very hallmarks of his life and death were his honesty and integrity.[1]

In point of fact, it was as *Colla Ciotach Mac Ghilleasbuig* ("Ambidextrous Coll, son of Archibald") that our subject was more formally known, and this identifies him as of noble rank, a high-born member of *Clann Iain Mhóir* ("The Descendants of Great John", the John in question being an important patrician of Clan Donald). His full pedigree, given by Ronald Black, was *Colla, mac Ghilleasbuig, mhic Cholla nan Capull, mhic Alasdair, mhic Iain Chathanaich, mhic Iain, mhic Dhomhnaill Bhallaich, mhic Iain Mhóir* ("Coll, son of Archibald, son of Coll of the horses, son of Alexander, son of John of the battles, son of John, son of pock-marked Donald, son of Great John". In the English language, his name is quite simply Coll MacDonald of Colonsay.

Clann Iain Mhóir ("The descendants of Great John")

From the eighth to the twelfth century, the Hebrides were under the thrall of the Vikings, but eventually there arose an individual whose personality and guile were sufficient to weaken their power. On the night of Epiphany, 1156, the fleet of Godred of Man sailed up the sound of Islay and into a trap; an enemy fleet, well armed and fitted with innovatory rudders, was hidden behind the Post Rocks at *Rubh a' Mhàil* ("Tribute Point"). With the full force of a spring tide behind them, the Viking ships could not turn back and worse, relying upon primitive steering-boards, they were unable to manoeuvre; for some hours the battle raged, the tide slowly carrying the fleets closer and closer to the fascinated spectators on Colonsay's eastern hills. The trap had been laid by the man now known as Somerled (*Somhairle*), and as a direct result he gained sovereign possession of a vast tract of land, from Ardnamurchan to Arran, including Kintyre, Morvern and all of the Inner Hebrides.

From Somerled sprang a number of important families, including the House of MacDonald, and by the 14th century, one of the mightier descendants set himself up as a feudal magnate, Lord of the Isles. This was John 1st who, by marriage, was able to reunite the mighty territory that had been Somerled's; he and his successors had great power and state, sent ambassadors abroad, made treaties with foreign potentates, made laws, endowed churches and abbeys – enjoyed all the panoply of sovereign independence. Not surprisingly, the Lordship was viewed with unease by the Scottish monarchy and within less than two centuries the title had been abrogated to the crown.

When this happened, in the Act of Forfeiture of 1493, the Lordship of the Isles came to an end and the great House of MacDonald was shattered into its component parts. The most important of these was the family of the MacDonalds of the South, or *Clann Iain Mhóir*, of which the MacDonalds of Colonsay were a branch.[2]

The headquarters of *Clann Iain Mhóir* were at Dunivaig (*Dùn Naomhaig* "Fort of the Coble") in Islay, a remarkable fortress lying just behind the present Lagavullin Distillery and now a National Monument, sadly neglected. The strategic importance of its location would be difficult to exaggerate, particularly in the light of contemporary conditions. Dunivaig lay at the centre of major communication routes – it controlled the North Channel, between Kintyre and Antrim; it controlled the entrance to the

Sound of Islay and also to the Sound of Jura, and thus the Firth of Lorne, the Sound of Mull and the Great Glen. Barely twenty miles from Ireland, Dunivaig lay at the heart of Gaeldom.

Since they are so important to the events which will follow, it is as well to consider a contemporary description of some of these localities; Dean Munro published his book in 1594 but the description is based on a tour in 1549:

"**Ila**. ... ane ile of twentie mile lenthe from the north to the south, and sixteen myles in breadth from the eist to the west, fertil, fruitful, and full of natural grassing, with many grate diere, maney woods, faire games of hunting beside every toune, with ane watter callit Laxay, wherupon maney salmon are slaine, with ane salt water loch callit Lochegunord, quherin runs the water of Gyinord, with high sandey bankes, upon the quhilk bankes upon the sea lyes infinit selccheis [seals], whilkis are slain with doges learnt to the same effect. In Ila is meikle lead ure in Mochyills. In this iyle there is a good raid [anchorage] for schipps, callit in Erische Polmoir, and in English the Mechell puill; this layes at ane toune callit Lanlay Vanych. Ane uther raid layes within Ellan Grynard, callit in English the isle at the poynt of the ness; the raid is callit Leodannis. Within this iyle ther is sundrie freshe water lochis, sic as Lochmoyburge, wherein ther layes an iyle perteining to the Bishopes of the iyles; the loch of Ellan Charrin, quherin ther is an iyle pertyning to M'Gillane of Doward [McLean of Duart]; Loch Cherossa, with ane iyle perteining to the abbot of Colmkill [Iona]. In this iyle there is strenths castells; the first is callit Dunowaik [Dunivaig], biggit on ane craig at the sea side, on the southeist part of the countery pertaining to the Clandonald of Kintyre; second is callit the castle of Lochgurne [Loch Gorm], quhilk is biggit in ane iyle within the said fresche water loche far fra land, pertaining of auld to the Clandonald of Kintyre, now usurped by M'Gillayne of Doward. Ellan Forlagan [Finlaggan], in the middle of Ila, ane faire iyle in fresche water.

"**ORNANSAY**. North from Ilay layes ane iyle callit Ornansay, it is twa myle lange, and neire alls meikle in breidth, quherin ther is ane monastery of chanons, mayne laiche land, full of hairs and foulmarts, with convenient havens for Heyland galeys, and shald at the shores. It lays eight miles of sea north from Ila. Beside this iyle Ornansay layes ane uther ile lesse then it, callit by the Irische Ellan Namuche, half ane myle lang, which is guid for swyne and alse uther bestiall.

"**COLNANSAY**. Northward from the iyle of Ornansay, be ane half myle of sea, lyes ane ile, callit Colnansay, seven myles lange from the northeist to the southwest, with twa myle bredthe, ane fertile ile guid for quhit fishing. It hath ane paroch kirke. This ile is bruikit be ane gentle capitane, callit M'Duffyhe, and pertened of auld to Clandonald of Kintyre."

Clan Donald of the South was descended through *Iain Mór* from his father John, 1st Lord of the Isles, whose second wife was Princess Margaret of Scotland; the property that had been granted to *Iain Mór* as Tanister (or second son) included the castles of Saddell and Dunaverty (both in Kintyre) as well as that of Dunivaig, and his extensive holdings included lands in Kintyre and the islands. *Iain Mór* further developed his position through marriage to Margaret Bisset, and thus acquired the fertile and valuable area of Antrim known as the Glens; his own title became that of 'MacDonald of Dunivaig and the Glens'.

Threats to Clann Iain Mhóir

Although *Clann Iain Mhóir* survived in the troublesome times which followed the Act of Forfeiture in 1493, and continued to occupy the ancient homelands, it was with increasing difficulty as a result of a relative inability to accept the new order or to indulge in intrigue. Relative, for example, to the ability of the Campbells or to that of the MacIans.

Following the Act of Forfeiture, King James IV had come to the West in person to exact obedience, since it was important for him to secure the submission not merely of the forfeited Lord of the Isles himself, but also that of his vassals. Many of the chiefs made immediate submission, and were rewarded with continued possession of their estates and within a year, the Lord of the Isles had also submitted. Government forces were now introduced to garrison the ancient castles of the clans, but the king's initiative in this respect was not universally welcomed and met with a particularly spectacular response from *Clann Iain Mhóir*.

At this time, the leader of *Clann Iain Mhóir* was another *Iain Mór*, and it was he who, with his son, *Iain Cathanach*, was required to recognise the sovereign's authority.[3] Having accepted the formal submission, the King went ahead and established his own garrison in *Iain Mór*'s castle at Dunaverty, on the Mull of Kintyre, regardless of the proprietor's own feelings in the matter. *Iain Mór* was outraged. No sooner had the King ridden away to his ships than he and his son *Iain Cathanach* raised their followers, stormed the castle and captured the new Governor; they then waited until the Royal Fleet was passing below the castle walls before hanging their prisoner from the ramparts, under the very eyes of the King.

The monarch's reaction was predictable enough, in that he sought both revenge and to make an example of these rebellious souls. The chosen agent is of interest, since for the first time in our story it exposes a Campbell actively working to set one branch of Clan Donald against another. In light of the Dunaverty protest, and through the agency of Argyll (the head of Clan Campbell), "Macian of Ardnamurchan was entrusted with the task of exacting retribution. The two heads of the Clan Ian Vor fell into his hands. He consigned them to Edinburgh where they were hanged." (1494). This account makes the capture sound very simple, but since *Iain Mór* and his son (the "two heads" of *Clann Iain Mhóir*) had taken refuge in the island fortress in Finlaggan Loch, MacIan could only have hoped to capture them through some form of deception. But MacIan was a member of the extended MacDonald clan and it was, of course, easier for a MacDonald than for a Campbell to invoke and betray their trust.

In his "History of the Western Highlands" Gregory records that, together with *Iain Mór*, no less than four of his sons were captured by MacIan of Ardnamurchan and brought to Edinburgh: "Here they were found guilty of high treason, and executed accordingly, on the Burrowmuir, their bodies being interred in the church of St. Anthony. Two surviving sons, who afterwards restored the fortunes of this family, fled to their Irish territory of the Glens, to escape the pursuit of MacIan." One of these sons, *Alasdair* ("Alexander"), was to be *Colla Ciotach*'s great grandfather – the vicissitudes of his forebears were to have a direct bearing on Coll's own position and probably helped to shape his own robust approach to life.

Loder, the author of an authoritative history of Colonsay, emphasises the point that "The most wholehearted convert to the cause of the King was John MacIan of

Ardnamurchan, who soon stood high in the royal favour. Like Angus, son of John of the Isles, he was married to a daughter of the Earl of Argyll. In this case the political as well as the matrimonial alliance was consummated." Although even quite conservative families could be linked through marriage to the house of Argyll, John MacIan seems to have gone altogether too far – in his personal ambition he was utterly unscrupulous.

MacIan had a sister who was married to Malcolm MacDuffie (*MacDubhshith*)[4] of *Dùn Eibhin* ("Evin's Fort") in Colonsay. Clan MacDuffie had been hereditary Record Keepers for the Lords of Isles, still held their tenancy of Colonsay from MacDonald of Dunivaig and the Glens, and were to remain overtly loyal for another century. Nonetheless it seems that now, in the pursuit of his own ambitions, MacIan managed to persuade Malcolm MacDuffie to betray his ancient trust; perhaps they both believed that by treachery they could enhance their standing, if not their honour. Not content with his treachery to date, MacIan was keen to curry further favour with the King and with the Campbells and an opportunity to do so was not long delayed.

In 1496, just two years after the executions of *Iain Mór* and his sons, a further attempt at resistance was led by Sir Alexander MacDonald of Lochalsh, nephew of the last of the Lords of the Isles. Following a reverse, he set out through the Isles to raise further support and reached Oransay, where he was the guest of the Prior. Malcolm MacDuffie, MacIan's brother-in-law, was closely related to the Prior and must have heard of Sir Alexander's presence; word quickly reached MacIan himself, and as a result his respected kinsman was surprised and murdered. The crime was committed in the building known as the Prior's House, a former barn in which the mediaeval carved tombstones of Oransay are now preserved. One of the two prostrate figures in high relief is locally accepted as the effigy of Sir Alexander of Lochalsh, and Sir Alexander's host in Oransay is thought to have been Prior Colin, for whom the magnificent High Cross is named.

One result of this murder was that it gave the King a pretext to cancel all the new charters that had been granted, and furthermore he then appointed the Earl of Argyll as Lieutenant, with the power to issue new leases on most of the former property of the Lordship (excepting Kintyre and Islay). This situation was highly satisfactory to Argyll and had been brought about by his son-in-law, MacIan. If the latter had indeed been helped by MacDuffie, one might reasonably expect to see signs of a reward and, sure enough, in 1506 the island of Colonsay was leased directly to "Malcolm MacKoffee". Loder points out that John MacIan of Ardnamurchan, the brother-in-law, stood caution.

MacDuffie quickly discovered the error of his ways, since in 1507, it was MacIan who accounted to the Exchequer for the rent; and by 1509 we find MacIan claiming the island for himself, by gift from the Earl of Lennox. Writing in 1935, Loder records a tradition that at about that time a number of MacDuffies were transplanted to Ardnamurchan "and that their descendants are still to be found at Kilchoan near MacIan's castle of Mingarry." Although the main branch of the MacDuffies managed to survive in Colonsay, it is noteworthy that they maintained close relations with Clan MacIan throughout the rest of the sixteenth century.[5]

Meanwhile, although *Clann Iain Mhóir* had not yet been forgiven for their flamboyant behaviour at Dunaverty in 1494, their current chief, Alexander of Dunivaig and the Glens, had had some successes and, in 1520, was rewarded when he obtained, from Sir

John Campbell of Calder (also known as "Cawdor"), a lease which once more included lands in Islay, Jura and Colonsay, in exchange for a Bond of Gossipry and Manrent. However it was not long before Alexander's peaceable enjoyment of these island properties was rudely shattered, as a result of a personal dispute between the same Sir John Campbell and Lachlan MacLean of Duart, in Mull.

Seemingly Lachlan, who was married to a sister of Sir John, had decided to separate from his wife; the exact reasons are unclear but one (sadly erroneous) account has it that he had become fascinated by the personal charms of a Spanish lady, whose ship had become separated from the great Armada and was sheltering in Tobermory Bay. According to this account, Lady MacLean arranged to have the galleon blown to kingdom come, complete with most of the company; so spectacular was the explosion that two of the victims landed on the Morvern shore. Although the dates do not fit this particular explanation, by a margin of almost a century, we can be confident that Lachlan must, in some way, have been sorely provoked by his wife, since she was tied hand and foot and exposed upon a tidal rock in the open sea not far from the southwest end of Lismore, and known to this day as "Lady's Rock". (MacLean sources maintain that it was a quite different rock, not nearly so far offshore and not quite so far under water at high tide.) By chance, she was noticed and rescued by the crew of a passing boat, and restored to the care of her brother. One way and another this episode led to a great deal of ill-feeling, in which it seems that Alexander MacDonald of Dunivaig and the Glens sided with the MacLeans – and of course the Colonsay people were aligned on the same side.

Colonsay certainly suffered for its involvement in the dispute, since it is on record that, in 1524, Sir John Campbell obtained a pardon for "the criminal burning" of the lands of that island, which he had so recently leased to Alexander MacDonald. Possibly he felt that the "Bond of Gossipry and Manrent" had entitled him to expect support against the MacLeans, but nonetheless he had to agree to pay compensation. All this was not without further benefit to the MacDonald interest, since the feud and the events that followed led to the personal intervention of the King, and enabled Alexander of Dunivaig and the Glens to improve his own position with the Crown.

Dunivaig and the Glens

As a happy result of the above events, the MacDonalds began to gain more security and further opportunities soon arose in which, by their apparent service to the crown, they earned further reward. Such an opportunity arose in a rising in 1543 centred on the person of *Domhnall Dubh* ("Dark Donald"), for although the Lordship had been forfeited, there were still those who sought to revive it and individuals able to rally them. *Domhnall Dubh* was one of the most important of these because through his father, Angus, he was acknowledged by the islanders to have rightfully inherited the ancient title.

Angus had died in 1490, assassinated by an Irish harper at Inverness. *Domhnall Dubh*, his heir, had been captured in infancy by Argyll and held throughout his childhood in close confinement in Inchconnell Castle on Loch Awe. In 1501 *Domhnall* had escaped, with the help of the MacDonalds of Glencoe, and he had then become the principal figure in a lengthy and well-conducted rebellion that was only finally suppressed in 1506.

He had then been re-imprisoned, this time in Edinburgh Castle, and had remained there for almost forty years.

Now at last, in 1543, *Domhnall Dubh* escaped from Edinburgh Castle and was proclaimed Lord of the Isles, the leader of a vigorous rising that took two full years to suppress. But James of Dunivaig and the Glens had by now succeeded his father Alexander, and was married to Lady Agnes Campbell, a daughter of Colin, 3rd Earl of Argyll. Prudently, neither he nor the MacDuffies, his dependants in Colonsay, seemed to become involved in open support for *Domhnall Dubh*. As clan historian Donald J. MacDonald recounts:

> "In April 1545 .... Arran (as Regent) rewarded James of Islay generously for his neutrality, and for services rendered to the infant Queen against the old enemy, England. He was given the heritage of the lands previously held by himself and his father on lease from the Crown. Some of these were erected into the Barony of Barr, in North Kintyre. Others were granted in Islay (91 merklands), in Jura (184 shilling lands), together with smaller allotments in Arran, Gigha, Colonsay and other isles."[6]

James of Dunivaig and the Glens, as he is most usually remembered, was a very successful chief who had established cordial relations with the Crown and even with the Earl of Argyll. He had also taken steps to extend his Irish estates by conquest and here Donald J. MacDonald describes the original territory:

> "The Glens (or Glynnis) open on the sea at irregular intervals along the east coast from Glenarm northwards to Ballycastle and lead inland to the watershed between the coast and the valley of the river Bush. Dotted along this coast are the castles of Glenarm, Red Bay, Kinbane and Dunluce.... the Irish accounts refer to the Glynnis as wooded places, which no doubt they were at the time. [A contemporary account] makes mention of the difficulty of finding their enemies in the thick woodlands of the Glens. They were thus an ideal place for fugitives to hide and defy pursuit."

James extended his influence dramatically when he overwhelmed the contiguous area known as The Route, the homelands of the O'Cahan and McQuillan families. This was the original *Dalriada*, a rich and fertile prize, and he appointed one of his brothers, *Colla nan Capull* ("Coll of the Horses"), as "Lord of the Route".

When James MacDonald of Dunivaig and the Glens died in 1565, having been wounded in a battle to protect his Irish estates[7], his son Angus inherited all that belonged to him in Scotland and came therefore to be known as "Angus of Dunivaig". Meanwhile it was one of James' surviving brothers who took possession of all his Irish interests, based upon an entrenched position in the Glens of Antrim. This brother was *Somhairle Buidhe* ("yellow-haired Samuel") or Sorley Boy, as he is normally known in English, a most remarkable and spirited individual who managed to retain these lands until his own death in 1589, when they passed to his son Ranald. For many years Sorley held his property by main force and in defiance of the crown; his exploits were remarkable and it will have been with some relief to all concerned that he was able to be confirmed in his possessions by the expedient of submission to Queen Elizabeth in 1586. For formality's sake, *Somhairle Buidhe* was then naturalised as an Englishman and in due course his son was created Viscount Dunluce in 1618. This Irish sept of *Clann Iain Mhóir* became known as the MacDonnells of Dunluce, eventually the Earls of Antrim.

Notes

1 It is noteable that Prof. Donald MacKinnon, writing in the last century, was confident that the meaning was either 'left-handed' or ambidextrous. As founding Professor of Celtic Studies at Edinburgh University, he was an authority on Gaelic; and being himself a Colonsay man born and bred, he was familiar both with his subject and with island traditions no longer available today. It is also significant that Buchan has no doubts and mentions "a Colonsay MacDonald, commonly called Coll Keitach, or "Coll who can fight with either hand."

Incidentally, Prof. MacKinnon points out that the nickname was not used in reference to the sons; in Gaelic and in Highland areas, one spoke of '*Alasdair MacCholla*' ("Alexander, son of Coll") for example, although elsewhere variations of '*Alasdair Mhic Cholla Chiotaich*' were to cause some confusion. One of the more pleasing errors turned 'Colkitto' into 'Colonel Kitto', whilst another writer came up with 'MacDonald of Colkitto', as if "Coll" were an estate or district.

2 *Iain Mór* ("Great John", after whom this house was named, had been the second son of John, 1st Lord of the Isles (popularly remembered as Good John of Islay), by his second marriage with the Princess Margaret of Scotland. *Iain Mór*'s elder brother, *Domhnall* ("Donald"), became 2nd Lord of the Isles after their father's death c. 1385, but *Iain Mór* had been granted a huge tract of territory in Kintyre and Islay, which thus became the heartland of *Clann Iain Mhóir*, Clan Donald of the South. It has been a tradition that *Carn an Eoin*, the highest point on Colonsay, is named for John, 1st Lord of the Isles (d. 1385), although others have it that the name means "Hill of the Birds" for more obvious reasons; and there is a tradition that *Dùn Domhnall* on Oransay is named for Donald, grandson of Somerled, who held both Islay and Kintyre and gave his name to Clan Donald itself. *Dùn Domhnall* is said by Grieve to have been at first his main seat, only later transferred to Finlaggan Loch in Islay.

3 The original *Iain Mór*, (who had been killed in 1427), had been succeeded by his son, Sir Donald Balloch, who died at Loch Gruinard on Islay, where he had a residence on one of the islands (1476); the leadership then passed to his own son, again known as *Iain Mór*, who married Sabina, the daughter of an Ulster Chieftain, Felim O'Neill.. His brief leadership was inextricably linked with that of his son, *Iain Cathanach* (perhaps "Warlike John", although Hill states that Iain Cathanach's name was properly *Cahanagh* "from being fostered in Northern Ulster with the O'Cahans").

4 The family name which is anglicised here as "MacDuffie" has more than fifty variations, including Duthie, Duphaci, MacFie, MacPhee, MacCathie, MacGuffie, Mahaffy. "MacDuffie" is reasonably close to one of the earlier Gaelic versions, *MacDubhsith*, but defies certain translation. The element "*sith*" suggests either "peace" or perhaps "knowe" in reference to the ancient turf-covered dwellings of the earliest inhabitants. Commonly, the female inhabitant of such dwellings has been remembered through folklore as a "*bansith*" or "banshee".

5 In 1517, the murder of Sir Alexander of Lochalsh was at last avenged by his son, when Mingarry Castle was burned and MacIan killed at *Creag an Airgid* ("Silver Crag"). His tombstone at Iona is a handsome affair, whose Latin inscription indicates that the stone was paid for "by Mariota MacIan, his sister, wife of Malcolm MacFie, Lord of Dun Eibhin in Colonsay" The MacIan stone in Iona, although now broken into a number of pieces, is a product of the Oransay school of sculpture and is illustrated in Drummond's "West Highland Monuments". Mariota was something of a patron of the arts, and her own gravestone may be seen in Oransay Priory: HIC JACET .../... [MAR]IOTA ALEX/ANDRI JOHA(NN)IS MACEAIN (Here lies ... Mariota, daughter of Alexander, son of John MacIan). This stone shows a female standing below a triple canopy, with angels supporting her pillow headrest; she has a long robe, a cloak and wears a cowl; in one hand she holds a bible, in the other a Rosary and her lap-dogs nestle into her cloak. It is fascinating to reflect on the cultivated artistry that was evidently still flourishing in Oransay just a few years before the Reformation; within a lifetime the reformers were to attack such monuments with sledgehammers and within a century Oransay Priory, although unsacked, was to be a crumbling ruin, little better than it stands today. With splendid irony, Mariota's tombstone has now been placed for protection in the Prior's House, the scene of Sir Alexander's murder, committed by her brother and probably through her connivance.

6 It is worth noting that this same 'James of Islay', whose position was so enhanced by his restraint in the cause of *Domhnall Dubh*, had a strong subsequent claim to have been Lord of the Isles in his own right. He was nominated as successor by *Domhnall Dubh* and also had the support of the Islesmen and of the Earl of

Lennox. Indulging in a little politics, he wrote to Henry, King of England, on 24 January 1546, describing himself as "aperand aeyr of ye Yllis". It is also recorded that he once used the title "Lord of the Yllis", in a letter to the Irish Privy Council; his grandson was to be the (Sir) James MacDonald, whose own claims would be so warmly supported by *Colla Ciotach* and a grand-daughter, Mary, was to become *Colla*'s wife.

7 "O'Neill gave the sons of Mac Donnell of Scotland a great overthrow, in which Angus was slain, and James wounded and taken prisoner, and he died in a year after of the mortification of his wounds; his death was very much lamented, and he was a man distinguished for his hospitality, feats of arms, liberality, conviviality, generosity, and bestowing of gifts, and there was not his equal amongst the Clan Donnell of Ireland or of Scotland at that time, and his own people would not hesitate to give his weight in gold could he be thereby ransomed; many others were also slain in that battle of Glen Taisi..." Annals of the Four Masters

Colonsay

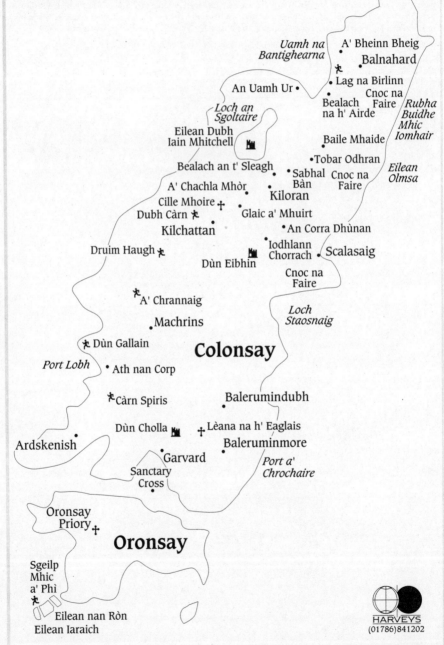

⚔ Leab' Fhalaich Mhic a' Phì
 (MacDuffie's Hiding Place)
🏰 Castle
✝ Church

Uamh na Bantighearna

A' Bheinn Bheig

Balnahard

An Uamh Ur

Lag na Birlinn

Cnoc na Faire

Bealach na h' Airde

Rubha Buidhe Mhic Iomhair

Loch an Sgoltaire

Eilean Dubh Iain Mhitchell

Baile Mhaide

Tobar Odhran

Bealach an t' Sleagh

Sabhal Bàn

Cnoc na Faire

Eilean Olmsa

A' Chachla Mhòr

Kiloran

Cille Mhoire ✝

Dubh Càrn ⚔

Glaic a' Mhuirt

Kilchattan

An Corra Dhùnan

Druim Haugh ⚔

Iodhlann Chorrach

Scalasaig

Dùn Eibhin

Cnoc na Faire

A' Chrannaig ⚔

Loch Staosnaig

Machrins

Colonsay

⚔ Dùn Gallain

Port Lobh

Ath nan Corp

Balerumindubh

⚔ Càrn Spiris

Dùn Cholla 🏰

Lèana na h' Eaglais ✝

Baleruminmore

Ardskenish

Garvard

Sanctary Cross

Port a' Chrochaire

Oronsay Priory ✝

Oronsay

Sgeilp Mhic a' Phì
⚔

Eilean nan Ròn

Eilean Iaraich

HARVEYS
(01786)841202

2

HEBRIDEAN STRUGGLES

Clan Donald of Colonsay

James of Dunivaig and the Glens had had three brothers in all, known in English as Coll, Sorley Boy and Angus. Angus was killed in the same battle in which James was fatally wounded, but Coll, the progenitor of Clan Donald of Colonsay, had predeceased them both. More usually known as *Colla nan Capull* ("Coll of the Horses"), it was he who had been appointed Lord of the Route by James and who, as elder brother, had taken precedence over *Somhairle*. In the natural order of things, *Colla nan Capull* should have been the one to take possession of all the Antrim lands, but he had died in 1558 and his teenaged sons could not hope to resist their uncle *Somhairle*. As a result, *Colla nan Capull*'s inheritance was lost to his immediate family some five years before the birth of his sole grandson. That grandson was to be *Colla Ciotach*.

Colla nan Capull, *Colla Ciotach*'s grandfather, was also often called *Colla Maol Dubh*, which identified him as "Coll the Dark Chief", whilst "*nan Capull*" is usually taken to refer to his cavalry skill but might recall the story that he and his men had at one time to exist on horse-flesh, during a campaign in Tyrconnell (Donegal). At all events he was known and respected as a fearless and formidable leader of Clandonnell. *Colla nan Capull* had had his base near Ballycastle, at Kinbane Castle (*Ceann Bán*, "White Headland"), named for the chalk cliffs on which it was built. Hill describes it thus in 1873:

> "Keannbann is a huge chalk rock of dazzling whiteness standing out in the channel some-what beyond the line of other adjoining headlands, and about a mile and a half westwards from the town of Ballycastle. It rises abruptly from the water about one hundred feet. The castle of Colla Macdonnell stood behind this immense rock, but connected with it by strong walls which were carried along the edges of the cliff so as to prevent any possibility of an assault from the sea. On the southern side it was protected by a range of cliffs standing considerably inland, but only capable of being descended by a precipitous path. This castle had a tower or keep, portions of which still remain."

The ruins have changed little to the present day – the setting is quite spectacular, with panoramic views of neighbouring Rathlin across the narrow but treacherous sound.

There is an interesting contemporary reference to Kinbane in papers of the reign of young Edward VI of England, whose successful invasion of Scotland had not endeared him to its inhabitants.[1] On 27 September 1551 John Dudley, Earl of Warwick, received a letter from Cusake, Lord Chancellor of Ireland, outlining attempted revenge by the English for a recent and humiliating defeat at the hands of *Colla nan Capull* and his brother:

> "Coll M'Connyll, seconde brother to James, had a stronge castill buylded upon a rock, with a strong baan [bawn] of lyme and stoon, over the sea, named the castill of Keanbaan, which my Lorde (Deputie) causid to be defaced, and brake much parte thairof, so as nowe it is not

defensible, which I am sure thai neid had for soe muche more displeasir doon to thaim."[2]

In fact, the damage to his castle seems to have left Coll neither up nor down, for he was already otherwise preoccupied in courting the lady who would become *Colla Ciotach's* grandmother. The turbulent events surrounding *Colla nan Capull's* marriage began with an expedition in which *Colla* had brought over a large party of *galloglaich* (mercenaries) from Scotland, and was making his way through The Route to the aid of The O'Donnell in his struggles against The O'Neill. He discovered that in his absence the MacQuillans, one of the families of The Route, had suffered at the hands of the O'Cahans, raiding across the Bann. As Lord of The Route, *Colla nan Capull* decided to launch a reprisal raid against O'Cahan, with consequences described by Donald J. MacDonald:

> "MacQuillan was living in Dunluce Castle at that time. Colla joined his force to MacQuillan's and the raid was successful: for every cow MacQuillan had lost, two were restored, and all done without the loss of a man. During the resulting festivities *Colla* courted MacQuillan's daughter, the fair Eveleen, whom he married later...
>
> "During the night, when heads were hot with wine and whisky, a quarrel arose between *Colla* and his host about the maintenance of *Colla's* mercenaries, who had been billeted on MacQuillan in accordance with the age-old custom of *bonaght*, by which mercenaries were fed and quartered, with their horses, at the expense of their employer. The feeding of so many of *Colla's* men no doubt imposed a great strain on MacQuillan's resources, and he planned to rid himself of the Scots by treachery. Eveleen heard of the plan and warned her betrothed in time for him to retire discreetly to Rathlin and safety."

The marriage took place about 1551, the very year in which Coll's castle was damaged by the English, but their attempt to ruin the place must have been sadly inadequate since he quickly restored it and lived there for the remainder of his life. *Colla nan Capull* died in mid-May 1558, at Bonamargy Friary (*Bunnamairge*, "Foot of River Mairge") where he was buried: "his dust no doubt reposes in the older vault under the abbey". He left two young sons, Ranald and *Gilleasbuig Fiacal* ("Archibald who was born with teeth"), both by Eveleen.[3]

The elder son, *Gilleasbuig Fiacal*, was fostered in the family of O'Cahan, MacQuillan's former rivals in The Route, perhaps with a view to healing the breach between the two ancient houses. This is confirmed in official records, since on foot of Sussex's raid in 1556 the following report was included: "On Sunday, the 19th, he removed to Collrahan (Coleraine); on Monday night came in Colloh (*nan Capull*) McConnell's son, a little child (of about 5 years), which was kept with O'Kanne".[4] In due course, young *Gilleasbuig Fiacal* courted and married a daughter of O'Cahan and his young wife was pregnant when he came of age in 1570.[5] *Gilleasbuig's* powerful uncle, *Somhairle Buidhe*, arranged the appropriate celebrations in Ballycastle. The festivities included a spot of bull-baiting, with unfortunate consequences when a bull broke free and, in the resulting confusion, one of the helpers managed to wound *Gilleasbuig Fiacal* in the thigh. He was taken the short distance to Rathlin Island for medical treatment, but died.. There were rumours that he was deliberately poisoned on Rathlin, so as to remove a possible threat to *Somhairle* for possession of The Route. *Somhairle Buidhe* was said to have been displeased that *Gilleasbuig* had married into an important local family, particularly as his father, *Colla nan Capull*, had done the same thing.[6]

Despite her bereavement, *Gilleasbuig*'s wife went her full term and gave birth to a baby son, having been first removed to the relative security of Glasineerin Island in Lough Lynch for her confinement. Her mother-in-law's family of MacQuillan had a fortress on that island, which was only about seven miles from Dunluce itself and much the same distance from the Bann and from her father's territories.[7] Her infant son, *Colla Mac Ghilleasbuig*, later to be known as *Colla Ciotach*, was now taken under the wing of his youthful uncle Ranald, *Colla nan Capull*'s surviving son. Soon afterwards, both mother and child accompanied Ranald when he moved from Antrim to the tiny Hebridean island of Colonsay, a move that was presumably at the invitation of his powerful but beleaguered Scottish cousin in Islay, known to history as Angus of Dunivaig.

One way and another, since the death of his father James some five years earlier, Angus of Dunivaig had been having rather a difficult time of it.[8] It was bad enough that his uncle *Somhairle Buidhe* had got possession of all his Irish inheritance, but even worse that in Scotland he was under mounting pressure from neighbouring magnates, what with MacLeans trying to take land and property by force, and Campbells trying the same thing in more subtle ways.[9] Angus may well have been very happy to offer prospects of future wealth to young Ranald and his wards, in exchange for the undoubted skills and loyalty that he would gain. Perhaps Ranald *MacCholla* was attracted by a simple but challenging role as leading lieutenant to his Scottish cousin, in contrast to a rather more dangerous Irish career. After all, his uncle Sorley might well have viewed him as little more than a threat to his own son, Ranald *MacShomhairle*, who was eventually to become the 1st Earl of Antrim.

MacDonalds and MacLeans

On his very doorstep, Angus was under pressure from the MacLeans of Mull, who were attempting to secure a title to the *Rinns* of Islay. The *Rinns* ("Peninsula" or "Promontory") is that large and fertile section on the west of Islay which is such a feature of any map – almost an island and geologically the same as neighbouring Colonsay. It is separated from the rest of Islay by two important sea lochs, Loch Indaal and Loch Gruinart, which in themselves formed part of an ancient and valuable trade route.

Following the Act of Forfeiture, the *Rinns* had come to be leased to the MacLeans, but only as a tenancy under the MacDonalds; the MacLeans now claimed that it should be theirs by permanent charter. Angus had succeeded to his own estates in his twenties, and having already been deprived of the Glens took a fairly robust attitude to this further threat. Unfortunately, as Professor MacKinnon remarks: "*Coltach ri cinn-chinnidh eile na Gáidhealtachd, bha sliochd Iain Mhóir 'nan daoine foghainteach, ach chan urrainnear a rádh gun robh iad daonnan ro-ghlic.*" ("Like other chieftains of the Highlands, the descendants of Great John were men of valour, but one could not say that they were always especially wise.") He continues:

"Seldom was seen so sorrowful a chronicle as was seen in the Western Isles after the rule of Clan Donald. MacLeans and MacDonalds to the south, MacDonalds and MacLeods,

MacLeods and MacKenzies to the north, all squabbling amonst themselves. Certainly there were Campbells on this hill and Gordons on that hill, energetically urging them on. But, cunning though they be, they would have achieved little had not the clansmen been ready and willing to dance to their tune".

Even before the time of Angus, Colonsay had had its share of these disturbances; the MacDuffies of Colonsay had fought for Angus's forefathers and for *Clann Iain Mhóir* and some of their battles are still remembered, as are countless such local skirmishes throughout the Highlands and Islands. No doubt the stories gained a little in the telling, but in all fairness they suggest that Clan MacDuffie and their adherents were prepared to sell themselves dearly.

MacLean raids on Colonsay

The Battle of Balavetchy arose through a 16th century raid on Colonsay by MacLeans of Mull, in pursuit of a supposed claim to the island; it is said to have been the last of their many raids, and Grieve gives the story as he heard it from Sir John McNeill in 1881:

"... a large party of them ... landed at Balnahard. They had several birlinns which were sent south along the east coast with instructions to wait near Isle Olamsey [Eilean Olmsa] until the result of the raid was known. The young chief and his followers proceeded down the west coast overland. News of the landing of the expedition had been sent to the chief of Colonsay, who lived at Kiloran. He took immediate steps to defend his possessions, and, as he had few followers at hand, he was placed at a great disadvantage. Hurrying off with his men, he reached the short glen or gap leading from Balnahard to the sand dunes at the head of Kiloran Bay, and arrived there before the Macleans. The warriors of neither party had guns, but were armed with pistols, bows and arrows, and spears. The Macleans, however, had with them a small piece of ordnance .... this weapon was much dreaded by the Colonsay people, who had no such equipment of their own. When fired, it made a great noise, which was possibly the most dangerous thing about it. The sound was peculiar and said to have been like an exaggerated *coo-what*. Hence the Colonsay men named it the *cuat* or cuckoo. It was held in superstitious awe, and if anyone was injured by it, he was supposed to have been guilty of some secret sin. In later times it got to be a saying when any injury befell an evil-doer that "it was the droppings of the *cuat* that caused it".

"The chief and his men had little time to make preparations before the MacLeans were upon them. The invaders were at a disadvantage as to position, but they did not hesitate to attack. The fight went on for some time, and was all in favour of the Colonsay men who, hidden among the rocks, were able to use their weapons with much effect. They, however, lost some men, but the Macleans suffered severely. A few of them managed to force their way through the pass and reach the sand dunes. Here they were attacked by superior numbers, and all the invaders were killed except their young chief. Seeing that his men were defeated, he fled from the field of battle across the island to its eastern shore. He was closely pursued and ran down the glen that opens upon the sea, almost opposite Eilean Olamsey. Here he expected to meet his galleys, and shouted to attract the attention of those in charge of them. His people saw him and made for the land, but they were a long way off the shore. Although much exhausted, the knowledge that his pursuers were near him made him plunge into the sea and swim towards his ships. The sea was rather rough, his strength gave out, and he was drowned." In another version, Murdoch McNeill has it that, threatened with capture, he "preferred voluntary death by drowning" at *Rudha Buidhe Mhic Iomhair* ("McIvor's Yellow Point").

This is by no means the only MacLean raid that was to be remembered in Colonsay and another is commemorated at Kiloran Bay where, among the sand dunes, is *Lag na Birlinn* ("Hollow of the Highland Galley") – also known as "McLean's *Birlinn*"[10] – a site which recalls a 15th or 16th century raid that failed. Here the islanders were left with a trophy in the form of a captured *birlinn* that was presumably damaged and of no practical use. An islander, Murdoch McNeill, notes that "The boat must have been dragged through the dunes for about a quarter of a mile before it was set fire to. Rusty boat rivets were found in the surface sands for many a long day after"; and Grieve, an antiquarian, has it that "the Macleans landed in their *birlinn* at the head of Kiloran Bay. They were defeated by the Colonsay men, and had to abandon the vessel which was pulled up on the sand dunes where it remained until it went to pieces from age and exposure".

Another famous Colonsay battle was that of *Blàr-an-Dèabhaidh* ("Field of the Skirmish"), beside *Loch Fada* ("Long Loch"); sufficient detail survives to be worth repeating at length. Grieve takes up the story:

"The descent of the Mull men was unexpected, and the Colonsay people were taken by surprise while working at their peats. The only handy weapons they had beside them were their peat spades and forks. With these they defended themselves as best they could until many were killed. At last neighbours bearing arms came to their assistance, and the tide of battle went in favour of the men of Colonsay across the field of Deabhaidh [*Blàr an Dèabhaidh*]. At this juncture there arrived sixteen men of the Clan Bell from Balnahard [i.e. MacMillans], who evidently had taken a vow against the M'Leans, as they had remained unshaven, probably under the impression that thereby they would obtain strength, like Samson. The fight was very bitter, and by the end of the day fifteen of the Bells had been killed, and the only one left alive had lost an arm and a leg."

Murdoch McNeill goes on:

"While the battle was in progress *Calum Caol Mac Mhuirrich* ("slender Malcolm Currie"), who lay ill of a fever in his house at *Iodhlann Chorrach* ("Steep Stackyard") on the opposite side of the loch, had his servant on sentry outside keeping him informed of how it fared with the combatants. At last, getting excited, he impatiently donned his kilt, grasped his sword, and hurried across to join in the fray. He killed the first of the foe that he met; and to instil a young native, whom he found hiding in a furze bush, with courage, he caught some of the gushing blood in the hollow of his hand and made the youth drink it. He then gave him a sword, and, inspired by Malcolm's example, the young man fought bravely until the invaders were vanquished."

Loder has an interesting contribution:

"Accounts differ as to how the struggle turned, but eventually such of the combatants as remained unhurt separated. Another and larger party of Bells put in an appearance when all was over. Ever afterwards they and their descendants were known as the Late Bells to distinguish them from the Early Bells, who had borne the brunt of the fight. When crossing *Bealach na h-airde* ("Pass of the Cape") on the path between Kiloran and Balnahard, the Late Bells had to go to the east of the cairn, while the Early Bells went to the west of it."

Murdoch McNeill concludes the tale:

"When the fight was finished, a friend, meeting Malcolm, remarked, "I thought you were ill with a fever." "Oh yes," he replied; "but I got relief." Returning homewards from *An Corra Dhùnan* ("The Steep Hillock"), Malcolm noticed a reflection on the face of a rock some distance to the north of the middle loch, and on arriving at the spot found, to his suprise, eight of the foe lying fast asleep. Taking advantage of their helpless state, he killed them one after the other. He then collected their swords, which stood against a rock and caused the reflection which had first attracted his attention, and took his departure". This place is still known as *Glaic a' Mhuirt* ("Murder Hollow") and is a sheltered gully with rocky outcrops beside the march fence at *A' Chachla Mhór* ("The Big Gate"), now heavily overgrown and protected by dense banks of gorse; the ruins of *Calum Caol MacMhuirich*'s house can still be traced on *An Corra Dhùnan*, overlooking Loch Fada; the bodies were said to have been buried in the graveyard of *Cille Mhoire* ("Our Lady's Chapel") nearby.[11]

The Strategic Importance of Colonsay

Although Clan McDuffie had looked after MacDonald interests in Colonsay for many generations, the MacLeans had not been deterred and had become a growing menace. Now that they threatened even his Islay possessions, the young Angus of Dunivaig determined to meet the challenge, with the help of his equally youthful cousin Ranald *MacCholla*. After the untimely death of *Gilleasbuig Fiacal*, Angus presented Colonsay to Ranald as a base, and thereby created a powerful buffer between the MacLean heartland of Mull and its outposts in Jura and in the Rinns of Islay. All this occurred in 1570 or soon afterwards, when Ranald *MacCholla* and Angus of Dunivaig were both in their early twenties.

It will be remembered that, just twenty years earlier, Dean Munro had noted that Oransay had good harbours for *birlinns*. There were (and remain to this day) very good reasons for traffic between Mull and the *Rinns* to pass along the east side of Colonsay, but the coastline lying opposite Colonsay, from Scarba along the whole length of Jura and right down to Ardnave (the entrance to Loch Gruinard), is a bleak and inhospitable lee shore. There is shoal water off *Rubha a' Mhàil* and off Oransay; the whole area is subject to a remarkable Atlantic swell, and a lengthy and dangerous bar lies across the entrance to Loch Gruinard. It was not by chance that the Vikings selected Colonsay as an important strategic centre, and nothing had changed in the intervening centuries. By manning just three lookout points on Colonsay (each still marked as *Cnoc na Faire* ("Lookout Hill"), on the O.S. map) it was possible to monitor and react to the movements of the MacLeans. In particular, no ship could enter or leave the vital Sound of Islay without the danger of interception by craft based in Colonsay.

Of course, Colonsay was also very vulnerable, since the three nearest landfalls are

Mull, the Rinns and part of Jura – which, by this stage, were all in the thrall of the MacLeans. Thus Colonsay was at the centre of a completely hostile triangle, and unless vigourously defended, would have been quickly annexed. Apart from the traditional troubles arising from clan rivalry, it is at this point worth noting that the MacLeans had been the first of the Western clans to embrace the Presbyterian faith, whereas the inhabitants of the territories of *Clann Iain Mhóir* would be amongst the last to do so. Although subsequently out-manoeuvred by the Campbells, the MacLeans will at first have hoped to enjoy rich pickings at the expense of their Catholic neighbours.

So it was in these circumstances that Ranald *MacCholla* MacDonald, by now a professional soldier, chose to make his home in Colonsay, accompanied by his O'Cahan sister in law and her infant son, Coll.[12] For a few years, they enjoyed relative peace and tranquillity but, unfortunately, the difficult relationship with the MacLeans deteriorated still further after *Lachlan Mór* of Duart became their chief in 1578, and inevitably the hostilities of the period will have dominated *Colla Ciotach*'s youth and upbringing, in the shadow of his uncle.

For the moment, Ranald's mere presence seems to have been enough to give security to Colonsay and he was able to maintain an interest in the proceedings of his allies and friends in Ireland. In July 1579, two Spanish ships landed in Dingle, carrying an armed expeditionary force complete with a bishop, some friars, a Papal Legate, an English priest, the Papal Blessing and the highest of hopes. The leader wrote almost immediately to *Colla*'s uncle and guardian in Colonsay but the letter, written on 31 July 1579, was intercepted by the English. It gives us a clear idea of the value of such a man as Ranald, then about 29 years old:

> "James Fitz Maurice, to Ranald MacDonnell – The custom of the letter [i.e. "Greetings"], from James, son of Maurice, to his friend and companion Randal, son of *Colla Maeldubh*, [alias *Colla nan Capull*] and tell him that I told him to collect as many *bonaght* men [professional soldiers] as he can, and come to me, and that he will get his pay according to his own will, for I was never more thankful to God for having great power and influence than now. Advise every one of your friends who likes fighting for his religion and his country, better than for gold and silver, or who wishes to obtain them all as their wages, to come to me, and that he will find each of these things."

Another, later, record confirms that, despite his base in lonely Colonsay, Ranald continued to be active in Ireland in those heady and romantic years, for he is known to have been fighting in Munster in 1586.[13]

Cattle Raid at Inbhir Cnoc Bhreach

Regardless of expeditions to Ireland, Ranald seems to have concentrated his efforts on the job in hand in Scotland, and was certainly prominent in support of his cousin Angus in the feud that arose with *Lachlan Mór*; for he accompanied Angus in 1585 on a peace-making visit to the MacLean Castle of Duart, trying to resolve a desperate and deadly feud which had been created through malice. *Donald Gorm Mór* of Sleat had been on his way to visit his kinsman Angus of Dunivaig in Islay, and had sheltered overnight in McLean's part of Jura, at *Inbhir Cnoc Bhreach* ["Speckled Hill Inlet"] in the Sound of

Islay, almost opposite *Bunnahabhain* ["Mouth of the Burn"]. Unfortunately one Hugh *MacGhilleasbuig Chléirich* ("Hugh, son of Archibald the clerk"), a relation but a vengeful outlaw, had sheltered in a neighbouring bay and, seizing the opportunity, stole away with some cattle. As he had intended, *Donald Gorm Mór* got the blame; the MacLeans discovered their loss before dawn and launched a savage attack on Donalds's unsuspecting men who had bivouacked on the shore. The party suffered heavy losses and, although Donald himself had slept on board and so escaped, he and his clan were outraged and sought revenge.

Angus of Dunivaig sought to prevent yet more bloodshed and undertook to visit *Lachlan Mór* MacLean to arrange some sort of conciliation; naturally he was accompanied by leading members of his own clan. It should be mentioned that *Lachlan* was brother-in-law to Angus, whose marriage to *Lachlan*'s sister had been intended to increase harmony between the two families. Incredibly, *Lachlan Mór* broke every known rule of hospitality and kidnapped the entire party ... except Ranald, *Colla Ciotach*'s uncle, who somehow guessed what was to happen and escaped. Eventually Angus was released, but not before he had been forced to assign his remaining rights in the Rinns of Islay to *Lachlan Mór*. Angus was obliged to leave as hostage his young son James (later to become Sir James MacDonald), as well as his own brother Ranald, known as Ranald of Smerby.[14] Young James, of course, was also the nephew of his captor, fruit of the marriage mentioned above.[15]

The ramifications of the dispute ran well beyond the horizons of the participants, for feuds such as these were of interest in the wider world. In a letter of 22 August 1585 Wotton wrote to Walsingham, Queen Elizabeth's Secretary, concerning a league of co-operation with King James, in which Scottish mercenaries were to be removed from Ireland. Wotton was acting on behalf of the English authorities, and made an interesting suggestion:

> "Hee [King James] ys presentlye to direct his lettre to Sorle boy, and Agnus Maconell, to commaunde theym to revoke their Highelande followers which ar passed into Irelande ... yet these Highelanders (as farre as I can see) care but little for the King, and will obeye him at their owne pleasure. But the thing that gevethe mee most hope of their revocation, ys a quarrell that ys latelye fallen out between Agnus and Macclan [MacLean], who have ben together by the eares within these 2 dayes (as I am informed) and Makklan hathe slayne 140 of Agnus his men. I am (for myne owne parte) of opinion, that yf her majestie wolde bestowe a yerelie pension of one hundred or two hundred poundes upon Makclan, yt wold save her 4000 or 5000 poundes everye yere in here Irish expences, – for this Makclan (being a great Lorde in the Highelandes) and having a deeidly fewde against Agnus, upon whom hee borderethe, were hee her majesties pensioner, wolde be redye at all tymes, whensoever eyther Agnus or Surleboy sholde sterte into Irelande, to spoyle and burne their countryes. So that the feare thereof wolde (as I thincke) keepe theym from goyng (or yf at any tyme they dyd go) wolde quycklye call theim home agayne....."

The Feast at Mulindry

Being forced to leave the hostages behind on Mull, Angus of Dunivaig returned to Islay, ostensibly to make arrangements for the MacLeans' ingoing to their newly secured property. In July 1586, Sir *Lachlan Mór* MacLean arrived in Islay, complete with young James as hostage, and established himself in the castle on the island of Loch Gorm. Angus invited *Lachlan Mór* and his retinue to move into a property of his own, the Longhouse of Mulindry (Mullintrae, not far from modern Bowmore), as being more comfortable, and gave earnest assurances of goodwill. Eventually, and after much persuasion, *Lachlan* agreed to take up the offer and there was a great and cordial feast. Later that night, when the MacLeans had retired, and after the house had been silently surrounded by 200 of his supporters, Angus went knocking at *Lachlan*'s door, pressing him to take a night-cap. *Lachlan Mór* made his excuses but Angus pressed so warmly that at last he emerged, bearing the 12 year old James on his shoulders; Angus, of course, had his sword ready drawn, but James pleaded earnestly for his uncle's life and *Lachlan Mór* was spared, although imprisoned in another room. Most of his men surrendered, but two of them put up a desperate defence; these were the two allegedly involved in the original trouble on Jura, one of them being a henchman of *Lachlan Mór* and the other, Angus MacDonald of Harris, being a close associate of Hugh *MacGhilleasbuig Chlèirich* who had actually stolen the cattle. Eventually, their attackers becoming impatient, the building which they were defending was put to the torch and they perished.

Word of these developments soon reached Mull, where *Lachlan*'s brother, Alan MacLean, had been left in charge of the remaining hostages, Ranald of Smerby and (according to Hill), Ranald of Colonsay, Coll's uncle. If anything fatal were to have happened to his brother *Lachlan Mór*, Alan's prominence would have become permanent .... so, nothing loath, Alan took the chance to inflame things by letting it be known (falsely) that Ranald of Smerby had been executed; Ranald's "brothers" on Islay immediately started to take a measured revenge, by executing two of their MacLean hostages daily. Since there were eighty-six of them, it took some time, but eventually they were so whittled down that only two were left, *Lachlan Mór* and *Iain Dubh* of Morvern. Angus of Dunivaig was determined to be present at their deaths, but suffered an accident on the way there (in which he is said to have broken a leg), and the delay was just long enough for Alan MacLean's ruse to be uncovered.

Coll's uncle Ranald had barely escaped the original treachery at Duart Castle, and he was presumably involved in the necessary negotiations to secure the release of Angus. In the confusion after the events at Mulindry, and whilst one or both Ranalds were apparently captive on Mull, the executions on Islay are said to have been conducted by Ranald of Smerby's "brothers" (presumably Angus and Coll). The senior brother, Angus of Dunivaig, was doubtless in control, but, as has been seen, tradition strongly suggests that he was not present throughout the proceedings, merely being minded to attend the *coup de grâce* for *Lachlan Mór* himself. Gregory is quite specific: "Coll McJames, under the impression that his brother Ranald [of Smerby] had really been executed, let loose his vengeance against the rest of the unfortunate prisoners. Two of these were executed every day ...." Very probably young *Colla Ciotach* will have been at his side, avenging one or both of his two "murdered" uncles.

At all events, it seems quite certain that both *Colla Ciotach* and his uncle Ranald were closely concerned in all these tumultuous events. Alan MacLean's deception being ultimately revealed, a truce was negotiated and in April 1587 Angus of Dunivaig released *Lachlan Mór* in exchange for a full pardon and eight substitute hostages, including *Lachlan Mór*'s own son and heir. No doubt Ranald of Smerby will have had some sort of family celebration when he was released, and it is pleasant to think that in such happy circumstances his daughter, Mary, will have noticed her seventeen-year old cousin, Coll, her future husband. It was also at about this time that *Colla Ciotach* made his decision to stay permanently in his adopted island, for he gave his Antrim home at *Ceann Bán* to a MacAllister of Colonsay who had gone to soldier in Ireland for *Somhairle Buidhe*.

Notes

1 The idea had been to marry the two infant monarchs to create a union between the realms; the Scottish nobility agreed, but discovered it was out of touch with the populace and had to renege: "if you had the las and we the lad we coulde be well content with it .... our nacyon, being a stoute nacyon, will never agree to have an English man to be the King of Scotlande. And though the hole nobilite of the realme wolde consent unto it yet our comen people and the stones in the strete wolde ryse and rebelle ayenst it." Sir Adam Otterburn, quoted by Sir Ralph Sadler some years later.

2 The English knew that Clan Donald had established the exclusive rights to supply mercenary troops in the north of Ireland, troops which had recently been used with good effect on behalf of O'Donnell and MacQuillan against Hugh O'Neill; the English believed that the MacDonalds had gained much booty and that it had been taken for safety to Rathlin. Thus for greed the English launched an attack by land into Antrim, and by sea upon Rathlin. At Rathlin, an attempt to reconnoitre fell into farce when "a soddaine sourde off the sea came at ebb and sett their boate upon the rockes". 25 men were drowned and 4 survivors captured by the Scots, who were afterwards exchanged for Sorley Boy (who had been captive) and a huge ransom. The Annals of the Four Masters confirm that James of Dunivaig and the Glens was in Rathlin at the time, together with *Colla Maeldubh* (Coll the Dark Chieftain), *Colla Ciotach*'s grandfather. The mortified English commander threatened that "he wolde complayne to the kingis Majesty, and certifie the governour of Skotlande of (James') evil demeanour in this behalfe" – i.e. in resisting an unprovoked attack!

3 There may also have been a third son, Alexander. The ruins of Bonamargy Friary are a short distance from the harbour of modern Ballycastle and the graveyard and well-preserved vaults will reward the interested visitor. The Franciscan Friary at Bonamargy was an important centre of the 17th century Scottish counter-reformation.

4 In certain MacDonald manuscripts another version of the name is given, as reference is made to fosterage "in the household of a gentleman of the O'Quinns of Carnrighe (Kilrea), near Coleraine"

5 Some years earlier, in his teens, *Gilleasbuig Fiacal* is specifically recorded as having been present when Shane O'Neill was allegedly murdered in revenge for the death of James of Dunivaig and the Glens. Shane had suffered a staggering reverse in *Tirconnell* (Donegal) and "he sent despatches inviting the sons of James, the son of Alexander, son of John *Cathanach*, the sons of Mac Donnell, from Scotland. That was the cause of shortness of life, and of death, for him to invite the sons of the man who had fallen by his hands on a former occasion. They accordingly came with a large fleet, and landed at *Bun Abhann Duine* (Cushendun), in Ulster, where they constructed a strong camp, with numerous entrenchments. When O'Neill received intelligence of that large force having come to his aid, without taking into consideration his former enmity towards them, he incautiously committed himself to the protection of that fierce and revengeful clan, without pledge or security, in order that he might avenge his enmity and hatred against the Tirconnallians. The reception he got from them, after being in their company for some time, and after they had detailed their former animosity and injuries, was suddenly to attack him, and instantly cleave him with their swords, so that they left him dead on the spot". After being buried for some days, his body was exhumed and his head was sent to the authorities "pickled in a pipkin", to be exhibited on a spike; but it was widely rumoured that the whole thing was an elaborate hoax, that Shane was alive and well and that the decomposing head was a substitute.

6 *Colla nan Capull* had earned the respect of O'Donnell and O'Neill as well as MacQuillan, whose daughter he had married. Now his son, *Gilleasbuig*, had married a daughter of O'Cahan, an important chieftain whose territory bordered that of MacQuillan, on the western side of the Bann. *Gilleasbuig*, like *Iain Cathanach* (the grandfather of both *Colla nan Capull* and *Somhairle Buidhe*) had been fostered in that family – any concern by *Somhairle Buidhe* might have been understandable. Territorial claims based on native alliances might have been more acceptable to Elizabeth of England than those of invaders from Scotland, the old enemy.

7 The Loch itself was named for the island in the middle (*Loch-Leithinnsi*, "Lake of the Half Island"), which

was taken to be half-and-half the property of the people on the opposite shores. The Loch no longer exists, having been drained in the course of agricultural improvements. (O.S. ref G991368)

8 In point of detail, the Scottish estates had passed to an elder brother, *Gilleasbuig,* before the death of James, but the elder brother had died by c. 1567, and Angus will have been getting to grips with his problems when his cousin Randal became available to help.

9 Although his father had married a daughter of the 3rd Earl of Argyll, and his grandfather had been married to a daughter of MacIan of Ardnamurchan, Angus will have been well aware that these alliances were more of a threat than a help to future generations.

10 Not to be confused with the site of the Viking Boat Burial nearby.

11 Interestingly enough, the late Peter McAllister, a Colonsay resident, once came across some old swords stacked in a cleft in the rocks on *An Corra Dhùnan* and they were eventually examined by archaeologists from RCAHM, who confirmed a late mediaeval date.

12 *Colla Ciotach*'s mother will, of course, have been accompanied by retainers and peers; the *O'Cahan* family remained prominent in Colonsay for generations and the records of 1624 mention some half-dozen individuals, including a noblewoman, just possibly Coll's mother. (See Appendix) That her family remained important may be seen from the Annals of the Four Masters, e.g. 1577: "O'Kane, i.e. son of Aibhne, the son of Cumaighe, son of Roderick of the Routes, was drowned in the Bann; and Roderick, the son of Manus, son of Donogh, was appointed his succesor. Meva, the daughter of Hue Roe O'Donnell, who was first married to Mac Gille Eoain (MacIan), of Scotland, and secondly to Donald Clerach O'Kane, a woman who enjoyed this worls in happiness, prosperity, and affluence, and was highly distinguished in fame and excellence, in hospitality, and elegant manners, and who spent a long time in piety in Donegal, died, after performing many virtuous deeds, in the 87th year of her age."

13 A large force of MacDonalds, some 2000 strong, went to the assistance of the Burkes of Mayo, but rather overstayed their welcome in Ireland that year and suffered serious losses against Sir Richard Bingham's force, at the Battle of Ardnaree. In the same year, *Somhairle Buidhe*'s son *Alasdair* was killed: "Alexander, the son of Sorley Buighe, son of Alexander, son of John Cathanach, the son of Mac Donnell of Scotland, who was brother of *Inghean Dubh* [the original "nut brown maiden"], the wife of O'Donnell, and mother of Hugh Roe, son of Hugh, son of Manus, was slain ... in the month of May precisely."

14 Rev. Hill states that Coll's uncle Ranald was also given up as hostage at this point and "thrown into a dungeon at Dowart castle", but this may be a confusion of names.

15 In order to appreciate how all this will have influenced his background, it is worth noting again how closely young *Colla Ciotach* (now fifteen) was related to all these individuals: Angus of Dunivaig and Ranald of Smerby were cousins of Coll's father, *Gilleasbuig Fiacal,* and also of his uncle Ranald, who had escaped from the initial trap. Ranald of Smerby was also to be Coll's father-in-law, for Coll eventually married his daughter Mary. Young James, as well as being second cousin to Coll, was full cousin to Coll's wife.

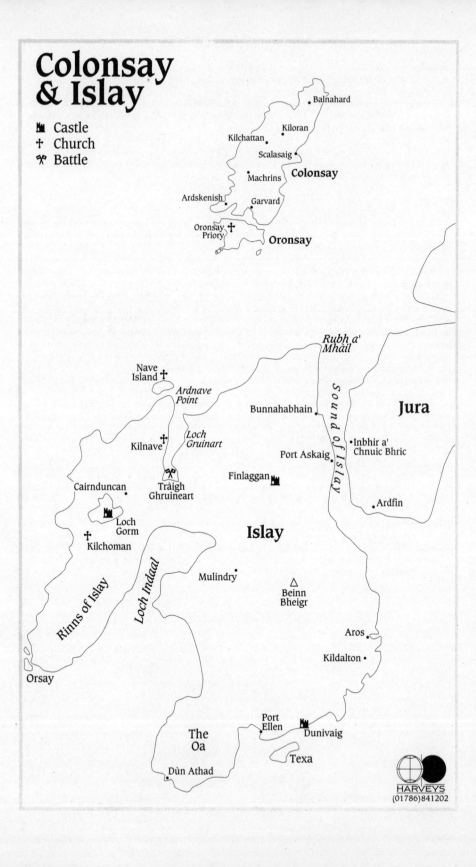

Colonsay & Islay

- 🏰 Castle
- ✝ Church
- ⚔ Battle

Balnahard

Kilchattan

Kiloran

Scalasaig

Colonsay

Machrins

Ardskenish

Garvard

Oronsay
Priory ✝

Oronsay

Rubh a'
Mhail

Nave
Island ✝

Ardnave
Point

Bunnahabhain

Sound of Islay

Jura

Kilnave ✝

Loch
Gruinart

Port Askaig

Inbhir a'
Chnuic Bhric

Finlaggan 🏰

Cairnduncan

Tràigh
Ghruineart ⚔

Ardfin

🏰
Loch
Gorm

✝ Kilchoman

Islay

Mulindry

△
Beinn
Bheigr

Rinns of Islay

Loch Indaal

Aros

Kildalton

Orsay

Port
Ellen

Dunivaig 🏰

The
Oa

Texa

Dùn Athad

HARVEYS
(01786)841202

3

THE GROWTH OF ROYAL AUTHORITY

The Forfeiture of Angus of Dunivaig

Now that he had secured the release of both the Ranalds and his own son, and had also gained important MacLean hostages (including the heir to their Chief), Angus of Dunivaig turned his attention to other affairs; but within a couple of months, in the summer of 1587 and whilst Angus was away in Ireland, *Lachlan Mór* fell upon Gigha and Islay and ravaged them with fire and sword in an orgy of revenge. Although Ranald MacDonald of Colonsay was also away in Ireland at about that time, Colonsay may have been adequately defended, since there is no record of it being involved in this reprisal.

On his return, Angus left his hostages unharmed but launched a campaign of retaliation, in which he and his men swept through Mull and Tiree, killing as many of the inhabitants and livestock as they could find. Meantime, *Lachlan Mór* MacLean was busy laying waste most of Kintyre. In no time at all, the whole of the west coast was embroiled since, in the words of Gregory:

> "It may easily be conceived that the effects of this deadly feud were not confined to the Clandonald of Isla and the Clanlean. Besides the Macdonalds of Isla and Sky, who were more particularly involved, there were numbered, among the opponents of the Macleans, the Clanranald, the Clanian of Ardnamurchan, the Clanleod of Lewis, the Macneills of Gigha, the Macallasters of Loup, the Macfies of Colonsay, and other tribes of lesser note. On the other hand, among the partisans of the Macleans we find the Clanleod of Harris, the Macneills of Barra, the Mackinnons, and Macquarries."

The Government sought to act decisively; Angus was ordered to hand over his hostages to the Crown, and both sides were to avoid all further gatherings or hostilities whilst the authorities sought to bring about a settlement to all the disputes. In pursuit of this an Act known as the "General Band", was passed: all landlords and chiefs had to put up a substantial sum as guarantee for their conduct and that of their vassals or clansmen, and injured parties were to be compensated from these monies, which were also to be subject to fines in favour of the Crown. For a brief period MacLean held the advantage, as he readily agreed to be bound by these terms, whereas Angus of Dunivaig was declared outlaw.

But *Lachlan Mór* was not the man to be quiet for long, and he quickly became involved in an extravagant outrage against John MacIan of Ardnamurchan when he committed such an enormity as to introduce a byword to the language. John MacIan had come to Mull in the role of bridegroom to *Lachlan*'s mother (a Campbell), and *Lachlan Mór* himself had been going along with the arrangements, since he rather hoped thereby to secure MacIan's support in his feuds. Although it had become clear that MacIan was going to prove a disappointment in this respect, the marriage went ahead as planned "at Torloisk in Mull; but the very same night John MacIan's chamber was forced, himself taken from his bed out of MacLean's mother's arms, and eighteen of his men slain", because he refused to assist MacLean against Angus MacDonald. "Although his life was spared through the urgent pleadings of his bride, he was imprisoned and subjected to daily torture". These proceedings came to be commemorated in the popular expression "MacLean's Nuptials", as describing festivities best avoided.

As if this was not enough, fate provided *Lachlan Mór* with the opportunity to commit further enormities when the "Florida", a large vessel from the remnants of the Spanish Armada, was forced to take shelter in Tobermory. *Lachlan Mór* arranged the refit and victualling, and accepted the temporary services of one hundred Spanish soldiers in payment, with whose aid he ravaged the whole of the Small Isles. It is said that he massacred the entire populations of Rum, Eigg, Canna and Muck and laid waste the lands of Ardnamurchan. Meantime, not to be outdone, the MacDonalds had augmented their own strength with a band of English mercenaries and fallen once more upon the lands of MacLean.

The situation had clearly gone beyond the bounds of all reason; desperate circumstances called for desperate measures and the government chose to sacrifice honour in pursuit of results. Full pardons under the Privy Seal were issued in favour of *Lachlan Mór*, Angus of Dunivaig and also Donald *Gorm* ("birthmarked") MacDonald of Sleat; with guarantees of safe conduct they were induced to come to Edinburgh in order to work out solutions to their differences. Yet as soon as they arrived they were immediately imprisoned, the remissions were waived and Angus and *Lachlan Mór* were charged with treason. (The very serious charge of treason arose because they had employed foreign mercenaries, rather than making do with local ones).

At this point, the financial difficulties of James VI came into play; he could not find a way to control the Western Isles without expense, and yet was convinced that they were an area of great potential. He had been heavily misinformed as to the value of the fisheries and the quality of the land and minerals; the internecine feuding had led to substantial arrears in rents and taxes and had prevented any economic development or exploitation of these imagined priceless assets. He agreed to release his prisoners in exchange for fines and financial guarantees, plus a series of detailed undertakings as to conduct and behaviour. The king retained the right to impose a sentence of death and forfeiture in the event of backsliding, and also insisted on holding hostages at Edinburgh to further guarantee the behaviour of the MacDonalds. John Campbell of Calder, guardian to the young Earl of Argyle, stood surety for the MacDonalds; and John Campbell of Ardkinglas performed the same office for the MacLeans.

Curiously enough, these two guarantors had their own differences. John Campbell of Calder was within a few years to be murdered at Knippoch, beside Loch Feochan, in 1592; three bullets pierced his heart, fired by a man called MacEllar from a "hackbut supplied by Ardkinlass".[1]

This murder was connected with much wider events, including the murder of the "Bonnie" Earl of Moray, and led to a significant feud between the house of Campbell of Calder and that of Stewart of Appin, who had been heavily involved in the plot. It affected the unravelling events in the islands by quite simply moving the centre of attention elsewhere, giving both *Lachlan Mór* and Angus of Dunivaig the chance to ignore their responsibilities. King James VI did issue various reminders, but Angus refused to submit and in 1594, just a century after the Act of Forfeiture had destroyed the Lordship of the Isles, the very estates of *Clann Iain Mhóir* were also declared forfeit.

Apart from the forfeiture, the king was fully engaged in the suppression of the revolt of the Catholic Earls and this prevented him from taking more forceful action until 1596. Early in that year, one of the king's hostages was authorised to visit Angus of Dunivaig, to persuade him of the gravity of his position. That hostage was James, now 22 years of age, Angus' eldest son and the same James that had been *Lachlan Mór*'s passport at the Longhouse of Mulindry.

Angus did now at last submit; the terms that he was forced to accept included provision for "plantation" of his lands, a concept that was later to be developed in the decision to grant Lewis and Harris to a group of Lowland adventurers for colonial exploitation, and eventually further refined in the more comprehensive Plantation of Ulster. The humble island of Colonsay was distinguished by being included in the provision of 1596, cited by Loder:

> "His Majestie sall have full libertie with the said Angus [of Dunivaig] and his sonis consent, to dispone upon the landis of Ilay nocht sett to Makclane, and also upoun the haill ilis of Jura and Colanza, and upoun the said fourtie merkland adjacent to Kilkarrane, as his Majestie sall think gud for planting of burrow townis with civile people, religioun, and traffique of merchandice thairupoun."

James MacDonald was knighted for the success of his efforts, although he continued to be held at Edinburgh as an hostage; but his father paid a high price for his delay, since the Rinns were granted to MacLean and he was also deprived of his properties in Kintyre; he kept the rest of his estates, but had to agree to surrender Dunivaig Castle to the Crown.

At this point a startling intervention from Ireland reveals just how serious had become the threat to the estates of Angus of Dunivaig, and therefore to the interests of the new Sir James MacDonald. On 26 October 1596 his kinsman, James MacDonnell [MacDonald] of Dunluce, wrote to King James; he was a younger son of *Somhairle Buidhe* and the cousin of Angus of Dunivaig.[2] In his letter he reminded the King of past services of his family and went on to suggest that he had a more valid claim to *Clann Iain Mhóir* estates in Scotland than did Angus, hinting that the latter was illegitimate. He also mentioned that he had rejected overtures from Angus, inviting him to assist in military adventures against the King. Clearly this letter was a big threat, not least to the scavenging interests of Clan Campbell, whose manoeuvring would be put at nought if the king obtained a more satisfactory tenant; not surprisingly, therefore, Argyll used all his influence to support the claim of Angus of Dunivaig, and thereby his own long-term prospects. Although his claim did not succeed, James MacDonnell was invited to Edinburgh and gained a knighthood together with 30 merklands in South Kintyre. Sir John Skene gives an account in a letter to the Lord Secretary:

> "James McConeill, aliter James McSorlie, hes, be ane supplicatioun gevin in to the secreit counsall, desyrit infestment of the haill lands possest be Angus McConeill to be geuin to him, be ressoun yat he allegis the said Angus to be bastard, and yat he is narrest and lauchfull [air] to wmquhill James McConeill, his father's broyer, and to wmquhill Allestar McConeill, his

guidsir. Quhilk petitioun was refusit. Alwayis the kingis majestie is veray desyrous to gif him sum piece of land upon this realme, fra the quhilk he may tak his styll of knychtschip, for his is to be maid knycht on sonday nixt cummis. Sum thinkis yat he sall haif inchgarvy, sua yat Johne fentoune consent yairto, because it is ane ile wpon ye see. ... Suirlie he is ane veray veill manert gentilman, and abill of body, and in yis toun veray temperat of his mouth.... In ye wery moment of tyme yat his bill was red in the counsall, my Lord Argyill com in, and eftir his reuerence done to the king, sat down in counsall, and ye said James McConeil beand present, schew na signe of reuerence unto his Lordship. Angus McConeil has bene heir, and his sone Sir James; he is past hame, and his sone is with the king at the hunting in Haltoun. .... My lord of Argyll is returnit hame this morning, very tymouslie, quha, as I persaue, dois all yat he may for Angus againis James McConeill." April 28 1597.

In the same letter, Sir John Skene confirms that the King had set out certain conditions for Angus, as negotiated through the intervention of his son, Sir James MacDonald: to pay up his outstanding rents; to remove "his wyf, barnes, and famelie, furth of the lands of Kintyre"; remove himself completely from the Rinns of Islay ("set to McClene in tak and assedatioune"); and to hand over the castle of Dunivaig to the King's representatives, "befoir the twentie day of the nixt moneth" i.e. before May 20 1597.

The Fire at Askomel

The political realities were changing quickly; the King was absolutely determined to get total control of the Highlands, and in that same year, 1597, an Act of Parliament ordered everyone to produce title deeds or charters to support any claim that they might have to occupy land. Once more, Angus decided to tough it out; but his son Sir James MacDonald had been held at court long enough to realise that these delays were exasperating the Crown and could lead to the final destruction of his patrimony. He was again released from Edinburgh, to encourage his father to accept the situation; Sir James went to Kintyre, insisting that his father should honour an earlier agreement and pass everything into his own hands, but Angus refused.

Relations appear to have been cordial at first; Sir James was staying at Smerby, his uncle's house, and his father was living just a few miles away in his own house at Askomel, and came over for a drink on at least one occasion. Negotiations proved fruitless, however, and when Sir James became impatient it so happened that one Gorrie MacAllister, Chief of Loup was at hand. Having just killed his guardian, he was now in hot pursuit of that guardian's sons, who had gone to Angus for protection, and it was natural that Gorrie would offer to help put pressure on the occupants of Askomel. It is said that Sir James went to Askomel under cover of darkness, with MacAllister and a force of 300 men, and set fire to the house, knowing that his parents were inside. Gregory states that "at length his father, endeavouring to make his escape, was made prisoner, after being severely burnt and suffering many indignities from Sir James' servants". But some say that Angus was growing old and wandered, and set fire to the place himself, in a confused re-enactment of the time that he had burned the houseful of MacLeans on Islay (at the Longhouse of Mulindry). Whatever the truth of the matter, the fire flushed him out and into the arms of his opponents. Although the older man was badly burned, Sir James held his father captive in irons at Smerby, and, with official sanction, took over the leadership of *Clann Iain Mhóir*.

During the next few months, Sir James put these harrowing events behind him whilst he sought to consolidate his position and it is interesting to see that he concluded bonds with certain of his tenants, who presumably accepted that his was a rising star.

"At Glasgow, the 19th day of January, the year of God, fifteen hundred, four score, and sixteen years, the which day we *Gillespik Makduffie*, indweller in Isla and John *Groiame Mac vic Eachene*, indweller in Colonsay, grants and confesses us by the faith and truth of our bodies to have taken and accepted Sir James MakConell of Knockrynsay, Knight, Master of Kintyre, as our only Lord and Master and promises faithfully never to leave the said Sir James during our life-time, and shall maintain, assist, fortify and defend the said Sir James, contrar all men whatsomever to the uttermost of our power, in all things, and at all times hereafter." This document was witnessed by "Alexander Makdougall, Parson of Kildaltone, John McCay and John Stewart, servitors to the said Sir James with others diverse."

A similar agreement was made the following summer, between Sir James MacDonald and "my loving servitor and native kynd man, Donald Makduphee, Pryor of Oronsay", who signed both for himself and his brother "At Simerby the 3rd of July, 1597, before these witnesses – Gillespic Mac vic Allister of the Largie, John MacGillespic vic Cay, John Oig Mac Marc Nis, and John Steward, writer hereinto with others diverse."

The Battle of Traigh Ghruineart

Meanwhile, Sir *Lachlan Mór* MacLean having noted that *Clann Iain Mhóir* was in a weak-ened condition through internal strife, took the opportunity to enhance his grip on the Rinns of Islay. He was no doubt secretly encouraged in this by the Campbells, and we may be equally certain that Sir James MacDonald was evenhandedly encouraged to resist. Professor MacKinnon puts the central problem neatly: "*Bha a' chrìoch eadar an dá oighreachd aig Port Ascaig an Caol Ile, ach có bu leis Port Ascaig?*" ("There was a boundary between the two territories at Port Askaig on the Sound of Islay, but whose was Port Askaig?"). Sir James was keen to avoid bringing matters to a head and made strenuous efforts to reach some sort of honourable compromise; but *Lachlan Mór* took this for a sign of weakness and refused to co-operate.

On 5 August 1598, the Battle of *Tràigh Ghruineart* ("Loch Gruinart Strand") was fought to determine the matter, between the forces of Sir James and the much greater forces of his uncle, *Lachlan Mór*; it was to be the last Clan battle ever fought and it was a bloody one. Before the battle, *Lachlan Mór* was given advice by a spey-wife: he was not to anchor at *Poll-nusaig* ("Anchorage Pool"), he was not to take a drink at the well of *Neil Neònach* ("Strange Neil"), and he was not to plant his standard on *Cnoc nan Aighean* ("Hinds' Hillock"). In the event, he decided to anchor well away from his usual spot, so as to avoid an immediate confrontation with the MacDonalds at *Tràigh Ghruineart*; he then made his way up past Ardnave ("Holy Point"), found the going thirsty and took a drink from the well at the foot of a wee green hill ... only to find that it was the one that he had been warned against, *Tobar Neil Neònach*. At this stage he discovered that the place where he had anchored was called *Poll-nusaig*. It gave him pause for thought, but he pressed on and a little later he found the ideal place to raise his standard, a beautiful sandy knoll ... no sooner was the flag unfurled than he discovered his error: the knoll, of course, was *Cnoc nan Aighean*.

Despite the portents, he went ahead with the battle and, of course, his forces met with their preordained defeat. Sir *Lachlan* himself was shot dead by a 'small, dark man' from Jura, whom we can assume from all evidence to have been a MacDuffie; before the battle *Lachlan Mór* had been offered the services of this man, but had rejected them with contempt. There are no contemporary records, but Arra Fletcher gives a distinctive account of the individual from his own family tradition: "There came to MacLean an ugly, hunch-backed dwarf called *Dubh Sìth* ("black fairy")[3], because of his dark skin and black hairy appearance. His father was a Shaw[4] from Lagg on Jura and his mother was a fairy woman." The dwarf, *Dubh Sìth*, is said to have hidden in a tree near a well, and to have shot an arrow through Sir *Lachlan*'s forehead when he raised his visor in preparation for a drink of water. The well is said to have been the one already mentioned, *Tobar Neil Neònaich*, and it is interesting to find that the name of "*Neil Neònach Makduphee* in Migirnes" appears in c. September 1606 as a signatory to a petition to the king.[5]

J.F. Campbell was given an account of this story by John Dewar, a labourer and self-taught man employed by the Duke of Argyll, which includes further details of the encounter: "*Bha duine ro bheag, ris an abairteadh Dubhsìth Mac Illesheaghanaich, 's theireadh cuid Dubh-sleabha ris, 's chaidh e dh'ionnsuidh camh Mhic Gillean 's dh'iarr e guth de Mac Gillean fein. Chaidh L. McGillean far an robh e, 's dh'fharraid e "Ciod e do ghnothach riumsa?" Thubhairt Dubh-sìth, "airm 's aodach gu dol leibh do'n cath." Sheall McGillean air le tàir, 's thubhairt se ris "ged bheireadh tu airm s'aodach leat, cha tugainn-se aite dhuit measg mo dhaoine." "Seagh, seagh" arsa Dubh-sìth 's e falbh.*

"*Chaidh Dubh-sìth 's raining e camh Mhic Dhomhnuil, 's dh'iarr e guth do McD. Chaidh McD. far an robh e, 's thubhairt e "ciod e do gnothnach riumsa?" "Airm 's aodach, ma bheir sibh cuid duine dhomh." Thubhairt McD. "Bheir mi àite duine dhuit, 's b'fhearr leum gu'n robh coig ceud de d'lei-thid agam.*""

(A very small man, known as Duffy, son of Shaw .... went and sought out MacLean's camp and asked to speak to MacLean himself. MacLean went over to him and asked "What is it that you want of me?" Duffy replied "arms and dress to go with you to battle." MacLean looked on him with contempt, and said to him "Even if you had your own arms and equipment, there would be no place for you amongst my men." "Aye, aye." said Duffy, and went away.

Away went Duffy, to the MacDonald camp, and asked for a word with Sir James. MacDonald went over to him, and asked him "What is it that you want of me?" "Arms and dress, if you will have me as one of your men." MacDonald replied, "I'll have you as one of my men, and I wish I could have 500 more like you.") In this account, MacDuffie had a gun, (the only gun at the battle), but otherwise the details agree.

Although Sir James MacDonald was himself badly wounded and lost about 30 of his men, the MacLean losses were catastrophic; they lost their chief and close to 300 dead. The spot where Sir *Lachlan Mór* fell is marked by a stone, *Clach Mhic'illean*[6]; he was buried at Kilchoman and on the way there, it is said that the cortège rested within view of *Loch Gorm*; he had spent his last night on earth in the little castle on *Eilean Loch Gorm*. As the bearers rested and took refreshment, it was noticed that Sir *Lachlan*'s jaw had loosened and fallen open; a callow youth took the notion to stuff some bread into his open mouth – and was instantly knifed for his pains, by the widow, Lady MacLean.

They put a cairn over him where he lay, where it still stands, and bears his name, "*Cairnduncan*". Dewar tells us that he was known as *Donnachadh Dubh-chasach* ("Black-legged Duncan"), "*gun robh fionna dubh a' fàs air a chasaibh*" (because there was black, shaggy hair growing on his legs); and that he was the servant of the lady who had looked after *Lachlan* when he was fostered in the Rinns, and who now had taken charge of his remains.

The MacLeans and their supporters were enraged at the defeat and the loss of their chief; their own records suggest that the boats carrying more than half their force had gone aground at Nave Island, at the entrance to the loch, and been neaped, thus leaving them shorthanded for the battle. Certainly there seems to have been some difficulty, but Dewar has it that it was *after* the battle that the *birlinns* were ashore, the crews having been too confident of victory. The fleeing MacLeans were unable to escape, and many of them took refuge in the chapel of Kilnave but their merciless pursuers burned the building and all within it, except one fellow, named *MacMhuirich*.

MacMhuirich leaped up on to the wall and out through the burning roof; he rushed to the shore, but by now the boats were leaving and he struck out for Nave Island. An arrow wounded him in the buttock, but he kept swimming and got onto a big rock, known as "'*Bhadag*" ("Drowning"', submerged at high tide), far out in the sea, where he was able to hide under the seaweed. He managed to remove the arrow, and stayed where he was until the rising tide forced him to swim back to the shore, where he landed safely. He spent the rest of his life on Islay, married and had family, known to this day as "*Clann Mhuirich na Badaig*"; his good fortune gave rise to an Islay proverb "*Cho math foighidinn ri fear na saighde*" ("As patient as the fellow with the arrow").[8]

Clan MacLean took a terrible revenge in a devastating raid in the vicinity of Dunivaig, when, according to their *seanachaidh* ("tradition bearers") they claim to have slaughtered many MacDonalds at "Ben Bigrie", the exact location of which is uncertain but could be Beinn Bheigir near the south end of the Sound of Islay. They are said to have had the assistance of Camerons, MacLeods, MacKinnons and MacNeills in this enterprise.

Although Sir James MacDonald had had permission to enforce his father's submission to the king, he had substantially exceeded his remit by holding him prisoner and by becoming embroiled in a fullscale battle against the MacLeans. He now tried to regularise his position with the crown, making an offer to vacate Kintyre and to pension-off his father, but as usual the Campbells were already in action. As Gregory states: "There is reason to believe that the influence of the Earl of Argyle and John Campbell of Calder was already, if not earlier, secretly used in thwarting the endeavours of Sir James to reconcile himself and his Clan to the Government." Certainly Sir James got nowhere with the crown, but he was allowed to be more successful with the Campbells, for in 1599 or so he married Margaret, the sister of John Campbell of Calder.

The continued struggle for leadership of *Clann Iain Mhóir* soon gave the Campbells further opportunities. By 1600 Angus was once more at the helm, and by 1603 he had captured his wayward son, Sir James, and had handed him over to Campbell of Auchinbreck and, through him, to the Earl of Argyll. The latter held him in private custody for some months, but eventually, early in 1604, Sir James came before the Privy Council at Perth, and was imprisoned, first at Blackness Castle and later, after an attempted escape, at Edinburgh, by which time he was held in irons.

Back in lonely Colonsay, all these events will have been followed closely; Ranald and

Colla Ciotach will have been present at most of the main events, together with some of
their tenants. Their preoccupation with matters elsewhere may have been taken as a
sign of weakness, for to some individuals it seemed to be time for new allegiances. On
7 March 1605 Malcolm MacDuffie presented himself and signed a bond for Ronald
Campbell of "Barrichbyand in Craignes (Craignish)":

> "It is contractit agreit and finallie endit for now and ever betwix the honorabill pairties
> undirwrittin, to witt, Gillecallum Makfeithe of Collisnaye and Johne growm McVcKechern
> his foster father and officear of Collisnaye on the ane pairt; and Ronald Campbell of
> Barrichbyand on the uther pairt: – That is to say that quhair the saidis Gillecallum Makfeithe
> and Johne growm McVcKechern byndis and oblissis thame, thair airis and all thair kyn,
> freindis and allya, men servandis, tennentis quhatsumevir that they may stop or latt, that they
> sall assist maintein, and defend the said Ronald Campbell of Barrichbyand his airis, his kyn,
> freindis, men, servantis, tennentis quhatsumevir in all things contrair all utheris quhatsumevir
> be law or by law [beyond law] in the maist straitest forme that can be usit or devysit be oure-
> selffis or onie utheris..." Witnesses were "Donald Mcdonald chrom alias Campbell, George
> Campbell brother to Ronald Campbell foirsaid, John Makfeithe brother to Gillecallum
> Makfeithe of Kollisnaye, Archibald McVcKerchern soune to John growm McVcKechern
> foirsaid, Gillecallum McVcKechern soun to the said Johne growm and Donald growm
> mcmorrachie. Sic subscribitur, We Gillecallum Makfeithe of Kollisnaye and Johne growm
> McVcKechern officear of Kollisnaye with our hands touching the pen becaus we could nocht
> writt. Ronald Campbell of Barrichbyand."[9]

Meantime King James VI was away in England being King James I, and although Angus
promised obedience and paid all his rent, the Campbells took the opportunity through
secret negotiation to secure a lease of Kintyre and Jura. It was granted to Argyll in 1607,
and provoked Sir James to make a further attempt to escape, with another prisoner,
Lord Maxwell:

> "One December evening they succeeded in disarming their immediate guards under the
> pretence of a game, locked them up in the room, and stole out into the dusk. Overcoming
> the keepers of the inner and middle gates, they scaled the outer wall, but Sir James, hampered
> by gyves on his legs, sprained his ankle in jumping to the ground. Lord Maxwell got away. Sir
> James, after trying to conceal himself in a dung-heap, was recaptured by the Constable as soon
> as the alarm was given."

The Submission of Dunivaig

Angus had so far failed to fully submit; the King was far away in London and royal
authority on Islay was vested in the Earl of Argyll. The Castle of Dunivaig was by now
occupied by *Aonghas Og* ("Young Angus"), the younger brother of Sir James
MacDonald, and so far he had refused to surrender it. In 1608 Lord Ochiltree was
appointed Lieutenant of the Isles, to be advised by a council under the leadership of
Andrew Knox, Bishop of the Isles. An expedition was mounted, and when it arrived
at Islay *Aonghas Og* peacefully surrendered the Castle and earned the commendation of
the King. The Castle was then garrisoned by the Crown, and the small castle on *Eilean*

Loch Gorm was destroyed. This same expedition continued to Mull, where a large number of the Western chiefs were invited on board the Bishop's pinnace, "Moon", where they had innocently expected to hear a sermon but instead were kidnapped, in a famous incident leading to the imposition of the Statutes of Iona.

On 6 February 1609 Lord Ochiltree promised the Privy Council that on 16 March he would produce before it Angus MacDonald of Dunivaig, together with two of his sons, and "Coill McGillespik"; Coll was by now in his late thirties and clearly a figure of some importance. Stevenson points out that although this is the first official reference to *Colla Ciotach* it is a significant one. Whether or not Coll came before the Privy Council is unknown, but the trial of Sir James MacDonald went ahead that spring, officially on charges of fire-raising and treason although, of course, the crux of the matter was his attempted escape from unjust custody.

The old story of the fire at Askomel was now raised in earnest; Angus gave evidence, but his wife was even more convincing; one must remember that she was not merely the mother of this troublesome son, but also the sister of *Lachlan Mór* MacLean, the uncle whom James had so decidedly destroyed at *Blàr Tràigh Ghruineairt*. Great detail was given to the court, not of the fire alone but even of "trees" set up as booby-traps outside the door, so that Angus would trip over them whilst trying to rush away from the fire. Sir James refused to use his main defence, a warrant signed by the King and dated at Falkland 8 August 1598, authorising him in the seizure of his father. His forbearance was of value to the King, and although Sir James was sentenced to death the execution was suspended. To his enemies, there was an advantage in keeping the threat of execution hanging over him and thereby over his clansmen.

Even if he was not brought before the Privy Council in March 1609, it is very likely that *Colla Ciotach* will have been present in August of that year when the Statutes of Iona were accepted by the chiefs. Those listed as present include:

> "Angus McDonald of Dunnoveg, Hector McCleane of Dowart, Donald Gorme McDonald of Slait, Rorie McCloyd of Hareis, Donald McAllane VcEane of Ilanterane, Lauchlane McCleane of Coill, Rorie McKynnoun of that Ilk, Lauchlane McClane of Lochbowie, Lauchlane and Allane McCleanis brether german to the said Hectour McClane of Dowart, Gillespie McQuirie of Ullowa, Donald McFie in Collonsaye, togidder with the maist pairt of thair haill speciall freindis, dependairis and tennentis...."

The main business of that day is commemorated in Iona itself in the place-name "*Iomair nan Acht*" ("The Ridge of the Statutes"). The chiefs had to agree obedience to the crown, to assist the forces of the Reformation, to limit the size of their own households, to suppress the bards, have their eldest children educated in the Lowlands and in English etc.[10]

Dunivaig Castle was still occupied by the royal garrison that had been established when it was surrendered by *Aonghus Og*, and Bishop Knox was now rewarded for his work by an appointment as Steward of the Isles; he became Constable of Dunivaig and established his headquarters there, taking possession on 10 August 1610. In the same year, the Earl of Argyll obtained a royal grant of the Barony of Ardnamurchan, but this was now held to include Colonsay and, even on paper, was a threat to *Colla Ciotach* and also to the interests of his close relation, Sir James MacDonald.

The time was not yet ripe, but it was to be against the above background that *Colla Ciotach* was to make his appearance as a key figure in a desperate enterprise, as a high-born member of an ancient and once-powerful family, now on the edge of final destruction. If there was anything to be saved, it would be by defiance of the corrupt Edinburgh administration and a direct appeal for justice to the King himself.

In the century that has been reviewed, the ancient House of MacDonald had endured a terrible ordeal whilst weak and vacillating monarchs had blown with every wind in the attempt to secure or enhance the throne, regardless of the dreadful cost to the inhabitants of the west. The Lords of the Isles had hitherto given security to the population, had encouraged religion, education and the arts. In a very difficult century their heirs had been as hard-headed and determined as most, but they had not cultivated power in Edinburgh and had failed to recognise the intensity of the ambition of the monarchs and their courtiers.

It has not been possible to touch upon every theme in this brief survey. The Lordship had been destroyed, and the forces of the Reformation had virtually annihilated the benefits of Church both in worship and in secular society – indeed those same forces were already intent upon the destruction of their own creature and would eventually plunge the entire nation into civil war. In the west, the security of the old order had been based upon a form of accessible justice, but even that had now been stripped away; central government could not provide stability or security in the Highlands or Islands, but by playing one family against another had come close to completing the total destruction of the old culture. That this was official policy was demonstrated in many of the provisions of the Statutes of Iona, and by the policy of "Planting". It was government policy to drive the indigenous population from the land, by fire and sword, and to confirm incomers in their place by authority of paper and parchment, rather than that of ancient possession.

Donald J. MacDonald completes the *mise en scene*:

"The Islay Chief (Angus) was now old and tired of his hitherto constant and fruitless struggle to secure titles to his lands and preserve his heritage. The last recorded transaction in his life is to be found in a deed of 1st January 1612 by which he surrendered his patrimony in Islay to Sir John Campbell of Cawdor [brother in law to Angus' own son, James] for the paltry sum of 6000 merks. The unhappy transaction marks the triumphant culmination of the process of insidious absorption by the Campbells of the lands of the Islay family."

Notes

1 Those involved in the plot included Duncan MacDougall of Dunollie, whose reward was to have been the lands of Luing. An interesting point is that Campbell of Ardkinglas, on being discovered, resorted to witches, by whose services he hoped to restore his position. The witches may have helped, since he escaped unpunished but he nonetheless felt driven to make a detailed written confession (28 June 1604).

2 James of Dunluce was also a cousin of *Colla Ciotach*'s own father. If there had been any truth in the suggestion that Angus was illegitimate, it would have meant that the rightful heir to the Scottish estates of *Clann Iain Mhóir* was *Colla Ciotach*, not James of Dunluce.

3 MacDuffie of Colonsay has a number of variations in English, of which the most obvious are Duffy and Mahaffey. In Gaelic there are two usual spellings, *Mac a' Phi* and *Mac Dubhsith*. Since a traditional forename in that family is *Dubh* ("Duff"), it seems that *Mac Dubhsith* may well be merely a fuller form of *Mac a' Phi*...

but it is also possible to suggest a connection with *sìth*, meaning fairy.

4 Here it should be mentioned that the Jura name "Shaw" is also locally associated both with the wee folk and with Clan MacDuffie.

5 Entreating for MacDonalds to be allowed to retain Islay: "We beseech your Lordships for the cause of God to let us have our own native said Master your subject during his lifetime, and thereafter his eldest son and heir Sir James ...." (no reply)

6 They say that a faithful page boy hid near the body of his chief, and as he watched, a looter tried to steal a massive gold signet ring from the corpse – the hand being swollen, the looter leaned *Lachlan*'s hand upon a tussock and was preparing to cut off the finger when the brave *gille* shot him through with an arrow. The same story may yet be heard, but now told about a *cailleach* in Islay said to have been robbing bodies washed ashore from the "Transylvania"; whilst about to cut the ring from a victim's finger ("a great big man, black as can be"), she died of shock when the "corpse" suddenly flopped onto its back, the arm going up, and a big, slow voice querying "Is that easier for you, ma'am?"

7 Dwelly gives *badag* (f) = small bunch, cluster or tuft... etc.

8 This story is of some further local interest as it also survives on Colonsay, where *MacMhuirich* was an important family; in the telling, the incident got 'moved' to Uragaig and sited at "*Bogha Mhic a'Bhastair*", but the tale is otherwise faithful and leads to the establishment of the new family on Islay.

9 Sad to note that the descendant of the hereditary record-keeper to the Lords of the Isles could no longer write, but hopefully he could read what he had accepted.

10 Any Highland hotelier will applaud the rather sensible provision which led eventually to the establishment of many of the inns that survive to this day: "The quhilk day the forsaidis personis, considering and **haveing found be experience the grite burdyne** and chairges that thair haill cuntreymen, and speciallie thair tennentis and labourairis of the ground, hes **sustenit be furnissing of meit, drink, and intertenyment to straingeris,** passingeris and utheris idle men without ony calling or vocatioun to win thair leiving, hes, for releif of passingeris and straingairis, **ordanit certane oistlairis to be set doun in the maist convenient placeis within every Ile**, and that be every ane of the foirnamit speciall men within thair awne boundis as thay sall best devyse; quhilkis oistlairis sall haif furnitoure sufficient of meit and drink to be sauld for reasonable expensis."

4

FAMILY LIFE IN COLONSAY

Colla Ciotach's Marriage

The Battle of *Tràigh Ghruineart* had taken place in 1598, when *Colla Ciotach* was about 28 years old, and it was the culmination of the inter-clan struggles that must have dominated his career to date; but of course his private life had been developing meantime, and for information we must rely mainly upon traditional accounts. We know that Coll must have spent much of his formative life engaged in the defence of Colonsay and other MacDonald territory against the depredations of MacLean, and we have seen how unlikely it is that he could have missed *Blàr Tràigh Ghruineairt*, taking place almost literally on his own doorstep. Whether or not he was present at any particular battle, he was certainly kept fully aware of all these events, he was aware of the threat to his ancient house and was conscious of the families and forces that seemed to lie behind it all. In a more immediate sense, he will have been aware that his own estate was at risk, particularly in Colonsay.

After the forfeiture of the Lordship, there had been a period of great confusion as to land tenure and, following the murder of Sir Alexander of Lochalsh in the Prior's House in Oransay, McDuffie and MacIan were briefly rewarded with tenancies of Colonsay, but the main struggle took place over their heads as the Campbells stalked *Clann Iain Mhóir*. We know that from at least 1520 Colonsay was recognised as being part of the territory of MacDonald of Dunivaig, and that in 1545 Queen Mary specifically included it in her grant to James of Dunivaig. The records show that the territory included land in north and south Kintyre (294 marklands and 53 shilling lands), land in Islay (91 marklands and 1064 shilling lands), land in Jura (184 shilling lands), together with allotments in Arran, Gigha, Colonsay and other islands. This grant was renewed in 1558 (the original title deeds having been destroyed in a raid on Saddell by Sussex, Queen Elizabeth's Deputy in Ireland), and this renewal included a provision that "remainder" or inheritance would be to James' brothers, Angus, Coll, Alexander and Sorley.[1]

It is clear, therefore, that the MacDuffies held their position on Colonsay from MacDonald of Dunivaig rather than from the crown, but it is also clear that in the early sixteenth century they had sought to gain the island for themselves. As we have seen, because of its strategic importance Angus of Dunivaig was anxious to retain Colonsay for the MacDonalds, and it was with this in mind that his cousin Ranald, *Colla nan Capull*'s son, was based there. Whether Ranald inherited the island in his own right or was established therein by Angus, it seems that his main function was to create a formidable opposition to MacLean incursions. He was a soldier rather than a farmer and Clan MacDuffie continued in pastoral occupation although with continuing attendant military obligations. On the death of Ranald without issue, his nephew *Colla Ciotach* inherited the lands in Colonsay, where he seems to have been a good landlord and to have put a stop to most of the more casual outrages of the MacLeans. Although he does not seem to have been personally involved in farming affairs in the early years, he eventually established himself and his household in *Sabhal Bàn* ("The White Barn"), a former monastic barn belonging to Kiloran Abbey.[2]

On the domestic front, there is a doubtful story that *Colla* was romantically linked with more than one lady. J.F.Campbell had it that *Colla* was married to a daughter of the Laird of Auchinbreck (i.e. a Campbell), but this seems to arise from later traditions in Kintyre which sought to portray both *Colla* and his son *Alasdair* in an unflattering light – i.e., in some way enthralled to Clan Campbell; another authority, Angus Matheson, thinks that story to be unlikely, but mentions other candidates including one of the *O'Cahans* of Dunseverick (presumably simple confusion here, since *Colla*'s mother was an *O'Cahan*), the daughter of MacDonald of Sanda, a daughter of MacNeil of Barra (possible confusion with *Macconneill*, as in "Marie *Macconneill*", below), and finally a daughter of Ranald of Smerby. Of these candidates, the latter lady fits the accepted tradition on Colonsay and is also favoured by Matheson; *Colla* and his wife Mary were both direct descendants of Alexander of Dunivaig and the Glens and therefore of the Lords of the Isles.

The belief in Colonsay is that Mary was *Colla*'s wife, but that she had been married before, to Ranald MacDonald of Clanranald. A traditional account has it that "she gave him a fine son, *Aonghus Mór Mac Raghnaill.* He repudiated her, and after that she married *Colla Mac Ghilleasbuig* (i.e. *Colla Ciotach*), and became the mother of *Colla*'s children – *Gilleasbuig, Raghnall (Aonghus)* and *Alasdair*, and a bevy of daughters that were married to fine gentlemen". Murdoch MacNeill gives more detail:

> "M'Donald of Keppoch had been married to a woman much younger than himself. For a slighting retort that she made when he was in a playful mood, "*Se sin miolaran an t-seana choin ris a chuilein,*" ("like an old dog trying to sport with the pups"), he sent her away, and she afterwards lived with Coll in Colonsay as his wife. M'Donald, later on, found his way to the island. Coll, on hearing of his arrival, went to apprise his wife, who had been but recently confined. Wishing to find out if she still had any regard for her former husband, he told her that M'Donald had been drowned off the Point of Ardnamurchan. On hearing this, she turned away her face and expired.
>
> "A dispute subsequently arose between Coll and Keppoch [i.e. Ranald McDonald of Clanranald] as to where the body should be taken for burial, Kilchattan or Oronsay; and to settle the matter they resorted to a duel of spears at the western entrance of the mansion-house, afterwards known as *Bealach an t-Sleagh* ("Pass of the Spear")."[3]

Loder suggests the date of this incident as being about 1615, since Keppoch was closely involved in the rising of that year and will have had business in the neighbourhood; but the records of Franciscan missionaries (which will be considered in a later chapter) show that "Maria Domhnaill, nobilis" was attending Mass and Holy Communion on Colonsay in 1624. Interestingly, the same record shows that the lady who was to become Ranald MacDonald of Clanranald's next (and fifth) wife was with Mary on Colonsay at that time, so Ranald may well have made a visit to the island in late 1624 which happened to coincide with Mary's death.

"Clan Donald" states that

> "the first Macdonald of Benbecula was Ranald, fourth son of Allan ix. of Clanranald and well

known by his patronymic of *Raonull Mac Ailein 'Ic Iain*". According to this authority he married "first: Mary, daughter of Ranald Macdonald of Smerbie son of James MacDonald of Dunnyveg and the Glens, and by her had a son *Angus Mor*, from whom sprang the Macdonalds of Ballypatrick in Antrim; second: *Fionnsgoth* Burke, and by her had three sons; third: Margaret, daughter of Norman MacLeod of Harris, widow of Norman *Og* MacLeod of Lewis, without issue; fourth: Mary, sister of Sir Donald MacDonald, first baronet of Sleat, and had by her a son Donald *Gorm*; and fifth: Margaret, daughter of Angus MacDonald of Dunnyveg and the Glens[4], and by her had Ranald, who succeeded him, and seven other children.... he died in Canna in 1636 and was buried at Howmore in Uist."[5]

David Stevenson, the historian, accepts that regardless of other relationships, Mary was the mother of all or most of Coll's children; and agrees that her first husband was indeed Ranald MacDonald of Benbecula, who had repudiated her in 1603 or thereabouts. Ranald must have been keen to keep matters within the family, because wife number five, Margaret, was first cousin to wife number one, the Mary that married *Colla Ciotach*. Margaret, daughter of Angus of Dunivaig and the Glens, is the lady mentioned above, shown by Vatican records to have been living in Colonsay in 1624, by which time her father was dead and her brother, Sir James, was living in exile. Ranald had been in exile together with Sir James, but managed to get permission to return to Lochaber and seems to have made straight for Colonsay. Documents of the Franciscan missionaries, now in the Vatican, record the Sacraments being administered in that year to: "*Margareta Domhnuill, nobilis domina ex magna familia Domhnaldorum, quae praecipua est totius Scotiae familia, antiquitate et potentia spectabilis*" [Margaret MacDonald, a noble lady of the great Clan Donald, which amongst all Scottish houses is principal in antiquity and notable power].[6] Perhaps Ranald went to Colonsay to seek Margaret's hand, coincidentally arriving when Coll's wife had just died, providing the pretext for the story about *Colla Ciotach* having tested his wife's true feelings.[7]

Colla Ciotach's children

Against the above background, and allowing for the turbulent situation in and around Colonsay, it is remarkable that *Colla Ciotach* and Mary were able to maintain any sort of settled family life; but they were both from the same stock, steady in their loyalty to both family and Faith. Stories such as that concerning Mary's death will have been created later in an effort to blacken their name, but there is no evidence that they were anything other than a devoted couple.

They were blessed with children, as has been noted, presumably all borne in the period between 1603 and 1620: The girls included one, named in tradition as either Jean or Sarah, who married MacKay of Ardnacroish; and another thought to have married a brother of MacDonald of Largie. The boys were *Gilleasbuig, Raghnall, Aonghus* and *Alasdair*; *Aonghus* is something of a mystery, but there seems to be a good case for believing him to be a son of Mary's first marriage and therefore stepson to *Colla Ciotach*. There was talk which suggested that there might have been another *Aonghus*, an illegitimate son of *Colla*, but there is no evidence for this. On the contrary, Ronald Black makes use of what evidence there is to suggest very strongly that there was only one *Aonghus*. He is remembered as *Aonghas mac Cholla* in Colonsay tradition and appears in historical record; he is sometimes said to have been executed in 1647, but it seems likely that an account in "Clan Donald" is correct and that he made his way back to Ireland, his issue becoming "the MacDonalds of Ballypatrick".

Gilleasbuig was clearly the eldest of Coll's own sons, as he is named for his grandfather; and *Raghnall* was the second legitimate son, named for Coll's guardian and uncle as well as for his father-in-law; the third, and much younger, son was *Alasdair*, with whom *Raghnall* seems to have been very close. Professor MacKinnon confirms that *Gilleasbuig* was indeed the eldest and had reached manhood by 1623; we know that he married, and was to be survived by a son, Coll, and a daughter, Sarah, who was to marry one *Aeneas* MacDonald. The Franciscan missionaries mention "*Nola Domhnaill, nobilissima matrona*" as well as three of the boys, "*Eneas Domhnuill*", "*Gillatius Domhnaill*" and "*Alexander Domhnaill*" (Angus, Archibald and *Alasdair*). The girls included "*Rosa Domhnuill*" and "*Menina Domhnall, nobilis*". [A full list of those Colonsay inhabitants that were "converted" by the Franciscans is given in an Appendix].

It has been mentioned that *Colla Ciotach* and his family eventually made their home in *Sabhal Bàn*, a former monastic barn at Kiloran; Grieve states that "this building was situated somewhere near the west wall of the fruit and vegetable garden of the present Colonsay House. The *Sabhal Bàn* is said to have been a thatched building with a cellar underneath which used to be filled with old empty wine bottles .... some of the bottles had "Colonsay" stamped upon them." Grieve goes on to describe the discovery of such bottles in the late nineteenth century, but there is, as yet, no firm evidence that the remnants in the walled garden were of anything other than an old vault or possibly a midden. Nonetheless, Murdoch McNeill accepted the same tradition and says that "Some stones at the base of an old elm are said to have formed part of Coll's drying-kiln." Archaeological evidence seems to place the main Abbey buildings some 150 yards northeast of this site, close to *Tobar Odhran* (St. Oran's Well), but of course the barn could easily have been exactly where it was said to have been.[8]

Wherever it stood, it was in *Sabhal Bàn* that *Alasdair MacCholla* was born, the most famous of all Coll's children; he was later to become a figure of international renown, and it is not suprising that stories of his birth and childhood survive. It is still a strong tradition that on the night of his birth the swords, mounted on the walls, leaped from their scabbards and the muskets fired of their own accord – although in view of the confusion that this could have caused, it might be better to accept the less dramatic version that the swords merely rattled whilst the muskets harmlessly cocked themselves. Either way, it caused a stir: "This is a portent", cried the midwife. "Indeed it is!", said Coll, "get a bucket – drown the child at once!"

In the event, Coll was persuaded that the portent suggested that his son would be a mighty warrior, rather than some evil being as he had at first supposed. When the child was a little older, his nurse conducted further research one Hallowe'en and "went out into the kiln with a ball of blue yarn to see what fate had in store for Alasdair. When she came into the house again she said to Alasdair, "*Ní thu móran gaisge fhathast agus théid gach blàr leat gus gun sàth thu do bhratach aig muileann Ghocam-gó, agus cha théid leat tuille 'na dhéidh sin.*" ("You will perform great deeds of valour yet and you will be successful in every battle until you set up your standard at the Mill of Gocam-gó, but you will never be successful after that.") Not much attention was paid at the time to what she had said, but Alasdair always remembered the Mill of Gocam-gó". This account, collected by

Campbell and translated by Matheson, confirms accepted Colonsay tradition.

There are a few other traditions concerning young Alastair. As a youngster, he is said to have got hold of a toad when out with his nurse in the garden; when she took it from him, he howled blue murder until his grandfather [sic, "*sheanair*"] heard all the commotion and told the nurse to give it back to him: "*Thabhair dha i, thabhair dha i, agus leig leis an dárna donas an donas eile itheadh*" ("Give it to him, give it to him, and let one devil eat the other"). Of course, it did him no harm, but was another portent for the future; the "grandfather", had there been any substance in the story, must have been his maternal grandfather, Ranald of Smerby. Sadly, there are no toads in Colonsay, so perhaps we should take it that the incident took place at Smerby itself, perhaps on a family visit.

On Rathlin, it was a tradition that Alasdair was able to twist the foot off a bull ("*a' toirt a mach an dórn bhuar*"), the contemporary equivalent of tearing a telephone directory in half. Campbell's account gives another account along the same lines, but with more detail, (translated by Matheson):

"*Alasdair* grew up to be a tall, hard, sinewy lad and he was an expert swordsman. He had almost attained manhood before he ever wore bonnet or shoes. There was one occasion when *Colla Ciotach* was going to slaughter a cow for winter food. The cow went wild and would butt with her horns anyone within reach, and *Colla Ciotach*'s men could not catch her or hold her and did not dare enter the park in which she was. *Alasdair mac Cholla* came, bare-headed and bare-footed, and said to his father, "*Ma bheir sibh dhomh – sa boineid, paidhir bhròg, agus paidhir osan, beiridh mise air a' mhart agus bheir mi staigh do'n taigh-mharbhaidh i.*" ("If you give me a bonnet, a pair of shoes and a pair of hose, I will catch the cow and bring her into the slaughter-house".)

"Coll said, "*Ma tà Alasdair, ma ní thu sin, bheir mise dhuit boineid 's brògan 's osain.*" ("Well, *Alasdair*, if you do that, I will give you a bonnet and shoes and hose.") *Alasdair* then went into the park where the cow was. The cow made for *Alasdair* and *Alasdair* made for the cow. He caught the cow by the horn and mastered her. He brought her into the slaughter-house, held her with the one hand, got an axe and killed her with the other. His father then gave him a bonnet and shoes and stockings and these were the first bonnet, shoes and stockings that he ever had."

Of course, there have always been 'Rites of Passage' and this incident does not reflect any suggestion of poverty in the household; until recently it would have been the equivalent of a young boy getting his first pair of long trousers and it might be thought that *Alasdair* would have been 10 or 12 yrs old at the time. The Irish tradition has it that he was born about 1620, so this incident might have occurred in the early part of the following decade.

Social, Domestic and Agricultural Conditions

Amongst the domestic activity on Colonsay in the early 1600's there may have been a little construction work, arising from the continuing strife. Loder draws our attention to the Register of the Privy Council, 15 June 1602: "Hector McClane of Dowart, failing to appear as charged to render obedience to his majesty, find caution to pay the King's maills and duties, and answer touching the 'slauchteris, heirschipis and depredations' committed by him upon the King's own tenants of His Majesty's Isles of Oronsay and Colonsay, is to be denounced rebel." Evidently the MacLeans were still a force to reckoned with and it is likely that their neighbours in Colonsay will have devoted a lot of care to their defences.

It may have been at about this time that the secret lairage was created on the summit of *a' Bheinn Bheig* ("The Little Peak"), on the north side of Colonsay's Kiloran Bay, since it is said that it was prepared as a place of concealment for cattle and the surviving remains seem to support that suggestion. Nearby, there are a group of caves including one, *Uamh na Bantighearna* ("The Lady's Cave"), which shows traces of modern occupation, and on the other side of the bay is *An Uamh Ur* ("The New Cave") which is rather better concealed and contains both a well and a smooth stone, said to have been used for sharpening weapons.

More substantial remains exist on *Eilean Dubh Iain Mhitchel* ("John Mitchel's Dark Island) in *Loch an Sgoltaire* ("The Loch in the Cleft"). The island is named after an itinerant priest of the Penal days, who seems to have used it as a place of refuge;[9] substantial fortifications were created there in 1615, and in the early 18th century the MacNeills are said to have lived there briefly. In the 19th century a bower or summer house was built within the walls of a well-preserved fortalice.

It seems likely that *Colla Ciotach* created the basis of this fortification in the years running up to 1614 and very possibly even lived there for a the time, only moving to *Sabhal Bàn* after 1615, when things became more settled. It was to some extent a replica of the little fort on the island in *Loch Gorm* in Islay, with which he was already familiar.[10]

Around this time, as has been noted, Argyll was attempting to secure legal title to *Colla Ciotach*'s estate, whether or not he could yet hope to occupy it. Although the Church lands of Oransay and Garvard are not included, an early document (Reg. Great Seal of Scotland) lists most of the farms on Colonsay and is of some interest since it gives information on rentals and an indication of military resources. The rental agreed suggests that the land was productive even by modern standards:

"Apud Quhytehall, 30 Mar. (1610)
REX, pro sevitio sibi et suis progenitoribus prestito, ac pro pecuniarum summis persolutis, – cum consensu &c., – ad feudifirmam locavit et quitteclamavit ARCHIBALDO ERGADIE COMITI domino Campbell et Lorne, heredibus ejus et assignatis quibuscunque, – terras et ilam de Colonsay (scil. 2´ mercat. terrarum de Ballenehard, 5 mercatas de duabus Killoderans, 2´ mercat. de duabus Gilcattingis, 2´ mercat de Mauchrenecleif et Balleveray, 2´ mercat. de Kilbreid et Maucherybeg, 2´ mercat. de duabus Arskyinis, 2´ mercat. de duabus Ballerymyn, 16 sol. 8 den. de Skallissage, cum castris, manerierum locis, molendinis, piscariis, lacubus, advocationibus ecclesiarum, beneficiorum et capellaniarum) ..... REDDEND, pro Colonsay 34 martas, 34 ververces, 255 petras casei, 255 pet. farine, 8 lib. 10 sol. argenti, et pro Ballerewmyn 4 bol. polenti, pro Ballerewmynmoir 4 bol. polenti, pro Maucherebege 4 bol. polenti, pro Killebreid 4 bol. polenti, pro Ballevoir 4 bol. polenti;..."

"THE KING – for services rendered to him and his forefathers, and for sums of money received – with the concurrence, etc. – has given in feufarm and quitclaim to ARCHIBALD EARL OF ARGYLL, Lord Campbell and Lorne, his heirs and assignees whatsoever – the lands and the island of Colonsay (namely the 2´ merklands of Balnahard, the 5 merklands of the two Kilorans, the 2´ merklands of the two Kilchattans, the 2´ merklands of "Mauchrenecleif" [that part of modern Machrins close to *A' Chrannaig* ("The Pulpit") and

preserved in the names *Machaire na Clibhe* and *Maol Chlibhe*] and "Balleveray" (Baile Mhuirich
or "Currie's Farm", the main part of modern Machrins), the 2´ merklands of Cille Bhríde and
Machaire Beag [the eastern and southern parts of modern Machrins], the 2´ merklands of the
two Ardskenish [one of which is now Ardskenish Glen with Turnigil], the 2´ merklands of
the two Baleromins [Balerominmór and Baleromindubh], the 16 shillings and 8 pence lands
of Scalasaig, with their castles, manors, mills, fishings, lakes, ecclesiastical rights, benefices
and chaplaincies) ....
PAYING for Colonsay 34 Cattle, 34 wethers, 255 stone of cheese, 255 stone of ground flour,
£8 and 10 shillings in silver, and for Balleromin 4 bolls of malt, for Ballerominmor 4 Bolls of
malt, for Machrins 4 bolls of malt, for Cille Bhríde 4 bolls of malt, for Baile Mhuirich 4 bolls
of malt; ..."[11]

The merkland was not a measure of land, rather it was a measure of the productivity of
the land. It could be divided into pennylands, but the actual area of land involved would
vary with its quality and it is interesting to note that the basic divisions and their relative value have remained almost unchanged over almost four hundred years. The total
rental was over 20 merklands, so one can see that the tenantry of Balnahard would have
to produce about 4 cattle and 4 wethers plus perhaps 4 cwt. of cheese and 4 cwt. of
grain just to meet the rental to be paid (through Argyll) to the Crown, but this does not
include profit for Argyll himself, nor that of his agent, nor even the administrative and
physical costs of collecting and transporting the produce.

Until the changes heralded by the Statutes of Iona, additional burthens lay upon the
land in obligations towards the costs of defence; Grant and Cheape give details from
Islay where, in addition to rentals in livestock, victuals and money rent "ilk merkland
man sustein daylie and yeirlie ane gentleman in meit and claith, quhilk dois na labour,
but is haldin as ane of their maisters household men, and man be sustenit and furneisit
in all necessaries be the tennent, and he man be reddie to his maisters service and advis."

Those details came from a report drawn up for James VI, in which Colonsay is
described as a 30 merk land, and Oronsay a 4 merk land "paying dues according to the
Ile of Ila." Unfortunately this document appears to be somewhat in error as it gives
other figures which, if accepted to represent rental and obligations, must be much
higher than the actual resources of the island would permit. They suggest that Colonsay
(with Oransay) could produce about 119 cattle, 476 sheep, 952 geese, 1904 poultry,
over 10 tons of malt, over 12 tons of meal, 4 tons of cheese and £45.6s.8d in cash.

Possibly they refer to the totality of the resources, rather than the rental ... thus the
"twa Iles will raise 100 men" seems reasonable as a statement of fact, but the document
makes clear that only 30 plus 4 persons were maintained in permanent armed readiness
at the expense of the farmers, for service due by MacDuffie of Colonsay to his superior, MacDonald of Dunivaig and the Glens. One third of those in readiness "aucht
and sould be cled with attounes [stuffed leather jackets] and haberchounis [coats of
mail], and knapshal bannetts [iron helmets]

Other obligations included that of "*calp of ceann-cinnidh*", the right of the superior to
the tenant's choicest beast when he died. Even after such charges had become mere
memories elsewhere, having been legally abolished in 1617, they continued to be levied
by the Campbells who tried to levy calps on Colonsay, through a factor, as late as 1646.

Dress at this period was on the point of change. In 1543 John Elder boasted in a letter that "goynge alwaies bair leggide and bair fottide, ... the tendir gentillmen of Scotland call us Reddshankes." The main covering was a checked cloak or plaid, belted about the waist and frequently worn over a linen shirt, usually yellow. Men wore their hair long, without headgear. As the seventeenth century wore on, exposure to English influence will have modified the costume, leading to the spread of hose, trews and flat bonnets amongst the general population of the west.

Food and drink seem to have been reasonably plentiful, and wine consumption was quite high. The Statutes of Iona contained provisions for restraint:

> "it being foundin and tryit be appeirance that ane of the speciall causs of the grite povertie of the saidis Ilis, and of the grite crueltie and inhumane barbaritie quhilk hes been practisit be sindrie if the inhabitantis of the samyn upoun utheris thair naturall freindis and nychtbouris, hes been thair extraordinair drinking of strong wynis and acquavitie brocht in amangis thame, pairtlie be merchandis of the maneland and pairtlie be sum trafficquaris indwellaris amangis thame selffis, ffor remeid quhairof it is inactit be commoun consent of the foirnamit personis that no persone nor personis indwellairis within the boundis of the saids haill Iles bring in to sell for money ather wyne or acquavitie, undir the pane of tinsale of the samyn."

The Statutes empowered anybody who could lay hands on such illegal imports of wine and spirits to help themselves, without payment. Home brew for domestic consumption was permitted, and chiefs and "substantious gentilmen" were exempt from restriction until 1644 when more draconian legislation restricted them to about 60 to 250 gallons a year, depending upon their importance.

The chiefs and greater men kept either *birlinns* or galleys, and made considerable journeys in them. MacNeil of Barra was able to raid Valentia (in southwest Ireland), and in 1545 *Domhnall Dubh* was supported in his rising by 17 chiefs with 4000 men in 180 galleys. The *"Birlinn Chlann Raghnaill"* is a most beautiful and evocative poem by *Alasdair MacMhaighstir Alasdair* which describes a journey from South Uist to Ireland (via the tip of Oransay) and includes an excellent description of the practical aspects of the seamanship involved. At one time these ships had been very common, but they fell under restriction in the Statutes of Iona and declined rapidly in number thereafter. A Privy Council document describes a "galley" as a vessel with 18 to 24 oars, and a *"birlinn"* as one with 12 to 18 oars. Grant & Cheape mention that MacLeod of Dunvegan had a *birlinn* built as late as 1706, but that "in an inquisition made by the Privy Council into the number of galleys and *birlinns* owned by the West Coast chiefs, the number of boats is suprisingly small. Duart had two galleys and eight *birlinns* and his brother one galley. Argyll himself, Coll and MacLeod each had one galley, and Coll also had two *birlinns*. Clan Ranald, MacLean of Ardgour and MacPhee each had one *birlinn*." The report itself stated that (modern spelling): "The burthen of a galley and *birlinn* and the number of men of war which they are able to carry is estimated according to the number of their oars, counting three men to every oar."

Colla Ciotach's prowess at sea was to become legendary; for lengthy periods throughout a span of 30 years (1615 – 45), he was reputed to have roamed the Hebrides undaunted and in defiance of alien law, operating from secret harbours and involved in incidents that inspired epic poems and songs. Although the truth is more prosaic it is true that in Colonsay and Oransay he took full advantage of the many harbours noted by Dean Munro as suited to the Highland galley; the finest of these is known now as *Port a' Chrochaire* ("Port of the Hangman's Victim"), presumably so named by the Campbells when they finally managed to usurp his property and plant the island with their own people.[12]

The following extract from a modern and very popular composition gives some idea of the heroic mantle that enveloped *Colla Ciotach*; the author has captured the power and surge of the sea, the motion of the boat, the vigour of the crew:

Birlinn Cholla Chiotaich
Ho rí ho ri á, hoireann á hoireann ó
O chí mi do bhàt' air Maol gàbhaidh na h-Odh'
A Cholla, mo ghràdh, rinneadh tàir air do chòir,
Thigeadh dhuit sa bhi dàn, 's iomadh nàmh th'air do thòir!

Thigeadh dhuit-sa bhi dàn, 's iomadh nàmh th' air do thòir,
'S glan, siúbhlach i 'snàmh; birlinn ràmhach nan seòl,
'S i 'sgoltadh an t-sáil' air bárr nan tonn mór,
I 'ga iarraidh roimh chàch 's muir a' rànail m'a sròin.

Ho ree, ho ree áh, horan áh horan óh,
I see thy lone barque on the wild Mull of Oa,
O Colla, mo ghrá, sacred theme of my woe,
Be ye daring and brave, for fierce is thy foe!

Be ye daring and brave, for fierce is thy foe,
Swift, smoothly she sails; the fair galley oh hó!
She cleaves the white spray o'er the mad racing foam,
She stems the huge wave; billows rave at her prow.

Duncan Johnston

Notes

1 As it transpired, James' Scottish possessions actually passed not to his brothers but to his son *Gilleasbuig* (Archibald). *Gillesbuig* died within four years and was succeeded by his brother Angus, who was chief from 1569 until his death in 1614 (apart from the periods during which he was usurped by his son, Sir James MacDonald).

2 It is likely that when Ranald first moved to Colonsay, he established his base at *Dùn Cholla*, where the ruins of late mediaeval buildings can be seen.

3 This place is just inside the gate to the old track which leads from the public road near Kiloran up towards Loch an Sgoltaire, identified by Dugie McGilvray.

4 This is the lady who is found living in Colonsay in 1624 under the protection of *Colla Ciotach* and his wife Mary McDonald.

5 This Ranald MacDonald was an extraordinary individual who seems to have been lucky not to have died a little earlier, not least because he failed to respond when he was called to trial at Inveraray in 1634, charged with Murder and Polygamy, as recorded in this document of 5 October 1633:

"Criminal Letters by Archibald Lord Lorne, Heritable Justice of the Sheriffdom of Argyll and the Isles on the complaint of Malcolm Fisher, Procurator Fiscall, directed to [blank] messengers against Rannald Mcallen VcEan alias Mcrannald of Castle Vorreiff [Borve, in Benbecula] who in August 1618 'having conceaveit ane deadlie hatred malice and Invy againes unquhile Allaster Mcrannald his servitour came to Loch skippart in Wyist quhair the said Allester wes in quyet and peciable maner doeing his lesome affaires and bussiness' etc. and took him captive and 'thaireftir Incontinent moist cruellie wickedlie and unmercifullie with his handis treassonablie with ane durk murderit and slew the said unquhile Allaster to the death being for the tyme his captive under his poware and trust.' "Item in the month if June 1609 he came to the Yle of Barra and there most cruelly etc. slew to the death unquhile Johnne Mcneill persone and minister of Bara. Item he and his servants and followers wherever he goes 'wearis and bearis about with him hakbuttis gwnes and pistollis.' Item contrary to the Acts of Parliament he is a common 'slayer of deare' and in the monthsof August and September 1632 with a gun slew '6 deare in the Yle of Rowme' and also in July and August last with a gun slew other 6 deare 'in the Yle of Rowme.' "Item having 'shakkin aff all feare of god and obedience to His Majesties Lawes he in 1603 with out any Lawful devorcement putt away [blank] nyn Rannald VcDonald his first mareit wyiff and mareit umquhile Margaret nccleoyd sister to umquhile sir Rorie Mccleoyd of Dounvegoune. Efter quhais deceis he mareit Marie Ncconnell sister to Sir Donald McDonald of Sleatt and keepit house with her Ten yeires and thaireftir in ane most godles and Lawles manner without any Decreit of Devorcement patt the said Marie away and mariet Margaret NcConnell sister to Angus McConnell of Dounnavaig with quhome he keipes present companie and societie **and sua at this present hour he hes thrie mareit wyiffes alive.**'

6 Ronald Black points out that by November of the following year, when they were visited by Fr. Ward, Ranald and Margaret were married; but they were related within the forbidden limits of consanguinity and it was not until December 1630 that a dispensation could be obtained, when Fr. Hegarty re-admitted them to the Sacraments.

7 We know how "Ranald of Benbecula" came to be parted from wife number four, the second Mary MacDonald. Pitcairn includes the details in his "Criminal Trials":
"Rapt and Ravishing" – (Forcible Abduction) – Adultery. "The following brief notice of an ancient Crim. con. Case, affords a specimen of the mode in which affairs of gallantry were managed in the Western Islands. Sir Lauchlan McFingane (MacKinnon) of Strathardill, having fallen in fancy with Mary McConnell (MacDonald), the wife of Ranald of Benbecula, makes the best use of his winning arts, and carries off the lady, by violence, from her husband. It would appear, from the charge of Adultery being also preferred against this knight errant, that the consent of the lady had in all probability been previously obtained to the arrangement. Ranald McAllan VcEan, the injured husband, was brother to Donald McAllan McEan, Captain of ClanRanald. This gay and captivating deceiver, Sir Lauchlan, was one of several Hebridean Chiefs, who had been knighted by King James VI, in the latter part of his reign, to ensure their more ready acquiescence in the schemes so zealously projected by him, for the civilization of their semi-barbarous tribes. A Gift of his Escheat was granted by the King, Dec. 12 1622.
"NOV. 8. – SIR LAUCHLANE McFINGANE OF STRATHARDILL, KNYt. "Dilaitit of the Rapt and Raveischeing of Marie Mcconneill, sister to Sir Donald McConneill of Slait, and spouse to Rannald Mcallane Vceane of Castelwirrie (Castletirrim); committing Adulterie with hir, and remanent crymes contenit in the Letteris. "James Logie, wryter, producet the Letteris deulie execute, indorsate, and registrat; quhairby the said Sir Lauchlane is denuncet rebell, and put to the horne, for nocht finding of cautioun, to haif compeirit to haif underlyne the law."

8. Incidentally, a building used to exist close to Kiloran, in *Pairc Bhaile Mhaide*, which is remembered variously as "a (pre-reformation) chapel" (Donald McNeill of Lower Kilchattan) and as "a barn" (late Peter McAllister, Glassard); this was a 19th century barn, but built in the same Gothic style as was the formal archway at Kiloran Farm. It was destroyed completely many years ago, but a photograph exists which shows a building, the proportions of which were very like the "Prior's House" on Oransay (which was itself originally built as a monastic barn). The O.S. 1st Ed. marks the site of this building (at NR 402973 on modern editions); the final stones were removed for use in the creation of a loggia at Colonsay House as 'they were flat on one side' (Dugie McGilvray, Kilchattan). The building was two-storey with gable ends, aligned east/west. On the west gable, there were three openings, one above and two on the ground floor; the heads of these window openings were pointed, being formed by flat lintel stones coming together. On the south side there were three openings with arched or 'Norman' heads. Each was the full height of the ground floor and the width of a door – say 8' x 3'. The central one had a lintel and door opening, the others had been reduced to form windows with splayed interior reveals. The arched heads were formed by flags laid side on side in conventional manner, keyed at apex. Overall, the building was about 35ft long by about 15ft wide, wallheight perhaps 9ft , gable about 20ft. Construction was of high standard and the surviving structure was noticeably sound in the photograph, although roofless and lacking the east gable. The O.S. Map showed no access track and aerial

photographs fail to show any detail. Fieldwalking after cultivation revealed a litter of very small slates and pieces of unglazed clay tile.

9 As yet, no corroboration has been found for the story of Fr. Mitchel, but silent testimony exists in the form of a desecrated altarstone. In the Victorian period a summer house was built on the island, and a consecration cross may be seen in the very stone that was chosen for use as a threshold. The family who were responsible suffered financial reverses and lost their estate.

10 Loder records a local story that there was a narrow underwater causeway leading out to the island, only passable by those with knowledge of the gaps, but this seems to be based upon wishful thinking. In the 19th century, the level of the loch was raised to improve the mill lade and at that time a field wall became partially submerged, whilst its terminus became a new islet. Local children used to walk along the top of the wall, and in course of time their antics led the antiquaries to embellish the facts; aerial photographs reveal no trace of any causeway to *Eilean Dubh Iain Mhitchel*.

11 A "boll" is equal to about 140lbs in weight.

12 It is unfortunate that the Ordnance Survey map is in error by some hundreds of yards; the harbour of *Port a' Chrochaire* is the sandy bay, sheltered from sight and from weather, below the house of *Baleromin Mór*.

5

RANALD OG'S RISING – 1614

The Rising at Dunivaig

In the early chapters, we traced the origins of Clan Donald of Colonsay and followed the story to that point at which, in January 1612, Angus of Dunivaig surrendered his patrimony in Islay to Sir John Campbell of Calder. It seemed then to be the end of all hope for the MacDonalds, but in fact there was to be a final spark – it was discovered that Angus had retained the right to overturn the arrangement with Calder, if only he could repay the monies advanced to him.

To Calder's suprise, this was just what Angus managed to do, through the help of Sir Ranald MacDonnell of Dunluce (*Raghnaill MacShomhairle*).[1] Thus in September 1612, and with Angus' enthusiastic support, Dunluce took effective control of the MacDonald estates on Islay; as he was not a Scot, his crown lease was issued through a nominee, Sir George Hamilton. This was a short lease, but Sir Ranald immediately began to negotiate for a more permanent arrangement and as Stevenson points out, all this must have been agreeable to the crown, and was therefore unsettling, to say the least, for the Campbells.

Angus of Dunivaig died in the following year, 1613, leaving two legitimate sons, Sir James (still prisoner in Edinburgh) and Angus *Og*, but there was also an alleged illegitimate son, Ranald *Og* (although he had been repudiated by Angus himself). Stevenson suggests that these sons stirred up resentment against Sir Ranald MacDonnell on Islay, hoping thereby to have their own interests restored. If so, it may well be the case that Calder will have encouraged them in this, since any hint of stability would have worked against his own cherished ambition to secure Islay for himself.

In any event, Professor MacKinnon is able to assure us that: "*cha do thaitinn riaghladh an Eireannaich ris na h-Ilich. Chuir iad gearann do Dhùn-éideann gun robb an t-uachdaran 'gan sàrachadh le màl is le mòd, le càin is cìs, is le riaghailtean na h-Eireann, an uair a b'e an còir-san a bhith fo riaghladh na h-Alba. Fhuair an gearan éisdeachd.*" (The rule of the Irish was not popular with the Islay folk. They complained to Edinburgh that the landlord was burthening them with rents and tribunals, with fines and taxes, and with the laws of Ireland, whilst they were entitled to be under the law of Scotland. The complaint got a hearing.)

In the midst of this uncertainty as to the future tenure of Islay, Angus' above-mentioned illegitimate son Ranald *Og*, "a vagabound fellow without ony certane residence", was persuaded to seize the initiative. In March 1614, with a few followers, he seized the castle of Dunivaig and evicted the garrison which had been maintained therein by Bishop Knox since he had taken it over for his headquarters in 1610. It seems that Ranald may have been duped into believing that this action would lead to some recognition of his claim to be an heir of Angus, but perhaps he had merely been promised some place to live, somewhere to have a "certane residence"..

The background to his action was very complex but from all the evidence it seems reasonable to say that the whole thing had its origins in a planned rising in Ireland, intended to restore land to young Irish nobles whose patrimony had been forfeited to create the plantation. An illegitimate son of Sir James MacDonald, *Domhnall Gorm*, had been party to these plans and it seems to have been he who persuaded his half-uncle, Ranald *Og*, to start the ball rolling with a rising in Islay. In fact, the assault on Dunivaig was not really connected with the Irish rising, but was a trap: once Ranald *Og* had captured Dunivaig, it was planned that he should be brought to heel by Angus *Og*, legitimate brother to Sir James MacDonald, and then the castle would be ceremoniously restored to a grateful monarch. In the scenario envisaged by the schemers, the grateful monarch would then accept loyal Angus *Og* as his tenant, displacing Sir Ranald MacDonnell of Dunluce; but the latter (who seems to have been innocent of the whole affair) would hopefully accept the development graciously and therefore might expect to be compensated by additional rewards in Antrim. And, of course, the King would come to see that the MacDonalds were not only more powerful in the west than the Campbells, but also more loyal. The unfortunate dupe, Ranald *Og*, fulfilled all expectations, but the plot was rather too intricate and Angus *Og* became hopelessly ensnared as matters spiralled out of control.

Returning to the actual assault on Dunivaig, one should note that in all conscience the word "garrison" is a rather imposing name for Ranald *Og*'s victims, a handful of folk who seem to have had no military aspirations and whose occupation of the premises seems to have been little more than a token. The significance of the occupation lay in the fact that elsewhere and at this date, the king had accepted physical possession of ancestral seats as establishing title to estates.[2]

The simple details of Ranald *Og*'s brief military adventure were later recounted in the statement made by Angus *Og* on 23 May the following year, when he was a prisoner in the Tolbooth:

> "Deponis that in Marche 1614 the castell of Dunivaig was keipit be Robert McGilchrist, Jonet Hammiltoun, spouse to Patrick Knox, and his dochter.
> "Depones lykwise that about the last of Marche foirsaid Ronnald Oig McAlester, of lait callit Ronnald Oig McAngus, bastard sone to umquill Angus McDonald, come in the nicht and brocht with him ane ledder on the whiche he himself, Gilecalem McGilmole, Donald Onnavenye, McIlveny, his brother and McLachlan come up to the drawbrig of the inverbahan of the castell, and all the nicht ludgeit thame selffis in ane grite quantitie of hedder that lay in the said bahan. On the nixt morning, the said Rannald and his complices finding the yettis of the castell oppin, Johnne Hairt and Johnne Mwre being past furth in thair awin busyness, he enterit in the castell with his complices with [where] Robert McGilchreist and Patrick Knox wyff and his dochter was, and perforce thrust thame out of the castell and maid him self maister thairof."[3]

Word of Ranald *Og*'s activities travelled fast. Angus *Og*, the legitimate son of Angus of Dunivaig, was living only 4 miles away, at *Aros* ("Mansion"), and he immediately "sent round the fiery cross, warning all those who were well affected to the King's obedience to rise and concur with him in the recovery of the House".[4] In addition to the general alarm, Angus *Og* particularly called upon *Colla Ciotach* of Colonsay for his help; this was hardly surprising in view of Coll's reputation down to the present day, but in case there could be doubt as to his contemporary standing, Professor MacKinnon makes it clear:

"Ré nam bliadhnachan 1606 gu 1615 an uair a bha na Domhnallaich, le cuideachadh chàirdean, a' srìth r'an greim a ghleidheadh air Ile, cha robh aon 'nam measg a dhearbh e féin cho gleusda is cho teòma ri Colla. Bha an duine gu nádurra foghainteach, misneachail, seòlta; is cha do chuir a choguis riamh a bheag de dhragh air. Chan fhairicheadh a cholann no inntinn sgìos no taise. Bu choingeis leis muir is tìr. Bha e cho teòma leis a' ghunna is a bha leis a' chlaidheamh." (During the years 1606 – 1615 when the MacDonalds, with a throng of relations, were struggling to retain their grip on Islay, there was not one of them that proved himself to be so skilful and adept as Coll. By nature, he was an heroic figure, courageous and ingenious; and not unduly troubled by an uneasy conscience. Unaffected in body or mind by tiredness or idleness, he was equally at ease on land or sea. He was as skilful with the gun as with the sword.)

Ranald Og ejected

Colla Ciotach answered the summons and laid siege to Dunivaig, "with ten or xij of the Clandonald"; once again the scale of the affair is of interest – the Bishop had left the place occupied by a mere handful, who had been ejected by another handful, now besieged by less than a dozen. Since Ranald *Og* had so few supporters he could not hope to defend the castle for long, but he had possession of the castle's store of ammunition and "were prodigal enough in bestowing the same upon the besiegers." Within six days he and his men were forced to make an escape by sea, using a six-oared boat and carrying what plunder they could.

Angus *Og* now took personal command of the castle in the name of the king and offered to restore it to the original garrison, but when the offer was declined he installed *Colla Ciotach* and his supporters to hold it meantime. Shortly afterwards, the fugitive Ranald *Og* and four of his men were captured by Angus *Og* and, in a mysterious incident, Ranald was seen to chew up and destroy a letter that had been hidden in his sleeve, the content of which was never brought to light. Although his men were executed, Ranald *Og* himself managed to escape his captors. Coll and Angus *Og* reported later that he had admitted to having been encouraged in his activities by Donald *Gorm*, which was probably no more than the truth. But Donald *Gorm* was the illegitimate son of Sir James MacDonald, and therefore Sir James (despite being still a prisoner in Edinburgh) might possibly be thought to have influenced the insurrection, whilst on the other hand Coll and Angus *Og* were demonstrably striving to uphold the interests of the crown.... All this subterfuge was insufficient to fool Bishop Knox, who was later to assert that on the contrary, it was Angus *Og* himself who had been behind the seizure of Dunivaig, with the aim of providing himself with a chance to shine and to discredit his brother, Sir James.

At all events, Angus *Og* declared himself ready to restore the castle to Bishop Knox, asking only for a remission for any offences that he and his supporters might have committed. At the same time, his brother in Edinburgh made a strong appeal for liberty, under whatever terms might be imposed, upon which the Council sent to London for advice, but retained Sir James in custody until the king's determination could be known.

Bishop Knox now made his way to Islay, but reported to Edinburgh that far from being ready to restore Dunivaig to the authorities, Angus *Og* had actually strengthened it and had prepared it for a siege. Sir James now began to be suspected of complicity in the affair and was more strictly confined; his papers were seized for examination, but they merely revealed that he had made diligent efforts to ensure that the castle was restored to the control of the authorities without delay. Sir James, of course, received no recognition or reward for his unsuspected fidelity and remained imprisoned. Bishop Knox having by now returned frustrated to Edinburgh, it was determined that he should put the integrity of Angus *Og* to actual test and in August he set out for Islay once more, bringing a pardon for Angus *Og* and his men on condition of immediate surrender of the castle (i.e. within 24 hours).

The Bishop's journey was dilatory in the extreme, and he received a stiff letter from Lord Binning, Secretary of State. He gave excuses, saying that he was delayed by the need to raise forces, so that he would be equipped to fulfill his commission of fire and sword if the surrender was not forthcoming. In fact he had delayed so long that it was now harvest time with the result that he was truly unable to raise sufficient support. It was not until 19 September that he reached Islay, and even then with an inadequate force of merely 70 men. Other support that he had been promised suddenly evaporated, whilst the MacDonald forces were swelling rapidly, and his difficulty was further compounded when an armed party of 100 MacDonalds, under the leadership of *Colla Ciotach*, seized and destroyed the four boats in which the prelate and his retinue had arrived. "And, so having us cut of frome our boittis, they directed a threatening to us, that they wald put us all to the edge of the sword without exceptione, or els it behovit us to deliver suche of our nomber to theme as they wald chuse."

Having surrendered two hostages, the Bishop was then forced to negotiate, and eventually to sign a formal contract: "It is aggreit and endit betuix the pairties under-wryittin, to wit, betuix the right honourabill Angus Oig McDonald, Ronald McJames McDonald, his uncle [i.e. Ranald of Smerbie, Coll's father-in-law], Colene Gillespie McDonall [i.e. *Colla Ciotach*], Ronald McSorle [Dunluce, the future 1st Earl of Antrim and current tenant of Islay], and [blank], on the ane pairt, and the reverend father in God, Andro, Bishop of the Ylles of Scotland, upoun the uther pairt: ...." The Bishop agreed to endeavour to obtain for Angus *Og* a seven year lease of Islay, " – in posses-sioun of the whilk Sir Ronald McSorle of Dunluse is for the present –", and since said "Sir Ronald McSorle" was a signatory to the contract, it must be accepted that this arrangement would be acceptable to Dunluce himself. He was also to try to procure permission to transfer Dunivaig Castle to Angus *Og*, and to obtain a pardon for the followers of Clan Donald. *Colla Ciotach* and others were to receive new leases of Church lands that they had held traditionally. It is notable that the negotiations do not seem to have been conducted on any wider basis than that of self-interest and that no attempt was made to advance the specific interests of Sir James MacDonald, but perhaps it was felt that to involve him in any direct way would only be to make his position worse.

This contract was dated 22 September, so Bishop Knox had been forced to make these and other concessions within just three days – he had to leave his son, Thomas, and his nephew, John Knox of Ranfurlie, as hostages, but was promised repayment of necessary expenses and safe return of the hostages provided he acted faithfully in his endeavours.

In a letter to the Privy Council, Bishop Knox mentioned that "They [Clandonald] have built a new fort in a loch, which they have manned and victualled. Angus Oig, their captain, affirms, in the hearing of many witnesses, that he got directions from the

Earl of Argyle to keep still the house [Dunivaig], and that he [the Earl] should procure him therefore the whole lands of Isla and house of Dunivaig to himself." This allegation was later repeated under oath by Angus *Og* himself, and was also repeated by him in conversation with George Graham, a representative of the Lord Chancellor. All this is persuasive that the MacDonald faction was being manipulated by the Campbells to bring about their own ruin, and supports the belief that there was as much intrigue as there was rebellion in Islay that year.

The Council was not impressed, and referred the matter to King James "to your Majestei's awne princelie consideratioun"; despite the views of the Bishop, they considered favourably an offer by Campbell of Calder to pay a substantial rent for Islay ("far above any thing any responsible man of quality did ever ... offer for it") in exchange for a permanent lease, and in the meantime commissioned him to reduce the rebellion by force. He undertook this commission at his own expense, save for the provision of artillery and men expert in "the battering of housis". The projected lease to Calder attracted the Bishop's criticism, not least because of the danger to the hostages, and he tried to persuade the king to refuse his consent: "All the trouble that is done to me and my friends is because of Archibald Campbell's diligence to procure the isle of Islay to the Laird of Calder." He further warned that he could not "think it either good or profitable to his Majesty, or this realm, to make that name [Campbell] greater in the Isles than they are already; nor yet to root out one pestiferous clan, and plant in another little better." Instead, he recommended a new plantation, as in Ulster.

The King accepted only part of his advice and, on 14 October 1614, ordered two hundred soldiers and six siege guns to be sent from Ireland, "sufficient for the battery and forcing of the said house of Dunyvege, which wee are informed is a place of good strength, being strongly built of it selfe, and, besides, it is compassed with iii stone walles, each of them conteyninge thirty and sixe feet in thickness." The rebels "we intend to punish with all severity"; and he confirmed that Sir John Campbell of Calder was to act as his lieutenant. As preparations continued for Calder to get to work, urgent representations by Sir James MacDonald were ignored. He made an offer of 8000 merks per annum for the crown lands of Islay, initially for a period of seven years to prove his obedience, or as an alternative, he undertook to remove himself and his kinsmen to Ireland for good, if he could be given one year's rent of Islay with which to buy land. Otherwise, if given 40 days freedom, he undertook to reduce the castle of Dunivaig, to release the hostages, and to hand over the principal "rebels" (including *Colla Ciotach* "to be keipt in irnes during His Majesties pleasour"!). He even offered that, with a free pardon and a recommendation to the Estates of Holland, he would remove himself and his clan forever. It is evident that Sir James was being deceived himself, for amongst his guarantors was his brother-in-law, the same Sir John Campbell of Calder as was actively working for his ruin.

On 22 October, Calder was issued with his commission, in which the offences of Ranald *Og* and Angus *Og* were described "... for the quhilk thay and Coill McGillespick, ane of thair rebellious compliceis, ar denuncit his Majesteis rebellis and put to the horne...". Archibald Campbell was appointed as administrative head of the expedition. "Perhaps," writes Loder, "it was his idea to borrow a petard from Edinburgh Castle. This was an engine which the authorities were anxious to try, but which was evidently considered as likely to be as dangerous to the users as to the rebels. James Anstruther, the expert detailed to accompany it, insisted, among other conditions, on a guarantee of provision for his family in case of his death or disablement."[5]

George Graham's Intrigue

As if the situation was not already sufficiently confused, it later became known that the Earl of Dunfermline, Chancellor of Scotland, was making private arrangements of his own, ostensibly for the good of the hostages, but secretly and in consultation with nobody. He had engaged one George Graham, from Ross-shire, to go to Islay and endeavour to rescue the hostages by whatever means. Graham was a Gaelic speaker who already had the acquaintance of Angus *Og*, and he was accompanied by Duncan Campbell of Danna, whose daughter, Katherine, was married to Angus and was with him in Dunivaig. Graham met Angus *Og* and seems to have used the Chancellor's name to achieve without difficulty the surrender of both the castle and the hostages, Angus *Og* being assured that Graham would then put a halt to Calder and his military expedition.

Having secured the hostages, Graham then restored the Castle to Angus *Og*, with an understanding that he was now to hold it as constable, on behalf of the crown, until he should receive further instructions. Angus had symbolically surrendered the actual keys of Dunivaig, and these were now returned by Graham, who handed them to *Colla Ciotach*. Angus was further instructed by the devious Graham that even if Calder, as King's Lieutenant, were to defy the instructions that he would receive from Graham and were to attempt to take possession of the place, Angus *Og* was to resist to his utmost ability.

At this juncture, the said Royal Lieutenant's herald approached, to issue a formal summons. At first, Graham tried to persuade Angus *Og* and *Colla Ciotach* to murder the herald out of hand, and then tried to turn him back himself, but when all this failed, Graham persuaded Angus *Og* to reject the summons and encouraged *Colla Ciotach* to adopt a violent and abusive attitude to both the herald and to the Prior of Ardchattan, who accompanied him. Graham then made his departure with the liberated hostages, but not without further misleading injunctions to the hapless and betrayed islanders.[6]

At the end of November, Campbell of Calder arrived at Islay, and it seems that he and his retinue spent a fortnight encamped on two small islands near Dunivaig, awaiting troops and cannon due from Ireland. At the end of that time, he had achieved nothing, although on 21 November he achieved his personal ambition when the heritable feu to Islay was passed under the Great Seal in his favour. Eventually he returned to Duntroon for further supplies, but no sooner was he gone than Sir Oliver Lambert arrived with the Irish forces, and came to anchor off Ardfin, in the Sound of Islay.

He had a substantial force which Gregory describes as including "his Majesty's ship called the Phoenix, a pinnace called the Moon[8], a hoy [a single-decked, sloop-rigged vessel] to carry the ordnance, and a Scottish bark with provisions; and these vessels carried a considerable number of soldiers". Lambert now sent his own summons to the castle of Dunivaig, whilst he awaited word from Calder, and he was no doubt surprised to be assured by Angus *Og* that he himself had a warrant from the Lord Chancellor and Council of Scotland to hold the castle, and would otherwise have been happy to surrender it. Meantime, the Lord Chancellor denied that he had authorised any such warrant, and piously asserted: "I will not meddle in the like of that but by special warrant and direction; His Majesty knows I ever professed ignorance in all Irische cabals".

Lambert saw a copy of the warrant "supposed to be given by the Lord Chancellor to Grymes, signed with the hands of Angus Ogge McDonnell and Coll McDonnell... in which I found neither frase nor matter likelie to fall from the pen of the Lord Chancellor". Although he recognised that Angus *Og* was acting in good faith, he also recognised that Graham had had no authority to issue such a document and resolved to impose a siege just as soon as Calder would arrive. Eventually, having been delayed by the bad weather which is common enough at New Year, Calder arrived once more in Islay on 5 January 1615 and within a few days had invested the castle. He had some 340 men at his command and some of the "rebels" began to be alarmed. Those who agreed to surrender were to be pardoned, on condition that they enlisted in Calder's ranks.

On 21 January "Ranald MacJames, who commanded the fort and island of Lochgorme, surrendered his post to the Lieutenant and, along with his son, received a conditional assurance of his Majesty's favour." This was Ranald of Smerby, father-in-law of *Colla Ciotach*, and his surrender suggests that by now the "rebels" really must have believed themselves to be acting on authority. It would be perfectly correct for Loch Gorm to be surrendered at this stage, since Graham's pretended warrant did not include anything other than Dunivaig. Unfortunately, it allowed Calder, uniting his roles as Royal Lieutenant and incoming landlord, to concentrate all his resources and fire-power on Dunivaig and its dwindling garrison.

The Bombardment and Surrender of Dunivaig

Landing the ordnance proved to be difficult, but eventually, on 23 January, the hoy was beached near Dunivaig although "somewhat subject to the shott of the castle." Over the next week "wee labored to unshipp and drawe the cannon, and on the soldiers' shoulders to carrie all our provisions of timber, delve boards, powder and bullettes to our colde campe, halfe a mile almost from the place they landed." There were a few casualties, including Captain Crawford, who "unfortunately received a shott that brake the smale of his legg all to shivers. After five or six daies he was dismembred, which he indured manfullie, and dyed within twoe howers after."

On 1 February, the ordnance was all in position, on the substantial platform that is still clearly visible near to the castle, and the battery opened fire. The "rebels" sent various messages to the Lieutenant, Campbell of Calder but these were all rejected. Fire was maintained all day, and the following day, whilst fire was witheld for two and a half hours, Angus *Og* and Calder met in person. Angus, "protesting that he and the rest were subjects and held the howse for his Majestie and the Councell of Scotland; and if they might see any warrant to deliver the howse to Sir John Campbell, they would obay the same; with muche other idle stuffe and imaginations infused into them by Grymes [Graham]". Calder patiently explained to Angus *Og* that he had been deceived by Graham, and when at last Angus *Og* came to understand what had happened he agreed to surrender with his followers. Lambert noted that he found "noe great substance in Agnus other than Coll McDonnell thrust into him."

Things were not to be just so simple. When Angus returned to Dunivaig "persuaded, as there is reason to believe, by Coll MacGillespick, he again absolutely refused to surrender." It seems that *Colla Ciotach* may have pointed out the dangers of an unconditional surrender to a lieutenant who was now the feu-holder of the entire island, had the power of life and death entrusted to him, and who might be tempted to treat them as rebels despite their warrant from the Lord Chancellor and their evident good faith.

The battery continued next day and, since the castle was utterly unable to withstand the bombardment, Angus *Og* determined on a leap of faith by accepting the demand for unconditional surrender. As was reported by Lambert himself: 'Three dayes batterye with the ordnance wee used was powerful to ruyne the whole howse, invincible without the canon and famyn." On the evening of the second day, Angus and Coll sent out their wives and children, together with their nurses and the rest of the womenfolk; and a message along with them, to say *Colla Ciotach* had also agreed to the surrender, subject to one condition: "to be carried too Edenburrough to aunswer for himselfe before the Councell." But in reality, this was a subterfuge, for Coll did not trust Calder and had determined on a strategic withdrawal.

Whilst the women and children had being making their way out of the castle, Coll had been preparing a boat for sea. Now, whilst Lambert was considering how to reply to his message, Coll and about twenty followers made a daring escape:

"Coll with all his abell men made a faire skape to the sea, neither daunted with the shott that came from the Hylanders lodged on a rocke fust before the arche, oute of which ther boat was launched into the sea. Soe they did as careleslie, having no other way to save their lives, passe under a rock wher our muskateers lay fortafied and shott freelie at them. Three boates well manned with Hylanders followed them. Wee might see them give fyer on both sides. The rebells roed themselves soone out of sight of them, and, being cleare of them, stoode back againe and landed some five miles from the castle in Ila, sunck ther boate, and marched away to shift for ther safetie. They are good men and abell to doe mischeefe before they shalbe suppressed."

It will be remembered that Ranald *Og* had made a similar escape, when besieged by Coll some months earlier. There is a water-gate at the castle leading into the bawn, which had taken the brunt of the cannonade; but it seems barely credible that such an escape could have been possible, given the narrow and difficult access to the open sea, unless some sort of collusion had been negotiated with the "Hylanders" who were guarding that route.[9]

Of course, the boat had been high and dry in the bawn, and had had no time to "take up", which explains why the fugitives just ran along the coast as far as the Oa and then landed again on Islay. Six of them were later captured by Calder's men and executed, Coll himself managed to make good his escape.

Meantime, back at Dunivaig, Campbell of Calder accepted Angus *Og*'s unconditional surrender on 3 February, and then, as Coll had anticipated, he immediately tried, condemned and executed fourteen "rebels", including ten members of the garrison and four men from the neighbourhood, known to be friendly to Angus *Og*. In addition, six of those who had held (and surrendered) Loch Gorm were also now condemned to die. In a report to the King, Lambert mentioned that Dunivaig had been much less strong than expected "walles ... eight foote in some places, less in others; only one corner fowerteene foote which wee hadd noe occasion to touche. ... The greatest enemye opposed us was cold wett and perpetuall stormes".

The immediate family of both Angus and Coll now became hostages, mentioned in a petition to the King: "That his Majestie may be pleaset to appoint quhat ordour salbe taken with Angus Oig his twa sones, Colle Mcgillespick his twa sones, and Archibald Dow Mcconill his sone". It seems that *Gilleasbuig* and *Raghnall MacCholla* were the two sons of Coll referred to, both young children, and this suggests that the older boy, *Aonghus* (if he was present) escaped with his step-father. (*Alasdair* would not have been a candidate for capture, since he is traditionally assumed to have been born in 1620 or shortly before). Angus *Og* and a few of his principal men were spared for examination by the Privy Council, and in the passing, Calder and his men found time for a spot of sacrilege. In his own words, Archibald Campbell of Glencarradale records that "Sence my cuming heir I fand owt a number of images whiche I hawe caussit to be bruntt: the religioun that the cuntrie pepill hes heir amongst them is Popishe for yair is newer a minister in the wholle Ille except wan poore man that the bishop did leaue heir."

The Privy Council turned its attention to the examination of Angus *Og*, enquiring into the background to the seizure of the castle and also into the details of the warrant issued by Graham. The evidence, including that which was ably given by Angus' wife, Katherine, indicates that both Campbell of Calder and the Chancellor had acted basely, and it supports the belief that Angus *Og* had initially been encouraged into whatever he had done and that having got started on the path, had then been adroitly manoeuvred into his present difficulty.

Despite the evidence, it is clear from his correspondence with Secretary Binning that King James was at pains to avoid either justice or clemency for the MacDonalds, and that both the Chancellor and Calder were allowed to obscure the details of their machinations. As a result Angus *Og*, together with several of his surviving followers, met the fate that had been courted by his poor misguided half-brother. That same summer Angus and the others were "tried and condemned for high treason on 3 July, and executed on the 8th of that month. Their fate excited great commiseration, which was mingled with a feeling of indignation, that no steps were taken to punish the villanous conduct of the Chancellor's emissary, Graham" (Gregory).

Although that was the end of Angus *Og*, *Colla Ciotach* had remained at large and far from idle. His decision to flee rather than to surrender had been vindicated, but his wife and children were being held hostage, many of his close friends and relatives had been or were about to be hanged and his powerful Irish cousins had been supplanted in Islay by Clan Campbell. Coll himself was unmoved; he was still loyal to his religion and to his people and still strove to right the wrongs that had been done to his ancient house. As the most senior member of *Clann Iain Mhóir* still retaining his liberty, he was ready to fight on, but for the moment he was weak and he and his followers needed time to regroup. Within a matter of weeks he had laid the groundwork for a new and audacious campaign and then, combining business with pleasure, *Colla Ciotach* took the opportunity to go stravaiging.

Notes

1 Sir Ranald MacDonnell of Dunluce (*Raghnaill MacShomhairle*) was later to be created 1st Earl of Antrim, and was of course the son of *Somhairle Buidhe* and first cousin to *Colla Ciotach*'s uncle Ranald.

2 As, for example, on Skye, where the MacDonalds had been in possession of Trotternish, Sleat and North Uist: "For seventeen years the MacDonalds retained possession until, for some inexplicable reason, the king chose on the 11th January 1613 to grant Sir Rory MacLeod charter right to the MacDonald lands. By this charter actual possession of the earth and stone at Duntulm (castle) would suffice for possession of all the lands mentioned."

3 The RCAHM Inventory describes the castle of Dunivaig, on a coastal promontory which commands the anchorage: "The existing remains comprise an outer courtyard or barmkin of irregular polygonal layout situated on low-lying ground immediately to the north of the rocky knoll at the tip of the promontory. The summit of this knoll ... is surrounded by vestiges of an enclosure-wall. It is crowned by the ... seaward side-wall of a substantial building of elongated hall-like proportions (internally 11.3m x 6m) which survives to a height of more than two main storeys. The upper and lower levels of the castle are linked by the remains of a stair which ascends from a small inner courtyard and traverses the site of a bridge built against the west face of the rock outcrop". This latter "bridge" is the "drawbrig of the inverbahan" referred to in the evidence of Angus Og; it seems that Ranald Og and his companions were able to walk up to the castle and use their ladder to bypass a drawbridge that was less than 4 metres above the ground and which in any case bridged a gap of only 1.5 metres. Even a watch-dog would have roused the occupants, who clearly must have felt no threat.

4 It is interesting to note the employment of the "fiery cross", which continued in to be used well into the 17th century; it is described by Alexander MacGregor: "When an emergency arose ... the *crann-taraidh* or fiery-cross was instantly called into requisition. It consisted of a piece of wood or pole half burnt, then dipped into the blood of a goat or lamb, and having at times a stained flag attached to it. Every chieftain had several of these significant beams of alarm in his possession to enable him to despatch them in every direction ..."

5 A petard was a bell-shaped device packed with explosives and intended as a replacement for the battering-ram; it would be attached to walls or defensive gates and then detonated. The blast would follow the route of least resistance, hopefully through the wall or gate but with the danger that in certain circumstances the blast would backfire, whereupon the operator would become "hoist with his own petard". In this case, before being taken to Islay, the petard was to be tested "at some gate within the Castle of Edinburgh where most commodiously and with least danger the same may be used."

6 The full details of this extraordinary episode are recorded in the Denmylne Manuscripts; it seems that the entire affair was an attempt by the Chancellor to orchestrate the destruction of both the Campbells and the MacDonalds, whilst at the same time covering himself in glory by the rescue of the hostages. He too cherished hopes to get possession of Islay, and must have been confident that his particularly nasty little scheme would never come to light.

7 Presumably one of these islands was Texa.

8 The "Moon " will have been familiar, since this was the ship that had been employed by the Bishop in 1608, when he had kidnapped the chiefs at Mull.

9 The only other possibility is that a small boat could have been concealed in a crevice in the rock upon which the castle stands; tied in such a way as to be hanging flush against the seaward wall of the castle, it would not be apparent to any observer from land but a major diversion would have been needed elsewhere to give time for it to be launched and manned.

6

A TOUR OF THE HEBRIDES

Colla Ciotach's Escape to Ireland

Following his daring escape from Dunivaig on 2 February, successfully accomplished *"ged a bha na peilearan a' feadalaich mu'n cluasan"* (despite the bullets whistling about their ears), Coll and his little party landed about 5 miles away, at the Oa, destroyed their damaged boat and scattered to the four winds. Campbell of Calder was anxious to catch them and, in addition to scouring Islay, ordered the destruction of all the remaining boats on the island. Coll, presumably accompanied by his stepson, Angus, was not to be so easily contained and, having assembled a small force of about sixty men, seems to have made his way across to Jura.

In a chance encounter with one Donald Campbell, son of Ronald Campbell of Craignish and an obvious opponent, *Colla Ciotach* appears to have tried to avoid confrontation. This is of interest, because it seems to reflect his natural behaviour – neither of the sieges of Dunivaig had seen him involved in wanton violence and even the wily Graham had not persuaded Coll to do physical harm to the Lieutenant's Herald. This helps to underline the fact that Coll's motivation was basically political, and that he was working in a committed way to protect the interests of the survivors of *Clann Iain Mhóir*. The details of the encounter on Jura are recorded in "The Manuscript History of Craignish":

"Donald his [i.e. Ronald Campbell's] eldest son, a very promising and high spirited young man, having gone with a company of 40 men to assist the Earl of Argyle (who was then in Isla to reduce the said Island from the MacDonalds and to put it fully in the possession of the Lairds of Calder in consequence of the agreement between the Earl and Calder), he I say upon a night as he had taken up his quarters at Ardnel in the south end of Jura and his cousine Inverlivers two sons with him as volunteers on his way to join the Earl in Isla, one of his centinels challenged a great body of men that passed by his post in the night and was answered that it was Coll MacDonald and his party, who bye the bye was then lurking having left Isla for fear of the Earl.

"Coll asked the fellow whom he belonged to; he answered and told to whom, upon which Coll is said to have replied, that tho' he designed to have lodged in that place that night yet he would leave it to the Campbells since they were in possession and march a little further to find other quarters for himself.

"The Centinel calls to his fellow and bade him alarm their leader at the head quarters that the grand Coll Kittick or left handed Coll his enemy was then marching by with a party; upon which they got to their arms and, hearing that Coll's party was but small, with a dozen or two of his men and Inverlivers two sons, without waiting for the rest, pursued Coll but caught a Tartar, for he had all his threescore men in a body, and gave many fair words to be rid of them; but to no purpose so Providence would have it, for like one seeking his end he would not be put off, broke in thro' the people and singles out Coll himself, who often shifted him, the vigorous young man being hard for the old man.

"Coll at length cry's to his men and said "since none of you dare face him have you never houghed (i.e. hamstringed) a cow". Upon which they came behind him whilst he was doubling his blows and cut his sinews; upon which he fell and Inverlivers two sons and about 20 of his men. McLavertich of Gartcharran who was with him carried home the dead bodies, whose son told me the story."

The authorities must have heard of this incident and of the likelihood of *Colla Ciotach*'s clear escape, and immediately made what arrangements they could. At Edinburgh on 17 February 1615 they issued a

"Missive to Donald Gorme, McClane, and Capitaine of Clanrannald that they suffer nane of the rebellis of Ila to be ressett [received] in thair boundis.

"The quhilk day Sir Rory McCleud of Hereis, and Rory McKanyee [McKenzie] of Coigache, Tutour of Kintaill, compeirand [appearing together] personalie befoir the Lordis of Secreit Counsaill, promeist that they sall send present advertisement and direction, viz. the said Sir Rory to his cuntreyis, landis and possessionis, and the said Rory McKanyee to the Lewis, that nane of the rebellis of Ila, especialie Coill McGillespik and Malcolme McRorie McCleude, salbe ressett in the saidis boundis; and, yf the saidis rebellis salhappin to come thair, that they shalbe huntit, followit, and persuit with fyre and swerd as rebellis to God, thair King, and cuntrey. Lyke as [likewise] thair wes delyverit to the said Rory McKanyee ane proclamatioun prohibiting the ressett, supplee and intercommoning with the saidis rebellis, and ane missive letter direct from the Lorde of Secreit Counsaill to Donald Gorme of Slatt willing him to keepe his cuntrey and boundis cleene and free of the saidis rebellis. Whilk proclamatioun the said Rory McKanyee promist to caus publishe deulie and ordourlie at the mercat croce of Innernes, and utheris placeis beidfull in the northe; as alsua he promeist to send the missive foirsaid to the said Donald Gorme with diligence."

The Irish Dimension

In fact, the fugitive band was heading in the opposite direction, at least for the moment. From Jura, Coll made his way to Ireland; he arrived at "Portrolock" in Antrim, before the end of February and stayed for three or four days.[1] Information on his movements is available because of that developing political situation in Ireland which had already become associated with the the events in Islay, and with which *Colla Ciotach* was closely related. The original Plantation of Ulster had been commenced by King James VI in 1609, when many of the Irish aristocracy had been forfeited and their land given to colonists. "The Lord Deputy of Ireland, Sir Arthur Chichester, was doing a brisk trade in plantations, and was still hungry for land." (R. Black).

An entire generation of young, dispossessed Irish noblemen were seething with anger and frustration, and the seizure of Dunivaig had prompted them to an initiative of their own; the two situations had much in common, not least that Sir Ranald MacDonnell's leadership was as unpopular with many of the Antrim MacDonnells as was his bid for Islay with many of his kinsmen there.

This Ulster movement was led by Alexander MacDonnell (*Alasdair Garrach*), nephew of Sir Ranald.[2] It involved leading Irish families, including that of the O'Cahans (the family of Coll's mother), and envisaged the projected capture of Derry, Coleraine, Lifford, Culmore and Limavady; the thirty-eight conspirators eventually identified

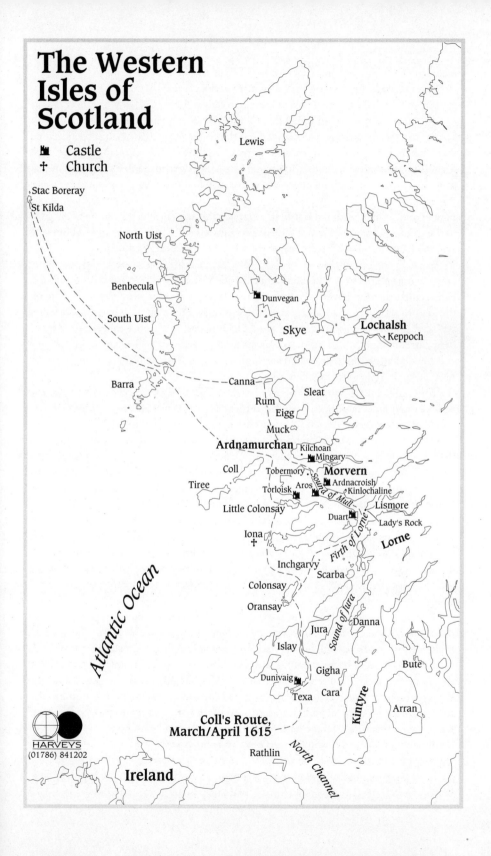

The Western Isles of Scotland

🏰 Castle
✝ Church

Stac Boreray
St Kilda

Lewis

North Uist

Benbecula

South Uist

Dunvegan 🏰

Skye

Lochalsh
· Keppoch

Barra

Canna

Sleat

Rum

Eigg

Muck

Ardnamurchan Kilchoan
Mingary 🏰

Coll

Tobermory

Morvern

Tiree

Ardnacroish 🏰

Torloisk 🏰 Aros 🏰

Kinlochaline

Sound of Mull

Little Colonsay

Duart 🏰

Lismore

Lady's Rock

Iona
✝

Firth of Lorne

Lorne

Inchgarvy

Scarba

Colonsay

Oransay

Sound of Jura

Danna

Jura

Islay

Gigha

Bute

Dunivaig 🏰

Cara

Texa

Kintyre

Arran

Atlantic Ocean

**Coll's Route,
March/April 1615**

🌐 ⚫
HARVEYS
(01786) 841202

Rathlin

North Channel

Ireland

included "Coll MacGillaspic MacDonnell" (*Colla Ciotach*).

Stevenson tells us that confessions which were eventually wrung from some of the participants told of a meeting held in Ireland in May or June 1614, by which time Angus *Og* had taken responsibility for Dunivaig and Ranald *Og* had allegedly "escaped". It seems that the Irish rising was planned for the following August, and it was decided that "when they went to burn and surprise Coleraine, they would send for Coll MacGillenaspie into Scotland, who was sure to assist Alexander and his kinsmen in that action". Thus in May or June it was already anticipated that Angus *Og* would refuse to surrender Dunivaig when the time came for him to do so, for it was agreed that "those of Scotland should begin the war first." Perhaps this was the impression that Coll gave to the meeting, since in May and June he was himself in military command of Dunivaig and will have been largely responsible for whatever was being planned.

As has been seen, the plans for Islay were later modified, as soon as the possibility arose that armed confrontation could be avoided. Because of Graham's deception, it had seemed that the government was not inobdurate and the hostages (indeed, even the keys to the castle) had been surrendered to him. Diplomacy and negotiation then replaced any idea of a genuine rising based on Dunivaig, and in consequence the dependent Ulster rising was also still-born. Now that the treachery of Graham, Calder, Argyll and (by default) King James had destroyed any hope of peaceful settlement, it was to his kindred in Ireland that Coll turned.

During the few days that he spent in Antrim, *Colla Ciotach* was making plans for the future, and it must have been then that the arrangements were made for a more determined protest, one with a stronger figurehead. Angus *Og* had done his best, but lacked conviction and gravitas; he had been hopelessly outmanoeuvred by Graham and it had become clear that his elder brother, Sir James MacDonald, was more suited as a "leader". He had experience of court procedure and diplomacy, was the eldest son of old Sir Angus (and was therefore a stronger claimant to the Dunivaig estates), and despite years of confinement in Edinburgh he had had the benefit of experience in battle since his early childhood. Whatever his reluctance, Sir James was now persuaded that the sole remaining chance for *Clann Iain Mhóir* to curtail the Campbell gains lay in a dramatic gesture of protest, to be followed by a direct appeal to the King himself. Thus it was that, in those few days in Antrim, Coll turned power-broker and made the arrangements that were to bring Sir James from captivity and to the forefront of a final campaign.

Having done everything that was needful, Coll then embarked on a short but spectacular new career – he became a pirate; it may perhaps have been as enjoyable an interlude as it was eventful, but was nonetheless undertaken for a serious purpose. It seems that he sought to create a smokescreen of activity in the Western Isles, compounding the difficulty of the authorities, who already had a full agenda in investigating and reviewing recent activities both in Islay and in Ulster. Coll had nothing else to do until Sir James could join him, and so took the opportunity to put the forces of the crown off-balance. To the authorities there seemed to be no rhyme nor reason to his movements in the following few months, and of course vigorous but random activity always puts maximum strain on the resources of an opponent.

The first thing that Coll required was a boat, and early in March he captured one, belonging to Henry Robinson of Derry. Fortunately for us, a seaman who was on board was also seized and put to work in the weeks that followed – he eventually escaped on 12th May and made a statement next day.[3] The detail that he provides enables us to follow *Colla Ciotach*'s movements very closely, and for anyone familiar with the western isles, it is easy to picture almost every detail of the voyage.

Robert Williamson's Testimony
"EXAMINATION of ROBERT WILLIAMSON taken before Sir Thomas Phillips, 13th day of May 1615

"This examinate, being duly sworn and examined by virtue of his oath, sayeth that he, being servant to Henry Robinson of Londonderry, was taken in a boat of his said master's by Collo M'Gillaspick, with whom he by force has continued the space of 10 weeks now last past, and that this last night he made an escape from him from the Raughlins [Rathlin].

"In the time he was with Collo he was a labourer, and wrought in the boat, and he with Collo was one day ashore at Laxsa [Texa], which is within a mile of the castle [Dunivaig] in Eyley [Islay], and Colla's men were one night in the Island of Eyley to confer with their friends there.[4]

"During examinate's being with Collo M'Gillaspick he was in many islands with the said Collo, as namely Collernessy [Colonsay], which is within eight miles from Eyley, but went not ashore there. From thence to Mulley [Isle of Mull], some 40 miles from Collornessy [perhaps to Aros?], and there remained four days, but went not on shore; from thence to Canna some 20 miles from Mulley, where they were about eight days; there they went ashore and feasted and drank with their friends, and chiefly with M'Callan [ClanRanald] (and?) O'Cahan's wife (her husband being in Scotland); from there they sailed to Ewest [Uist], which is 40 miles from Canna, and there Coll went ashore and lay on land with two of his men in his company one night. The boat stayed there eight days; from there they sailed to the Isle Art [Hirta, i.e. St. Kilda], which is from Eross 100 miles, whereof Maylon [McLeod?] is commander. There they landed and took great store of barley, and some 30 sheep for their provision.

"This island is in length two miles or thereabouts, and there were but 10 men and 10 women inhabiting therein. There they remained a month. From Art they sailed to another island called Burribaugh [Stac Boreray], which is six miles from Art, of some half a mile in compass. There is no dwelling therein, but only is a rocky strength; there Coll had a purpose to keep himself, for it is of such strength as not to be gained but by famine.

"And from thence they returned back the same way they went thither, and touched at every place as formerly they had done on their voyage outward. On Saturday 6th May, Coll M'Gillaspie went ashore at the Isle of Collumkelle [Iona] and there did drink aqua vitae with Laughlin M'Gleane [MacLean], M'Gleane's brother, and stayed there about two hours, and there bought some five or six pounds of powder, and as much lead, but of whom he knows not, because he was not suffered to go ashore. This island was called Collown [Little Colonsay?], and is about a quarter of a mile from the Isle of Mull.

"And they came to the Raughlins and landed there, taking the principle men of the island, and having them bound all night, and loosed them in the daytime, and they broke all the boats they found at the island to prevent their going to the main [land] to give intelligence of his being there.

"Coll M'Gillaspie, with two of his men in his company, went from the Raughlins in a fisher boat of his, and landed at Port Britas [at the head of Ballycastle Bay] called Bonavargie [now

Ballycastle], the 10th of this month being Wednesday, and sent the boat back to the Raughlins, and they took a fisherman's boat of some five or six tons which was laden with oats for Scotland.

"Coll M'Gillaspie after he was put on shore at Bonavargie, which was about 10 o'clock in the forenoon, they [went] as far as Lough Chichester [Lough Neagh], and returned not until Friday the 7th [sic; actually 12th] of this month [May], but with whom or in what places about the Lough they were, knows not.[5]

"When Coll and his company returned they made a fire on a hill in sight of the boat that lay at Raughlins, being a token between them, that on sight thereof he should bring the boat for him, which was accordingly done. The boat came to the shore and fetched them about 10 o'clock in the forenoon, and in their way towards the Raughlins they took a boat which was bound for Loughfoyle with salt, which they gave chase to, and in the chase, with a shot of a caliver, they killed one of the Scots' mariners, and then took the boat, being about the burthen of 12 tons.

"There was in her besides salt, five hogsheads of wine, eight hogshead of beare [beer], and three score Scots gallons of aqua vitae, and some money to pay the fishermen for their labour besides other necessaries for fishing.

"There came from the shore with Coll M'Gillaspie, one Sorley M'James M'Donell and six men in his company, the names of two of them he heard called, the one Alexander M'Donnell, the other Rory Oge O'Cahan, but for the other four he never heard them called by their names.

"He did oftimes hear Coll M'Gillaspie say he would disperse his company and live himself in the Island of Eyley and Keintier [Kintyre] in secret manner among his friends, and would have a small boat that should carry him away upon all occasions if he should by any means be discovered, and that this was his full resolution when he went into the county of Antrim from Raughlins as aforesaid; but it should seem that he was otherwise advised when he was among his friends about Lough Chichester aforesaid, for that at his return with Surly M'James M'Donnel he vowed to pillage and rifle all those that he could overcome without sparing of any, and he heard those in the company of Coll say that Sorley M'James was the first that entered upon the Glascoe boat, and that the Scotchmen that lost that boat did confirm the same to be true.

"After Coll M'Gillaspie did return with Sorley M'James M'Donnel to the Raughlins he heard Coll say that he would make himself as strong as he might with all speed, and would attempt the regaining of the castle in Eyley, and having effected the same, he would put the Scotts that should be there found to death without sparing any living creature of them.

"At the time examinate came from Coll M'Gillaspie as aforesaid with the small boat of five or six ton formerly taken, he had in his company some 30 men and boys, mariners, and had among them 14 calivers [guns], 24 swords, 17 targets [shields], and every one had a long skiene [knife], and every one of them that had calivers, had some 20 shot of powder and not any more.

"Lastly he came not in the boat with Coll M'Gillaspie when he landed in the county of Antrim, but he came in the boat to fetch him aboard, which was near the place where the quarry of freestone is, and it was about 10 o'clock in the forenoon, and in that place he was likewise put ashore.

"*Signed*: Thos. Phillips."

The above account is remarkably clear and detailed, and is reproduced faithfully (with the exception of the transposition of two small sections not in narrative sequence in the original). It is interesting to notice the humanity of Coll – we are told of his romantic wish to live quietly and even remotely; we find that he is very happy to feast and drink with his friends; and we see that despite his measured manner, he was moved to great anger on the second visit to Antrim. We cannot be sure exactly what it was that so upset him, but there were plenty of possibilities: Angus *Og* was prisoner in the Tolbooth, there were rumours that Sir James himself was to be executed, Coll's two young sons were being held hostage, and in Antrim his relations were the victims of an inquisition. Perhaps he had even got word of the King's letter of approbation to Calder, from Whitehall on 20 April: "we decern that the name and repute of that infamous tribe [Clan Donald] ... be altogether abolished, rooted out, and supressed, or reduced to our obedience."[6]

Williamson's account is very coherent; it does not suggest that Coll was guilty of any excesses and he stresses that it was only in hot pursuit of the Scottish trading boat that a shot was fired and a seaman killed. In later years, attempts were made to suggest that Coll was some sort of mindless man of violence, yet such incidents as are recorded seem to show that although well able to look after himself, it was Coll's policy to avoid violence wherever possible. In fact, there is a lot of evidence to show that Coll was a man of strong religious convictions, one who would see himself as answerable to God for his actions.

Sir Rory McLeod's Version

Besides Williamson's account, further details are given in a letter to Lord Binning, Secretary of State to the Privy Council. It seems that Sir Rory McLeod, who had been particularly instructed to harass *Colla Ciotach* when he made his own personal appearance before the Privy Council, was rather vexed to hear of Coll's visits to Uist and St. Kilda, so he wrote urgently to Lord Binning to present his excuses in the following terms, 18 June 1615:

"MY LORD – My homble dewtye after all reverence and seruice remembered, in the beginning of Apryll I left Edinburgh and passed till Glasgow the viste my barnes who ar at the shoole there, where I remained the space of fyifteinth dayes, and thereafter I passed till Stirling and going in to the toun I mett my lord Fleming comeing out of the toun, who had a ledd courshour [lit. racehorse, i.e. hunter] besyd and I rydand on a other courshour, both the courshours brailes togidder, and I was forced to leave and fall af my horse, where I brack two ribbes in my syd and lay for the space of XVth dayes in Perth vnder the cure of physik, and thereafter I reteired to my owne countrey.

"And in the meantyme of my absence Coill Makgillespik and his companie come to the north Illes, and stoppet the first night at the yle of Cannis [Canna], and thereafter passed derectlie to North Wyest Donald Gorme his landis, where he was reseat [received], his men enterteaned, and Makintoshie's dochtar, Donald Gorme's wyff, beeng for the tyme in that countrey, togidder with Donald Gorme, Makkenyees good brother, send to the said Coill beeng scant of viueres, four horse load of meat, in the whitche there wes two swyne, on salted and one vnsalted, and the said Coill and his companie was perswaded, moved and requested by the saide Donald Gorme's wyff and young Donald and clann Neill vaine the speciall tenents of north Wyest to pass to a yle of myne called Hirta [St. Kilda], a day and a night sailing from the rest of the north yles far out in the ocean sea, and to that effect derected two of the tenents on north Wyest to be there guyd and pyllats there for they wer vnknowen thame selues there, and coming to the ylle they slew all the beastiall of the ylle both kowes and horses and sheepe and took away all the spoolyee of the yle, onlie reserved the lyves of the inhabitants thereof.

"And when all wes done they returned to North Wyest againe, where they randered there guyd and pyllats agane, and gave to the inhabitants thereof all and whole the spoyle of my yle, and afore my comeing to the yles the said Coill Makgillespik passed away south to Ila againe ...."

Certainly Sir Rory McLeod was not slow to try to point the finger – whilst he was on holiday in Glasgow or in his bed in Perth, he had a perfect excuse for inaction; and it was some compensation for his loss that he could so comprehensively accuse so many others of complicity with Coll and his men. Yet once more we find that even Sir Rory, trying to curry favour with the crown, fails to suggest that Coll was guilty of any violent or intemperate act, whilst from other sources we know something of just how he passed his time in St. Kilda: "*A' teagasg an t-sluaigh!*" [Giving religious instruction to the people!]

Colla Ciotach in St. Kilda

This rather endearing tradition was one that was long-preserved in St. Kilda before it was first recorded by Rev. Alexander Buchan, who went there for the Society for Propagating Christian Knowledge as a minister, in 1705. Rev. Buchan was a devout man but not, of course, an adherent of the Old Faith, and he therefore tells the story in a certain way:

"'Tis commonly reported by the Natives, and others more concerned in this Affair, that about the beginning of the last Century or thereabouts, there happened to be One in St. Kilda, who went under the Name of a Popish Priest; but was so ignorant, that he was not capable to teach them the Repetition of the Lord's Prayer, the Creed, and ten Commandments, aright; yet was this nominal Priest it seems skilful enough to teach those poor ignorant people, who then might receive an impress, Superstition and Idolatry, by giving them Beads, Images, Observing of Superstitious Days, Erecting idolatrous Monuments, etc. among them: with this Teacher and Religion they continued until the Irish Rebellion, which broke out in the year 1641 [*sic*; there was an important rebellion in that year, but it seems likely that the date of this incident was actually 1614, (old style)], where there was one Coll Mackdonald, alias Ketoch (for he lost his right Hand in the then late Wars, whose Son called Alaster Mackdonald, was slain in the following Irish Rebellion) a commander in chief of the Irish Army, and was of the Mackdonalds in Ireland, or of the Family of Antrum, the Mackdonalds Chief there.

"This Coll Mackdonald alias Ketoch being defeat in Battle, loosing his right-hand, and his Army which he had raised for the Popish Interest routed, was forced, with a few, to flee for his Life; and getting his Foot in a Vessel, comes to land in St. Kilda, whom when the Inhabitants saw, they run away from him and his Men, into a Cave in some remote Corner of the Island, where they thought they might be most safe from him, whom they thought to be an Enemy come to destroy them; but he sending some few of his Men after them, told them of his friendly Designs, and he himself advancing gradually, enforces what his Men had said, by telling them he had no hostile Design against them, and that tho' he had, he was not in a Condition to effect it, since he wanted the right Hand (shewing them the stump;) so pulling out his Mill, and giving them a Snuff, with which, and some other significations of Kindness, they came to be delivered of their former Fears; so that he lived in Safety and quietness with them for the space of three quarters of a Year:

"This Col Mackdonald at length examining them of their Religion and Principles, found that the Priest was very ignorant, and had not taught the People the Lord's Prayer, Decalogue, and Creed aright: So rebuking the Priest, he corrected this, by causing them to repeat these aright: he likewise established them in the Superstitious and idolatrous Practices, being himself a bigotted Papist. The poor People, judging the Priest to be in the Wrong, and looking on him to be Ignorant, resolved to depose him; for the doing whereof, they referred it to the Sentiment of this Coll Mackdonald, whether they should do it or not; but this Coll put them off such Thoughts, by telling them, he never saw a Priest deposed in his Country for Ignorance; with this and other such like reasonless Reasons they were satisfied. And this was all the Religion they had till the year 1697....."[7]

The Rev. MacAuley, a later minister to St. Kilda, also recorded the tradition, as he received it in 1758 when he arrived there for SPCK:

"Col. McDonald ... having made himself obnoxious to the laws, fled to St. Kilda. An impostor there claiming a right to tithes or some religious perquisites, a part of the people refused to pay the tax, and pleaded that he was absolutely unqualified for the priestly office. Their great objection was, that this ghostly father was not able to repeat the Pater Noster. The pretended teacher had a faction to support his cause, at length the two contending parties, after many hot altercations, submitted the matter in dispute to the more learned stranger. Mr. McDonald, either attached to the new doctor of divinity, or willing to divert himself and others with a witty conceit, declared to the whole assembly, with a very serious air, that in the whole course of his life and reading, he had not seen a Clergyman deposed, or turned out of his living, for being unacquainted with the Lord's Prayer. The party in the opposition were either satisfied or silenced, and the intruder began immediately to levy his taxes".[8]

Sir James MacDonald breaks ward

Returning again to our narrative, we rejoin *Colla Ciotach* and his companions at Rathlin, 12th May 1615. Williamson made his escape that very night, by means of the small boat that *Colla*'s men had captured on the way back from Ballycastle two days earlier, and he at once made his report to the authorities. According to Black: "It seems the plan at this stage, such as it was, was that Alexander and Sorley were to hold Rathlin for a month or so while *Colla* and Malcolm MacLeod used it for a base for making further depredations on the shipping route between Ireland and Scotland, and while another "conspirator," Ludar MacDonnell, sought assistance in Spain. However, an unexpected development arose. This was the news that Sir James MacDonald had escaped from Edinburgh Castle and was making his way to the Isles. So *Colla* set sail again for the north, taking young Sorley with him. Meanwhile Alexander was arrested at Dunluce. He was eventually acquitted, but others – including *Ruarí Óg Ó Catháin* – were found guilty and executed."

Perhaps Sir James' escape was "an unexpected development" in some circles, but not so unexpected that *Colla Ciotach* could not be there to greet him at a rendezvous. Coll's recent activities had certainly prepared the ground for what was to follow and can hardly have been entirely fortuitous. The escape and subsequent developments were clearly carefully planned, and Sir James received the help of *Alasdair* MacRanald of Keppoch and his eldest son, as well as that of the Captain of Clanranald, all of whose territories had recently been visited by *Colla*. "The enterprise [i.e. Sir James' escape] appears to have been very skilfully conducted. The fugitives crossed the Firth of Forth, in a small boat, from Newhaven to Burntisland, and directed their course thence to the Highlands of Perthshire. On the 24th of May, a commission was given to the Marquis of Huntly and the Earl of Tullibardine for the apprehension of Sir James and his companions .... a reward of two thousand pounds was, at the same time, offered for Sir James, dead or alive."[9]

There was a determined pursuit, and at one point, near Loch Rannoch, the huntsmen actually came within sight of their quarry, at which stage Sir James and his party took to the woods and escaped on foot, abandoning their horses and possessions and even some of their servants (who were later released, through the good offices of the Earl of Tullibardine). The party made its way through Lochaber, and the Privy Council redoubled its efforts, determining: "That a missive be written to the Marquis of Huntly desiring him to send his son the Earl of Enzie [Lord of Badenoch] to Lochaber with diligence to pursue the rebels if they be there, to take, demolish and cast down MacRanald's houses, to confiscate all his goods and what else belongs to him, and to mell [forfeit] with the goods of such persons within Lochaber as has received Sir James McDonald since his escape out of custody."

The fugitives continued through Morar and Knoydart, and eventually to Sleat in Skye "where they had a lengthened conference with Donald Gorme. This chief did not join them openly himself, but a number of his men of Sleat followed Sir James, who sailed to the south in a large boat which he procured in that district". It is probable that this boat had been left for him by arrangement, perhaps by *Colla* himself ... certainly it is inescapable that the path of Sir James and his party seemed to run along lines that crossed Coll's recent tracks.

Sir Rorie Mcleod's letter to Lord Binning, on 18 June, which was quoted above, continued:

"Now sence I persave Sir James hes brocken warde, and come to Lochaber, and out of that come to Morar and Knoydart, where he took per force a young youth, the secund sone of Glengarrie on-a-worse [unawares], and keepes him still in custodie; and the Captanes sone, a son of Donald McAllan McEan, Captain of the Clan-Ronald.

"And thereafter, come to Sleat, to Donald Gorme's bounds, where he got a bigg boat, with oares, saile, and taikleing; and intercomoned at lenth with Donald Gorme there; and a number of Donald Gorme's folks of Sleat, called *Clann Tarlich*, is gone with him. And thereafter, passed till the Yle of Egga, where he met Coill and his companyee, togidder with his base sone [*Aonghus MacCholla*], and a sone of Sir James Maksorle of the Route [Sorley MacDonnell]. And they ar in number, as I lerne, tuelfue or thretteinth score, at the present tyme. And whidder they go South or North I can not tell, at the writteing heerof...."

The rendezvous on Eigg was a scene of jubilation. The Earl of Tullibardine forwarded an account of it in his own letter to Lord Binning a week later, on 24 June 1615 (spelling somewhat modernised):

"I hear he [Sir James] landed into the Iles of Rum and Eigg, where Coull McGillespic did meet him with a company of hagbutteris [armed men], about the number of seven score of men. Their form of meeting, as I hear was this. Sir James and his company stood in one place by them selves, where the other with his company went round about him, once; and at the next going about, saluted him with their volley of shots; and continued so shooting [firing volleys] and encircling him, for the space of half one hour; and thereafter come to him every man, particularly [one at a time], chapping hands [i.e. swearing fidelity to death]. Upon the morn, they conveyed all the whole beasts, horses and cattle, to one place, which they thought to have slain entirely; but upon better advisement, they slew only a number of cattle, for meat, which they carried immediate to their boats; and thereafter took the sea [set sail], to the number of Three hundred men, in all. Coull brought him two crearis [crayar, a type of large galley], with them were boats that Sir James him self got in Ardnamurchan, and suprised in their parts [pressed into their service]. It is thought that they have taken their voyage to Islay; and if the country be upon their guard, as they should, I think they shall not profit greatly."

In fact, Sir James and his host had not "taken their voyage" directly for Islay but for Colonsay, where they are said to have landed on 18 June 1615, a Sunday.

Notes

1 Portrollock is in Island Magee (Cahal Dalat, pers. com.), close to modern Larne. This is 25 nautical miles from Kintyre, but presumably Coll suspected that the more accessible landing places were under surveillance.

2 And therefore second cousin of Coll, and of his wife, and of Sir James MacDonald, and also, of course, of Angus *Og*

3 Now in the Stearne Mss. of Trinity College, Dublin

4 An interesting tradition suggests that *Colla Ciotach* may have been almost captured at this point, when he enquired as to the lie of the land. No doubt he was well warned that Dunivaig remained in enemy hands and it may be that this tale arose in connection with the visit:
"Piobaireachd Dhunaobhaig", "The Piper's Warning to his Master".
The story is well told by Duncan Johnston of Islay, songwriter and author of "*Birlinn Cholla Chiotaich*": "As soon as Coll's advance party arrived at the castle they were made prisoners. Next day, Coll furtively left his secret lair [in Texa?] and sailed away for *Dunaobhaig*, and when his galley was seen sailing directly for the castle the conspirators were delighted. Their deadly foeman was sailing right into the muzzles of the guns of the stronghold. In order to allay any suspicion Coll might have regarding their good intentions they conceived the idea of releasing the piper, so that Coll might see and hear him playing the pipes on the battlements, and thus get the impression that all was well. Little did they know that Coll and his piper had perfected a system whereby the piper, by means of his chanter, could warn his master of danger. As soon as the piper saw his beloved master almost within the jaws of the trap, he struck up and played the celebrated "Piper's Warning to his Master", or *Piobaireachd Dhunaoghaig*.

A Cholla, mo rùn,	Coll, my love,
Seachain an Dùn	Shun you the Dun,
Freagair a' ghaoith	With wind turn round
'S thoir ort an Caol	Make for the Sound,
Tha mise 'n làimh	A captive, I
Tha mise ' làimh!	A captive, I!

As soon as Coll heard the warning notes of *Mac-an-Riabhach*'s chanter, he at once put about and sailed away. The plotters were extremely chagrined when their quarry escaped them. The sudden manner in which Coll had turned away could only allow of one explanation. Suspicion fell on the piper and he was cruelly tortured...."

The significant part of the story is that the tune as played was defective, *piobaireachd* being a very formal type of music, played according to an exact system of rythm. The tune as played had been deliberately mutilated and although it would be possible to restore the missing phrases it is a temptation that has been resisted since, to the present day, "*A Cholla, mo rùn*" is played without emendation, a lasting tribute to *Mac-an-Riabhach*.

5 It is unlikely that Colla Ciotach really made a round trip of 80 miles cross country in two days without some very pressing reason. More likely that Williamson was deliberately misled.

6 In Canna, Coll's host "McCallan" was *Mac 'ic Ailein*, i.e. Clanranald; it will be remembered that Coll's wife Mary had at first been married to *Raghnall* MacRanald of Benbecula, and that *Aonghus MacCholla* was thought to be their son. The party that joined *Colla* in Antrim clearly represented the leadership of the abortive rising of the previous year. It included Sorley MacDonell and his brother *Alasdair Garrach*, who were both second cousins to Coll, and they were accompanied by one "Rory O'Cahan"; Coll was, of course, an O'Cahan on his mother's side. Possibly this "Rory" was the O'Cahan whose wife had been one of the convivial little party on Canna in mid-March, but Black believes that Williamson must have been mistaken in the name, since other records show that the *Ruarí Òg Ó Catháin* who was prominent in the Ulster conspiracy could not have been present with Coll on 12th May. Black suggests that a likely candidate is the famous blind harper *Ruarí Dall O' Cathain* who flourished at this time and spent most of his life in Scotland. Then again, perhaps Williamson was deliberately misled, since he encountered this "Rory O'Cahan" on the very day that he "escaped" – or, possibly, was deliberately allowed to get away; it seems odd that after ten weeks captivity he should suddenly manage to get away, complete with information that could be important to the authorities.

7 Although Coll was offering snuff, to which he was extremely partial, in remote St. Kilda barely 30 years after tobacco first reached fashionable London, it was probably made from the root of *Corra-Meille* or "Bitter Vetch" (*Lathyrus montanus*), a versatile plant which was still used for flavouring whisky in 19th century Colonsay. The story of the priest remains popular in the island, the punch-line always being delivered in Gaelic and with particular relish: "*Thuirt e nach cual e riamh iomradh air sagart a bhith air a chur as a dhreuchd air son aineolais!*" (He said that he never heard tell of a priest being removed for ignorance).

8 Martin Martin did not record this story in St. Kilda, but he was able to give a detailed account of the doings of a later divine, one whom even Buchan can hardly have associated with Papists: "Roderick the Impostor", who flourished some 130 years after the Reformation, engaged the females of the island in very particular exercises of his own devising. As a Penance for the recalcitrant, he had the unfortunate lady stand naked below a stopped-up burn, which was then released on top of her; but mercifully enough, this was only in extreme cases – "The ordinary Penance he imposed upon them, was making them stand in cold Water, without any Regard to the Season, during his Pleasure; and if there were more of them upon whom this Severity was to be inflicted, they were to pour cold Water upon one another's Heads till they had satisfied his tyrranical Humour"....

9 Quotation from Gregory. Also note: "Sir James McKonnell escaped out of the Castle of Edinburgh, where he had been wairdit the space of eighteen years, upon the 24th of Maij, the day after Angus Ooge, his brother, and eight or nine of his complices, were brought to Edinburgh. It was thought that he escaped not without the privity of these who had credit." – Calderwood, M.S. Church History, cited by Pitcairn in his "Criminal Trials".

7

SIR JAMES MACDONALD'S RISING – 1615

Interlude in Colonsay

When Sir James MacDonald's forces landed in Colonsay it was at the suggestion of *Colla Ciotach*. No doubt they decided to enlist the support of Malcolm MacDuffie and his levy of 40 men, to gather intelligence, and to secure this strategic position. Whilst they were there they are known to have made improvements to the small fort on *Eilean Dubh Iain Mhitchel*, at *Loch an Sgoltaire*. Even with 300 men at his disposal it is unlikely that *Colla Ciotach* could have built it from scratch in a few days, and so we may suppose that the works were confined to completing or upgrading an existing structure.

The Privy Council were well informed by their spies, and a letter of 20 June reported that Sir James "was four nightis in ane little yllan, callit Collinsaye, and slew ane numir of merttis [cattle]. He has maide ane strenth in it upon ane fresch wattir loch in ane eylanne".[1]

This brief visit to Colonsay was further enlivened in a most extraordinary way, the circumstances of which are preserved in a contemporary petition. It seems that after Campbell of Calder had regained Dunivaig, he had appointed one Alasdair MacDougall as constable and the latter's garrison had included a Duncan MacDougall and three of his brothers. Duncan had designs upon the Prior of Oransay's daughter, but his suit having been rejected by her reverend father Duncan and his brothers decided upon a more forthright approach and sailed across to seize and ravish her, little knowing that the lovely lady now shared her remote habitation with some hundreds of heavily-armed rebels. The events were graphically described in the following statement made some months later, on 11th January 1616:

"**COMPLAINT** by McDonald McAllaster of Largie as follows: –

The cause pretended [put forward] by Archibald, Earl of Argyll, his Majesty's Lieutenant over the Isles, for the taking and detaining of the said complainant as prisoner so long was his receiving [harbouring] of Duncan MacDougall, one of the assistants, as he alleged, of the traitor MacDonald in his treasonable courses; whereas if the said Lords understood the certain truth, the said complainant is sure the said Lords would not think he had offended in that point.

"For so it is that, this MacDougall and three of his brothers being the chief and principle men that assisted the said Laird of Caddell in his first employment against Coill McGillespik [*Colla Ciotach*], and who kythit most on action against Coll at that time, they were therefor appointed by the Laird of Caddell to assist Alasdair MacDougall, Captain of Dunnyveg, in the keeping of the said house, and remained there with the Captain all this winter, and until the month of May last.

"And, the eldest of the four brothers being in suit of the Prior of Oransay's daughter in marriage, and finding no likelihood that he could come to his intent, he therefore, with the advice of his three brothers, resolved to ravish the gentle-woman: and for performance thereof, the four brothers came out of the Castle of Dunnyveg in the month of May last to the Isle of Oransay, where the gentle-woman was at the time, 'resolved to haif revisched and tane hir away'.

"But so it was that Coll and Sir James MacDonald happened to be in the Isle at the time, and heard tell of the landing of these men, and what was their purpose. And the said Coll found that occasion very fit and proper unto to him to be revenged on them for their former service done to the Laird of Caddell against him the previous year. He therefore, with some of his force, came and made a cruel onset upon the four brothers and such as were in company with them, and hurt the eldest brother 'deadlie' upon the head; and, having them all in his mercy to have slain them, yet, out of the malice of his heart resolving to have their lives by a more shameful death, he brought them to Sir James; and, he and the said Sir James consulting together, they resolved presently to hang them for the intended ravishing of the gentle-woman.

"Whereupon a gibbet was immediately set up, and the four brothers, bound and fettered with withies [willow or osier branches], were brought to the gibbet, and the eldest was set up upon a barrel, with a tow [rag] about his craig [neck] fastened to the gibbet, because they lacked a ladder; and, being at the very point to have been wirreyed [strangled], McRannald, whose wife is a MacDougall, made great entreaty with Sir James for their lives, and Coll, upon the other part, urged their present [immediate] execution, – so that there was a very great trouble and business like to have fallen out between them, had not some wise men in the country took up the matter between them with this condition, that Sir James should keep the four men with him as prisoners until the dissolution of His Majesty's force; at which time, with common consent of the principle chiefs that followed Sir James, it should be resolved whether it were more expedient to spare or save them.

"And so they were kept as prisoners with Sir James all the time that he was on the [battle]fields. And, when he fled, this MacDougall came to the said complainant, unto whom [MacDougall], for the respect he carried to his Majesty because he [MacDougall] was troubled for his Majesty's service in assisting the Laird of Caddell against Coll, he [complainant] shewed some favour. And, as soon as the said complainant understood that the Earl made a quarrel of the matter, he offered to deliver the man to him; and the man himself was very willing to have come to the Earl for his exoneration; but the Earl would not take him off his [complainant's] hands. And now, at the said Earl his going away, the said complainant earnestly entreated him either to take the said MacDougall off his hands, or then to exonerate the said complainant of him; and his answer was that he had given order in that matter to his brother, the Laird of Lundy." (The matter was put back for review on 26 March, when witnesses were to be called.)

This interesting little vignette was only to come to light months later, but whilst the unfortunate MacDougalls stood in the shadow of the gibbet decisive attitudes were already being struck in Edinburgh. On 27 June 1615, Campbell of Calder was rash enough to make a promise to the Privy Council:

"The which day in presence of the Lords of Secret Council appeared personally Sir John Campbell of Caddell, and promised to be answerable for keeping of the Isle of Islay from Sir James MacDonald, Coill McGillespik, and the rest of their rebellious accomplices, and that they shall have no reception, aid nor comfort within the same, but shall be pursued with all rigour and extremity if they shall happen to come there, in such form and manner as the remaining landlords of the Isles are obliged to answer for their lands. And, touching the house of Dunnyveg, he undertook to be answerable for the safe keeping of the same; and, if any of these rebels shall happen to come in Islay and commit any insolence there, he promised to try and use his own power and forces against them before he would crave any assistance or aid from his Majesty or his Council."

Dunivaig seized again

Fine words, but rather empty since at the time that Calder was making his "promise", Sir James MacDonald and *Colla Ciotach* were already in Islay and investing Dunivaig. One of Lord Binning's spies was Hector McNeill of Taynish, who had already reported the activity at Colonsay, and who now wrote again (26 June):

"MY LORD – Your Lordship, accepting so well of my last news of the Isles, has emboldened me now, with most speed, to inform your Lordship of this latest development, for the 23rd of this month Sir James MacDonald landed in Islay and came unperceived near Dunnyveg and by 'traine' [lead] of a crafty fellow of the country, the Constable of the Castle by name Alexander MacDougall brother to Rory, was brought out by this fellow and five soldiers with him and going a little space from the Castle was set upon by Sir James and Coill Mcgillespik and all their companie. The gentleman spying them, made for the house and is slain and three of [his men]"....

Sir James and his men had then invested part of the defences, set fire to the gates and gained control of the only water supply, a well in the inner courtyard; the next day the castle was surrendered to them. The besiegers had lost just three men, but one of them was Ranald *Og*, the very man who had started the whole chain of events the previous year and who had himself been expelled by *Colla Ciotach*. Calder's men were driven from Islay and Sir James's force was swollen by the arrival of waves of his clansmen. Once again we should note that there seems to be no suggestion of excesses, the whole undertaking being tightly disciplined. As Stevenson remarks: "At last, he [Sir James] hoped, he could negotiate with the king for possession of Islay from a position of strength, not as a helpless prisoner, and the island would be preserved from the Campbells – "I will die befoir I sie a Campbell posses it." Unlike the unfortunate Angus *Og*, who was left passively awaiting counter-attack in Dunivaig, Sir James resolved to retain the initiative by occupying Jura and Kintyre."

Colla Ciotach undertook the responsibility for this in Kintyre, where he encouraged and organised ready support amongst the inhabitants of these ancient *Clann Iain Mhóir* lands – lands to which his clan had title but which had been held for eight years under the yoke of Argyll. In Jura, the principal leader was *Domhnall Giogach MacIain*, who followed the lead of Malcolm MacDuffie in Colonsay by supporting Sir James; the first report of this came in a letter to Lord Binning from Archibald Campbell, son of the Prior of Ardchattan (29 July): "I am certainlie informit be my spie that McFie of Collinsay, [and] Donald *gigache* in Jouray, hes gone with the rebels and are earnest transporting thair gudis to Ilay."

Campbell's report was confirmed but with a more alarming twist in a message sent on the same date by Hector McNeill of Taynish:

> "Two speciall men that held of Argyle befoir ar newlie rebellit with thame, Mcduphe of Collinson, and his haill name [clan], and Donnald Gigaich Makean who held Jura of Argyle, those two chiftanes ar gaine with the rebels thriescore and foure and remaines in Kintyre in pairtis neirest Argyll as zit making thair boast and vowing to be at the Tarbert quhilk is nyne myls within Argyle's boundis this night or the morne."

MacDuffie had provided forty men from Colonsay, and from McNeill's report it can be seen another twenty four were raised by MacIan in Jura. Even on their own, these two small forces compared favourably with the forces as yet available to the crown: "From communications made by the Prior of Ardchattan and Archibald Campbell, his son, to the Secretary for State [Lord Binning], it appears that the people of Argyle and Lorn refused to proceed against the rebels till the arrival of a Royal lieutenant; and that, in the middle of July, there were only forty men in arms for the protection of that part of the country against the Clandonald and their abettors." – Gregory.

On Islay itself, Sir James organised the repair and strengthening of the fortalice on the island in Loch Gorme, where spies reported that he had engaged a force of 120 men on a non-stop basis, creating a massive bawn or earthwork of great thickness: the rebels "ar all bissie fortiefying the eyllan of Ellan loch gorme with ane baoune of feall [turf] of ane greit breid, as the reportis, tuanttie foote bread. Sir James is bissie about it sex scoir of men euerie day."[2]

Elsewhere in Islay, other working parties were engaged in additional preparations for defence and Sir James was reported to be creating another fortification at "Dunand", a site which it is tempting to identify as *Dùn Athad*. This dramatic beacon-site on the lofty Oa is within clear view of Rathlin and the Antrim coast and was certainly important to Sir James; his efforts in preparing it were worthwhile, for a signal from that beacon was shortly to save his life.[3]

Sir James pledges his fealty

Although Sir James MacDonald clearly found plenty of morale-building activity with which to engage his enthusiastic and ever-growing body of supporters, he did not pin his hopes on military success. Perhaps in this he made the same mistake which had plagued his generation; both Ranald *Og* and Angus *Og* had chosen gesture-politics and negotiation, and now Sir James, even from a position of strength, was reluctant to commit himself to open defiance and revolt. It should be remembered that having spent many years in Edinburgh and at Court, he was as cultivated as he was well bred; characteristically, when he had been forced to break custody and to fly to his native heath, he had been accompanied by a small retinue of domestic staff and had even brought the nucleus of his library.[4]

In addition to general sensibilities, it was natural that Sir James would seek to avoid rebellion since he remained a lifelong loyal Catholic, and as such accepted that the King ruled by Divine Right. Elsewhere, forces of the Reformation sought to challenge this tenet, but for Sir James to defy the King openly would be for him to deny his own Faith.

Thus he contented himself with preparations for self-defence and limited operations against the territories of Argyll and Calder, both of whom were, in his eyes, guilty of treason in their abuse of the King's trust, but his true hope rested in the pursuit of reconciliation.

The Earl of Tullibardine was to be the chosen conduit for almost all of Sir James' correspondence at this critical time, but sadly, instead of forwarding letters as addressed, Tullibardine saw it as his duty to convey them directly to the Privy Council, as a result of which they were all suppressed. In the first of these communications, soon after leaving Edinburgh, Sir James had given a simple and compelling explanation for his action, and had sought reconciliation with the King under any terms. He explained that he had received direct and convincing evidence that Campbell of Calder had obtained a secret warrant from King James himself, which, if produced, would compel the Privy Council to implement the outstanding sentence of death under which he lay. In effect, his life had been given into the hands of the man who had already gained possession of his patrimony and Sir James had felt himself obliged to flee.

These letters produced no effect, but after he had regained Colonsay, Oransay, Islay, Jura and much of Kintyre – in fact, most of his ancestral territory – Sir James chose to write again. He wrote to Lord Binning, to the Marquess of Hamilton, to the Earl of Caithness and to the Earl of Crawford among others. His letter to the Bishop of the Isles is as suitable as any in expressing his sincerity (quoted by Loder):

"And now, my Lord, I protest, albeit I was twelve years in ward and all my kindly lands disponed to strangers, my life left in His Majesty's hands, yet the same made me not so much to break ward as it did when I was offered by the Laird of Calder's own friends, who cannot deny it, that His Majesty, by his secret warrant, had given over my life in the Laird of Calder's hands. And now, my Lord, I protest to God my desire is not to rebel or trouble the estate of the country, but serve His Majesty with all humility, and make my kin and friends peaceable men, if I may have His Majesty's peace, with the assurance of my life and the life of my poor friends, and some means to sustain us rather nor to force us for want to oppress others.

"Herefore I beseech you, seeing my race has been ten hundred years kindly Scotsmen under the Kings of Scotland, and willing to live upon one poor part of that which our forbears had, and I to find good surety for all that becomes loyal subjects to do, both for myself and my whole kin that follows me, that your Lordship will, as you ever did, intercede for me at His Majesty's hands to see what grace or favour your Lordship may obtain to me, and in special, to see if, without diminishing His Majesty's commodity, I may have the island [Islay] to myself and my kin to sustain us; otherwise that your Lordship will get that favour that no hasty course shall be taken against me, by giving employment to my unfriends [enemies, i.e. Campbells], till your Lordship may have time first to speak with me; at which time, albeit I get not the island, yet, providing His Majesty will hold it in his own hand, I will show your Lordship how His Majesty's commodity here may be increased, and I to be satisfied, and His country to be free of any trouble of me or my friends."

Since this and other letters failed to reach their destinations, the "rebellion" became a reality; the Privy Council rushed ahead with the execution of Angus *Og* and his companions, blithely ignoring the compelling evidence of their innocence. Now that Sir James had escaped, they sought to use the escape itself to justify the original imprisonment;

they ignored his evidence about the secret warrant, and of course had long "forgotten" that his original offence, in capturing and restraining his father, had been in pursuit of the King's interest and with the King's consent. Now that they had intercepted and suppressed his explanations to the Crown, the members of the Privy Council were in a position to act against the very situation that they had themselves created.

The Privy Council felt that so serious a revolt must be sternly opposed by the "loyal" chiefs and by the principal landlords; they issued instructions accordingly, but their leading candidate, the Earl of Argyll, was at this time in London, financially embarrassed and very unwilling to return to Scotland to face his creditors. His brother, Colin Campbell of Lundie, was called before the Privy Council and asked to undertake to keep the Earl's properties free from the "rebellis", but he too made his excuses, having "no warrand nor commissioun frome his bruther to that effect; always he declairit that he wald write to his brutheris baillies and chalmerlanis that they wald haif a care of this mater." The Privy Council decided to report this to the King, and to entreat the King to arrange for the Earl of Argyll either to come home at once or to appoint "some gentleman of credite, pouer, and freindschip who will tak the burdyne of keeping his cuntreyis".... In the meantime, Sir Dougal Campbell of Auchinbreck was induced, however reluctantly, to act in Argyll's absence, for which purpose he had to be released from prison where, Stevenson informs us, "he had languished in connection with his chief's debts.".

Another early move by the Privy Council was an offer of a bounty to anyone at all "that salhappin to be in company with the said Sir James and Coill McGillespick or ather of thame, will tak, apprehend, or present to justice, or slay, ony of thair societie and company being of better rank and qualities nor thame selffis." The reward to any such traitor was to be a free pardon for that and all previous crimes, regardless of their extent. The Privy Council was particularly keen to destroy the leadership of the "rebellion" and offered significant rewards, dead or alive, in ready cash: "for the said Sir James fyve thousand pounds, for McRonald [Keppoch], his sone, and Coill McGillespick, and for everyone of thame, fyve thousand merkis [£3000 Scots], and for every ane of the saidis Gillicallum McRorie and Ronald Oige thrie thousand merkis [£2000 Scots]."

By late July, an impasse had developed. Sir James himself had by now crossed from Islay to join *Colla Ciotach* and his forces in Kintyre, had sent round the fiery cross and was making a show of preparations for an attack on Tarbert, but still he held back, still hoping for a positive response to his various attempts to avert confrontation through conciliation. Campbell of Auchinbreck had meanwhile failed miserably in his command .... he had the use of barely three hundred men, and the fencible men of the districts had simply ignored the blandishments of the Privy Council. Neither side wanted to make a move, but eventually (22 August) Argyll himself was persuaded to accept his commission, and it may have been in token of his distaste for the task that he acted swiftly, efficiently and almost mechanically. It was clear to him that the Privy Council would almost certainly welch on the costs of the enterprise,[5] and there is also the possibility that his second wife, an English Catholic, had re-awakened long-dormant sensibilities in his character.

Argyll's military campaign

Be that as it may, when Argyll reached his demesnes, he found that his resources now amounted to about 400 soldiers and some cannon, together with a few naval vessels that were already in the area, they having been put on station in the spring as a response to *Colla Ciotach*'s earlier activities. Once he had established his headquarters at Duntroon (opposite Crinan), Argyll moved on to Tarbert with his own force, and sent Calder ahead by sea to occupy the islands of Gigha (held by McNeill) and Cara (a property of MacAllister of Largie), just opposite the site of Sir James' mainland camp in Kintyre. With a total force of some seven or eight hundred men, he would be well placed both to hold the islands and to make use of them as a base for a sudden attack. It is notable that Sir James and his supporters remained south of Tarbert, always within their ancestral lands – in any moral sense, their activities could not be described as rebellious.

Sir James MacDonald and his men were aware of Argyll's arrival, but they lacked intelligence reports and, as a result, Sir James moved forward with half of his force, in the direction of Tarbert, whilst *Colla Ciotach* and about 60 men advanced in three boats to the mouth of the loch. Coll's naval base was already established in the island of Cara, and in a sad comedy of errors the opposing forces of *Colla Ciotach* and Campbell of Calder seem to have passed each other unawares (Calder's fleet must have been moving south along the east coast of Gigha at the very time that *Colla Ciotach*'s boats were moving northwards along the west coast of that tiny island). Coll made a successful raid at Loch Tarbert and captured Campbell of Kilberry and a few companions, who seem to have been out on reconnaisance, but on his return spotted Calder's fleet. Part of that fleet then made an attack on Cara, but was driven back by the defenders under the command of Keppoch and Sorley MacDonnell who also, by means of lighted beacons, managed to pass an alarm to the mainland camp. Coll himself is known to have become embroiled in some aspect of this conflict at Cara, but managed to get free again, complete with his boats and prisoners.

At this stage, *Colla Ciotach* seems to have attempted to rendezvous with the main body of Sir James' force, further south in Kintyre, but Argyll's forces were pressing them closely and Coll's landing was so severely opposed that he lost some of his boats and about 15 or 16 men. The planned retreat became a rout, in which Keppoch was flushed from Cara, pursued the length of Kintyre and barely escaped. Sorley MacDonnell made for Islay, and "in his retreat was pursued by Calder to within shot of the Castle of Dunyveg".[6]

Although Coll himself managed to make a successful withdrawal and returned to take overall command in Islay, Sir James was put to open flight. Having escaped to Rathlin, he returned soon afterwards with Keppoch to see if he could salvage anything of his position, but strong easterly winds forced him to make his landfall at the tiny islet of Orsay (off the Rinns of Islay). Having quickly realised that his position was impossible, Sir James then tried to parley with Argyll, in the hope of delaying long enough to gain a more favourable wind. This ruse was bound to fail, not least because *Colla Ciotach*, by now the acknowledged leader of the remaining clansmen, and in command of both the forts, insisted on conducting peace negotiations in person. Regardless of the wind, Sir James was quickly forced to flee once more, and for the final time. Campbell of Calder was with the government fleet at "Lodoms" (modern Port Ellen), and ideally placed to take advantage of the very wind that had frustrated MacDonald. He set out by night with a force of 1000 men, intent on surprise but, fortunately for Sir James, his sentinels were still at their posts at *Dùn Athad* on the Oa, and by means of beacons he received good warning of the raid.

We are told that it was upon their bended knees that his clansmen begged him to stay and fight, so that they could all die by his side. Sir James was somewhat more pragmatic, and knew that to stay would be to bring utter ruin upon his people;[7] so it was that, with a heavy heart, he bade his last farewells and boarded his galley, stepping aboard from a rock in Orsay still known to *Ileachs* as "The Ledge of Lamentation". He made his escape with a few companions, including Keppoch and Sorley MacDonnell, and in a near gale made for the open sea and the relative safety of tiny Instrahull, some 30 nautical miles away to the southwest, off Malin Head. The rest of his small company, a broken rabble, fled to the four corners of the island.

Colla Ciotach's treaty with Argyll

Now that Sir James MacDonald had fled from Scotland, never to return, the leadership of *Clann Iain Mhóir* passed instantly, clearly and unequivocally to *Colla Ciotach*. The circumstances were not auspicious, since the new clan leader found himself and his followers besieged and at the fag-end of a failed revolt, without lands and effectively at the mercy of their deadly enemies. These circumstances are very clear and should not be ignored. The events which followed immediately upon the flight of Sir James and his close companions are critical to *Colla Ciotach*'s reputation, and have been almost universally interpreted to his disadvantage. It is worth considering the way in which the matter was treated by Gregory, whose extraordinary rendering seems to have been seminal:

> **GREGORY** (1881): "Sir James finding it impossible either to resist the Lieutenant's forces, or to escape with his galleys to the North Isles, which was then his principal object, sent a messenger to the Earl, desiring a truce for four days, promising, before the expiry of that time, to surrender himself without conditions. To this request, Argyle yielded conditionally, providing Sir James gave up the two forts he held within twenty-four hours; otherwise, the proposal of a truce would be looked upon in no other light than a scheme for obtaining time, in the hope of a south wind arising in the meantime, which would give the rebels an opportunity of escaping as they intended. Sir James, finding himself now much straightened, urged Coll MacGillespick, who at this time had the command of both the forts, to give them up to Argyle; but this Coll flatly refused to do. .... [after the flight of Sir James] Coll MacGillespick surrendered the two forts and his prisoners, upon assurance of his own life and the lives of some few of his followers. .... Coll .... became an active partisan against his former associates, and crowned his treachery by apprehending and delivering to Argyle Macfie of Colonsay, one of the principal leaders of the rebels, and eighteen others."

This account begins with a simple statement of the circumstances leading up to the flight of Sir James, in which the facts are plain and the positions of the various parties are easily understood. However the account is critical in its conclusion, where Gregory becomes the first historian to accuse *Colla Ciotach* of treachery. That specific charge is based upon an erroneous reading, and as for the rest of the complaint, it is hard to see

that Coll should have taken any course other than one which would be in the best interests of himself and those under his command. It must be remembered that Sir James
had offered to make an "unconditional" surrender, whereas *Colla Ciotach* achieved
important conditions, not least to save the lives of all his men. Those people, including
MacDuffie, who were later captured (with or without Coll's help) were not under his
command but were amongst that broken remnant of the force which had been put to
headlong flight. In fairness to both Gregory and to *Colla Ciotach* we should now consider
the actual evidence that exists and upon which Gregory based his comments.

On 13 October 1615, Argyll reported to Secretary Binning:

> "Coll McGillespic having the keiping of the castle of Duneveg and the ile of Lochgorme, he
> stayed in his strenthis and fallowed not Sir James [in flight]. Before the landing of his Majesties
> cannoun to the castle, Coll submitted him selff and cam in. He hes renderit both the castle
> and ile to me, and hes delyverit Coline Campbell of Kilberrie, who was his prisoner. Lykwayes,
> he hes undertakin to do such service as may releif him selff. I have apprehendit all the prin-
> cipall ringleadaris...... I have presentlie imployed Coll McGillespik in service against these that
> ar owtlawis, whois succes your lordship will know at my next adverteisment."

On the 16th, Binning replied in terms that were cool and disappointed. On the 20th,
Argyll's secretary wrote and confirmed that "Those that ar already execut ar not of the
number that Coll McGillespick hes apprehendit." This letter may have been in response
to a follow-up letter from Binning, in which he further stressed his displeasure: "For,
since Sir James and his sone, with McRannald and his sonne, and Glengarries son, and
McSorle, ar all escaped, and Coll pardoned, I know not quhat ringleaders these ar
whome ye wryt ye ar to bring in."

Clearly under pressure, the secretary, Archibald Campbell must have persuaded
Argyll to take steps to justify himself. On 29 October Argyll wrote to Binning in very
business-like terms, commencing:

> "My verry gude Lord – As I wrait to your Lordship in my last letters from [Dunivaig] the xiij
> of this instant that Coill McIlespick befoir the landing of his Majesties cannon had geiven up
> the castell of Dunovaig and ile of Lochgorme, haid delyverid Colin Campbell of Kilberrie,
> and wes gone about to do forder service for himselfe, so this day he hes returnit to me, and
> hes brocht withe him nyneteene of the rebellis that followit Sir James. Of thir thair ar tua or
> thrie of the cheif and principall that were withe Sir James. One of thame had the comman-
> dement of fourtie men; his name is McDuffie....."

This story, possibly composed by Archibald Campbell, seems to have been intended
to get Argyll out of a hole, and the confusion was compounded in a report on the
campaign given to the Privy Council on 24 November, not by the Earl of Argyll, but
by Archibald Campbell on his behalf. In modernized spelling, the account contains the
following section:

> "So, as Sir James MacRannald and his sons and Sorle McJames flies away that night to
> Inchedachole [Instrahull], an isle off the coast of Ireland, Coll McGillespik, having the keeping
> of the Castle of Dunivaig and the Isle of Lochgorme, rendered them both to the Earl of Argyll,

and Colin of Kilberry, whom he had taken captive, and apprehended McPhie, one of the principles who followed Sir James and delivered him to the Earl of Argyll. And I have presented
him this day before your Lordships, with other five Sir James' complices. After that the Castle
of Dunivaig and fort of Lochgorm were taken, my Lord [Argyll] apprehended fifteen of the
principle men of Islay who were leaders of the poor ones to follow Sir James; whom he caused
to be executed there."

Note that there is no reference here to *Colla Ciotach* capturing and betraying anyone
other than McPhie, and as will now be clearly seen, the Earl of Argyll himself put the
record straight on that account, on 21 December 1615, when he appeared in person
before the Privy Council. This is the crucial evidence, not from a third party but straight
from the horse's mouth; after describing the escape of Sir James and his company, and
the scattering of his supporters, Argyll went on to report that:

"The rest of his companions were forced to take the hills in the night. McFie's boat was taken.
Which is in service as a ship's boat to his Majesty's ships.

"On the morrow after, Coll McGillespik made offer of the two forts and two prisoners
[i.e. the hostages that he had captured at Tarbert] for the safety of his own life and some few
others; which I did accept, in respect of the unseasonable weather, the extreme sickness of
the most part of the soldiers, and the great scarceness of provisions, without any hope of
supply.

"**The forts were no sooner rendered but McFie**, at present prisoner in Edinburgh, and
Johnne McEane Voir, **desired protection** while they were about **to do his Majesty service**,
wherein they desired no limitation but enduring [restricted to] the merit of their service and
my pleasure; which I suspended [maintained] during my abode in the country. But, howsoon
I was to repair towards your Lordships, I durst not to leave such remarkable ringleaders behind
me without assurance of their loyalty to his Majesty. In consideration whereof I have presented
them to your Lordships."

It really is perfectly clear – Coll surrendered his hostages and **"McFie** and Johnne
McEane Voir **desired protection**", i.e. surrendered themselves. As far as we can see,
the Earl of Argyll allowed *Colla Ciotach* to use the little bargaining power that was available to him to make a simple agreement that was acceptable to both parties, and one
which was honoured. Since MacDuffie's boat was captured at the Isle of Orsay, it is
likely that MacDuffie had been with the party that had fled precipitately to Rathlin, and
that he either failed to join Sir James in his final flight or was thwarted in the attempt.
He was amongst those who were forced "to take the hills", and next morning came
forward and offered to "do his Majesty service", and desired protection. There is no
hint here that Coll acted dishonourably, although one can speculate on MacDuffie's
own intentions – the forts had already been surrendered, so what can he have had to
offer other than to give evidence against his companions-in-arms?

Argyll himself stressed (with evident surprise): "The forts were no sooner rendered
but McFie ... desired protection "! Is it possible that Gregory took the "two prisoners"
that were mentioned to refer to MacDuffie and MacIan, rather than to the two hostages
that Coll had been holding? As has been seen, Argyll's motives in negotiating with *Colla
Ciotach* and his general leniency to the "rebels" had been sharply questioned by the

Secretary to the Privy Council and, in his own interest, Argyll had briefly exaggerated the extent to which *Colla Ciotach*'s pardon had been of value. Naturally, this tended to blacken Coll's name, but the plain fact is that he had negotiated an honourable truce. It is unfortunate that Gregory's comments have been followed somewhat slavishly by other writers (see Appendix 3).

The resolution of the crisis in Islay said a lot for *Colla Ciotach*'s ability as a commander, but it also brought credit to the memory of Argyll himself. Whilst it is true that token executions were carried out, they were limited in number: "… my Lord apprehended fifteen of the principle men of Islay who were leaders of the poor ones to follow Sir James; whom he caused to be executed there". *Colla Ciotach* did not hand them over, and they appear to have been local people rounded up by Argyll's own men, probably selected by Campbell of Calder from amongst his more difficult tenants. In fact, the Privy Council insisted on very detailed explanations from Argyll and seems to have been almost disappointed that matters had been resolved without resort to more draconian measures.

It has long been the practice to condemn all Campbells evenly and out-of-hand, but it is not reasonable to judge all individuals in this way and the behaviour of Archibald Campbell, 7th Earl of Argyll throughout this campaign may well prove that there is some good even in the worst of us. Perhaps it was pragmatism, perhaps he really wanted to avoid a prolonged and expensive winter campaign, but just possibly he chose to act honourably and disinterestedly either in pursuit of the public interest or even through more profound motives. Certainly Argyll engaged in sensible negotiations with *Colla Ciotach*, with the result that needless further hostilities were avoided and Coll himself was able to return to Colonsay.

As Coll accepted his role as the latest chief of *Clann Iain Mhóir*, a mighty family now stripped of all its possessions, it was perhaps fitting that he did live in that small island of Colonsay, so beloved of the early leaders of Clan Donald and which had been such a bulwark to the descendants of *Iain Mór*.

Notes

1 The RCAHM report describes the "strength" or fortification: "It consists of a roughly concentric system of defences, incorporating outer and inner thick-walled curtains. The outer enceinte is a pentagonal enclosure measuring 33m in maximum extent from E to W by over 30m from N to S. There are the remains of roughly circular drum-bastions at all except the W salient, and a pair of partly rebuilt towers of this kind flank a round-arched entrance-gateway in the N sector. .... The inner enceinte is a compact and irregular but approximately square enclosure, measuring about 15m from E to W by 14m over opposite faces of the curtain wall. It incorporates four rounded angle-bastions which are from 4m to 4.5m in diameter. The curtain-wall stands to a maximum external height of 2m along the N front, and is also about 2m in average thickness. .... A narrow intramural stair gives access to the wall-head of the NE bastion .. "

2 The island in Loch Gorm is roughly circular, about 50m in diameter and the surviving ruin is described in the RCAHM Inventory Report: "The fortification occupies the central area of the island and stands to a maximum external height of about 2.4m... it is of an overall quadrangular layout incorporating boldly-projecting and roughly circular bastions at each of the four angles. .... The curtain-walls and towers are of drystone boulder construction, and portions of the walling are much wasted and reduced to debris or a rubble core." The account goes on to describe a "turf-backed" curtain-wall, and the remains of the three central buildings. "The principal building ... is floored below the mean level of the interior and is reached by a sunken stepped approach ... the building is rectangular on plan, measuring 7.5m in maximum length from NW to SE by 4m transversely within drystone walls just over 1m in average thickness. The walls survive to a maximum internal height of 1.8m, and there are three cruck-slots in the W sidewall with the visible remains

of two corresponding slots in the opposite wall. ... the absence of fireplaces in the end-walls may be an indi-cation of the former existence of an open hearth." The account is of particular interest as it gives a good idea of the original arrangements at the fortalice on *Eilean Dubh Iain Mhitchel*, in Colonsay. In the 19th century, whatever ruins remained of the central buildings therein were used to build the present summer house, only the curtain-wall being preserved. From the remains at *Eilean Loch Gorm* it is reasonable to suppose that one or more thatched blackhouses provided accommodation for the garrison, protected by a bastioned curtain-wall and the natural defence afforded by the loch itself.

3 Archaeology has not yet identified the site of "Dunand" with certainty. A place recorded as "Downand" is mentioned in the RCAHM Inventory as a likely candidate, and is said to have been identified in rental records of 1686 and 1722, wherein it was closely associated with Kilchoman. The writers of the Inventory therefore expect it to have been somewhere close to Loch Gorm, and feel that it should not be confused with *Dùn Athad*; nonetheless, this latter site, high on the clifftop of the Oa, bears witness to extensive works having been carried out at about the time of Sir James' rising, and even if it was merely used for lookouts and beacon fires it played a vital part in his communications system. The RCAHM description of *Dùn Athad* is most interesting and includes the following: "These remains occupy the summit of a large and impressive coastal promontory which is situated about 2 km SE of the Mull of Oa... Rocky cliffs rise sheer on each flank of the promontory to a height of over 105m and the summit-area is an irregular linear platform.... The approach from the landward or NE side is across a narrow neck of land about 2m in minimum width, and thence obliquely by a sloping ascent along the W edge of the main ridge, skirting the remains of a massive forework.... It may have served as one of the beacon-stances used by the supporters of Sir James MacDonald in 1615. A slightly later topographical account refers to the 'great fortress called Dunaynt', which with 'small expensis .... might be maid ane Invincible strength.'" (Of course, to the lay-person, a "Dunaynt" which can be physically identified sounds at least as likely as to be the "Dunand"of 1615 as does an unidentified "Downand" first mentioned in 1686.) As it happened, Sir James did not require an "Invincible strength", but what he did need was a signalling centre, which would be for use only in the short-term, but which must be completely impregnable; *Dùn Athad* was perfect.

4 This library had had to be abandoned under hot pursuit, and its loss was bitterly regretted; the incident was close enough, as he commented in a later letter to his pursuer, the Earl of Tullibardine: "I protest I was never so hardly followed; and was so near taken that your lordship's self, and some few with you, was within three pair [paces?] to me. But I am much obliged to your lordship, for in faith you made me a better footman in one hour nor I thought to have been in one year."

5 As indeed it did – See Appendix 1

6 He would have been able to make a safe landfall despite the difficult approach, even in the dark – Wallace Clark notes that in the surviving ruin at Dunyvaig one can see a small, angled aperture, so positioned that a light placed therein will act as a guideline through the dangerous reefs.

7 He had the example of the Outer Isles to influence him, where the Marquis of Huntly already possessed a commission from the king by which he had been granted, rent-free for a year, all the Outer Isles (except Lewis) on condition that he utterly exterminate every man, woman and child within that year! King James might well be prepared to repeat the experiment against Sir James' own faithful supporters in Islay.

8.

THE WIDER WORLD

Author's note: The life and times of Colla Ciotach can be divided into three sections. From his birth in 1570 until he became the most senior survivor of the broken Clann Iain Mhóir in 1615, he had been involved in the constant struggle to retain or regain the ancestral territory of his clan; throughout that period his struggles against the McLeans and the Campbells had also brought him into conflict with the crown. After 1615 he sought to come to an accommodation with his neighbours and in consequence became a better subject, but a third period was to begin in 1638, when Argyll died and Colla Ciotach and his family became engulfed by the turbulence of the times, to rise again and take their places beside the most loyal and courageous citizens the country has ever known.

Having looked at Sir James MacDonald's abortive rising, this may be a suitable point to reflect briefly on contemporary political developments elsewhere. These developments affected and eventually came to dominate Colla Ciotach's life in the Western Isles, but he himself played no part in them. This chapter is merely an aide-memoire and many of the details are gleaned from William Sanderson.

After James VI gained the English throne in 1603, he and his court became firmly established in the south. In the first part of his London reign he relied upon the counsel of his chief minister, Sir Robert Cecil, formerly Secretary to Queen Elizabeth. From 1614 to 1625, in contrast, he reverted to his earlier behaviour in Scotland and embraced a series of favourites, allowing them to rule regardless of their competence. The central theme of his reign continued to be his claim, common to all the Stuarts, to rule by Divine Right. Inevitably he created and cultivated enemies who resented the influence of the favourites and, especially in Scotland, their own loss of access to the court, and at the same time his genuine belief in the Divine Right of Kings led to an inevitable clash with ambitious Parliamentary figures in England and with reformed religion everywhere.

1603–1614

On April 5, James set off for England and "Brings with him those of the greatest birth and most interest in the blood royall, who though farr enough off to follow after his Numerous issue, of a teeming fruitfull Consort, yet too neer to be trusted at home. And each one of them begat trouble and charge upon him, ever after, to reward, or to raise them up, beyond any desert; in both he was wisely regarding. Those were Lenox, Hamelton, Arguile ..."

Even as he travelled south, James was presented with a petition signed by 1000 Puritan ministers, urging him to support their reform: "... No popish opinion to be any more taught or defended: no ministers charged to teach their people to bow at the name of Jesus..." James held a conference in 1604 to debate the matter, his bishops vs. the Puritans, the outcome of which was a stalemate and the King's declaration to the Puritans that: "If this be all your party hath to say, I will make them conform themselves, or else will harry them out of the Kingdom."

Despite his conservative position, he was pleased to authorize work on a radical new translation of the Bible (on which work began at once and was complete by 1611), a translation both elegant and convenient – inasmuch as it tends always to support that crucial doctrine of Divine Right. More ominously, in 1604 his Archbishop insisted that all clergymen must subscribe to the Thirty Nine Articles of Faith, with the result that by December about 30 clergy had been ejected, creating the first major schism within the Established Church.

The various interested parties became involved in plots and intrigues – even Sir Walter Raleigh was disgraced and sent to the Tower, where he remained for many years. The period after 1604 was much occupied by the Guy Fawkes affair and its aftermath. Penal Laws then passed against devout Catholics continued to be rigorously enforced until 1619, and the common people were whipped up in hatred against Catholics of every degree. The Parliament that Fawkes had sought to undermine ran from 1604–11 and was notable for constant and growing friction between the King and the Members as the monarch sought to prove that all rights and privileges flowed from him, whilst his subjects sought to prove that Parliament had certain basic and inalienable rights of its own, developed through constitutional practice. He dissolved it in 1611 and over the coming decade concentrated his rule through personal favourites on revenue-raising by novel and non-parliamentary means.

In 1612 the death of Salisbury broke the last link with the Elizabethan period, and in the same year the death of staunchly Protestant Henry, Prince of Wales, made certain the succession of Charles, Duke of York, no enemy to Catholicism. Such was the spirit of the day that his father was rumoured to have had Henry poisoned, but details of the post mortem examination given by Sanderson in his History (1656) refute the charge, concluding: "He dyed in the rage of a Malicious Extraordinary burning Feaver." The following year Charles' sister Elizabeth married Frederick V, Elector of the Rhine Palatinate and a noted Protestant.

Plans for Charles to marry a French princess were thwarted by his father's need for cash. Parliament was recalled in 1614 but members failed to toe the line and vote the money that was needed... after a few weeks this 'Addled Parliament' was dissolved and James began to explore the prospects for a marriage between Charles and the wealthy Infanta of Spain. Meanwhile, Parliamentary factions were well aware that James' own wife was a devout Catholic, and that his mother Mary had remained true to her faith even as she approached the block, begging "that her poor servants might be witnesses to the world, of her patient suffering; and that she died a constant Romane Catholick." Charles himself had been raised as a Catholic and the prospect of his union with the Infanta was not welcome to all his future subjects.

1614–1625

Throughout the second period of his reign, James allowed himself to be influenced by his current 'favourite'. The first of these to come to prominence had been Robert Carr, a Scot who had accompanied the court when it first came to England in 1603 and who held the king's confidence 1612–1614, by which time he had become Earl of Somerset. In the autumn of 1614 he was supplanted in the king's affections by the lovely George

Villiers, whose own meteoric rise led him to become Duke of Buckingham in 1623; this particular favourite became a firm and close friend of Prince Charles.

In 1616 Raleigh was released from the Tower to prepare for a fantastic expedition to El Dorado, where he promised to collect enough gold to restore the king's fortunes; in 1617 he set sail, subject to many conditions, not least a positive undertaking to do nothing to upset the Spanish. In this he failed, for he returned in 1618 empty-handed and having attacked a Spanish colony. He was executed in October.

In 1617, whilst Raleigh was away looking for El Dorado, James made his long-promised visit to Scotland, apparently in search of a personal Holy Grail, the compliance of his subjects. He met with the clergy at Edinburgh and agreed to authorize a general assembly so that his Five Articles could be accepted, but when they were rejected his disdain for Presbyterianism reached new levels.

Back in London by now, James was becoming desperate for cash and he appointed Sir Lionel Cranfield to reform his finances. Great economies were introduced and the Admiralty came in for particular and rewarding attention, under a new Lord Admiral ... Buckingham.

Troubles now arose in Europe where James' son-in-law, the Elector Palatine, had crossed swords with the Holy Roman Emperor and with Spain. He was driven from his inheritance and James sought once more to arrange a marriage between Prince Charles and the Infanta, the price of which would include the withdrawal of the Spanish from the Palatinate. His subjects became concerned at the prospect of alliance with Spain and her hated Catholicism, and their anger was increased by the thought that their princess and her husband had been ousted by such enemies. The Spanish would not make a deal and an appeal to the populace for funds was met with little support. In this tense atmosphere James called his third Parliament, January 1621.

The new Parliament was no more compliant than the last; James had been raising revenue by various dodges, not least by the sale of monopolies, and the members of the new Parliament took action against the worst abuses. Things came to a head when they sought an assurance that Prince Charles would marry a Protestant and that the King would be more robust in his attitude to Catholics both in Britain and overseas. Advised by his favourites (including the Spanish ambassador), James first allowed matters to escalate, then came to regard his difficulties as an attack against Divine Law and dissolved Parliament in dramatic circumstances in early 1622.

Central to James' concern was his wish to have foreign forces removed from the Palatinate and his daughter and her husband restored to their rightful position, but if at all possible this was to be achieved peacefully and without expense. He believed that marriage between Prince Charles and the Infanta could achieve these ends and help to spread Protestantism within the Catholic states. It was in pursuit of this goal that in February 1623 Prince Charles and Buckingham left for Spain, travelling under assumed names, hoping to achieve great things but really just tilting at windmills. The wily Spanish had plans of their own, and it was not until October that the adventurers returned to London, disappointed and perhaps a little wiser.

James was now persuaded to embark upon a course that might be more popular and he resolved to arrange a general alliance against Spain, based upon marriage between Prince Charles and the French Princess, Henrietta Maria. A new Parliament was called, for February 1624. This time, the king seemed conciliatory as he asked the members for advice and himself proposed a show of hostility to Spain. He received rapturous support but unfortunately Buckingham, in pursuit of a private dispute, made tactical errors which greatly enhanced the powers of Parliament. A compromise was reached which tightened up on the abuse of monopolies, and thereby made the King even more dependent upon "supply" voted by Parliament.

Thus ended the last Parliament of James. Negotiations with France led to the suspension of the worst anti-catholic laws and the wedding between Charles and Henrietta Maria was formalized on May Day 1625, but James missed it, having died of an ague on 27 March:

> "The world which late was golden by thy breath
> Is iron turned, and horrid, by thy death."
>
> Drummond of Hawthornden

Scotland and Ireland

King James had not been sorry to get to London; he was a man of undoubted intellect and found no stimulus in provincial life. More to the point, he resented the poverty of his Scottish kingdom and the unpleasant Presbyterian affectations of many of his subjects – in his own words: "A Scottish Presbytery agreeth as well with a monarchy as God and the Devil." The main feature of his personal rule was to be his constant struggle with the clergy – as he saw it, order and hierarchy were needed in the Church as in the secular world; but the recalcitrant clergy sought anarchy and chaos: no fixed altar, extempore prayer, no structure. He left the day-to-day running of the country to his Privy Council, acting on his instructions from London and regardless of the inadequacy of his own information. In 1607 he boasted in London: "here I sit and govern with my pen, I write and it is done, and by a clerk of the council I govern Scotland now, which other could not do by the sword."

He was a dangerous and untrustworthy man and his servants did not rush to impart intelligence that might be unwelcome. Meanwhile, powerful men within the Privy Council resented their subordinate role, far from a glittering Court and with little reward other than that which they could gain for themselves by intrigue. Throughout the country, landowners became increasingly unsettled as first James and then his son sought to dispute their titles and in many cases determined to revoke existing grants, particularly of former church lands. Even the Campbells, always ready with a piece of parchment to prove their title, could not contemplate actual revocation with equanimity and it is hardly surprising that they eventually provided the leadership and initiative that was to gain control of the Covenanting movement and pervert it to their own ends.

A curious feature of the period was the climate of warped morality. The Reformers took a prudish and unhealthy interest in the sexual lives of their neighbours and all punishment was made to centre on ritual humiliation. In 1605 "... the Session ordains a more public place of repentance to be biggit with all dilligence .... that therein fornicators and adulterers may be distinguished and better discerned, both by their place and habit." This prurience was widespread, but more localized was the cult of witch-hunting, largely associated with the eastern parts of the kingdom, the centres of Calvinism. With extraordinary zeal, the very people who mocked "superstition" employed witch-prickers and delighted in the anguish of their victims: "The accused were hung up by their thumbs, lighted candles were set to the soles of their feet, hair shirts dipped in vinegar were put on them to 'fetch-off' the skin, needles were thrust up to their heads in their fingers." There were periodic waves of such atrocities, but "witches" were also useful in explaining misfortunes which affected the king and therefore weakened his claim to rule by Divine appointment – thus in 1590 and in 1633 witches were burned as punishment for causing storms at sea inconvenient to the reigning monarch.

Throughout the reigns of both James VI and Charles I, a punitive war was waged against the indigenous population in Ireland and the sickening policy of annihilation, which had been pioneered by James in the Western Isles, was brought to its apogee at this period. Lands throughout Ulster were seized and "planted" at the will of the regime; elsewhere paid officials were sent to scrutinize titles to land, increasing the sense of instability and fear. The "Discoverers", as they were known, were a threat to many of the old-established Norman incomers as well as to the native Irish. Penal laws against the Catholics were harshly invoked, and priest-hunts were organized, although with limited success. The Reformation had never been preached in Ireland, in fact was of no particular interest to most people, and therefore the Catholic clergy continued to be welcomed in the homes of all, natives and settled incomers alike. A degree of resentment was created by religious persecution, but the burning issue was that of property and persons dispossessed or threatened became a growing and dangerous enemy to the state. A contemporary of *Colla Ciotach*, Geoffrey Keating of Tipperary, summed up the bitterness:

"*Is leo gan gráscar lámh ar ndonna-bhruíona*
Gach fód is fearr dár n-áitibh eochair-aoibhne"
(Without a fight, they own our finest mansions,
(Each sod that's best of our pleasant lands there.)

As a result of the Plantation, lowland Scots came to take an increased interest in the affairs of Ulster, whilst the ancient links with Antrim continued to be significant to the inhabitants of the Western Isles, particularly those who lived in the homelands of *Clann Iain Mhóir*. Equally, the Earl of Antrim and his family persevered in their attempts to gain title to Islay and Kintyre and developed connections at Court. Although Antrim had made himself acceptable to the Crown, the vicious Ulster campaigns at the dawn of the century eventually led both The O'Donnell of Tyrconnel and The O'Neill of Tyrone to flee to the Continent (the "Flight of the Earls"), whereupon six entire counties were forfeited and planted, thereby sowing the seeds of the great insurrection of 1641. Of course the Scots gallowglass mercenaries were a regular feature of the Irish campaigns, where they were happy to fight for whoever would pay the best; many of their battles involved large numbers and were set-piece affairs, but frequently entailed little loss of life or even injury due to the disinterested professionalism of the individual warriors. The fate of the native Irish inhabitants was very different, as the forces of the Crown whipped up the very Horsemen of the Apocalypse and famine stalked the land – not a natural famine but one deliberately created by the British Crown. Fynes Moryson, private secretary to Lord Deputy Mountjoy gave an eye-witness account of its success:

> "Now because I have often made mention formerly of our destroying the rebels' corn, and using all means to famish them, let me by two or three examples shew the miserable estate to which the rebels were thereby brought. Sir Arthur Chichester, Sir Richard Moryson, and the other commanders of the forces sent against Brian MacArt [O'Neill] aforesaid, in their return homewards saw a most horrid spectacle of three children (whereof the eldest was not above ten years old) all eating their dead mother, upon whose flesh they had fed twenty days past ..."

Further details from this and other sources may be omitted here, but these atrocities were not easily to be forgiven.

As *Colla Ciotach* made his way homewards in the autumn of 1615, there was as yet little sign that the Union of the Three Crowns would provide any great benefits for the population of these troubled isles, but at least the worst effects of King James' inadequacies and infatuations lay in the future. Perhaps it would be possible to live quietly in Colonsay until the wheel would turn again and present some new opportunity for what little was left of *Clann Iain Mhóir*.

9

COLLA CIOTACH'S FEUD WITH MACDUFFIE

The Aftermath of 1615

After the 1615 campaign, *Colla Ciotach* returned to Colonsay and devoted himself to his domestic life, and he seems at first to have sought to live quietly enough, although his responsibilities were increased by the changed circumstances. Some of the main players in the 1615 "rebellion" withdrew permanently from the scene, such as Sir James MacDonald who, with a few companions, made his way to Ireland and thence to safety in Spain, where he remained; in 1621 he was allowed to return to London, where he died in 1626. Keppoch was also allowed to return from exile, and was even permitted to go back to his home in Lochaber. Argyll, still troubled by financial burthens, withdrew to England, but became a Catholic and found it prudent to remove himself to Spain as well, where he was known to be in touch with Sir James MacDonald and with Keppoch. Although Argyll was also permitted to return to London in due course, where he remained until his death in 1638, he had fallen under suspicion and was never fully restored to favour. There seems to have been little doubt that his Catholic connections were important to him and that he could have dealt more harshly with the "rebels" of 1615, and there is evidence a few years later that he may have made a contribution to the work of Catholic missionaries in Scotland. At all events, he was not to be trusted by the Court and the religious sensibilities of his successors came under particular scrutiny.

Of course, Malcolm MacDuffie of Colonsay had also withdrawn from the immediate scene, if somewhat involuntarily. As we have seen, he had surrendered himself to Argyll, with a view to doing service to the Crown. Having appeared before the Privy Council in November 1615, he seems to have been detained in Edinburgh until he received a pardon on 13 January 1618, in the following terms:

> "THE KING – for faithful service rendered unto him and his forefathers, by Malcolm MacDuffie of Colonsay and his forefathers without any suspicion of crime, and remembering the said Malcolm's assiduous perseverance in serving the King on all occasions, and particularly his having followed Sir John Campbell of Caddell, Knight, the King's agent and commissioner, in prosecuting the rebellious and predatory Clandonald;
>
> "which Malcolm, at the time of the late rebellion of Sir James McDonald, was by the said James and his accomplices taken secretly prisoner by violence from the house and the lands of Colonsay as a prisoner of the said Clandonald, and, while Archibald Earl of Argyll was the King's agent, desired to give his services against the said rebels (the said commissioner in the King's name, having given to the said Malcolm the King's protection and remission), and during this time the said Malcolm acted always as the King's most obsequious and energetic servant, wishing to incite him [i.e. Argyll] to pursue the remaining Clandonald outlaws,

"has granted, with the concurrence of the Privy Council, a free pardon to the said Malcolm for the duration of his life, for his connection with the said John, James and Archibald, and for all other offences committed before the date of these presents."

As Loder observes, Malcolm had "persuaded the authorities that he only joined the rebellion under force majeur. To earn his pardon he also [*sic*] had not been above giving away some of his associates." Perhaps it was Malcolm MacDuffie who suffered from divided loyalties, rather than Coll MacDonald.

MacDonald Tenure of Colonsay

Argyll had been active for many years in attempting to gain title to the MacDonald properties and in 1607 he had urged his claim to be the most suitable person "be resoun he is heretabill Justice, Colonell and Chamberlane, and his Lordshipis predicessouris had heretabill infestment of the landis thameselffis disponeit be King James the Fourt of worthie memorye." On 30 March 1610 he had achieved his ends when "Archibald Earl of Argyll, Lord Campbell and Lorne" obtained the coveted charter, including all of Colonsay except the lands of Garvard and Oransay (which were Church land). Despite all their efforts, Clan Donald had failed utterly in their efforts to rectify the injustice and had now no option other than to accept the *de facto* situation.

Thus it was under a lease from Argyll, and whilst Malcolm MacDuffie was detained at Edinburgh, that it fell to *Colla Ciotach* to take direct control of Colonsay. The spirit of the age suggested that he should concentrate on farming, and this may have been part of a personal agreement following his "safe-conduct" from Argyll. It is difficult to be sure of the exact relationship between Argyll and *Colla Ciotach*, but we know that it involved Sir James MacDonald, who was married to a sister of Campbell of Calder, and that all of them and all their wives were Catholics, or were soon to become such. Whatever relationship there was may have explained Coll's tenure of Colonsay, a tenure that would become less secure as Argyll's influence was eclipsed by his Protestant and Covenanter son, Lord Lorne.

Malcolm MacDuffie's return from Edinburgh

When Coll and his mother were brought to Colonsay by Ranald in the 1570's, they lived near the east coast of the island at *Dùn Cholla*, within easy reach of the main territory of *Clann Iain Mhóir*. A few years later, the stronghold at *Loch an Sgoltaire* may have been created as a refuge, but was unlikely to have been intended for permanent use.[1] Although the MacDuffie chieftains had lived at *Dùn Eibhinn* for centuries, by the early years of the 17th century that family had moved to Kiloran where they occupied *An Sabhal Bàn*, part of the old Abbey.[2] When *Colla Ciotach* took over the agricultural management of Colonsay in 1615, he moved his own residence to *An Sabhal Bàn*, where his most famous son, Alasdair, was born soon afterwards (in or before 1620).

So it was that when Malcolm MacDuffie returned to Colonsay from Edinburgh in January 1618, he will have found himself at something of a loose end since *Colla Ciotach* and his family were in firm possession of the island, had the home farm in hand and were actually living in what had been Malcolm's own house. These circumstances would probably have caused difficulty enough, without reference to whatever bitterness had arisen from the recent military campaign and its conclusion, and the difficulty was compounded by the fact that both families had been involved in intrigue with a variety of powers in recent years. MacDuffie had signed bonds with the Campbells, but had supported the MacDonalds and had fought against the crown forces, after which he had offered to betray his companions in arms, and had eventually gained a pardon. *Colla Ciotach* had been a major figure in organising and co-ordinating the "rebellion" and had recruited MacDuffie, but had then reached some sort of an accommodation with Argyll and on 18 June 1619 was given a safe-conduct to Edinburgh where, on 14 March 1620 he submitted and was pardoned.

Perhaps the two cases looked rather similar to Malcolm MacDuffie, who may have felt that the old order was at an end and that *Colla Ciotach* could be challenged with impunity. The exact circumstances are no longer remembered, but a feud developed between the two families which seems to have lasted until February 1623. Matters then came to a head, and surviving tradition describes the last chieftain of Clan MacDuffie as the fugitive in a desperate man-hunt.

Death of Malcolm MacDuffie

According to the story, MacDuffie was hunted the length and breadth of the island of Colonsay, and many of his refuges are remembered. These hiding places are called *Leab' Fhalaich Mhic a'Phì* ("MacDuffie's Hiding Bed") and they are all quite small, nearly always one such *Leab' Fhalaich* is within sight of another, and they overlook the pathways that existed at that time between the various clachans. One can imagine that the fugitive will have watched to see signals or where supplies might be stashed by any who dared to help him. The chance of escape was slight – there were few boats and they would have been carefully secured.

The sites that are still remembered can be listed starting from the most northerly, the *Leab' Fhalaich Mhic a'Phì* on the southern slope of *Beinn Bheag*. This is a natural cave, a kind of gully in the tumbled rocks, reasonably sheltered. Another is said to have been on the northern slope of *Dubh Chàrn* at Kilchattan, but it is hard to identify the exact spot now – possibly the vegetation was much stronger then, or possibly there were stone outcrops that have been quarried away for field-walls at some later date. There is another *Leab' Fhalaich* nearby, near the top of a low cliff behind Druim Haugh (said to be the oldest inhabited house on the island). This provides little shelter from the elements but can conceal a prostrate figure.[3]

The next one is close to the golf-course and is easily found from written references: "the Crannaig, or Pulpit, is situated at Maola-chlibhi" (Grieve); "a recess above a narrow gully leading to the big corrie below the hill called a' Chrannaig" (Loder). The old foot-path from *Port Mór* runs from the present *Gart a' Ghobhainn* through a disused water reservoir and may be easily followed until it crosses the corrie mentioned by Loder, where one can see a small cave overlooking the path. It is a little deeper than it looks and provides reasonable shelter and concealment.

A very similar cave can be found on the north side of the promontory of *Dùn Gallain*; and near the summit of *Càrn Spiris* is a hollow covered by a massive rock which might have been a useful lair before sheep destroyed the vegetation. MacDuffie is said to have been hunted from place to place "as if he had been a wild beast", even crossing to Oransay where he hid over the large chamber to the north side of the High Altar of the Priory Church.

Finally, in February 1623, he was hounded from all his hiding-places, and "in the darkness of the early morning he crossed the Strand from Colonsay and fled to the south-west part of Oronsay, and at low tide swam to Eilean-nan-ron." (Grieve). He must have been able to take advantage of a spring tide to struggle through the reefs to *Eilean nan Ròn* (Seal Island), since at any other state of tide there is a considerable expanse of water, completely exposed to the full force of the open Atlantic and subject to powerful currents. This remote and uninhabited island is really divided into three smaller islets, of which *Eilean Iarach* is the furthest one. By now *Colla Ciotach*'s men were evidently hot on the trail, since it is said that MacDuffie had no time to strip off, but had to swim with his boots on. Professor MacKinnon continues the tale:

> *"Lean na mortairean an t-allabanach truagh do'n Eilean Iarach. Rùraich iad gach fròg dheth, ach cnaimh de Mhac a Phì cha d'fhuair iad. An uair a bha iad a' tilleadh air an ais thug faoileann sgreuch aisde anns an Eilean Iarach. 'Tha rud-eiginn aig an fhaoilinn,' arsa fear de na sealgairean, is air an ais thug iad. Fhuair iad Mac a Phì 'na crùban for bhile creig os cionn a' chuain air sgeilp air an gann a sheasadh faoileann fhéin. "'Fàbhar, a Thamhais,' thuirt Mic a Phì ri Tamhas Mac 'Ille Mhoirche, a chunnaic an toiseach e. 'Fàbhar no fàbhar,' fhreagair Tamhas, 'is beag fàbhar a gheibhteadh o t'fheusaig ruaidh mu'n àm so an dé.'"*

("The assassins pursued the wretched wanderer onto Eilean Iarach. They searched every cranny of it, but could not find a hint of MacPhie. Just when they were returning, a seagull let out a screech on Eilean Iarach. "There is something upsetting that gull" said one of the pursuers, and back they went. They got MacPhie crouching under the lip of a rock at the edge of the ocean, on a shelf that the gulls themselves could scarcely stand on.
"Mercy, Thomas," cried MacPhie to Thomas McGilvray, who was first to see him. "Mercy indeed", replied Thomas, "it's little mercy would be got from your red whiskers this time yesterday.")

Tradition mentions that the pursuers had not tried to swim after him, but had come out by boat, whereupon MacDuffie is said to have covered himself in a great heap of seaweed. And although Professor MacKinnon's account[4] goes on to say that MacDuffie was put to death without further delay, a persisting account is more specific. His captors are said to have brought him back to Colonsay, landing at *Port a' Chrochaire*[5] and dragged him up to the standing stone at *Lèana na h-Eaglais* (Church Meadow) where he was tied to the stone and shot.

The chapel at *Lèana na h-Eaglais* is "said to have been at that time the only place of worship on Colonsay, and seldom used."[6] The standing-stone is known now as *Carraig Mhic a' Phì* (MacDuffie's Standing Stone), although at the time of the execution it stood some yards to the east of its present location, upon a low knoll. Having been used by generations of cattle as a scratching-post, it was eventually knocked over and broken. In recent years it was repaired and re-erected at the new site, but unfortunately upside-down and no longer properly orientated.

It is believed that Malcolm MacDuffie, the last chieftain, was buried along with four other victims in the small graveyard of *Pàirc na h-Eaglais*, now owned by the Clan

MacDuffie Society. Grieve gives interesting supporting evidence in a conversation recorded in 1881, for it seems that until perhaps 60 years earlier, MacDuffie descendants from Islay had maintained a custom of visiting *Pàirc na h-Eaglais* to keep it trim ... "shaving the graves of their ancestors."

It may be significant that the most sacred site on the island, and one where Mass was still said, was chosen for the execution. Significant also that the very stone to which MacDuffie was tied was not without symbolism, since it bore the carved image of a crucifix.[7]

Interestingly, David Stevenson gives an essentially different account, one which is unknown on Colonsay and which, although even more injurious to *Colla Ciotach*, seems also to be unknown to the descendants of the late Malcolm. The details are as follows:

"In February 1623 the prior of Oronsay, Donald MacPhee, lay dying, and his kinsman Malcolm MacPhee came to visit him. But Coll heard of the intended visit, and secretly landed on Oronsay with his eldest son, Gillespie, and about twenty men armed to the teeth with bows and arrows, two-handed swords, dirks, muskets and pistols. On Oronsay they hid ready to ambush Malcolm, who came from Colonsay by boat. But on landing Malcolm sent two servants ahead of him to announce his approach, and Coll's men opened fire on them, killing them both, thus warning Malcolm that something was wrong. Instead of fleeing, however, he moved forward to investigate, and came under heavy musket fire. One of his companions, Donald Og MacPhee, fell dead, but Malcolm managed to escape. His line of retreat to his boat must have been cut off, however, for he fled to the southern tip of Oronsay. Cornered there, he scrambled over the rocks and swam out to low rocky Eilean nan ron, the Isle of the Seals. There the last chief of the MacPhees of Colonsay spent his last night, alone and without food or shelter in wet clothes in mid-winter. The following morning Coll and his men came out by boat and, according to tradition, after a long search found Malcolm hiding under seaweed on the shore. He fled but his enemies caught up with him after he had been twice hit by musket bullets, and finished him off with swords and dirks. The thrifty murderers then carefully dug the musket balls out of the corpse; lead was scarce. Another leading MacPhee, Dougal, had surrendered on Oronsay on promise of his life; but after twenty days of captivity on Colonsay he too was murdered."

This version seems to combine elements of a number of other tales, which is hardly suprising after a lapse of some 350 years, but it differs significantly from the normal Colonsay version. Certainly it would have been easy enough to have murdered McDuffie in *Eilean Iarach*, as suggested above, or just to have thrown him overboard on the way back. To have gone to the trouble of dragging him all the way back to *Lèana na h-Eaglais*, as every other account has maintained, suggests that his fate was intended to be publicly witnessed, possibly as a result of a quasi-judicial process. Some twenty years later, an unscrupulous factor was to be executed at the same spot and in a similar way, as a punishment for criminal behaviour on behalf of the then Argyll when the latter was in open revolt against the crown. In these remote areas, landlords were held to be responsible for the maintenance of the public peace and *Colla Ciotach* may have believed himself to be exercising lawful authority[8]. If so, he was not unchallenged, as is recorded in Pitcairn's "Criminal Trials":

"Jun. 27 [1623] – Coill McGillespik McDonald in Collansay, Archibald McDonald, his sone, and four others, 'servitouris to the said Coill'.

   "Dilaitit of airt and pairt of the fellone and crewall Slauchter of vmqle [erstwhile] Malcolme Mcphie of Collonsay, Donald Oige Mcphie, Dougall Mcphie, Johnne Mcquhirrie, and Ewir Bayne, alias Quhyte; committit in Februar last.

   "Persewaris, Marie McDonald, the relict; Donald Oig Mcphie as sone; Katharene, Anne and Fynwall Mcphies, as dochteris to vmqle Malcolme; Murdoche Mcphie in Ilay, as brother to vmqle Donald Oige, and Dougall Mcphie, and as nerrest of kyn to vmqle Johnne and Ewir.

   "Johnne Quhyte, wryter, producet the Letteris duelie executed, &c. and protestit for releif of Archibald Campell, brother to the Laird of Caddell, cautioner for repoirting thairof. – Coll Mcallaster, ffiear of Dounskey, as cautioner for the said Coill, &c. unlawit, for nocht entrie of ilk ane of the saidis persones, in the pane of ane hundreth merkis. And siclyk, the Justice Ordanis that the said Coill, &c. sall be denuncet our soverane lordis rebellis, and all thair move-abill guidis to be escheit, &c."

The charge shows that more than one MacDuffie was executed, Malcolm and two sons plus two other males (close enough relatives that a third, surviving son, was their "nearest of kin"), which no doubt explains the plural in the tradition of "shaving the graves of their ancestors"; and that same tradition supports the belief that they were buried at *Pàirc na h-Eaglais* rather than in the traditional family burial ground at Oransay. The proposed forfeiture of Coll and his accomplices does not seem to have been carried out and the MacDuffies got little satisfaction. Although Malcolm's immediate family removed themselves permanently from Colonsay, other members of the clan remained on the island and are represented by direct descendants to the present day.

   Grieve records that "the story still current in the island is that the wife of Malcolm Macphie, having consulted a fortune teller, was told that if she could have seven daughters the islands would return to the possession of the clan. She was most anxious to have this prophecy fulfilled, but only succeeded in having six daughters, and as there were no sons the inheritance remained in other hands." Some of the MacDuffies were thought to have gone to Lochaber and to Nether Lorne, and in some cases became "travelling people" (itinerant smiths etc.).[9]

   Whatever lay behind the killings, Coll seems to have shown no remorse and regarded his own position in Colonsay as being beyond dispute. Not everyone shared his view and, with the benefit of hindsight, Professor MacKinnon was amongst those who felt that he had been too ruthless: "*B'i coir Cholla air Colbhasa coir Ahaib air fion-lios Naboit*" ["Coll's rights to Colonsay were like the rights of Ahab to the vineyards of Naboth"].

Notes

1 *Dun Cholla* is a very ancient hill-fort, locally believed to be named after one *Colla Uais*, an Irish king (and a direct antecedent of *Colla Ciotach*), said to have lived there for 14 years. Grieve believed that this tradition could be identified with records of the Irish annalists, and that it refers to a period c. 315 – 326 A.D. It is just possible that the traditions have become confused, and that the noble Irish occupant was indeed just *Colla Ciotach* himself, but however it got its name there seems to be no doubt that it was occupied in the late medi-aeval period, the remains of the buildings being clearly visible. *Colla*'s association with the spot is recorded in tradition and is further highlighted in the events surrounding the demise of Malcolm MacDuffie.

2 In the 18th century, Kiloran House was built on the site of the old Abbey. *An Sabhal Bàn* ("the white barn")

was at the west end of the present walled garden.

3 Dugie MacGilvray, one of the most senior Colonsay inhabitants, has drawn attention to a neighbouring site of interest, not so well-known. It is almost opposite the track to *Goirtean* and as one climbs a gully leading towards *Uaigh an Fhomhair* [Giant's Grave], the gully levels out and there is a flat place which bears the silhou-ette of a man and his dog. Seemingly the grass will never grow there, but this may be associated with another, earlier episode as Dugie mentions it as being the imprint of "Murdoch [MacDuffie] and his Black Dog".

4 Published in Cape Breton about 1903.

5 *Port a' Chrochaire* ("Port of the Hanged Man") was presumably so named at a later date, and commemorates the eventual fate of *Colla Ciotach*. It provides an excellent and sheltered refuge, with a narrow entrance, easily defended. Being close to *Dun Cholla* it was probably the normal base for *Colla Ciotach*'s birlinn, and was also the normal landing-place for boats from Islay. The Ordnance Survey map has misplaced *Port a' Chrochaire*, it is really at NR390907.

6 In these words Grieve confirms the accuracy of tradition, for he had no access to supporting information which has been subsequently revealed in Vatican archives. Reading the reports of the Franciscan mission-aries, it seems likely that it was near this spot that they spent a night without shelter or fire, with no food except the raw shellfish from the rocks.

7 Unfortunately no longer readily apparent since, with the stone being upside-down, merely the beginning of the cross-shaft can be seen. Interestingly, in recent years a partially completed Celtic cross was discovered during excavations at the site, which had broken during the course of construction. Perhaps stone-masonry was carried on there, or perhaps a damaged cross was better than nothing.

8 In this connection, see T.C. Smout, "A History of the Scottish People"; in a very interesting case, contem-porary with that of Malcolm MacDuffie, he cites the Baron Court of Campbell of Glenorchy, before which Campbell was accustomed to arraign people in a regular way. In 1623 "at a solemn and important trial before a jury of fifteen the laird accused a couple of stealing cattle, sheep and other goods from within the barony; the woman, who was a MacGregor, was ordered to be scourged and banished, and the man was hanged." Thus, in his own court and before his own jury, Campbell was able to obtain redress for anti-social behav-iour in his own territory.

9 In later years the name often became changed, so that Duffy, Dufficy, Mahaffey, Cathey are all now accepted as versions of the same name and eligible for membership of the modern clan society.

10

COLONSAY YEARS

Colla Ciotach and his neighbours

When Sir James MacDonald escaped to Spain and Coll became the head of *Clan Iain Mhóir*, he had had to take what steps he could to secure his personal position. This would be hard enough at any time but was made much more difficult by the political situation. Whilst King James was juggling with the complexities of three kingdoms and an awkward international situation, Colonsay was a long way from Edinburgh and even further from London. With Argyll himself in exile, other Campbells who remained in important positions became more powerful and utterly ruthless in their greed. The King's inevitable preoccupation elsewhere created endless scope for intrigue.

Although the 7th Earl had obtained physical possession of the *Clan Iain Mhóir* lands in Kintyre, Islay was an exception, being in the hands of Campbell of Calder. No doubt this was begrudged by the ambitious Lord Lorne, and it may have been he who ensured that Calder would never get peace to enjoy it, a situation reflected in the following petition to the Privy Council (27 January 1618):

"My Lordis of Secreit Counsaill, unto your Lordschipis humelie menis and shewis I, your servitour, Sir Johnne Campbell of Caddell, knyght, that quhair your Lordschipis knowis upoun quhat hard conditionis I haif undertane the rycht and title of the landis of Ilay, and how I am subject in a greit yeirlie dewytie for the same and am ansuerable to his Maiestie for the obedyence of the tennentis and inhabitantis of the saidis landis, and althoght I intend, God willing, to keepe ane honnest dewytie in all that I haif undertane and promeist in that matter, **yitt the inhabitantis of the nixt adjacent yllis repynning that civilitie or obedyence sould be established or setled in Ilay, bot that the wounted barbaritie and incivilitie of the same sould be intertenyed and continewed, they have resolved to do quhat in thame lyis to unable me outher to pay his Maiesteis dewyteis or to keepe the yle in obedyence; and for this effect nombaris of thame pretending to be maisterles and lawles personis comes in companyis to the said yle armed with invasive and forbidden armour, spoyles my tennentis, persewis thame of thair lyves, bindis thame, dimolishes thair housis, and sua oppressis, wrackis, and overthrawis thame that thay ar not able to pay thair dewyteis to me and wilbe constrayned for verie necessitie to brek lowse, without remeid be providit.** Herfoir I beseik your Lordschipis that I may have letteris direct to command, chairge, and inhibite all and sindrie personis inhabitantis of the Yles and Heighlandis nixt adjacent be oppin proclamatioun at all places neidfull that nane of thame presoome nor tak upoun hand to resorte nor repair to Ila at ony tyme heirefter without a pasporte or testimoniall in write under the hand of thair maisteris and landislordis, testifeeing quhose men they ar, and what is thair earand to Yla; certifeeing all and sindrie personis of the Yles and Heylandis that shall come to Ila without the said testimoniall that thay salbe repute, haldin, and persewit as brokin, lawles, and maisterles men and as commoun theevis, and salbe takin, apprehendit, and presentit to his Maiesteis Counsall or Justice accordinglie. And your Lordschipis ansuer."

One can only wonder whether Campbell was really suffering from the attentions of *Colla Ciotach* and Clan Donald, or whether he was victim to the intrigues of his own kinsman, Lord Lorne. Although at first sight *Colla* seems to be the chief suspect (and MacDuffie was evidently in the clear, being at that date still detained in Edinburgh), it still seems odd that *Colla*, not yet reconciled to the Crown, should have time or resources to devote to fomenting trouble on Islay. There is also the fact that Campbell of Calder's own sister, Margaret, was the wife of Sir James MacDonald and every reason to think that *Colla* would prefer to see Islay in the hands of Calder rather than Lorne. By 1626 Sir John Campbell had converted to Catholicism and was possibly a more sympathetic neighbour to Coll, but Lord Lorne was never to become anything of the sort, and may have been acting secretly to drive a wedge between Calder and the Colonsay laird.[1]

Campbell of Calder's troubles, already quite serious, went on from bad to worse. He had financial difficulties everywhere and had undertaken to pay an enormous rental for Islay, which was far from productive following the recent military conflicts. He found himself two years in arrears with his Crown dues and the result was that on 22 May 1618 he was **"denuncit rebell and put to our horne ... for not payment making of the soume of sex thowsand pundis money as for the fewdutie of the landis of Iyla, Rynnes and Middilwaird thairof ..."** In the difficult months that followed, it was in marked contrast that *Colla Ciotach*'s rehabilitation went on apace and Calder was reassured in a letter from James Mowat, his faithful agent that: "As concerning Coill his remissioun, feir not I am walkryfe [vigilant] anoughe thereanent, and sall be, God willing." (4 April 1619) "Walkryfe" or not, Colla Ciotach got a safe-conduct to Edinburgh in June and was granted his remission.

Meantime, Calder's confiscated estate was granted to his own agent, James Mowat, but within a couple of years the continuing financial difficulties led his creditors to appoint Calder's younger brother, William Campbell of Brachlie, as chamberlain of Islay, with particular responsibility for the "ingathering of the kingis dewtie." In June 1621, the Privy Council ratified Sir John Campbell of Calder's grant of Islay (in the terms of his grant of 21 November 1614), but by the following year it became clear that he was anxious to sell. On 5 February 1623 James Mowat wrote to Calder in connection with prospective purchasers: "The Merques [?]... writis he is not in the world shall give yow moir nor he, and better payment ..." Interest had also been expressed by Lord Erskine and "the Erle of Mar and Clandonald is great and intendis ane course anent Illaye". It seems likely that Coll could have acted for his Irish cousins, perhaps as a nominee, since by then (about 1621) he had publicly expressed his resolve "to become ane obedient and dewtifull subject" and "to present himselff befoir the Lordis of his Majesteis Previe Counsall for giveing unto thame satisfactioun and contentment anent his future obedience." But the exact timing was most unfortunate, since it seems clear that Islay came onto the market precisely whilst Coll was in trouble over the MacDuffie affair. Could it be that both the MacDonalds and the MacDuffies had been the victim of another plot? That, like the participants in the Dunivaig "rebellion", they had been manoeuvred into an utterly self-destructive course? As things stood there was little that could be done and, eventually, in July 1626, Calder passed Islay into the hands of his own elder son, John, known now as "the Fiar".[2]

The Fiar's term in Islay (1626–1639)

The Fiar was a man of business, strengthening and enhancing his possessions, and he seems to have been loyal to his family, since he appears to have ignored instructions to banish his uncle William, his Chamberlain in the island and a prominent Catholic. The following Order of the Privy Council was issued 28 July 1626:

> Forsamekle as Mr. William Campbell, brother to Sir Johne Campbell of Caddell, ane obdurit obstinat papist, hauntis and frequentis within the bounds of Ila, and by reasoning and other wayes corrupts the ignorant inhabitants of the said boundis both in their religioun and alledgeance to his Majestie: Thairfoir the Lords of Secreit Counsaill ordainis Johnne Campbell, appearand of Caddell, who was personallie present, and who now has the charge and commandement of the said yle, to bring and exhibit the said Mr. William before the saidis Lordis upoun the first Counsell day of November nixtocum, and failying thairof, that he putt and hold the said Mr. Williame out of the ile."

Not only did the Fiar ignore the command, but subsequent events were to show that he would continue to harbour Catholics in Islay, at least until 1639. The fact that his own father was now a convert may have coloured his judgement, together with the fact that the old religion remained almost universal in Islay and most of the neighbouring isles. The Fiar had other and more pressing troubles, one of which was an attack on Dunivaig Castle in the summer of 1630.[3] The attack certainly did not suit the Fiar, who decided that Dunivaig was too much of a liability and provided a perfect rallying-point for disaffected parties, so he now sought permission to demolish it, the pride of Clan Donald; permission was granted "so as it serve not theirefter for a beild, ressett, or starting holl to the rebellis of the Ylles", but in the event he never got around to the actual demolition. [4]

Throughout this period, *Colla Ciotach* continued to live in relatively peaceful possession of Colonsay, but from his surviving reputation and a few historical records we may suppose that he retained his vigorous zest. An example may be seen in the decree awarded against a party of reivers on February 21, 1635:

> "Action at the instance of John Campbell, brother-german of Alexander Campbell of Lochnazell [Lochnell], against **Coll McGillespick *alias* McDonald, in Colonsay,** Donald McGorme McRonald VcCoill *alias* McDonald, Duncan Dow McAllister, son of Archibald McAllister, in Arran, and Neill Bwy McKy, in Lochheid, for spoliation from the land of Crossage of cattle and horses pertaining to said Alexander Campbell.."[5]

Whether or not he had the support of the distant Earl of Argyll, there can be little doubt that *Colla Ciotach* and his supporters must have been an embarrassment to Argyll's heir, Lord Lorne. A possible explanation of Coll's survival throughout this period was that he served a useful purpose, in the creation of additional opportunity for the Campbells. This point is illustrated by Sir Alexander Hay, Lord Clerk-Register, whose telling comment on Clan Campbell was quoted by Smith in "The Book of Islay":

> "By many it is thoght that, if goodewill did secunde the dewtye which they ar bound to do, thir frequent iyland employmentis wald not occurre so often ....When their employmentis ar

so proffitable in present pay, and a preparatioun for making suite at Courte for service done, how easie a mater it is to haif some of these unhallowed people with that unchristiane language readie to furneis fresh wark for the tinker; and the mater so caryed as that it is impossible to deprehende the plotte."

The Counter-Reformation

Whatever the truth of the matter, Coll was busy enough in trying to protect the position of his family and of his wider dependants, yet he still found time and opportunity to travel extensively through the Isles, and he became actively involved in the work of the Counter-Reformation. We know something of his activities at this time through ecclesiastical records, many of which have been gathered together by Cathaldus Giblin O.F.M. Before turning to *Colla Ciotach*'s own activities, it is worth remembering that the Reformation of 1560 had been followed in Scotland by a period of virtual anarchy in which a number of forces struggled for supremacy. Although religion was involved, the real prizes lay in wealth and power, a situation that brought conflict between the nobility and the crown.

The King believed that he continued to rule by Divine Right, as had been sanctified by Catholic dogma, and even under the new arrangements it was important for him that his position should be supported by an hierarchical structure, but with his own placemen serving as bishops. It was also important to the King that order and traditional values were maintained; only thus could his own position be assured. Structured forms of worship, respect for authority and tradition, use of authorized liturgy were all important in the preservation of the social order, so he sought to use the former resources of the Church to achieve his aims, rewarding those noblemen and "bishops" who were prepared to support him.

The nobles had a slightly different viewpoint. They had gained enormous wealth through the appropriation of Church properties (lands, tithes, benefices), and were more concerned to retain these benefits than with the niceties of religion or the social order, but they had also gained in power through the evaporation of the Third Estate.

To make matters worse, on the death of Queen Elizabeth in 1603 King James had wasted no time at all in shaking the dust of Scotland from his royal feet and, pausing only long enough to borrow money for the journey, made straight for London. The Scottish nobles were effectively denied access to their monarch in his new Court and left to themselves to make the best of things at home. Not suprisingly, these nobles struggled to extend both their wealth and power, regardless of the effects upon the nation and frequently in open defiance of the King.

Meantime, there had arisen a new middle-class of private individuals, sons of merchants and lawyers, who saw the opportunities that lay in social change. They threw their energies into support for Calvinism, gaining for themselves some precious local power over the lives of their fellow-citizens and these were the people who became involved in local session-courts, who set themselves up in judgement over others and who used the hysteria of the time to foment persecution of "witches", beggars and other disadvantaged groups. Their influence was at its greatest in the East of Scotland, and also in the areas that had already suffered a degree of "plantation". The genuine Ministers and Presbyterians were hopelessly outnumbered by the fellow-travellers, the tragedy lying in the fact that being so close to the situation they failed to see how they were being manipulated.

In practical terms, the result was the creation of a spiritual wilderness in the West; few Presbyterians were willing to labour without payment, hence the islanders were left to make their own arrangements and in many areas, ecclesiastical structures no longer existed to regulate marriage, education, taxation, the day-to-day minutiae of normal life. Many of the people made their way to Ireland on annual pilgrimage, especially to Croagh Patrick, but the bulk of the population had to rely on a faith that had been received through tradition and was liable to drift into superstition. The sacraments were not available and of course one of the biggest difficulties arose with the sacrament of marriage .... some sort of ceremony could be arranged, but the validity was unreliable and frequently led to legal and domestic turmoil.[6]

All these circumstances created both need and opportunity to oppose the new religion and indeed the Catholic Counter-Reformation in Scotland had begun almost before the Reformation itself, although there had been many reverses. The ultimate objective may have been the restoration of the Church in all her glory, but this was a process only to be achieved through diplomacy and careful negotiation and in the meantime, pastoral workers were desperately needed. For example, in Lent of 1567, 12,606 persons attended Mass and Holy Communion in Edinburgh alone, and when the Bishop of Armagh made a brief visit to Scotland in 1585, he administered the sacraments to more than 10,000 persons. The resources of the secular clergy were totally inadequate to meet the demand, and of course the position slowly became more desperate.

From about 1611, various appeals were made to Rome, seeking Irish Franciscans to be sent to minister to the faithful. In 1612, John Ogilvie O.F.M., a Scot, came to Scotland from St. Anthony's College, Louvain, to serve as a priest and to gather background information and, in the following year, he was joined by a lay brother, John Stuart. The reports that they sent back to Rome began to attract attention to the plight of the faithful in the Highlands and Islands. Together, they laid the foundation for work that was to have a direct effect in Argyll and the Hebrides.

That their mission was dangerous was emphasised by the fate of another Scot, who happened to have the same name, John Ogilvie S.J., who arrived in 1614 but was captured by the Reformers and suffered martyrdom. In his introduction to the Book of Islay, Smith notes that this particular priest seems to have had a shadowy connection with events in the Isles and speculates on St. John Ogilvie's possible political connections:

"The Jesuit martyr, John Ogilvie, had come to Edinburgh in the summer of 1614, had gone to London on some mysterious business at Court, had met a man from the West and had returned to Edinburgh, had privately visited Sir James MacDonald in the Castle, had gone, later, to Glasgow, had been bound for Kintyre on the supposed business of buying horses, but had just then fallen into the clutches of Archbishop Spottiswood. Had he met the crypto-catholic Argyll during his visit to Court? Was it only of Philip's "Controverted Heads" that he had talked with Sir James in the Castle? What took this amateur horse-dealer to Kintyre? .... We should be wary to attach too much political importance to the wanderings of the impolitic Ogilvie, but this strange concatenation of events, the contemporary distrust of

Argyll, and the Earl's open confession of the Catholic faith and association with the quondam rebel justify the suspicion, even if future research prove it groundless."

The unfortunate Fr. Ogilvie was hanged on 28 February 1615; in a fine distinction, King James had remarked that "popery was a disease of the mind and puritanism a disease of the brain", but he did not hesitate to act against either.[7]

Despite such alarming events, the Franciscan mission in the West of Scotland laboured on. Eventually the Pope himself became involved and, upon his instructions, Cardinal Borghese wrote from Rome on 24 March 1618 to Lucio Morra, Papal Nuncio at Brussels. He explained that there were many Catholics in Scotland who spoke only Gaelic, and that there were no priests left in Scotland who could minister to them. The pope was aware that there were many Gaelic-speaking priests in the college at Louvain, this college having been established by the King of Spain, for Irish Franciscans and to help serve the Faith in Ireland. The Pope wished priests from Louvain to be sent to Scotland, there to be guided by a Scottish laird, *Colla Ciotach* MacDonald: "*et li persuadesse a mandare i detti religiosi in quelle parti sotto la guida del Baron di Marandal, scozzese, come vedra dalla copia del memoriale datone a sua santità.*"

The pope's suggestion was heavily endorsed by the Infanta. It must be remembered that Spain had a very long-standing and arguably legitimate interest in the affairs of England. Queen Mary's mother had been a Spanish Hapsburg and Mary herself had married Philip, the Emperor's son; although they had had no children, England had come under the dominance of Spain and had gone to war with France on her behalf. King James VI, who had supported Spanish naval interests against Elizabeth, had now assumed the triple crown and inevitably Spanish interest now extended to Scotland. Mary Queen of Scots had encouraged this interest when, in 1586, she wrote "Considering the great obstinacy of my son [James] in his heresy I have resolved that, in case my son should submit not before my death to the Catholic religion, I will cede and make over, by my will to the king [of Spain], my right to this [English] crown...". In more recent years, Spain had welcomed countless political and religious refugees from throughout King James' realm. For all these reasons the Infanta, the intended future bride of Charles, heir to the kingdom, helped to promote the Scottish counter-reformation.

The Franciscan Mission (1619–1629)

There were difficulties about finance as it was intended that the missionaries should not become a burthen to the faithful, so the pope agreed to meet the cost from Vatican resources. When everything was ready, the Nuncio issued his instructions to the missionaries (summarised by Giblin):

"They are to visit particularly the people of the islands, as these are more inclined than others to embrace the faith, and only Irish priests can be of any help to them; they have no priest of their own .... one priest is to be stationed in the Hebrides especially; in Kintyre, at a place called Carskey, there dwells a laird named Hector MacNeill who is very well disposed towards catholics; Coll MacDonald, the laird of Colonsay, is a catholic, and he can provide the mission-aries with information, and give them directions as to how to visit the other islands; the missionaries are to take advice from MacDonald as well as from the governor of the island [MacDuffie]; another leading man in the Hebrides is Roderick MacLeod of Harris, who is a catholic; the missionaries can find out from the governor of Colonsay how they are to reach the laird of Harris, who, fervent catholic that he is, will attend to their needs. ... each missionary is to have a notebook in which he is to write down the names of those he has converted or baptized, as well as other items which pertain to the salvation of souls..."

At last, on 4 January 1619, two priests set out from Louvain, Patrick Brady and Edmund McCann. Arriving in Scotland in mid-March, Fr. Brady made for the Highlands while Fr. McCann went to the Isles, where he enjoyed huge success. Of course, the Calvinist authorities were outraged and within 18 months had captured McCann who, after two years imprisonment, was banished under pain of death were he to return.

More volunteers were sought from Louvain and from the twenty who came forward, four were selected. Remarkably, Fr. Edmund McCann determined to return to Scotland once more, and those chosen to accompany him were Paul O'Neill, Patrick Hegarty and Cornelius Ward, approval being given by Pope Urban VIII on 4 September 1623.

In view of the difficult conditions and clandestine nature of the mission, it is remarkable that any contemporary record survives but Fr. Hegarty sent a progress report to Louvain, writing from Kintyre on 29 December 1624, (summarised by Giblin):

"On 14 July 1624 Hegarty and his companions left Ireland for Scotland, and, next day, landed on the isle of Sanda, where Hegarty explained the meaning of the sacred vestments to the islanders, and preached to them.... during the eight weeks which Hegarty spent in Kintyre, he converted 206, and baptized twelve adults and two babies; his days were spent hiding in caves, and by night he preached, baptized and administered other sacraments. ... from Kintyre Hegarty went to Arran, where no priest had set foot since the Reformation; he remained there eight days, living in a cave on butter, cheese and water, and during that time he brought eighteen back to the faith, and baptized two; from Arran he was compelled to fly to Gigha, but because of the opposition of the minister and the smallness of the island, he had no success there; however, he converted the assistant of the minister, and his son; from Gigha Hegarty went to Islay, and, in danger of his life, laboured there for fourteen days, during which he won over 119 to the faith, baptized eighteen, and exorcized four; he was in danger of being captured, but was saved by a band of thirty Catholics; he fled to Jura, where he remained twelve days, and won over 102 to the faith, and baptized twelve, including the leading man on the island [probably Daniel MacIain] and his wife; then he passed on to Colonsay, where he brought more than 133 back to the faith and baptized ten; in all more than 600 were brought into the true church by him in those places."

Thus it would appear that Fr. Hegarty arrived in Colonsay on or about 16 October 1623. He kept a careful record of those who received the sacraments there, so that the Colonsay and Oransay population of that date is recorded in great detail (see Appendices).[8] It will be recalled that Frs. Cornelius Ward and Paul O'Neill had parted from Hegarty in Kintyre, and their own efforts had also led to remarkable results. Whilst they were in Kintyre, one of those converted was

"one of the gentry who was prominent among the heretics; when he was gravely ill, Ward and

O'Neill succeeded in winning him over to the true faith, and on his recovery, he confounded the heretics every time he got a chance; a certain minister, who was a friend of the man in question, was enraged when he heard of the conversion and that the missionaries had said mass in the man's house; accordingly he planned to attack Ward and O'Neill, but *Colla Ciotach* MacDonald came to the aid of the missionaries and saved them; however, the two missionaries fled to the isle of Cara, which is six miles from the coast of Kintyre; there they found a building dedicated to St. Columba; there were only fourteen people on the island, and the missionaries converted all of them, as well as six of the oarsmen who had come with them, and they gave holy communion to all."[9]

"Ward and O'Neill remained in Cara for twenty-four hours only, and then went on to Oransay; the journey was very dangerous and took twelve hours; night had fallen when they reached Oransay; without having anything to eat, they took shelter in a hut till morning;... [*Colla Ciotach*] MacDonald, the laird of the island, was a catholic; during the two days they stayed there the missionaries brought forty back to the faith, and, as usual, administered the sacraments to them; they then went to Colonsay, where within two days, they converted nineteen; they had to leave the place because there was no food to be had there, and as the laird was not at home, there was nobody to come to their aid; they spent their last night there on the beach in the open, and their only meal consisted of shellfish which they collected on the shore..."[10]

A further report by Cornelius Ward, dated 19 August 1626, gives an account of social conditions, superstition and much else besides. The missionaries clearly laboured in great hardship and with scant finance, but they were men of great courage and resource. Fr. Cornelius Ward was known in secular circles as *Conchobhair Mac an Bháird* ("Con, the Bard's Son"), and was from a Donegal family, and it was in his own role as a bard that he gained access to the house of Sir John Campbell of Calder (the Laird of Islay), where he entertained the household for three days, and then revealed his mission. His enterprise was well rewarded, for it was as a result of this visit that Sir John was formally received back into the faith soon afterwards, by Fr. Patrick Hegarty. The conversion must have occured near the end of Sir John's tenure of the island, just before it passed to the Fiar and about the time when he had been trying to sell it.[11]

At about the same time (mid August 1625), Fr. Ward had visited Colonsay again, when he mentions that the island was almost entirely Catholic and that the laird, *Colla Ciotach* MacDonald, with his wife and daughter, were Catholic before the missionaries ever visited Scotland. On this occasion Ward was obliged to move out after three days as he was being pursued by the protestant bishop ("pseudoepiscopus"). Of course, Coll was only one of the many powerful men who clung to the old faith, but by this time the Franciscans had established their headquarters at Bunamargy in Antrim, were travelling the seaways of which Coll was an acknowledged master and had even been joined by at least one of his near relations, Francis MacDonnell, a natural son of the Earl of Antrim (their supposed patron). Bunamargy itself became a centre of religious devotion, replacing Iona which had been both devastated and desecrated by those who pretended to follow Knox. To this day, many of the Catholic inhabitants of the Hebrides owe the survival of their religion to the strength and support that Coll MacDonald was able to give to those early missionaries.

The following testimonial bears witness at least to the practical aid that *Colla Ciotach* gave to the missionaries [the original text is given in Appendix 5], and one wonders if activities such as this, in 1629, helped Argyll's heir in his efforts to gain title to the church lands of Oransay and Garvard (in Colonsay), which finally fell into his family's hands the following year. The document has a certain style that makes it interesting, for it is faintly reminiscent of a famous Charter granted by Donald, Lord of the Isles:

> "I, *Colla Ciotach* MacDonell, *[note use of his familiar name]* laird of Colonsay and Oransay, faith-fully witness that Rev. Father and Brother Cornelius Ward, respected secular priest, in the service of the Congregation for the Propagation of the Faith, on the Scottish Mission, visited our island thus thrice separately and once with Fr. Patrick Hegarty and Fr. James O'Neill; bringing together fortification to all the inhabitants of this distressed homeland by conver-sion of those aspiring to the sacred Christian faith.
>
> "I further testify to all which has been said in two other letters of testimonial by other Scots witnesses, (one on 17 May 1629 A.D. written in Islay, the other on Colonsay, 25 March the same year) to be true and not exaggerated, which is known to be true only by the facts.
>
> "Indeed, this same year 1629, nobody is better acquainted with the need for protection and defence of Fr. Cornelius Ward (I actually saving him from the heretics and ministers in imminent and virulent proximity, acting in person, and happily exposed in his place to danger). Wherein I suffered a permanent injury; these concealed and armed heretics would have surely carried him off had I not been hard-by and rushed in.
>
> "In the truth of which is signed in the island of Colonsay, April 1 1629
>
> "... Coll MacGillespie, who has signed, is laird of Colonsay. I, Daniel MacMhurrich, witness it."[12]

Colla's Tenancy Under Threat:

One of the results of the 1615 campaign had been that the provisions of the Statutes of Iona were renewed and enhanced, in a manner that must have heavily circumscribed such men as *Colla Ciotach*. David Stevenson summarises the new arrangements:

> "The island chiefs were to appear annually (and more often if summoned) before the [Privy] council with their leading kinsmen, to answer any complaints against them. They had to agree to limit strictly the size of their households, to reside in named houses and themselves super-vise the cultivation of home farms 'to the effect they might be thereby exercised and eschew idleness'. No chief was to have more than one large galley, and on their voyages they were not to oppress the country people; indeed they were to lease all their lands (except the home farms) to tenants at fixed rents, instead of vague traditional exactions, and were to free their lands of all sorners and idlers who lacked lawful occupation. Carrying of arms was closely regulated, and the annual wine consumption of chiefs' households was limited. Schools were to be established in every parish so that 'the Irishe language, which is one of the chief and principall causis of the continewance of barbaritie and incivilitie amongis the inhabitantis of the Iles and Heylandis, may be abolisheit and removit.' Chiefs were to send all their children aged over nine years to be educated in the Lowlands; sons who had not received such schooling would not be allowed to succeed their fathers."

That *Colla Ciotach* was forced to comply is suggested in one of the many Gaelic songs that were composed in his honour, where reference is made to his children being parted from him, in the Lowlands.[13] The exact date is unclear, but there is evidence that the bulk of the work was composed in or about 1625 (when Coll's wife Mary was still alive), and that it was updated to 15 March 1636, when news of the death of her first husband was included.[14]

As has been noted, *Colla* had held most of the island of Colonsay from Argyll, Lorne's father, but, since Oransay Priory and its lands had been seized by the crown in the aftermath of the Reformation, it was through that agency that he held the balance of his estate. Fortunately, the Reformation itself had not reached the island and unlike Saddell and Iona, Oransay Priory and its treasured sculptures were never desecrated, merely allowed to slip slowly into decay. The Franciscan missionary, Cornelius Ward, described it in 1624:

> *"Insula haec satis amaena egregium habet monasterium per S. Columbam olim exstructum, cuius modo exstantes paribus cum chori et tecti par, aedificium persuadent quondam fuisse pulcherrimum."*
>
> ("... this island has the ruins of a monastery which was once built by St Columba; judging by the walls and the parts of the choir and roof which remain, it must have been a very beautiful building.")

Although Oransay was of little interest to the reformed divines in a religious sense, its property was worthy of attention and on 15 February 1616 Oransay and Garvard "which before belonged to the Priory of Oransay" were included in a charter granted to Andrew, Bishop of the Isles. On 10 April 1623 Thomas, Bishop of the Isles, assigned that property (which he had received from Andrew "his brother"), to William Stirling of Auchyle (Argyll's agent), in a grant that was confirmed by Royal Charter on 19 December the same year. As might be expected, a further change was not long delayed and, on 5 August 1630, a charter of Charles I confirmed the transfer of the property to Archibald, Lord Lorne.

The Bishop continued to have an interest in the non-monastic church property on Colonsay, because in 1632 he granted to *Colla Ciotach* a lease on "the teinds of the parsonage and vicarage of the parish of Kilchattan and of all other teinds attached to Colonsay lands" (Loder), whilst in 1633 and 1634 we find that the Earl of Argyll leased the rest of Colonsay and Oransay to him for £480 (Scots) per annum. Thus, although *Colla* had full possession of both islands, he normally held the property from more than one superior and was responsible for all rents.

Perhaps the rents were too high, or perhaps *Colla Ciotach* was just not a good payer, since on 25 March 1635 a decree was registered against him by the Earl of Argyll and Lord Lorne (possibly on the insistence of the latter). The following year a new lease was issued, and for the first time *Colla* was no longer dealing with Argyll himself:

> "Contract betwixt Archibald Lord Lorn and Coll McGillespick in Collonsay and Archibald MacDonnald, his eldest sone, ratifieing the Decreet of Improbation at the said Lord's instance against them, whereby thair takes of that Isle maks no faith; quilk Contract containes a tack of the said Ile to the said Coll for 880 marks yeerlie dureing his lyftyme 25 March 1636. Registrat 13 Aprile 1636."

The little legal skirmish with *Colla Ciotach* was only a sideline, but the allegations of non-payment of rent may well have been fraudulent since Lorne did not hesitate to indulge in the basest of deceits. An interesting and contemporaneous example has been researched by Rev. Hill in connection with the estates of Lord Lorne's brother, Viscount Kintyre and may be summarised as follows:

In 1607 the peninsula of Kintyre had been usurped by the 7th Earl of Argyll when the MacDonalds were driven from it and, although there was still a valid MacDonald claim, there was no hope of obtaining redress through the corrupted legal channels. Argyll had been married twice and in 1617, after he fled to Spain, he made it known that in his will his possessions in Kintyre and Jura would pass to his son by his second (Catholic) wife, then known as James Campbell (but who in 1622 was created Lord Kintyre). The rest of Argyll's estate (including Colonsay) was to go to Lord Lorne (the primogeniture heir, by his Protestant wife). Argyll actually transferred the property in due course and the arrangement was later ratified by the crown in 1626.

The estate in Kintyre that thereby fell into the hands of Viscount Kintyre was unprofitable and in 1630 he offered it for sale. Notwithstanding his own, unrecognised, legal claim to the estate, Lord Antrim (possibly on the private advice of King Charles) decided to pursue the simpler and probably cheaper option of simply repurchasing his own property (the same course that he appears to have contemplated for Islay, in 1623). Lord Lorne having declined the chance of first refusal, Kintyre accepted Antrim's offer together with security of £1,500 and £250 expenses. On 16 January 1635, the "lands of south and north Kintyre and also Jura" were signed over to Antrim in the person of his son Ranald, Viscount Dunluce, the deeds being signed "At the Tour and Fortalice of Dunnavartick" [Dunaverty].

Kintyre must have expected trouble, because he specifically mentioned, in connection with the main residence ("my house in Kinlochcheran"), that "in case the key be either lost or put out of the way, I tollerate [Dunluce's agent] to breake open the doore and put on another loke, and possess himself." No sooner was the contract signed than Lorne tried to persuade Kintyre to dishonour it, but in vain since the latter protested that it was too late and that he was legally obliged to fulfill the bargain. Lorne then adopted a joint strategy: through the Privy Council, he transmitted deliberately misleading information to the King and at the same time set out to destroy his own brother. "He made all his [Kintyre's] creditors to putt att him at once, and cawsed his own agent, Andrew Darleing, to putt Kintyre to the horne upon an old chardge of ane Debt of three hundred markes Scotch"; Darling was then "cawsed to keep himselfe out of the wy untill the horning was registrate" [i.e. told to disappear so that the debt could not be repaid to him before the time limit elapsed].

The story continues in twists and turns of Balkan complexity, until the whole issue was overtaken and made irrelevant in the light of the general civil and religious upheaval that was to come, but it serves to remind us that the legal dispute over property in Colonsay and Oransay was just a tiny part of a much greater undertaking. Having fired a warning shot, Lord Lorne may have found it convenient to leave *Colla Ciotach* in occupation for the moment, for he was by now in his late sixties and could surely be rooted out at a moment's notice. Then, in 1638, and to the undoubted satisfaction of his son, the seventh Earl of Argyll died. He had at least been benign in his dealings with *Colla*, and possibly their relationship had been sometimes rather closer to that of kindred spirits than of rank opponents, but with the elevation of Argyll's son the situation was to change very quickly.

Notes

1 On the other hand, the disaffected persons causing trouble on Islay may in truth have been no more than victims of the times, leaderless bands of individuals including those made homeless and vagrant during the reprisals following Argyll's campaign of 1615 on Islay and in Kintyre. Following the execution in Islay of nine "rebels", we are told that "Argyle proceeded to Kintyre, where there were still a number of men in arms of those who had joined Sir James from this district. Some of the chief of these he apprehended soon after his arrival; and by the severity of his measures, and the number of persons he executed, seemed determined effectually to prevent any chance of a future insurrection in Kintyre." (Gregory). Argyll had presaged this in his own words to the Secretary of the Privy Council, trying to excuse himself for any earlier lack of enthusiasm: " I hoip now dayly to be busie in executioun whill his Hienes rebellis be brocht to ruine."

2 Old Sir John lived on until 1653, but his straitened circumstances were to prevent him playing any further prominent role.

3 Those involved seem to have included "Neill Makean, Dowie VcDuffie, ... Mak Finla VcIllichallome and Murdoch Makphaill"; "Dowie" is the ancient forename of MacDuffie, and MacIan was the family with which they had been associated for 150 years.

4 Letter from the Fiar to the Privy Council on 20 May 1631: "The late King had recommended the casting down of the house of Dunyveg to the said supplicants father, who being than bot newlie enterit in the ile, and the yle not weele plenished with civile people of his awne freindschipe, and having no sure place of residence within the yle bot the hous foirsaid, he wes thairfore and upoun mony other interveining occasionis withholdin from downe casting of that hous. And now the right of that illand being established in the said supplicantis persone by dispositioun maid to him by his said father, and the supplicant haueing peopled the said ylland with a number of his awne freindis, so he thinkis himselfe able aneugh to withstand and resist ony new assault that sall be intendit aganis him so long as he remaynis within the ylland. And, quhairas the necessitie of his adois doeth ofttymes invite him to the Lowlandis, he is in continuall feare of some new surpryse of the said hous, as wes practised this last summer when he was attending his actionis before the Lordis of Sessioun; at whilk tyme a number of thir disordourlie theeves and lymmaris of the Yles gaif ane fearefull assault to his said hous, and, if the care and diligence of hie servandis had not prevented and disappoyntit thair treasonable designe, by geving unto thame a feirce and couragious repulse, they had not failled to haif tane the house of new, and so haif interteyned ane new commotioun and rebellioun in these pairts .... And, whairas (supplicant) hes noe intendit to build a more commodious hous for his awne dwelling and in a more proper pairt of the yle, and seing the hoip of surprysing of that hous furnisches ever new matter to the rebellis off the ylland, **humblie desireing thairfore the saidis Lordis to give unto the said supplicant thair warrand for demolisching and casting downe of the said house...."** The Fiar's unease was well-founded, since sixteen years later the ancient castle was to be seized once more, when it served as the last Royalist stronghold in the Western Isles.

5 Duncan Dow McAllister was ordered to make restoration and the action against the other defendants was suspended.

6 In Colonsay, these impromptu weddings came to be celebrated in the open air, at Ardskenish. The chosen spot was *Sithean Mór* ("The Big Fairy-Knowe"), and it remained in use into the 18th century.

7 Donald MacLean,D.D. informs us that "Ogilvie, debonair, witty, truculent and unctuous, in turn, faced his judges and his doom bravely, and with a courage, even if marred by an unseemly pedantry, worthy of his Order .... Ogilvie's nonchalance, and, at times, arrogant defiance in unsympathetic courts, disturbed seriously the judicial calm requisite for a clear and balanced judgement in his case." But he goes on to quote from Scotichronicon, confirming the humanity of the victim: "Ogilvie endis his prayer, arose to goe up the ladder, but strength and courage, to the admiration of those who had seen him before, did quite forsake him; he trembled and shaked, saying he would fall, and could hardly be helped on the top of the ladder." His beatification took place on 22 December, 1929.

8 It is interesting to compare the family names of 1623 with those of more recent times, and to note just how heavily the island was "planted" in the 18th century. The list of names helps to support certain Colonsay

traditions, as in "Margareta Domhnaill", a 'noble lady of the great family of Clan Donald, which is principal amongst all Scottish families, of particular antiquity and power'. This was the sister of Sir James MacDonald, daughter of old Angus of Dunivaig, eventually to become the fifth wife of Keppoch (Ranald McDonald of Clanranald). It is the Colonsay tradition, given above (Chapter 3), that a visit by Ranald to Colonsay coincided with the death of Mary, Colla's wife. If so, then it must have been in 1625 or shortly before, since "Maria Domhnaill, nobilis" is also recorded as a living communicant at that time. (Keppoch having been prominent in 1615, had made his escape with Sir James MacDonald but in 1620 he was recalled from Spain by King James and granted a pension of "200 merks sterling". In October 1621 he was allowed to return to Scotland, and he was married to Margaret by November 1625.)

Other names recorded by Fr. Hegarty include three probable sons and daughters of Coll and Mary, and 'Nola Domhnaill, nobilissima matrona'. There is a large representation of the MacKay family ...It is recorded by *Niall MacMhuirich* that one of Coll's daughters (Jean, or Sarah) married a MacKay of Ardnacroish, who was eventually to die at the Battle of Auldearn, fighting for *Alasdair MacCholla*. (Another daughter is said to have married John, brother of MacDonald of Largie). After the defeat of 1615, large numbers of MacKays and MacAllistairs had had to fly from Kintyre and the list of names that survives suggests that some of them subsequently found refuge on Colonsay.

9 Twelve MacAllisters are said to have been hanged beside that little chapel, after the defeat in 1615; it still stands.

10 The original Latin text was published in full, but this summary is as given by Giblin.

11 In 1615 Sir John's own report had specifically stated that Islay was an entirely Catholic isle and a kinsmen had recorded that " the religion that the cuntrie pepill hes heir amongst them is Popishe for yair is newer a minister in the wholle Ille except wan poore man that the bishop did leave heir".

12 "Daniel Muireadh" can be found in Fr. Hegarty's list of "converts".

13 Ronald Black comments upon this poem in "A Manuscript of Cathal Mac Muireadhaigh". The original mss. is in Trinity College, Dublin.

14 At the earlier date, both Alasdair and Angus "are parted from you" and Gillespick "is held captive from you without cause". Very possibly Gillespick ("Archibald") was singled out for special mention as being Coll's eldest son, named in honour of Coll's own father. He was possibly being held as surety for good behaviour, in the light of the MacFie affair, in which he had been one of the accused and "without cause" may reflect the eventual verdict. Perhaps Angus, was being held as surety for his natural father, Keppoch, rather than for Coll. As for Alasdair, traditional accounts say that he was held as a child in a Campbell household and received a conventional education; if this part of the poem was written about the end of 1625, it suggests that Alasdair was born a little earlier than is popularly believed, perhaps about 1617. The internal evidence of the poem suggests that Coll was under great pressure from his enemies at the time, perhaps a reference to the machinations of Lord Lorne.

11

THE PRELUDE TO WAR

The National Covenant

The death of Argyll, *Colla Ciotach*'s benign protector, was followed in 1638 by the succession of his heir, Archibald, now the 8th Earl, a man of a very different character. He had already decided that the King's difficulties could be his own opportunity and in that same year had shamelessly allied himself with the nascent Covenanting movement. In a political development that is almost incredible today, a faction of religious zealots had become so fired with the spirit of their own sanctity as to see themselves as God's Elect, specially chosen to be His instrument in establishing a perfect form of worship. Their honest and enthusiastic spiritual leaders allowed their own pure motives to blind themselves to the reality of events – they took support wherever they could get it, largely from an emerging class of tradespeople and petty burghers, people anxious to distance themselves from the peasant class from which they had themselves so very lately sprung. Such supporters found it easy to deny the ancient beliefs of their forefathers and were swept along by the new and fashionable doctrines. Alarmingly, the reformers accepted support from members of a small group of sophisticated opportunists, of whom the new Earl of Argyll was the most dangerous. He saw, and seized, opportunity everywhere, as the authority of the King weakened and as a mindless, bigoted majority revelled in its own enormities. Rabble-rousers hunted Jesuits, destroyed churches, desecrated tombs ... Argyll quietly moved with the flow, content always to take advantage, but never to make any contribution that would make inroad upon his own resources.

The real explanation of the upheaval was of course not religious fervour itself but the discontent of a number of nobles, a discontent which had been created through Charles' own policies. From his accession in 1625 he had behaved in a manner that one might quite reasonably describe as cavalier. As had been the case with his father, his policies sought to render Scotland a mere province of Britain, and of course he ruled from distant London, treating his Council in Scotland as an agency to implement his will rather than as an advisory body. But perhaps his single worst move was his Act of Revocation in 1625, in which he proposed to revoke all grants of crown lands since the Reformation. The people most threatened were the most powerful of nobles, since it was they who had got possession of the bulk of the Church lands and livings, the teinds and even the very buildings.

These powerful people now began to manipulate the forces of the Reformation in Scotland, and in this they were ably assisted by blind but ambitious men of the kirk. It was made a matter of complaint that Charles had never called a General Assembly of the Church of Scotland, that he had curbed many of the powers of the divines, and that he had increasingly devolved civil and judicial power upon bishops, his own nominees. The eventual response came, on 28 February 1638, in the carefully-orchestrated introduction and adoption of the National Covenant, on a day that was greeted by many as "the glorious marriage day of the Kingdom with God". The details cannot concern us

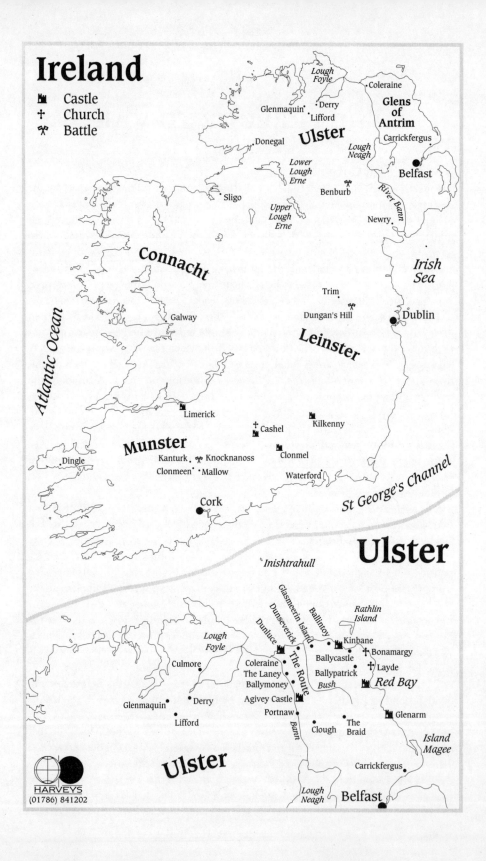

Ireland

- ♜ Castle
- ✝ Church
- ⚔ Battle

Lough Foyle
Coleraine
Glenmaquin
Derry
Lifford
Glens of Antrim
Donegal
Ulster
Carrickfergus
Lough Neagh
Belfast
Lower Lough Erne
Benburb
River Bann
Sligo
Upper Lough Erne
Newry

Irish Sea

Connacht

Galway

Trim
Dungan's Hill
Dublin

Leinster

Atlantic Ocean

Limerick
Kilkenny
✝ Cashel
Munster
Clonmel
Kanturk ⚔ Knocknanoss
Clonmeen Mallow
Waterford
Dingle

Cork

St George's Channel

Ulster

Inishtrahull

Glasmeerin Island
Dunseverick
Dunluce
Ballintoy
Rathlin Island

Lough Foyle
Culmore
Kinbane
Coleraine
The Laney
Ballymoney
Ballycastle
✝ Bonamargy
✝ Layde
Red Bay
Ballypatrick
Bush
Agivey Castle
Portnaw
Glenmaquin
Derry
Lifford
The Route
Glenarm
Bann
Clough
The Braid
Island Magee

Carrickfergus

Ulster

Lough Neagh
Belfast

HARVEYS
(01786) 841202

here, but in effect the leading nobles and some hundreds of lairds, at Greyfriars Kirk, signed a bond of unity between themselves as God's Elect, binding themselves collectively to a contract with Almighty God for the enhancement of His Kingdom on Earth. Copies of this document were then distributed throughout Scotland and these were freely signed by those who wished, and also signed, less freely, by many others.

The consequence was that a large body of people had now sworn allegiance together and to God, cutting out the middle-man, so to speak, the King. Referring to Calvinism, they swore "by the great name of the Lord our God to continue in the profession and obedience of the aforesaid religion; that we shall defend the same ... to the utmost of that power that God hath put into our hands, all the days of our life." Lord Lorne (as he still was, his father being still alive) was one of the Scottish councillors summoned to London in the aftermath of the Covenant, and is alleged to have been very frank with the King. Famously, Lorne's own father is said to have warned the King against him, else he would "wind him a pirn". His warning was ignored and Lord Lorne was allowed to remain at liberty.

In the autumn of 1638 Charles, in a serious misjudgment, resolved to put down the dangerous Scottish rebellion by the use of English forces. When he found that he had neither the money nor the support that he required, he temporised, in 1639, for a truce. The following year, the rebellious Covenanters seized the initiative and invaded England, occupying the northern counties[1]. By now the gravity of the Puritan threat in England forced Charles to try to come to an accommodation with the Presbyterians in Scotland and he agreed to a devolution of Royal powers.

Antrim to the aid of the King

In the midst of these and the other difficulties that faced him, Charles I was offered help from Ireland, by *Colla Ciotach*'s near kinsman, the Earl of Antrim.[2] Antrim, in association with Sir Donald Gorm MacDonald of Sleat, undertook to invade the territory of the Earl of Argyll, in an action which in itself would be a pleasure since these were usurped lands, rightfully the lands of Clan Donald. There was the reasonable additional incentive that, in the event of overall success, such lands as they could liberate and hold would eventually be confirmed to them by the victorious monarch.

> "On 5th June 1639, the king signed a commission appointing these associates "conjunctlie and severallie his Majesties lieutenants and commissioners within the whole Highlands and Isles of Scotland" for the purpose of arresting the progress of the king's enemies throughout that kingdom".

Wedgwood's description of the episode suggests that it merely confirms Charles' lack of political awareness and the feckless nature of Antrim who "pranced about the Court, boasting in his delightful brogue how he would land with a great host upon Kintire and make mince-meat of the Campbells." She accepts the fact that the MacDonald territories had been unjustly appropriated for the benefit of the Campbells, but says that the incident "gave gratuitous offence to Lorne whose doubtful loyalty should have been strengthened, not undermined." Perhaps the "doubtful loyalty" of a traitor had lost its appeal to the beleaguered monarch, and it is a fact that Antrim was to do much more for the Royalist cause than many less "delightful" individuals.

Loder mentions that *Colla Ciotach* had refused to subscribe to the Covenant[3], and that he and his sons were probably "already in league with their Royalist kinsmen in Ulster", although it would be surprising if it had been otherwise. The forces of the Covenant stood not just against the King but also against Catholics and indeed against all men who failed to give their support, genuine or feigned. As so often in history, the worst instincts of the mob were harnessed and manipulated by their leaders. There was, however, a difficulty in Scotland, where the "Highland Line" is almost tangible. The Covenanting leaders needed towns and cities in which to do their work, and in these places they did well enough, their influence also spreading quickly through the dour but prosperous villages of the east coast.

It was different in the Highlands and Islands. Extempore preaching and prayer, although frequently rambling and incoherent, was not objectionable in itself; but there were other and peculiar aspects to the Covenanters that could not commend them to the average Gael. The Covenanters refused to bow their heads to the name of Jesus, they perversely insisted on re-orienting churches, they forbade mourning for the dead, they forbade music and celebration, they forbade the celebration of feast-days, they devoted themselves to the Old Testament (virtually rejecting the Word of the Risen Lord) – in a nutshell, they sought to take all joy from religion and from life.

Naturally enough, all this was alien to right-thinking Gaels. To them the old ways had been best and, despite the difficulties of recent years, it was clear that the rule of King Charles would be better than the anarchy on offer either by the forces of the Covenant in Scotland or by the Parliamentary forces in Ireland. In both cases, these forces were wielded by cunning and ruthless operators and although on the face of it they were engaged in sectarian strife (always popular with the masses), more specifically they were the instruments which could be used to dispossess the Catholic population in both countries, to the aggrandisement of the rebel leaders.

Colonsay laid waste

So it is hardly surprising that *Colla Ciotach*'s sympathies lay with his annointed monarch, who had been brought up as a Catholic, had married a Catholic and was, by all accounts, a supporter of religious toleration for all. As it happens, Antrim's projected invasion did not take place (through the machinations of the jealous Wentworth), but word of it was leaked in order to put pressure on the Covenanters, and Argyll took the initiative. He appointed Duncan Campbell of Auchinbreck to arm and prepare those of his supporters whom he could trust, and (as reported by Wentworth's spies) fortified "those isles which are within three hours sail from the north of this kingdom [Ireland]. There are, as is reported, brought thither sixteen pieces of ordnance well provided and mounted in places of best advantage for the defence of his country, and the people taught the use of their weapons." With remarkable speed, on 17 June 1639, barely twelve days after the King had appointed Antrim and Sir Donald Gorm to be his "lieutenants and commissioners", Argyll launched a pre-emptive strike against Antrim's kinsmen on Colonsay. This was the more easily accomplished since the Fiar, laird of Islay, had become ill in early 1637.[4] Since the rightful heir was only a child, the management of his estates had been entrusted to the Fiar's younger brother, Colin Campbell of

Ardesier.

The 8th Earl of Argyll had the distinction of being a ruthless traitor, but he was also one of those manipulators who prefer to lead from the rear, so it will have been with some satisfaction that he could enjoin this Colin Campbell, his cousin, to do the dirty work. Although Colin was accepted as being the "laird" of Islay for the moment, no doubt he will have had to follow Argyll's instructions if he wished to be ratified in that position. Details of the action that ensued are recorded by one Richard Owen, an English naval officer, in a report to Antrim's rival, Wentworth, by now Earl of Strafford and King Charles' Lord Deputy in Ireland:

"25th June 1639

"The Wind being come about Southerly I stood for the coast of Scotland, arriving upon the 17th of this present in the Sound of Islay where I came to an Anchor. Immediately after there came a Boat on Board of me from the shore to see what we were, the men whereof I used at first with Courtesy; but seeing that by that means I could not gain knowledge how the island stood affected [i.e. Royalist or rebel], I threatened to hang them, which wrought more for my purpose, they telling me the strength among them to be about seven hundred men, the chief being a near kinsman to the earl of Argyll, by name Colene Campbell who was then absent, and had committed the charge to Mr. William Campbell, his unkle. Him I wrote unto in a courteous manner to come on Board, which at first took no effect. But after understanding him [quite correctly] to be a fervent Papist, I gave myself out to be the like, and that I had on Board of me a Priest. I caused a letter to be drawn as from this Priest to him, protesting he should have Liberty at Pleasure to return. This took; for on the morrow he came on Board, where I gave him the best Entertainment I could, which so well pleased him, having withal Liberty to return, that the next Day following he came again, and his Nephew [i.e. Colin Campbell, laird-apparent of Islay] who was returned from Coll's Isle [Colonsay], whither he went as I well understood with an hundred men, having brought with him the spoil of the island, killing all their cattle, and taking all their corn, butter, and cheese in boats, which were discerned to come thenceward, rowing closely along the shore .... Both the aforesaid Campbells I have brought with me, either to be examined by the Master of Ordnance, or to be sent to your Lordship. I have likewise brought a man with me that gives in evidence against them, being present with them in Coll's Isle [Colonsay], upon this barbarous usage of the inhabitants. I perceive that most of the Islands are more for fear than affection on the Earl's side, which appears by complaints made against his heavy Taxes on them."

Argyll duly rewarded Colin with the feu of Colonsay, for an annual duty of 800 merks (or £560 Scots), but by 1642, Colin was dead and the rental was paid for that and the following year by or on behalf of his heir. The rental exacted by Argyll was no bargain, since it was little less than *Colla Ciotach* had been paying and of course the island had been laid waste meantime. Colin is said to have been assisted in the raid upon Colonsay by Sir Donald Campbell of Ardnamurchan, and Sir Donald was later involved in the exploitation of the inhabitants.

As a result of this attack many of the old Colonsay families were forced to flee, to be replaced by Campbell "kindly men" or kinsmen. *Colla Ciotach*, now 70 years of age, was taken prisoner and handed over to Argyll, together with two of his sons, a son-in-law (John MacDonald of Largie) and that kinsman, Donald Gorme MacDonald (son of Sir

James MacDonald), who had been among those involved with *Colla Ciotach* in the *creach* on Campbell of Lochnell a few years earlier. The two sons now held captive with their father in Dunstaffnage Castle were *Gilleasbuig*, his eldest son, and *Aonghas*, his step-son. Unfortunately for Argyll, both *Raghnall* and *Alasdair* eluded him and immediately threw themselves into a new life, dedicated primarily to the release of the prisoners and, secondly, to vengeance on the traitor, Argyll.

Irish Rebellion 1641

Alasdair and *Raghnall* may have made their way to join the Earl of Antrim in the immediate aftermath of the attack on Colonsay and the seizure of their father, but perhaps they had been already in Ireland. Either way, the brothers established themselves in Antrim and we are told by Stevenson that "in November 1640 *Alasdair* led a raid on Islay with about eighty men, but was soon driven out; he had evidently been trying to seize hostages to be exchanged for his imprisoned father and brothers." It is not immediately clear what sort of hostages *Alasdair* might have hoped to seize since, at the best of times, Islay would be a strange resort for persons of political consequence. Possibly it was a reconnaissance mission, testing his men, seeing what sort of local support he might harness; or possibly he was demonstrating his military ability and his loyalty to the crown. Conceivably he was just testing the quality and current disposition of Argyll's ordnance, newly obtained the previous year.

The Earl of Antrim had removed with his Sovereign to Oxford at the end of 1639 but by June 1640 he was occupying his seat in the Irish House of Lords and there he remained, in Dublin, until the outbreak of the famous Irish rebellion on 23 October 1641. This rebellion, further complicating King Charles' unhappy situation, had been stimulated by growing fear of the anti-Catholic fanatics whose recent successes in both Scotland and England seemed likely to lead to further repression in Ireland. The "Old English" had remained largely Catholic, as had the MacDonald and other settlers; they now felt badly threatened, and of course the Catholic native Irish had already been dispossessed and now feared for their very lives. Thus were uneasy bed-fellows created – the rising was sudden and very successful, the work of the native Irish, who then repossessed their lands. The alien planters were everywhere evicted, normally unharmed but stripped of everything, even their clothes. Unpleasant though this may have been, few of them had to walk more than a few miles to gain the security of a town but nonetheless, terrific stories of atrocities were put about, and the distracted Protestant settlers, frightened and confused, largely believed them

Although Antrim had been involved in planning a Royalist *coup* in Dublin, he did not associate himself with the rebellion, and in fact disappointed many people when he condemned it. Because of the Royalist sympathies of Antrim and his adherents, there was no rebellion in his territory but Protestants in the Glens were apprehensive and Stevenson tells us that:

"on the outbreak of the Irish rebellion in October 1641, Alasdair (being a Catholic) was arrested, but was freed on the intervention of Archibald Stewart of Ballintoy, the Earl of Antrim's agent. Stewart, a protestant, raised a regiment to oppose the rebels but, though mainly protestant, the regiment contained catholic elements – native Irish, Macdonnells of

Antrim, and Macdonald refugeees from Scotland. There were two catholic companies, captained by Alastair MacColla and Tirlough Og O'Cahan, and Alasdair's brother Ranald also served in the regiment."

In the months that followed, this regiment was deployed to prevent the rebellion from spreading from across the Bann, which became a *cordon sanitaire*. At first, the shared responsibility seemed a sensible idea, but slowly the rumours and fancies of each side fuelled the fires of distrust. The seven Protestant companies were becoming uneasy about living and serving alongside the two Catholic companies, the only openly armed Catholics on that side of the Bann, and the Catholic companies felt increasingly unhappy at their exposed condition and also at their inability to assist their co-religionists. The situation was further confused by the fact that the rebels insisted that they were acting as loyal subjects, for the support of King Charles and with his approval.

The Portnaw Massacre

Matters seem to have come to a head when, in December 1641, part of the regiment having been briefly re-deployed at the Braid (north east of Ballymena), Archibald Stewart sent orders to the remaining companies to send detachments to Cross. It transpired that they were to be used to relieve one George Canning, a Protestant settler in Derry who had been held under siege at Avigey Castle, and unhappily enough, the siege was being conducted by Manus Roe O'Cahan, the brother of *Tirlough Og* and a relation of *Alasdair* (whose grandmother had been an O'Cahan). Naturally this put the two company commanders in an impossible position – they refused to send detachments, although realizing that this would lead to serious reprisals.

What happened next can be gathered from the evidence of a member of the same regiment, Robert Hamill of Ballymoney parish, given to an inquiry a decade later, on 4 March 1652:

"Who, being duly sworn and examined, saith that he was one of Captain Peebles' company in the British regiment under command of Archibald Stewart, Esq., and that to secure this side of the Bann that regiment lay on the Bannside. That upon Tuesday, the 2d of January, 1641, [old style, nowadays 1642] to his best knowledge, James McColl McDonnell and Alexander MacColl MacDonnell [*Alasdair MacCholla Chiotaich*], persuaded and took some of the Highland company of the same regiment, and drew together some Irish, and early in the morning of the same day (the British hearing an alarm but suspecting no danger) drew up towards one side Coope's house, where they heard Mr. Stewart was drawing his regiment together, and in their march thither they espied a great number of men, with the Highland and other colours of British regiments their friends as they supposed, and they the British then sent one Murdoch to the said men, whom they by their colours supposed to be their own men, to see what news, which man coming up to them, they saw one come out of the said Highland company, and the other forces with them, and run him the said Murdoch through with a sword. And he saith that he saw the said James MacColl MacDonnell and the said Alexander MacColl MacDonnell lead on the said Highlanders and the Irish whom they had gathered with their head pieces on. And that when they came near where the British forces were drawn up, they went to the right and to the left hand, well-nigh encompassing the British, who until then, by reason of their colours, did not suspect them, and poured in upon the British a volley of shot upon which they seeing themselves so betrayed ran for their lives. And he saith, that of eleven files of Captain Peebles' company, he never could hear of any that escaped except himself and six more men. And this examt. saith that he believeth that the number of those who were gathered together to murder the said regiment was about two thousand. And further he saith not."

In point of fact, Archibald Stewart seems to have attempted to isolate the two Catholic companies, exposing them to probable annihilation. In a pre-emptive strike, *Alasdair MacCholla* had enabled both companies to remove themselves from a dangerous position and, in a logical development of the situation, he had aligned his force with the body that now represented the King's loyal army.

There were exaggerated accounts of the death toll arising from this action and although, in truth, somewhere about sixty of the Covenanters were killed, numerous witnesses recorded that *Alasdair MacCholla* and other leaders had personally intervened to protect various individuals. The so-called "Portnaw massacre" was followed by a reciprocal event, the Island Magee massacre and, typically, Argyll was quick to turn the situation to his advantage: on 25 January 1642 the records show that the Privy Council gave him permission to strengthen his recent fortifications and even agreed to pay him the cost of the continuing illegal captivity of *Colla Ciotach* and his sons:

"Supplication by Archibald, Marques of Argile, as follows: – during the late troubles "he caused big a fortification in Loch Kilkerran [Campbeltown], opposite to the kingdom of Ireland, whilk he wes of intention to demolish"; but he has thought it better to advise with their Lordships as to this. The Lords, "**having tane to thair consideration the great rebellion in Ireland unto the which diverse of the clan Donald, speciallie Coill McGillespicks sonnes and others, followers of the Earle of Antrim, have joynned thameselves**, and there is great suspicion of the said Earle his accession thereto, thairfoir and becaus of the knowne inmitie of the said Earle of Antrim and the Clan Donald aganis the said Marques of Argile and his friends, and of the neernesse of thair bounds to the said Marques his lands of Kintyre and other parts, the said Lords ordains the said Marques to keepe up the said fortification and to doe everie other thing requisit for strengthening himselfe, his freinds and followers and defence of thair bounds frome the incursions of the rebels in Ireland and thair adherents."

"Supplication by Archibald, Marques of Argile, as follows: – **In the time of the late troubles he caused apprehend Coill McGillespick McDonald and two of his sons,** [also] John McDonald and Donald Gorme McDonald, for not finding caution to answer certain criminal charges made against them, **and he has ever since kept them in ward at great trouble and expense.** He has been lately informed that other two of his sons, with a number of their friends, broken and lawless men, who during the late troubles committed many insolences against himself and his vassals, have joined his Majesty's rebels in Ireland, doing there all the mischief that in them lies. He therefore craves that, as these persons named, who are now in his ward as heritable Justiciar within the bounds, have had no means to maintain themselves nor their keepers this long time past, their Lordships would prescribe what should be done with them, whether they should be brought to Edinburgh or what otherwise they should think best, and for the meantime and the past time that they should allow him his expenses.

The Lords approve of what the Marques has done, and ordain him still to keep these persons as public prisoners on his Majesty's expenses. They also modify to him the sum of forty merks weekly for the maintenance of the said five persons and their five keepers since Whitsunday last and in time coming till order be taken further in the matter. And they ordain the Lords of Exchequer and Commissioners of his Majesty's rents to make payment of this allowance."

Alastair's Ulster Campaign

Meantime, *Alasdair MacCholla* and his men continued to give of their best, being joined by regular and irregular forces which swept across the Bann, and they quickly gained control of almost the whole district. When they seized the town of Dunluce "the inhabitants, who were nearly all Scottish settlers, were supplied with boats and sent across the channel to their own land." Hill describes the assault on the castle at Clough, belonging to one Donnell Gorm Macdonnell but which had been seized as a refuge on the orders of Archibald Stewart. Although the place was filled with refugees and all their valuables, the garrison had neither the skills nor the stomach for a siege as it saw the joint approaching forces of *Alasdair MacCholla* and Art Oge O'Neill. It was Art Oge who summoned the garrison commander (one Walter Kennedy) to surrender, and in an adroit response was told that he would:

"'"never surrender to an O'Neill the castle that belonged to a Macdonnell!" Kennedy, a cannie Scot, took care, of course, that his words were spoken so as to be heard by Alaster Mac Coll, and the latter was so pleased and flattered by the reply, that he swore to Kennedy by the "cross on his sword", that, provided the castle were peacefully surrendered, the garrison would be permitted to pass out in safety, and that the multitude of non-combatants who had sought refuge therein, might carry away all their effects and retire to their own houses. This was more than Kennedy could have hoped for. He surrendered, therefore, without delay, and so far as Macdonnell was concerned, or had the means of controlling others, the terms of this surrender were faithfully carried out."

Archibald Stewart himself was not at Clough, but was closeted with a strong body of men at Coleraine. Just nine days after Alasdair and his men had been forced onto the offensive, a mutual relative, Sir James Macdonnell of the Cross, wrote as a cousin to this Archibald Stewart, erstwhile friend and neighbour. His letter is transparently honest and re-iterates the simple story: the native Irish Catholics had been forced to take action to try to recover their lands and their religion and out of loyalty to the crown but, recognising the great difficulties of trying to control large numbers of armed and angry civilians, Sir James offers his personal good offices, if only Stewart will accept the hand of friendship:

"COSEN ARCHEBALD, – I receaved your Letter, and, to tell the Truth, I was ever of that Opinion, and soe was most of all these Gentilmen, that your owne selfe had noe [deception?] in you; but certainly had I not begun when I did, I and all these Gentilmen, with my Wiffe and Children had been utterly destroyed; of which I got Intelligence from one that heard the Plott alayinge; and those Captayns of yours (whom you may rather call Cowboyes) were, every daye, vexinge ourselves and our Tennants, of Purpose to picke Quarells, which noe Flesh was able to indure: And judge you whether I had Reason to prevent suche Mischefe; And I vow to the Almightie, had they not forct me, as they did many others besides me that would rather hang than goe on as they did, I would stick as firm to your side as any one of yourselves; though I confess it would be the worse thing for mee and mine that ever I sawe.

"To speake to you really the Truth, and the true Information of the whole kingdome – upon my Creditt I nowe doe it. All the whole Kingdome in generall are of our Side except Dublin, whoe hath 2000 Men about it, in Leager [siege] of it, if it be not now taken; Drogheda whoe hath 1600 Men about it, and are these ten Days past eating of Horse Flesh; Carrickefergus, Coulraine, and my Lord Clandeboyes, and my Lord of Ardes. This is the Truth on my Creditt; Ballemenagh, Antrim and all the Garrisons between this and Carrickefergus are fled to Carrickefergus; soe that it is but a Follie to resist what God pleaseth to happen; But certainlie they will have all Ireland presentlie, whatever [length of] Time they [manage to] Keepe it.

"You may truely inform my Friendes in Coulraine that I would wish they [unharmed?] and if they yielde me the Towne, it shall bee goode for them and me, for the Booty shall be myne, and they shal be sure of goode Qurtrs [terms], for I will send for all the Raghlin [Rathlin] boates to Portrush, and from thanes send all the People away into Scotlande, which, if it bee not done before sir Felim [O'Neill] his army comes to the Towne who comes the next week [with some?] thousand Men and Peece of Artillery, all my desire of doeinge them good will be to noe Purpose, therefore sende mee Word what you doe therein:

"As for Both your Houses they shall bee safe, and soe should all the Houses in the Countrey, if they would bee persuaded by mee: the Oldstowe was rendered mee, and they all within had good Quarters, onely the Clandeboyes Souldiers and the two Regiments from beyond the Ban were a little greedy for pillaginge, which could not bee healpt; As for Killinge of Women, none of my Souldiers dare doe it for his Life, but the common People that are not under Rule doth it in Spight of our Teeth; But for your People, they Killed of Women and Children about 3 score.

"My Lord and Lady [Antrim] are gone to Slain – to whom I have sent; tell my bror. Hill and Mr. Barwicke that their people are all in good Health, but [secure?] in my owne company. I desyre you not to stirr out of that till I be neere you myselfe, for feare you should fall in the hands of the seaven Hundred I have in the lower Part of the Countie, whoe would give you noe quarter at all; but when I have settled thinges here, you may come to me yourselfe, and your dearest friends [also?], and the rest to transport them with the rest into Scotland;

"As for goinge against the Kinge, wee will dye sooner, or my Lord of Antrim either, but their only Aim is to have their Religion settled, and every one his owne antient Inheritaunce; Thus wishinge you to take my Counsell, whiche I proteste to God I will give you as reallie as to myselfe, and haveing the hope of your beleivinge mee hereinn, I reste your verie loveinge Coussen still – JAMES MACDONNELL

"From the Catholic Campe, at Oldstowne, the 11th of January 1641 [old style, i.e. 1642]

"Black Friday"

Perhaps predictably, Archibald Stewart declined to take the advice and within the month (11 February 1642) he marched out of Coleraine at the head of nine hundred men – three hundred English and six hundred Scots – to attack *Alasdair*'s camp at Ballymoney. The alarm was raised, *Alasdair*'s men took up their weapons and the conflict was joined at the Laney, about a mile outside the town of Ballymoney where, in a staggering turn of events, Stewart's aggressive little army was utterly destroyed. The effect on the Covenanters morale, and the battle itself, is described in a contemporary account by Rev. Clogy (quoted by Hill):

> "The Scots then throughout all the province of Ulster, where they were most numerous, betook themselves to [strong]holds, leaving all the open country to the enemy. For the first attempt of Coll Kittach had so frightened them that they thought no man was able to stand before that son of Anak.
>
> "In his first encounter, at the head of a few Irish Highlanders [i.e. Gaelic-speaking Scots] and some of Antrim's Irish Rebells, that were Brethren in Evil, against Eight hundred English and Scotch, **having commanded his Murderers to lay down all their Firearms**, he fell in among them with swords and durks or scanes, in such a furious manner, that it was reported not a man of them escaped of all the Eight hundred."

In fact, as Hill points out, one hundred must have escaped to scamper back to Coleraine, but the scale of the defeat was nonetheless awesome and, for generations, the day was grimly commemorated as "Black Friday".

Stevenson highlights a particular significance in the description of this battle, since *Alasdair* seems to have employed the "Highland Charge" for the first time, a military manoeuvre which was to stand him in good stead in the coming years and to serve Scotland for a century. Clogy accurately described the way in which, after firing one well-delivered round, the Highlanders threw down their empty weapons and hurled themselves into an irresistable assault.

By now, *Alasdair MacCholla* had become a considerable figure in his own right. By all accounts, he was a veritable giant of a man, six foot six inches tall and built to match – Stevenson quotes the description given by Patrick Gordon of Ruthven, who had probably met *Alasdair* and who said he was "of such extraordinarie strenth and agilitie as there was non that equalled or came neire him", whilst Alexander Clogy (above), described him as "that son of Anak". [*"A people great and tall, the children of the Anakims, whom thou knowest, and of whom thou hast heard say, Who can stand before the children of Anak!"* Deuteronomy, 9.2] Loder describes his sword, which was preserved at Loughan Castle in Co. Tipperary until the mid-19th century, and "was furnished down the back of the blade with a rod along which an iron ball weighing 10lbs. rolled from hilt to point to give extra force to its stroke".

So great did he become in the legend of the native Irish that his stature came to represent that of all his men, for in 1993, in Co. Cork, the author was told of a priest who had re-interred the bones of some of Alasdair's fallen comrades and had been impressed by their size – "they had been mighty men, those Scotsmen, every one a giant."

Argyll's Intervention

Soon afterwards Argyll began to make plans to send his own troops into Antrim, (under Sir Duncan Campbell of Auchinbreck, as colonel), and secured the King's agreement for the expedition. In April 1642 Antrim took that threat as a cue to return to his own demesnes and relieve the beleaguered Protestants. At the time, *Alasdair* seems to have been engaged in the siege of Ballintoy, some 10 miles from Dunluce and many years later one Gilduffe O'Cahan, of Dunseverick, was forced to give evidence about it. His evidence was largely against individuals that he knew to be safely dead, but it gives us an idea of the vigour with which the campaign was being prosecuted:

> "After the Irish had beaten the British in the Layney and killed very many, and taken several colours, he this examnt. and his sons, Henry MacHenry and Tirlogh Oge O'Cahan, wrote a letter unto Mr. Fullerton and Archibald Boyd, then in Ballintoy House, for surrender of it….and … promised they would conduct them with a good convoy from thence to Coleraine…
>
> "That the British in the said house not surrendering it upon the said letter, this examnt's. said son, Tirlogh Oge O'Cahan and Alaster McColl McDonnell, as was threatened in the said letter, soon after sent for cannon and brought it against Ballintoy, and shot two shots at the said house, and also caused a sow to be made, but it did no service."[5])

On Antrim's return, and in the expectation of the arrival of Argyll's royally sanctioned reinforcements, it became politic to lift this and other sieges. At Coleraine, Antrim provided help at his own expense and

> "On this occasion, Alester MacColl, who was chief in command, consented so to relax the severity of the siege, that the inhabitants not only got ample space for themselves and their cattle, but were supplied with the best descriptions of food – beef and oatmeal. Alester MacColl, who had here the fate of so many presbyterians literally in his hands, thus dealt with them very much more humanely than even the rules of modern warfare would permit…The presbyterians were taught to regard him and his adherents simply as the enemies of God… They would have gladly hewed him in pieces, had they got him into their power, even as Samuel hewed in pieces Agag, when he rebuked Saul for sparing the king of the Amelekites." (Hill).

Alasdair now withdrew from the Glens, and on 16 June, under Sir Phelim O'Neill, was in the vanguard of an atttack on an inferior British force at Glenmaquin, near Raphoe in Co. Donegal. This attack was ill-judged and *Alasdair* was badly wounded, being shot through the thigh: "with much ado O'Cahan brought of MacDonnell in a Horse-Litter" (Stevenson).

Meantime Antrim, having relieved the citizens of Coleraine, sought by parley to protect his lands from the attentions of the swelling army sent over from Scotland to defend or reinstate the beleaguered Protestant planters. These forces, sent by anti-royalist Covenanters, landed initially at Carrickfergus, and comprised 2,500 men in the first wave with a further 7,500 to follow in August. They were virtually unopposed by the unarmed peasantry and did not trouble to negotiate with Antrim, whose lands they quickly overran. At the end of May he himself was treacherously seized in his own castle of Dunluce by Monro, the Scots commander, whom he had just entertained at a banquet. Within a few weeks Antrim was moved to Carrickfergus and Dunluce was occupied by Sir Duncan Campbell of Auchinbreck, Colonel of Argyll's regiment.

The Scots army was empowered to use Rathlin as a base with "full authority to take possession of the said island and plant a garrison there." As Hill notes: "Although Argyll's regiment, like each of the other nine then raised, was to number one thousand

THE PRELUDE TO WAR

men, yet 1600 of the Campbells made their way to the little island of Rathlin, and literally swept it bare of every living thing. A vivid and harrowing tradition is still told there of this Campbell invasion, which is represented as having been more remorseless than any similar event that ever previously happened in that island. At a place known as *Port na Cailliagh*, many women are said to have been thrust or hurled alive from the cliffs...."

Alastair's treaty with Leven

At this stage, the Protestant forces were carrying all before them and the native Irish forces had retreated to their wildest fastnesses, whilst *Alasdair* was still recovering from his injuries "in the house of a priest called O'Crilly. This was, it seems, Patrick Crilly or Crelly, the Cistercian abbot of Newry ... an agent of the earl of Antrim." (Stevenson). Owen Roe O'Neill had lately arrived from Spain to take command of what native forces survived and was engaged in transforming them into an effective army. About the same time, in August 1642, the Earl of Leven, landed in Ireland to head the Covenanting army, now 10,000 strong, This was the same Earl of Leven, "a little, rather deformed man, and very rich" (Linklater), better known perhaps as General Alexander Leslie who, having humiliated his king had been ennobled for his pains. It is important to note that the King had consented to this particular Scottish expedition, no doubt content to divert potentially hostile forces from his growing predicament at home – it was in that very month that Charles raised his Royal Standard at Nottingham and declared the Commons to be traitors.

In original research, Stevenson has drawn our attention to this period and has made challenging suggestions; his work is so interesting that some of the relevant passages are considered here, opening with the words of Patrick Gordon of Ruthven [already quoted in part]who says that:

"when generall Lesly [Leven] went ouer to Ireland, he fand that there was non of the Irische commanderes so much to be feared as this man [Alastair] for actiuitie and strenth of bodie. He was of such extraordinarie strenth and agilitie as there was non that equalled or came neire him. He was of a graue and sulled carriage, a capable and pregnant judgement, and in speciall in the art militarie, and fror his wallour, all that knew him did relate wonders of his actiounes in armes; wherfor generall lesly, being well informed of his invincible courage, his great judgement in the art militarie, and happie successe which did euer accompany his interpryses... like a craftie warriour sends to him [Alastair], and dealles that he may **serue his own nation**, and takes vpon him to pacifie Ardgyll, to relieue his father and brethren, and gett them restored to their ancient inheritance. **Upon these terms he [Alastair] returns to Scotland with the general,** being so generous as he would in no terms take service against the Irish, with whom he had once sided." But Argyll would not release his prisoners, so Alasdair returned to Ireland **"vowing to write his revenge in blood."**

Stevenson mentions that although there had been otherwise slight evidence to support this account hitherto, he has subsequently unearthed three documents in the Bodleian which confirm that a deal was really made. The key document is the treaty itself:

"The heads and articles of the parley and intercommuning underwritten:

Imprimis, upon promission and conditions after spoken that there be first a full and firm pardon and [remission] of all former faults and guiltiness whatsoever procured, obtained and granted to Coll Kittagh McDonnell's children Randoll and Alexander, and to all their followers and adherents, making them in all time hereafter to be free and peaceable lieges to the king and his laws.

That a relaxation and enlargement from prison and captivity be granted to the said Coll their father, and their incarcerated brethren and friends, who in the common challenge of their guiltiness in Scotland are detained captives.

That the said Coll and children be repossessed and restored to their former integrity of estate, in lands and goods and others, as they were before their outbreaking in Scotland, or as good in al respects.

That whatsoever of them shall be able to acquire and make up a company of faithful and loyal soldiers in this his majesty's war against the common rebels of this nation shall have as good and due payment to themselves and their companies as any that are upon the said employment and service, pro rata according to their numbers.

For the which the saids Randoll and Allester with their foresaids shall before they cross the Bann instantly act and do some points of service against those rebels, both entering in their blood and spoiling of their goods and cattle, and use all other hostile courses and plots against them as shall clearly induce and prove their present fidelity and forwardness, and betoken the future countenance and loyalty in all time afterward in the said service. Copia vera. LEVEN"

The other documents are an undertaking by Campbell of Auchinbreck, 19 September 1642, to secure Argyll's ratification of the treaty and that his side of the bargain will be met; and a set of orders issued by Leven, 11 November 1642, specifying the sort of service that he requires *Alasdair* to perform as a sign of good faith. Between those dates, on 7 October 1642, it was reported that "Col Kitto and divers rebels have submitted and brought in many cows for pledges"; but a fortnight later, 21 October, Antrim managed to escape from his captivity at Carickfergus and the whole situation changed again.

Stevenson suggests that at this time *Alasdair* had "deserted" the Irish, and that his motives are clear: "hopes of gaining freedom for his family and restoration of their property". The charge of "desertion" seems rather hard, since it would be difficult to say that *Alasdair* had ever actually "joined" the Irish and indeed, it would be hard to actually define "the Irish" themselves in this turbulent period. Really it seems more plausible to suppose that *Alasdair* was buying time for Antrim by muddying the water, but in any event he did not act in any way that was inconsistent with his personal and military goals. It is possible to identify four important cords in the net against which *Alasdair* struggled at this time, some constraining him and others entangling him, and all linked to the 8th Earl of Argyll. The faction which had imprisoned his family and enslaved his lands was answerable to Argyll and, in effect, was personified by him, and it is fair to say that Argyll's was a rival noble family; that Argyll was a staunch and very dark Protestant; that his "kindly men" and planted incomers, with their social mores were in effect Sasunnach (English-like), and that he was a leading anti-Royalist.

These were the issues that counted with *Alasdair*; nationality would scarcely be a relevant factor between Irish and Scots, although of course the newly planted residents of Ulster were largely both Sasunnach and Protestant; but when *Alasdair* joined Antrim's regiment he was not joining that of a rival family, his own company was not Protestant, the area that he was protecting included family lands and Antrim was a noted Royalist. Again, at Portnaw he was forced to defend his company against the Protestant forces, and he engaged in action against the Sasunnach settlers, in defence of the interests of his kinsman, the Royalist Earl of Antrim.

Subsequently, Antrim had been imprisoned and his lands occupied by Argyll's regiment, at a time when *Alasdair* had been *hors de combat* and the forces with which he had been allied had afterwards been largely dispersed. By the time that *Alasdair* had recovered, new forces were emerging, those of Owen Roe O'Neill and those of General Leslie [Leven]. Leven, on this expedition, was acting with the consent of the King, and was offering the release of *Alasdair*'s captive father and siblings, whereas O'Neill had less to offer. Did *Alasdair* take Leven at face value? Or was he engaged in a desperate attempt to double-bluff him?

The negotiations must have been tricky and during that vital period of two months, there must have been confusion and delay. When *Alasdair* "came in" with the cattle, it may have seemed like a success for Leven, but was it? In an Irish account cited by Stevenson, *Alasdair* and *Raghnall* instructed their men "to take away [from] the people of every house where they might be on coyne [billetted], their cows and their horses along with their household furniture, their sheep and their goats along with their accoutrements. They did so, and carried the plunder with them to Coleraine." But, in part, the cattle were merely the cattle that had been seized from the planters themselves, and in any event, once *Alasdair*'s men had withdrawn there would have been nothing to prevent Leslie from seizing the animals without any help from *Alasdair*. There will have been more delay as *Alasdair* affected to dither about "entering in the blood" of the Irish. This must have been for effect, since Gordon of Ruthven (quoted above), had already commented about *Alasdair* "being so generous as he would in no terms take service against the Irish, with whom he had once sided." All the same, *Alasdair* proved to be as wily as his father in these proceedings: Leven's own men will have wondered what was happening... and could Argyll's men be certain that they themselves were not being betrayed?

There are hints of these events in "West Highland Tales", collected by J. Campbell and translated by Matheson:

"Alasdair MacCholla was very desirous of getting into the army. He first went to speak to the Earl of Argyll to obtain a post from him. The Earl of Argyll made him a promise. But the other gentry of Argyll were very much against giving Alastair MacDonald a post in the army of Argyll and they opposed him so strongly that the Earl did not give him a post.

"When Alasdair MacCholla reached Inveraray expecting to obtain a post in the army from the Earl of Argyle, the Earl said to him *"Chan 'eil e freagrach dhomh-sa oifig a thabhairt dhuit aig an am seo"* ("It is not convenient for me to give you a commission at the present time.") Alasdair MacCholla did not say anything to that, but went. When he was at Douglas Water a messenger came running after him and the messenger told him to come another time to Inveraray and that the Earl would try to do something for him. Alasdair turned round and said *"Fuich! Fuich! mar fhiach facal Iarla Earra-Gháidheal anns a' cheart am seo fhéin, chan 'eil e ro choltach gur fhiach e a rithis."* ("Fie! Fie! unless the Earl of Argyll's word is worth something at present, it is not likely that it will be worth anything hereafter.") And he turned his back on the messenger and went."

The other traditional tale has *Colla Ciotach* imprisoned at Dunstaffnage, and *Alasdair* (having taken Leslie's bait), serving as an officer in Auchinbreck's regiment; a servant is sent from Argyll, with a message for Auchinbreck, instructing him to have Alastair killed. The servant will know Auchinbreck for his height and his black hair and locks ... and of course delivers the message to Alasdair in error: *"Bha falt dubh 's ciachan mór dubh air fàs air Alasdair Mac Colla, mar a bh' air a' Chòirneal"* ("Alastair MacCholla had black hair and long black locks like the Colonel"). Alastair has the message sent on to Auchinbreck and next day is invited to a regimental dinner but, forewarned, escapes his doom and, nobly, takes no revenge: ***"Cha dean mise ort-sa 'san mar a bha thusa a los a dhèanamh orm-sa. Bha thusa a los mise a mharbhadh. Cha mharbh mise thusa aig an ám seo, ach fan ás mo rathad 'na dhéidh seo."*** ("I will not do to you at present what you intended to do to me. You intended to kill me. I will not kill you now, but keep out of my way after this.")

These tales support the evidence that *Alasdair* was indeed negotiating with the Covenanting leadership. It seems to have been a dangerous game that he was playing, and may well have ended in some such incident as an intercepted message revealing to *Alasdair* that his cover was blown. By that time however, Antrim again was at large and in England, in the confidence of the King and ready for revenge, Leven had returned to Scotland with nothing to show for his efforts, and *Alasdair*'s reputation, far from being harmed, had been even further enhanced. Throughout the episode, there had been no inconsistency: *Alasdair* had struggled with the power of his established opponent, the anti-royalist Protestant rival Argyll and if, on this occasion, he did not play "cricket" it merely helps to highlight the difference in the cultural tradition.

Notes

1 The Covenanting forces were under the command of Alexander Leslie (1582 – 1661); in his subsequent campaign of appeasement, Charles raised him to the rank of Earl of Leven. Leslie had been amongst the many Scottish mercenaries who had campaigned in Germany for Gustavus Adolphus of Sweden, and who had returned for the Civil War in which they "did a little to dignify a futile squabble between unforgiveable intolerances with the discipline learnt in the honesty of mercenary service." (Eric Linklater). Even after his elevation, Leven was to betray his King again; he led the invading forces of the Covenanters in late 1643, which were joined by Argyll and his regiment. At the battle of Marston Moor (July 1, 1644), Leven was supported on the left wing by two men of supreme evil, Cromwell and his own name-sake, David Leslie. As things transpired, David Leslie was to succeed Leven at the head of the Scots army, after Cromwell turned upon his old allies and defeated them; imprisoned in the Tower, Leven was released at the request of the Queen of Sweden and allowed to retire to Balgonie in Fife.

2 Ranald, second Earl of Antrim, was born in 1609; he was to play a prominent part in Irish affairs and the following biographical details have been taken from Hill, who begins with a contemporary quotation: "' The Lord Marquis has told me that he wore neither hat, cap, nor shoe, nor stocking, till 7 or 8 years old, being bread the Highland way, He was a proper clean lymmed man, first married to the Dutchess of Buckingham, and after to Rose, daughter of Sir Henry O'Neill of Shane's Castle.'" Having travelled on the Continent as a young man, he returned in 1634 and was introduced at court, soon after the assassination of Buckingham, the former George Villiers, had suddenly left his duchess "in the possession of fabulous wealth, and still retaining the nobler dowry of youthful beauty .... her numerous portraits represent her as possessing more than the ordinary share of personal charms." In fact, Villiers had been assassinated in August 1628, but nonetheless everyone was still very jealous at Antrim's match, not least Wentworth (the Earl of Strafford).

3 Loder dies not mention that Lord Lorne had also failed to sign the Covenant, despite his overt support.

Although he did sign the 1580 Confession, he avoided signing the National Covenant even after he publicly defied the King at the Church Assembly in December 1638 and when, as Earl of Argyll he became leader of the Covenanting movement, Scotland's Cromwell.

4 Indeed, on 19 September 1639 the Fiar was formally adjudged to be hopelessly insane.

5 A "sow" was a mobile structure, heavily protected, used to permit engineers to undermine walls.

12

ANTRIM MOVES AGAINST THE REBELS

Alastair's Royal Commission

Alasdair MacCholla now entered that phase of his life which was to win him enduring fame and, amongst the Highlanders, heroic status in his own right. Even as Leven issued his order, on 11 November 1642, specifying the type of service that he expected from *Alasdair*, larger events were already overtaking all concerned. The Civil War that had broken out in England earlier that year was approaching the end of the first campaigning season, although with no definite sign of the eventual outcome. Meanwhile, Argyll and his Covenanters were firmly entrenched in Scotland and had energy and resources to spare, sufficient to have invaded and maintained a presence in Ulster; and in Ireland the Confederate Parliament in Kilkenny was involved in delicate manoeuvres aimed at establishing an independent state which would continue to recognize the crown, but with the Catholic faith fully restored. *Alasdair* and Clan Donald had every reason to be Royalist since it was well-known that Antrim was in the confidence of King Charles and that any success for the King would be rewarded by the restoration of some at least of the ancestral lands, now held by the King's enemy, Argyll. A Royalist uprising in Scotland would be a check to the Covenanters and might well dishearten the Parliamentarian rebels in England, and it would certainly make it difficult for the Covenanters to maintain their expeditionary army in Ulster.

The complicated history of the Civil War is not something that can be closely followed here, but the interaction of apparently disparate events throughout the three kingdoms cannot be ignored and so a brief chronological sequence has been included as an *aide-mémoire*, and will be found in Appendix 7. Equally, the details of the amazing campaign conducted by Montrose are beyond the scope of this book, and only some aspects directly relevant to *Alasdair*'s own family and personal reputation can be considered. In reference to this personal life, it should be remembered that *Alasdair* and his brother *Raghnal* had been forced from their home in 1639, had had little life since then but the life of a soldier, and that their father and brothers had been held in captivity by Argyll throughout the intervening years.

In the opening months of 1643, King Charles had begun to make plans that involved both Ireland and Scotland and, although some of his negotiations were in secret, it was public knowledge that he had had Parliament's commissioners ejected from Dublin and that he had instructed Ormonde to treat with the Confederate Irish. He may have been prompted in this by the knowledge that, in November 1642, the Kilkenny Confederation had contracted to supply and deliver no fewer than 10,000 men for service in Spain! A confused situation had arisen in Ireland, largely through the fault of Charles himself: Ormonde had been authorized to raise an army in 1640 to assist the King against the Scots and, by July of that year, 9000 were in arms and ready for despatch when, with the advent of Charles' new policy of appeasement they became redundant.

This army remained in arms, billeted upon the King's indignant English planters, and costing him £860 per day until in May 1641 Charles decided to solve the problem by demobilizing it and giving permission for up to 8000 Irishmen to be taken abroad into foreign service.

Not surprisingly, a lucrative trade became quickly established since men were happy enough to go as mercenaries to a Catholic country and the planters were glad to see the back of them. By 1643 it began to dawn upon Charles that he needed help in his Civil War and that these men could provide it, provided that he could get the support of the Kilkenny Confederation (in whose gift they lay).

It was in this connection that, in May, Antrim was received by the Queen and undertook both to arrange a truce in Ireland and to raise 20,000 men to serve against the Covenanters. By a strange turn of events it was very soon afterwards, in July, that Montrose was contacted by Argyll and offered a command in a Covenanting Army to be sent into England in open defiance of the King. Shocked at this treachery, Montrose informed the King and offered him his own service (thus turning his back on the faction that he had so recently represented, when he had led forces to counter those of the Royalist Earl of Huntly in 1639).

In fact, the Covenanting Army now launched by Argyll was justified by him as the echo of another, one that was conjured up when Antrim had been forced to reveal something of his own plans. He had been captured on his way back to Ireland after meeting the Queen, and his mission to raise Royalist support there had been discovered. Antrim, perhaps foolishly, had sought to make a play that his Royalist Army, to comprise both Irish and Scottish elements, was for service in the King's cause, but only in England (rather than in Scotland). Unfortunately, under torture, one of his servants had revealed that "Collkittoch's sones" were to be involved in the enterprise, and it was not difficult for the Privy Council to fill in the blanks. Assuming that *Alasdair* and his men could be readily contained in Scotland, Argyll and his henchmen pretended to believe Antrim's own story, and used it as a justification for their own military incursion into England!

By the end of the year, the Covenanting Army was in being, under the command of Lord Leven (General Alexander Leslie) and Argyll, who had put up £12,000 towards the cost, was established in the force as Colonel of his own regiment. Meanwhile, Ormonde had signed a truce in Ireland and Antrim had at last been formally commissioned (by the King himself) to raise an Irish force and to bring it into Scotland, to join a Royalist force to be raised there by Montrose.

Anticipating some of these developments, *Alasdair* made an incursion into Scotland in November 1643. He seems to have hoped to raise support in the isles, and no doubt it was intended that a guerilla campaign in the area would help to create a diversion whilst Montrose organized a more conventional campaign in the Royalist heartlands. The Irish movements were reported anxiously to the Privy Council in Edinburgh, and must have been a humiliation for Argyll. *Alasdair* brought over a force of some 300 men and seems to have made Colonsay his base, as is revealed in the following details recorded in the "Tanner Letters" (published by the Irish Manuscript commission in 1943):

"Edinburgh 12 Dec. 1643

"The Paul of London, 180 tons, Robert Paul, master, having delivered her goods at

Londonderry and Dongale for the soldiers there, and freighted herself with salmon, hides and such commodities as that country affords, was driven upon an Island [Colonsay] on the coast of Scotland, where fifty Irish rebells [sic] accompanying the MacDonnalds who came lately out of Ireland and by reason there is no [Parliamentary or Covenanting] ships on those seas pass at their pleasure in long boats from island to island and are ready to draw more [men] out of Ireland at their pleasure, the said master, his mate and one other of their company were taken prisoners by them as you may perceive by these inclosed papers."

This distressing information summarized that which had been forwarded direct to Argyll by his agent, George Campbell. Earlier that same month, Argyll had launched himself on his treacherous campaign against his Sovereign and was unlikely to be best pleased to learn that the long-threatened Royalist force was now established and in his own demesnes so Campbell, anticipating that his devious master would expect others to be as crooked as himself, enclosed some proof and a disingenuous explanation:

"Most honble. and noble Lord,
Please your Lordp. to receive this letter and declaration whereby your Lordp. may perceive that the MacDonnalds are begun to do wrong by sea. And **least some may perhaps think this is an invention to be a motive for sending out ships to pursue them**, we thought best to send to your Lordp the London Charter party and bills of lading, the other papers, as we are informed, were in the master's pocket, whom they have captive. The storms have been so great that we have had no further word concerning these people, nor yet anything from Archibald Campbell anent them. We rest ....
     "George Campbell
     "Inneraray 4 Dec. 1643
"P.S. They have written to have the ship kept safe till they hear from his lp."

The "charter-party" or contract had been drawn up on 3 March the same year; the "Paul" had ridden at anchor in the Thames for over a month and by 10 April her cargo had included the following:

"10 runlets of strong waters, marked; 4 barr. raisins, rice and figs; 1 tierce of clarett, 2 barr sacke, 2 barr coddes, 30 fferkins of butter, 2 butt off sacke, 290 cheeses, 700 haberdins, 300 rod fish, 500 Colefish, 21 couple of ling, 60 sacks, 1 box containing 70lb of soap, 1 box with 2 trumpets, 1 small runlet of vinegar, one truncke, one Hampeir, one cloakbag, marked & numbered as in the margin, to be delivered at Donghall ..... [also, bill of lading] 136 qrs malt, 51 qrs. wheat, 103 qrs. barley & 2 bushels of water measure, and 200 qrs. pease of Chandlers measure." "Another bill of lading ... 12 butts of sacke, 4 packs of shirt, 3 Chirurgeons chests, marked and numbered as in the margent, to be delivered at the port of London-Derry, to Sir Rob. Stewart Kt. & Col. or his asignees..."

By then, the master and purser had signed (in triplicate) a total of 21 such bills of lading, and the total cargo must have borne some resemblance to that of the "Irish Rover". Evidently the goods were delivered safely to Derry and Donegal, and new cargo was found; what happened next is described by one of the sailors (a Campbell from Islay!):

"Decemb. 4th 1643. The Declaration of Lauchton Cambell, Sayler in the ship called the Paule of London.

"On Wednesday afternoon, 22 Nov., the ship, being almost laden with salmon and hides, loosed from London-Derry for London. But was driven by storm towards the Isles of Scotland and on Thursday they anchored hard by Collonsey, being 14 men and boys with 6 piece of iron ordnance. The storm was so great that none in the isle offered to come to them till Saturday.

"On Saturday 25 Nov. 6 men came in a boat "to speare news and told them they were come from the (Tutor) of Caldor," and enquired whence they came, to whom they belonged, were they for King or Parliament. The Master returned them an answer that he was a Merchant Traveller and intended harm to no man. They told him that on the morn being Sunday the Tutor of Caldor would come and confer with him.

"On Sunday afternoon Alistar MacDonnald, son to Coile Mac Gillespicke, accompanied with fifty men came into the ship, and the master, thinking is was the Tutor of Caldor and his company let them all in purposing to make them welcome.

"But as soon as they came in Alistar laid [hold of the] master and told him he must arrest him **in the king's name** [emphasis added] and presently hurled him down to his boat and caused likewise lay hands on the Master's Mate and one more of the company.

"Some of Alistar's men lifted the door of the overlap under which some of the crew were at meat; six of his Hagbutters shot down and deadly hurt one in the head and one in the arm. The Master gunner would have blown up the overlap, but not having things ready, he only let fall some powder and fired it, which so terrified Alistar and his company that they took to their boats, leaving one of their men and one of the crew slain above the hatches. Before they left they cut the cable with their swords thinking the ship would be driven ashore: but the crew put out another anchor, and it blew so hard that none could come off land that night. Fearing Alistar and his company should come back the crew made sail before day on Monday and were driven on the coast of Lorne beside Downnolliche [Dunollie Castle, Oban Bay] where they then lay.

"Since they came "thunder and fire" broke their main mast, and so shook the ship that she is unseaworthy till dressed.

"Lauchton knew Alistar, being born in Ila and 13 years ago a sailor in Ireland."

The above details reached the English Parliament on Christmas Day, which under the new regime was no longer a Feast, just a normal working-day. That *Alasdair* was present on Colonsay must be undoubted, although there may be doubt about "Lauchton Cambell" and his claim to recognise a man that he last saw some thirteen years before, as a child of about 12 years. Archaeological evidence may someday be found in the shape of the missing anchor, since from the internal evidence, it appears that the "Paul" must have been at anchor in Loch Staosnaig. *Alasdair*'s choice of Colonsay as his base will not have been fortuitous as the obvious advantage of local knowledge would be heavily enhanced by being based where he had strong native support.

Now that his whereabouts were known, Colonsay became too dangerous and *Alasdair* and his men began to move ceaselessly from isle to isle, harrying the Covenanters and encouraging all who remained loyal to the crown and to their own faith. Campbell of Ardkinglas was commissioned by Argyll to contain the situation, and seems to have been led a merry dance before *Alasdair*'s men slipped away back to Ireland in the spring. By then *Alasdair* had received new instructions, upon which his men retreated to Rathlin, to be at hand for the next enterprise. That island, whose population had been massacred so recently for the convenience of the Covenanting Army, had been vacated in the backend of the previous year when Leslie withdrew his troops, preparatory to his expedition into England.

Frustrated, Ardkinglas contented himself at first with the execution of civilians in the isles who were held to have given comfort to *Alasdair*'s men, but then got word that his quarry was in Rathlin and immediately launched an attack which dispersed the force in disarray. Many of those that fled to Jura and Islay were unfortunate in that he captured them there: "I took them and causit cut of above ane hundredth and ffyifteine of them and took some prisoners." By 28 June, Ardkinglas was able to report that he had accounted for all of the rebels except for thirteen who were said to have fled to the Outer Hebrides.

Major – General Alastair McDonald

If nothing else, *Alasdair*'s initial campaign had tied up James Campbell of Ardkinglas and his men for more than half a year, but he had also created a diversion during which Montrose had been able to make his first moves, encouraged by Royalist sympathies which had been expressed in Aberdeen. In Ireland, King Charles had advanced his position and Lord Inchiquin (Murrough O'Brien, a protestant and a turn-coat) had been rejected in a gesture clearly encouraging to the Irish Confederacy

Although his initial efforts may have been contained with relative ease, *Alasdair* had obtained his limited objectives. When he returned to Ireland in the early spring of 1644, it was to accept the rank of Major-General and the charge of another and larger force, arranging to combine it with with that rump of his original force which was to await him in Rathlin.

A popular story is still told in Argyll, describing the way in which the Council of the Confederation of Kilkenny selected the leader for the King's expeditionary force, a story which was recounted by Norman McLeod in "*Teachdaire Gaidhealach*",and quoted by Professor MacKinnon. The gist of the account, in English, is as follows:

> "When the nobles of Ireland gathered to appoint the man to lead their army into Scotland, there were two noble Irish heroes who expected to have that honour, through having many of their friends at the assembly. Properly, by long tradition, the honour should go to the strongest sword-arm in Ireland. "*Seo e!*" ("Here it is!"), claimed Alasdair, drawing his sword and in defiance of all who would oppose him. "*Càite bheil an ath ghàirdean?*" ("Where is the next strongest?"), queried the council. "*Seo e!!*" ("It is here!"), replied Alastair, passing the sword to his left hand. No man would dare oppose him, and Alastair came to be commander of the company."

The arrangements in Ireland were delayed by practical and political difficulties and when, at the end of May, *Alasdair MacCholla* sent supplies for the relief of his men in Rathlin, it was only to find that they had been expulsed by Ardkinglas. Eventually, on June 24, *Alasdair* was able to set sail once more in earnest, this time from Waterford, with four ships and about 1500 men. Delayed three days by storm, on July 3 he had the slight consolation of capturing a shipload of Covenanters, making its way from Ireland to Scotland. This was exactly the sort of prize that he sought, since he needed hostages if he was ever to gain the release of his father and brothers. Of the forty passengers on board, *Alasdair* contented himself with eight prisoners, including four ministers, one of whom, John Weir, was accompanied by his pregnant wife.

John Weir, a Scottish minister who had been busy in imposing the Covenant in Ulster, seems to have seen himself as particularly devout and he maintained a diary in captivity which was (ostensibly) a record of his personal Covenant, that contractual relationship that he felt himself to share with God. Following his unfortunate death one of the survivors, Rev. Hamilton, continued the journal (and also took the opportunity to hagiofy the deceased, even going so far as to record a selection of his utterances in clear parallel with the Passion of our Lord). The "Diurnal" is a poignant document and the balance of the material is included *in extenso* as Appendix 6.

Journal of Rev. John Weir

We have cause to be very grateful for the dedication of John Weir, whose thoughtful prayer rings true despite his worries for his wife and child, his parents and his parish: "Yet Lord, keep us from making ane heavn or a God of our libertie". Sadly, he was struck with a fever and his diary thus came to be preserved for us through the fact of his dying in captivity and it being discovered amongst his effects. The early days of *Alasdair*'s campaign are now well known – the nervousness of the Highland chieftains, the rendezvous at Blair Atholl, the flow of military successes; it is interesting to see the same story without the benefit of hindsight, the contemporary account of a captive who did not survive to modify his words:

> ### "diurnals of our captiviti
> we were taken prisoners on wedsday 3 july 1644 (*eleven*) hours by Alaster Makcoll in the "*Harp*" of Wexford
> 4 july: we anchored between Ila & Jura, where we heard of news that five score of Alaster's men wer lateli slain by the Laird of Ardkinglass
> 5 july: we anchored above Duart
> 6 july: at Duart; other four ships overtaken with wheat, rye & sack
>
> ### [Alasdair lands, takes 2 castles]
> 7 july was the fast of Scotland; we sailed a little forward, & som men wer landed, & went to Loch Allen [*i.e. Kinlochaline Castle*]
> 8 july: they hold in Lochaline, we sailed forward to Loch Sunder [Sunart] where the rest of the armie landed
> 9 july: we lay at anchor there
> 10 july: we came fornent the castle of meagne [Mingary]
> 11 july: we cam much nearer to the castle of Mingary
> 12 july: the kowes wer takne from Mingary castle
> 13 july: the castle was assaulted by land & sea
> 14 july: it was rendred upon quarter
> 15 july: we wer brought out of the ship to the castle & began the exposition of psalms

16 july: Collonell James was sent with copies of the king's commission to Sir James Makdonald of Slait & later we heard Captain Mortimer read the commission

17: the frigot persoued a pryz

19: it was chased back by Captain Swanlye [Swanley, a Parliamentarian who, off Bristol, had captured a ship bound for England with Irish reinforcements for the king; he had had the Irish troops tied back-to-back in pairs and thrown into the sea]

20: they had ane conflict at sea in which ane dutch ship was taken, the other frigot cam under the shelter of the castle, & Captain Turner stood our [*illegible*] that time of the conflict mass was said in the castle

22 july: mass was said in the hall. Alaster made us writ to Mgr. Martin Mckilvra & Mgr. Hecter Makclean anent our captivitie & to see if they would travel for us to the state. [Rev. McGilvary was minister in Iona, Rev. MacLean was minister in Morvern]

26 july: Ar[chibal]d Campbel was sent from Argyl & got back our letters to his lordship

29 july: Alaster & the armie went away in the night

Alasdair having left, Argyll lays siege to Mingary

1: [*Ships?*] wer seen in ye sound

3 aug: the koues wer taken from castle Mingary

7 aug: Argyl with 5 ships & mani boats came fornent Mingary & shot divers times at it

8 aug: he sends sumonds to render the castle & prisoners in 24 hours or else to have no quarter

Argyll tries psychological pressure

12 aug: Captain Turner's ship & the other dutch ship being takn by Argyles ships at the Ile of Seale [Seil] came fornent Mingary

14: Mr Dougal Cambel was sent in by Argyl & reported of the victorie at York [Marston Moor] & Munro's march in Ireland, & burning divers castles in his voyage. [Munro was commander of Scots expeditionary army]

15: aug the dutch ship was cast away upon the rocks at Mingary

16: aug Mr Dougal & Archibald Campbel were sent in to us from Argyl with blankets & linen

19 aug: meal and aquavite was sent to us from his lordship

20 august: the marquess Argyl went away & left Sir Donald Cambel to block up the castle

23 aug: we received letters from Argyl that (at his return) he would deliver Colkittoch & his sons for us, & that we should in the mean tym call to Sir Donald for ani thing we neided, whereupon we wrot for victuals

29: we writ to him again for the sam effect

30 aug: we got in some meal with a letter from the marquess

3 septr: Mistress Weir got leave to goe home being neir hir tyme of deliverie

10 septr: we wrot to Sir Donald for more provision

12 septr: we got som meal with news from Ireland of the Lord Inchiquinn's rysing for king & parliament; Sir Donald wrot that the captain of the castle ought to furnish us victuals, whereupon they gave us two dayes provisions

Pressure begins to have its effect on the garrison

– Septr: the soldiers of the castle refused to give victuals to ani of us that are ministers but to the other prisoners onli, to whom they then gave four dayes provision, but would give them no more

17 Septr: Sir Donald sent in som meal with ane letter from Mistress Weir out of Inverari

18 sep: John Mckeller, & the rest of the old warders of the castle of Mingary got al libertid, but without weapons, whereas they should have gone with their weapons [on the] 14 july when the castle was rendred by them

19 Sep: Sir donald sent us in some fresh meat & revived ye motion anent our relief

20 Sep: we agreed withthye captain that Wm Hamilton, Wm. Irving & Archd. Bruce should be set at liberti, Sir Donald Cambel giving his bond to pay ten pound sterling upon the 12 of october & we being bound to Sir Donald for his relief & to the captain of Mingary for Sir Donald's fulfilling

23 Sep: our said 3 fellow prisoners, wer set at liberti upon the terms foresaid, 3 ships & four boats cam in our view & anchored at Mul, Captain Tallemby & Captain Brown came to Sir Donald's camp

24 Sep: Sir Donald sent us in the news anent (*Inchiquin?*) in print & som meal & bread readie prepared for us

27 Septr: some of the ships went northward

28 Septr: the people of the castle wer drinking al day & fought amongst themselves at nyght & 3 wer wounded

29 Septr: the like drinking was al day & meal & beaf was sent in to us & ane motion was revived by Sir Donald for our relief

30 Septr: that motion ended thus: that if Colkittoch & his sons wer delivered in the (*garrison?*) of Mingary, with Argyl & Sir Donald their passes to goe where prefer they pleased, and if they did accept that we should be set at liberti; and if they would not accept that – the captain of Mingary would enter on some other terms with Sir Donald; 3 soldiers & a woman wer put to lodge with us

Hitherto Mgr. Weir had writn according to al above writn

2 October: Mr. Weir took siknes. what follows wer obs. by Mgr. James Hamilton

3 Oct: We certified Sir Donald Cambel thereof who promised prompt to certifi Argyl whereupon we wrot also for our releif. Sir Donald sent in writing with news of Inchiquin's, (Fairfax') & General Loftus' armies

4 Oct: We got in tallow & straw

The siege is lifted on word of Alastair's approach

5 Oct: In the night & before 6 o'clock in the morning, Sir Donald's camp was (*removed?*)

6 Oct: The things that wer in the camp wer spoyled, we kept sabath

7 Oct: News came that Alaster was approaching, divers went from the castle towards him

8 Oct: a commanded partie went to bring som goats for the castle

9 Oct: they brought them the goats

10 Oct: Mgr. Weir got ane coole of his fever

11 Oct: Fourti kowes cam from the captain [of] ClanRanald to the castle

12 Oct: Killed beeves all the day

13 Oct: Report cam that Alaster was in Lochaline; Mgr. Weir fell in the fever again

14 Oct: We got leave to write to the comittee of estates & the comyssioners of the grat assembli, the marquis of Argyl, Sir Donald Cambel, Mgr. Weir's wyf & (−), also ane further was sent to ani that should come to us

15 Oct: Captain Farli & the rest of the men from the castle to meit Alaster returned

16 Oct: Alaster came back to the castle having burnt Lochaline, at which tym Mgr. Weir died at full assurance of God's rich love to him.

17 Oct: Mgr. Weir was buried at Kilcowankirk. Alaster's people reposted their sentories at (*posts?*) and after noon, 100 kowes was brought to ye castle."

Since his departure on 29 July, *Alasdair* had achieved great things; he had been joined by Montrose at Atholl and, together, they had raised a greater force and swept through Scotland, enjoying one mighty success after another. For a variety of reasons, Montrose has gained the personal credit for these triumphs, but the fact remains that at almost all his victories *Alasdair MacCholla* was at his side, whereas without *Alasdair* he encountered little success, despite his own personal valour and undoubted loyalty.

They had marched from Atholl to the field of Tippermuir, 3 miles from Perth, where they encountered 7000 infantry and 700 cavalry famously animated by their minister, Rev. Carmichael: "If ever God spoke certain truth out of my mouth, in His name I promise you today a certain victory." An incautious pronouncement, since by nightfall 2000 of his flock were dead and most of the others captured, save that "most of the cavalry saved themselves by the speed of their horses"!

From Perth the Royalists had continued to Aberdeen, on hearing that Lord Burleigh lay there at the head of a considerable force of "traitor rebels" (Montrose). In fact, Burleigh had 2000 foot and 500 horse on the morning of 12 September 1644, but by nightfall he had neither: the infantry had been annihilated and, once again, the cavalry had run away – "The victors, unable to pursue, much less to come up with them, let them escape in safety." It was at Aberdeen that Dr. Wishart describes:

> "an Irishman ... trailing his leg, so shattered at the thigh by a cannon-ball that it hung by a mere shred of skin. Observing his comrades somewhat dismayed at his misfortune, he hailed them with a loud, cheery voice, "Ha, comrades, such is the luck of war; neither you nor I should be sorry for it. Do your work manfully As for me, sure my Lord Marquis will make me a trooper, now I am no good for the foot." With these words, he coolly drew his knife, without flinching cut away the skin with his own hand, and gave the leg to a comrade to bury. Eventually he recovered of his wound and was actually made a trooper... ...The discipline, courage, endurance, cheerfulness, and fun of the Irish through this campaign are evidenced by all contemporary authorities, and should have secured for them the treatment due to true soldiers."

After Aberdeen, Montrose moved by way of Kintore, Strathdon, Glenavon and Tomintoul to Strathspey, then back to Atholl, which he reached on October 4 1644. He "despatched [*Alasdair*] MacDonald with a party to the Highlanders, to urge them to join, and force such as refused", and it was on this mission that *Alasdair* returned to Ardnamurchan and raised the siege of Mingary Castle, as described by Rev. Weir. Meantime Montrose made his way up into Badenoch, constantly on the move and trying to avoid outright battle whilst he awaited *Alasdair*'s return.

John MacDonald, the Captain of ClanRanald, had sent 40 cows for the use of *Alasdair*'s men, and when *Alasdair* returned to his rendezvous with Montrose his force was augmented by the Captain and 500 of his clansmen. Winter was upon the Royalists by now, when with incredible audacity Montrose decided to visit himself and his army upon the personal estates of the arch-rebel, Archibald, eighth Earl of Argyll. Noted for his cowardice, or perhaps, in Wishart's kinder words, merely "destitute of physical courage", Argyll now surpassed even himself. He was quietly ensconced at Inveraray on 13 December 1644, believing himself to be utterly protected by the sheer expanse of his demesnes and the difficulty of the terrain, when word reached him that the King's forces were almost literally at his very door, barely two miles away.

He appears to have been completely stricken by panic: "Irresolute and well-nigh beside himself with dread, he scrambled into a fishing-boat and saved himself by flight, abandoning his friends, clansmen and the whole of his country to fate and the mercy of the enemy." There was little mercy – Montrose divided his force into three parts, commanded respectively by himself, by *Alasdair MacCholla* and by the Captain of ClanRanald. Throughout the next six long weeks, those of Argyll's rebels that were caught in arms were put to death, and "they then gave their villages and cots to the avenging flames and burnt them to the ground, an act of retaliation on Argyll, who had been the first of all to wage this cruel war of fire and sword upon his countrymen."

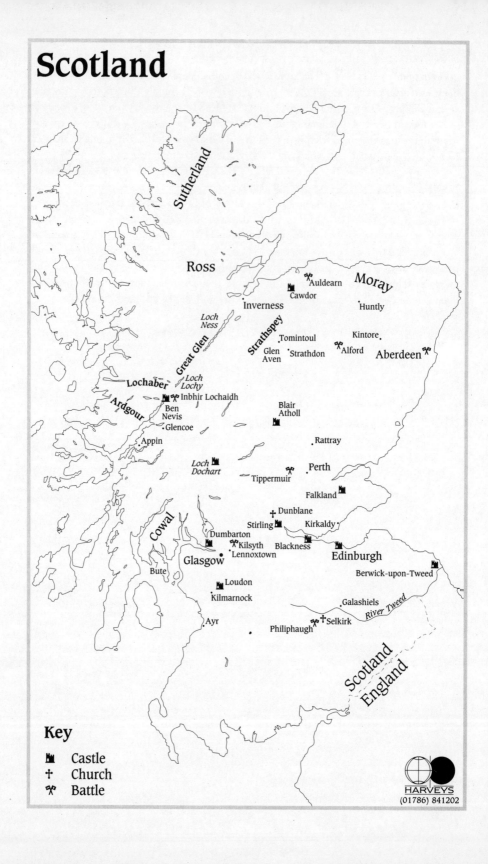

Scotland

Sutherland

Ross

Moray

Auldearn �֎

Cawdor 🏰

Inverness

Huntly

Loch
Ness

Strathspey

Tomintoul

Kintore

Great Glen

Glen
Aven

Strathdon

Alford ✖

Aberdeen ✖

Lochaber

Loch
Lochy

Inbhir Lochaidh ✖🏰

Ardgour

Ben
Nevis

Blair
Atholl 🏰

Glencoe

Appin

Rattray

Loch
Dochart 🏰

Perth

Tippermuir ✖

Falkland 🏰

Cowal

Dunblane ✝

Stirling 🏰

Kirkaldy

Dumbarton 🏰

Kilsyth ✖

Blackness 🏰

Glasgow

Lennoxtown

Edinburgh 🏰

Bute

Berwick-upon-Tweed 🏰

Loudon 🏰

Kilmarnock

Galashiels

River Tweed

Ayr

Philiphaugh ✖

Selkirk ✝

Scotland

England

Key

🏰 Castle

✝ Church

✖ Battle

HARVEYS
(01786) 841202

13

THE YEAR OF GLORY – 1645

Fear Tollaidh nan Tighean

The great ravaging of Argyll's territory was comprehensive and sustained, lasting from 13 December 1644 until 29 January 1645; the forces of Montrose had been encouraged by the words of Angus *Mac Ailean Dubh*, a volunteer from Glencoe: "I know every farm belonging to *Mac Cailinmhor* (i.e. Argyll); and if tight houses, fat cattle, and clear water will suffice, you need never want". Col. James MacDonnell gave a contemporary account, preserved in the *Carte Mss.* in the Bodleian Library: "...(we) burned and preyed all this country from (Lawers) to Auchenbrake's, whose land and country we burned and preyed; and so throughout all Argyle we left neither house nor hold unburned, nor corn nor cattle that belonged to the whole name of Campbell. Such of his Majesty's friends as lived near them joined with us ..."

It was probably at this time that *Alasdair* gained the name of *"Fear Tollaidh nan Tighean"* (Wrecker of Houses). It is perhaps not suprising that many of the traditions of Kintyre represent *Alasdair* and his men as harsh and cruel, for this was an army on the move, trying to divide the energies of the King's rebels and, no doubt, many individual members of that army were anxious to gain personal revenge for past wrongs. *Alasdair MacCholla* had a personal interest in putting increased pressure on Argyll, for his father and brothers remained captive and Argyll had preferred to countenance the death of *Alasdair*'s own hostages (the clutch of covenanting ministers) rather than come to terms.

Despite all this, there are a few tales of *Alasdair*'s generosity and humanity, such as when he was encamped at *Maol Dubh* (between Tarbert and Loch Gilp), plundering the countryside and burning houses. There was an inn at the roadside, *Taigh an Draighnein* (House of the Thornbush), and when *Alasdair* asked for water, the landlady brought him milk. He told his men to be careful to spare the house *"oir cha mhór ged a dh'fhàg sinn aon taigh ann an dùthaich gus luchd gabhail rathaid a dh'fhaotainn fàrdaich ann."* ("for it is not a lot for us to leave one house in the locality where travellers can get shelter.")

Other sources give quite detailed insights into the course of events and Patrick Gordon, in "Britane's Distemper" recalls that it was the "McNabes, or rather M'Enabotes, there first dissent being from ane abote", who had facilitated the entry of the royalist forces into the fastnesses of Argyll, by deceiving and overpowering the Campbell garrison of the island castle in Loch Dochart. *Neil MacMhuirich,* quoted by Stevenson, summarised the whole campaign: "In short, all the territories of *MacCailin* (Argyll) were spoiled and burnt on that occasion, and eight hundred four score and fifteen men were killed in these countries without battle or skirmish having taken place in them." Whatever the truth about civilian atrocities, it seems quite clear that such of Argyll's military followers as could be found were routinely executed.

"When they had wasted Ardgyll, and left it like a desert, they marched to Lorne", where a number of the Stewarts "comes in to the general promising from henceforth to be good and faithfull subjects, as [also] many others of good quality, upon whose submission they were spared; one of the which was M'Condachie Anrain... this M'Condachie being secretly a malcontent.... who with a forseeing and politic providence esteems this but a violent tempest which should have an end, and that Ardgyll would again be master of all... M'Condachie there-fore betrays his trust and attacks a party of unsuspecting royalists, but the latter manage to hold their ground until help arrives and then respond with vigour. M'Codachie himself is sore wounded, and not able to stand, [and] is carried off with a shameful retreat, although he was twice their number. After this his base proceeding, he thought it not safe to return to his own house, but retires to the strong castle of Dunstaffnage, a place that of old the kings them-selves had built and dwelt in."

Frustratingly, this must have been as close as *Alasdair* was to get to his father and brothers, who had been held captive in that very castle. Although Dunstaffnage never fell to *Alasdair*, he was too close for comfort and Argyll had his prisoners removed to Dunbarton for greater security.

The battle of Inbhir Lochaidh

At the end of January, the Royalist force made its way through Glencoe and into Lochaber "being come as far as the head of Loch Ness, where there came certain intel-ligence that Ardgyll was entered Lochaber with three thousand men.." A council of war ensued and it was decided not to continue against Inverness and Moray but to "returne to Lochaber and discusse that armie first."…. "and because it was to be feared that, if he got intelligence of their coming, he would shun the fight till he might join with those forces [of Ross, Sutherland and Moray], or to have them ready to fall on at one time with, therefore they return an other way than they came, and that was through the hills, although they were at [the] time covered with snow." In these simple terms, Patrick Gordon explains the reasoning behind one of the most remarkable military manoeu-vres yet on record; in the depth of winter, bare-legged and with minimum equipment, *Alasdair MacCholla* was to lead his men across some of the most difficult terrain in Europe and then, without rest or pause, to launch an attack upon a mighty force of fresh, well equipped men, united in defiant and open rebellion.

> "They marched two days through the mountains, in great extremity of cold, want of victuals, and in necessity of all things, yet their great courage and patience did bravely sustain it. Nor ought their extreme sufferings at that time ever be forgotten; for that day they fought, the general himself, and the earl of Airely, who had stayed with him since the battle of St. Johnestoune, those two noblemen (I say) had no more to break their fast before they went to battle but a little meal, mixed with cold water, which, out of a hollow dish, they did pick up with their knives for want of spoons, and this was those noblemen's best fare. One may judge what wants the rest of the army must [have] suffered. The most part of them had not tasted a bit of bread these two days, marching high mountains in knee-deep snow, and wading brooks and rivers up to their girdle. About the shutting in of the night, they fell upon the skirts of Ardgylles army, two or three miles from the castle of Inverlochy, where himself lay. Those retiring quickly gave the alarm to the whole camp."

Having lost the advantage of surprise, Montrose (on *Alasdair*'s advice) sent out "ane forlorne hope, who, with continuall fyre and shote held them sturreing so as they gotte no tyme to resolve [draw up a plan] in this confusione." All the same, Argyll himself managed to find time to come up with a "resolve" in short order – losing not a moment, he withdrew himself to the safety of his galley, the "*Dubh-luideanach*", accompanied only by Sir James Rollocke, his brother-in-law, Sir John Wauchope of Nithrie and Mr. Mungo Law. "It is reported those two last was sent from Edinburgh with him to bear witness of the expulsion of those rebels, for so they were still pleased to term the Royalists." Archibald Colquhoun of Port Appin told J.F.Campbell a traditional account in which Argyll then sailed to Corpach, where he was joined by Lochiel (who was married to a Campbell). "*Théid mi féin leat, ach cha gheall mi gun théid mo dhaoine leat*"; (I will go with you myself, but I cannot promise that my men will go with you). "Lochiel went into the galley with Argyle and they sailed to a place on the Ardgour side, called *Camus nan Gall* (Strangers' Bay), where they had a view of the battle."

They were not the only ones who chose to view the proceedings from a distance, for the Gaelic bard *Iain Lom* ("Satirical John") had already established himself on the slopes behind Inverlochy Castle and, according to Archibald Colquhoun, it was he who encouraged Lochiel's men down from the braes of Corpach and into the action. "When the battle began the Campbells set on fiercely and it seemed as if they would route the MacDonalds. *Ian Lom* shouted as loudly as he could *"Tha Alasdair mac Colla a' dol air ais!"* ("Alasdair MacColla is retreating!"). Immediately, Lochiel's men came to the assistance of the MacDonalds."

The battle itself is too well-documented to bear further detailed review. The contemporary account by Patrick Gordon is as succinct as any and is given here to speak for itself (spelling modernised):

"Upon Sunday, the second of February, being Candlemass day, *anno* 1645, about the sun rising, both the armies draws up in battle. By Auchinbreck, as general for that day, the two regiments Argyll had brought from Stirling were placed in the right and left wings, and some highlanders with them; their van was a strong battalion of highlanders, with guns, bows and axes; in the rear or main battle, were all their prime men, and the greatest strength of the army, with two pieces of ordnance.

"The Marquis of Montrose divides his army also in four battles, the major, Alexander M'Donald, had the leading of the right wing; Colonel O'Cahan ["Occaen"] had the leading of the left wing, both those were Irish [forces]; the Stewarts of Appin, with those of Athol, Glencoe and Lochaber, had the van. Donald Farquharson was gone to raise more forces in Badenoch and the rest of Huntly's highlands. MacDonald, the captain of Clanranald, and Glengarry had the rear brought up by Colonel James MacDonald. The Marquis had a reserve of Irish [troops] and other highlanders. It fell to O'Kane, with the left wing, to charge Argyll's right wing; he [was] commanded by the major not to give fire till he gave it in their breasts, and this course in the right wing he rightly observes also; and thus patiently receiving their shot, without giving fire, till they fired their beards, both wings made a cruel havock of the enemies; leaping in amongst them with their swords and targes [shields], they quickly put them to disorder, and disperses them over all the field. Their van, by this, perceiving themselves naked, and their wings broken and dispersed that should [have] flanked them, did hardly withstand the shock of Montrose' van, who charged them, and followed their charge in a close body, with such strength and fury as they were forced to give back upon their rear; who, instead of opening their ranks to receive them, and give the enemies a new charge, they quit their standing, breaks their order, and flies confusedly towards the castle, wherein they had placed fifty soldiers. Sir Thomas Ogilvie, with a troop of horse, affronts two hundred of them that made for the castle, and forced them to flee with the rest up the side of the lake or firth. In this conflict, this brave gentleman received a shot, whereof he died soon after, to the no small regret of the whole army.

"The Marquis of Argyll, standing off a little in the sea, and had seen this overthrow, to his great grief no doubt, not staying to see his enemies pursue the flight, which continued for seven or eight miles; and if they had not been wearied with a long march, standing all the night after in battle [formation], and fainting for want of food, there had few or none escaped. In this battle, the laird of Auchinbreck was killed, with fourten barons of the name of Campbell, two and twenty men of quality taken prisoners, and seventeen hundred killed of the army.

"In the castle of Inverlochy there were fifty of the Stirling regiment, with their commanders, that got their lives; but of two hundred highlanders, none escaped the clan Donald fury. This happy and fortunate leader, having set all things in order after the battle, retires towards Moray with his small but victorious army."

The battle of Inverlochy took place on "the day of the Purification of the Blessed Mary, mother of God and ever Virgin", as Bishop Wishart helpfully reminds us and is famously celebrated by *Iain Lom*, a contemporary of *Alasdair* and a kinsman; as mentioned above, he accompanied the Royalist force on that heroic march through the snow-covered hills and was an eyewitness of the bloody encounter.

> *"Alasdair nan geurlann sgaiteach,*
> *Gheall thu 'n dé a bhith cur ás daibh;*
> *...Alasdair mhic Cholla ghasda,*
> *Làmh dheas a sgoltach nan caisteal,*
> *Chuir thu 'n ruaig air Ghallaibh glasa,*
> *'S ma dh'òl iad càl chuir thu asd' e....*

"Alasdair with your sharp-edged blades, yesterday you pledged to confound them ... Alasdair, handsome son of Coll, accomplished destroyer of castles, you put the gallowglasses to flight and knocked the very stuffing out of them..."

Less formal was *Iain Lom*'s delighted quip as he watched the fleeing Campbells struggling across the ford at the foot of Ben Nevis, swollen by winter snows, unable to keep their feet and their headgear floating off at their ducking: "*A Dhuimhneacha Dhuimhneacha, cuimhnichibh 'ur boineidean*" ("Campbells, Campbells, mind your bonnets...")

Alasdair's personal success at Inverlochy included a final confrontation with Sir Duncan Campbell of Auchinbreck, who had been recalled from Ireland to lead Argyll's forces and thereby meet his doom. With his father and brothers still held hostage, *Alasdair* is said to have offered Auchinbreck his choice between the sword and the noose, eliciting a response which was to become proverbial "*Dà dhiù gun aon roghainn*" ("two choices, no pick"), upon which *Alasdair* despatched him at his own hand. In fact, although *Alasdair* in person killed Auchinbreck, it must surely have been in heat of battle since, regardless of any other consideration, Auchinbreck would have been a valuable prize and *Alasdair* would not have wanted to waste him. The actual event is described graphically by Grant: "the gallant Sir Duncan Campbell of Auchinbreck was slain by Major-General Alester MacColl, who, by one blow of a two-handed claymore, swept off his head and helmet together."

Release of the hostages

As it was, a number of valuable hostages were taken, including "Bearbrick", the infamous Sir Donald Campbell, an ardent henchman of Argyll. He had destroyed Clan MacIan and usurped their lands, he had personally participated in the raid on Colonsay which had destroyed *Colla Ciotach's* family, and it was his castle of Mingary which had been overthrown by *Alasdair MacCholla* and which was now a royalist stronghold. This must have been a sweet encounter for his captor but short-savoured; negotiations began immediately for the exchange of hostages.

Argyll himself, having prudently avoided the field and deserted his men, re-appeared at Edinburgh a few days later, on February 12th, where he was observed to carry his left arm in a sling. Having been under pressure from the kirk to secure the release of *Alasdair*'s clerical hostages, Argyll now found himself under additional pressure from his own clansmen. By now, two of the ministers had already died in captivity at Mingary, to the fury of the Commissioners of the covenanting General Assembly, who expressly:

> "lay it home to the Marquess of Argyll's door that his Lordship might have gotten these holy men of God liberated, if his Lordship, for the three Ministers, would have set at liberty old Coll Kittach and his two sons Archibald and Angus ....Now Argyll (though too late) acknowledge's God's justice against him in the loss of his best friends and wasting of his lands for his too small respect to these faithfull men of God, whom he might have gotten restored to him at first on reasonable conditions, but his deep hatred against old Coll hindered all."

In fact, by this time arrangements for Coll's release were already under way. At some point during the ravaging of his territories, Argyll had moved his prisoners from Dunstaffnage to Dumbarton Castle for greater security, where the keeper is recorded as having complained to the Estates that he had neither manpower nor resources to hold them, and requested that he be relieved of them. Almost as soon as Argyll reached Edinburgh, on 14 February 1645, he was commissioned by Parliament to transfer Coll and his two sons to the Tolbooth, in Edinburgh, but it quickly became clear that they must instead be returned to Dunstaffnage Castle, from which convenient location it would possible to arrange an exchange with the hostages at Mingary.

No doubt there was an element of secrecy in the arrangements for the transfer, and at some point an inquisitive bystander who spotted *Colla Ciotach* and the other prisoners was fobbed off with an unlikely yarn. This bystander was taken in by the story and passed it on, and so created a rumour which eventually reached Edinburgh and the Commissioners of the General Assembly, who thereby gained the impression that Coll was no longer available for exchange, having been murdered in captivity:

> "While Montrose and Allaster MacDonald was wasting and burning his bounds, he [Argyll] sends his prisoner, old Coll, to Captain Gillespie in Kirkcaldie with order to keep him sicker

[securely] under the deck till he, and no other but he, should send written orders for his re-delivery, which order was sent soon by one of Argyll's captarons, who upon the sight of the order received him and hanged him over the ship's side, betwixt Innerkething and Kirkcaldy. So was he both hanged and drowned. My author [authority] says that he was in Gillespie's ship when he saw old Kittagh delivered to the captain, and when he came to shore at Kirkcaldie he heard that he was hanged."

Presumably Argyll's officers had not wished to parade the fact that they were moving such important captives through a war-zone. Even at sea, they were very vulnerable; indeed throughout this period the North Channel was haunted by fast and well-armed Royalist privateers from Dunkirk, hence the attempt to have their charges spirited away with the minimum of fuss. The prisoners were successfully transferred and on 1 May Argyll's agent, William Stirling of Auchyle, arrived at Duart Castle in Mull to meet with *Alasdair MacCholla*'s representatives. He was authorised to negotiate an exchange for the prisoners in Mingary Castle and at long last *Colla Ciotach* and his two sons, Angus and Gillespie were released, together with Gillespie's own son, Coll, and *Colla Ciotach*'s son-in-law, brother to MacDonald of Largie. So it was that Rev. James Hamilton of Dumfries finally obtained his freedom, to the relief of the Covenanting clergymen at Edinburgh, and to the discomfiture of Argyll.

In "Memorialls of the Trubles" we are told that "Mr. McDonald, his father and his tuo sones, was sett to libertie, keeped be Argyle in strong firmness most wrongously diverss years bygone. Bot how soon they wan free, they glaidly came in to Montross' service, who was brave cavilleires and weill willed doubtless." This accords with Professor MacKinnon who states as tradition *"gun robh Colla 's a dhithis mac, Gilleasbuig 's Aonghus, anns gach blàr a chuir Alasdair le Montròs"* ("that Colla and his two sons, Gillespie and Angus, were at every battle that *Alasdair* fought for Montrose"). In fact, since we know that they were in captivity until May, it seems that the only major battle available to them will have been Kilsyth, but nonetheless we can be confident that they were fully committed to the Royalist cause.

Certainly *Alasdair* was unable to join his family immediately after they were released, for matters had moved swiftly since Inverlochy and he had been fully occupied. On 19 February, Elgin surrendered to the Royalists, but on 4 March, Lord John Graham, Montrose's eldest son, died at Gordon Castle, apparently exhausted by the stress and rigours of the campaign. Meantime, *Alasdair* had been on yet another recruiting drive through the west: "To recruit the ranks, Alaster MacColl, now a general, taking with him a regiment of his trusty Antrim men, went off even further than before into the Highlands, to obtain fresh levies." Rev. Hill states that the recruits included Sir Lachlan MacLean of Mull, at the head of eleven hundred men.

Battle of Auldearn

Alasdair and his men had rejoined Montrose after that foray and now, 9 May 1645, just a few days after *Colla Ciotach* was released, there came another splendid victory for Montrose, this time against the army of General Hurry. This was the battle of Auldearn, not far to the southeast of Inverness, and once more *Alasdair* excelled himself, with all observers combined in his praise. Even Rev. Wishart, no strong supporter, writes thus:

"Macdonald, a brave man, but readier with his hand than his head, hasty in battle and bold to rashness, stung by the taunts and scoffs of the enemy, disdained to shelter himself behind dykes and bushes, and, contrary to orders, threw himself with his men outside of their strong position. His rashness cost him dear. The enemy, who were far stronger both in horse and numbers, and most of them veteran troops, drove his men back pell-mell, and had he not withdrawn them to a neighbouring enclosure just in time, they would every one of them have been lost, and the royal standard with them. Rash as he had been, he atoned for his error by his splendid courage in bringing off his men. The last to retire, and covering himself with a huge target, single-handed he withstood the thickest of the enemy. Some of the pikemen, by whom he was hard pressed, again and again pierced his target with the points of their weapons, which he mowed off with his broadsword by threes and fours at a sweep..."

It is a magnificent image, entirely worthy of *MacCholla Chiotaich*. All told, about 3000 of the Covenanting rebel foot were killed, although much of the cavalry escaped "by a flight more timely than honourable".

At the end of May, *Alasdair* parted from Montrose again, in order to visit eastern Ross-shire and to bring the clans of Lovat back to their rightful loyalty. Subsequently he made his way to the western seaboard, on a recruiting drive that must have been quite exhilarating – he was an acknowledged hero, at the head of a victorious force whose wave of victories seemed likely to drive the hated Covenanters from the Highlands and bring about the restoration of the ancient order. Those who joined his force had tasted excitement, victory and spoils as well as hardship.

It was on this same trip to the west that *Alasdair* rejoined his father and brothers, freed at last after some six years of captivity. Despite the story that *Colla Ciotach* then followed *Alasdair* and was present during all his remaining battles, this seems unlikely for a man of 75 years (and increasingly mentioned as "old Coll" in contemporary sources). More probably, *Colla Ciotach* made his way to the islands of the west and passed from isle to isle, renewing old friendships and basking in the success of a youngest son whose exploits so closely reflected those of his own prime. He will have been a powerful recruiting sergeant and no doubt his other sons will have played their own part, not least in monitoring the position in Ireland and assessing the best hopes for the remnant of Clan Donald of the South.

His commitments in the west prevented *Alasdair* from participating in Montrose's next great success, the battle of Alford on 2 July 1645, but his friend and kinsman Manus O'Cahan was there to represent him and, although as usual *Alasdair*'s "Irishes" bore the brunt of the battle and ensured the victory, they were ably supported by the clansmen of the west and by the Gordons. Lord Gordon himself fell in the battle, a loss that was keenly felt by all who knew him, not least by Montrose. The battle of Alford was on 2 July 1645, the Feast of the Visitation of the Virgin, a fact that was noted by both sides in the conflict.

Battle of Kilsyth

After Alford, *Alasdair* returned once more to join Montrose and the main force, which was now augmented by some 1400 additional men whom he had raised in the west. The forces of the Covenanters were by now concentrated in the vicinity of Stirling, to which town their administration had removed now that Edinburgh was wracked by plague. Adroitly, Montrose was able to lure those forces into an ill-judged attack upon him at Kilsyth, and was helped in this by disunity amongst the rebels. The Covenanters had a peculiar fascination with committees (all being equals under God) and their general, Baillie, had become so disenchanted by this lack of authority that he had resigned his commission and was by now merely working out his notice. Wishing to avoid blame for any possible reverse, he now allowed his responsibilities to be shared with a campaign committee, one that actually included Argyll!

Having pressed for an engagement at Kilsyth, the rebel "tacticians" decided at the last moment to alter the disposition of their army and for a brief period there was confusion in their ranks. In that moment lay the Royalist opportunity and, without waiting for any command from Montrose, *Alasdair MacCholla* seized the initiative and launched his red-blooded Highland Charge. Montrose understood what was afoot, immediately ordered the rest of his army to advance on all fronts and, being caught completely wrongfooted, the rebels were thrown into total disarray and overwhelmed. Some 4000 were certainly slain, perhaps as many as the 6000 suggested by Rev. Wishart:

> "Of the Covenanting nobles, who were present in large numbers at this battle, some saved themselves by a timely flight, and, thanks to their good horses, reached the strong castle of Stirling. Others slipped away to the Firth of Forth, and got aboard some vessels at anchor near the shore. Among these was Argyll, who now, for the third time, took boat and escaped aboard a ship. Even then he did not think himself safe till they had weighed anchor and stood away far out to sea."

The battle of Kilsyth was fought on 15 August 1645, the Feast of the Assumption of the Virgin Mary. After Kilsyth, all Scotland lay at Montrose's feet: using the army that *Alasdair* had brought from Ireland, and strengthened by the clansmen that had been raised through the power of MacDonald, Montrose had conquered a kingdom. It was all the more incredible when one remembers that Montrose himself had been forced to enter Scotland in disguise and had failed to raise any significant force – indeed would not even have revived the support of the Gordons had not *Alasdair* given him the aura of credibility. Now that Montrose had achieved his aim he had to secure the realm and, although he recognised that his army would have to develop a wider base than Highlanders and Irishmen could provide, he was not the man to underestimate his debt.

In the immediate aftermath of the victory, Montrose moved to Glasgow whilst, on 19 August, *Alasdair* led some 600 of his men on a sally through Kilmarnock and Ayrshire and "met with a hearty welcome, even at Loudon Castle, where the Chancellor's lady embraced him, and having entertained him very sumptuously, sent her servant John Halden with him to present her service to the Marquis." The purpose of the expedition was to forestall the efforts of the Earls of Cassilis and Eglinton, who sought to rally opposition and "were reported to have raised a tumultuous body of about 4,000 men" but such was *Alasdair*'s renown that they would not face his much smaller force and instead dispersed "in the greatest terror" on word of his approach. The inhabitants of the region fell over themselves in their anxiety to disown the Covenanters and to acknowledge the rightful authority of the King. Meantime, Montrose had established his own authority and subsequently felt strong enough to remove his forces from

Glasgow. He encamped at Bathgate on 20 August, which is where *Alasdair* rejoined him on his return from the southwest.

Sir Alastair MacDonald, Knight

On 2 September, Montrose received the King's commission as Lord Governor of Scotland, given under the Great Seal and proclaimed by herald. "Then in a short but stately speech he commended the valour and loyalty of his soldiers, and assured them of his warm esteem. Before the whole army he singled out Macdonald for special praise, and by virtue of his royal commission conferred on him the honour of knighthood." It was with pride and hope that the new Sir Alastair MacDonald set out on his travels once more, on 3 September, although now accompanied by only a small portion of his own force, about 120 men.

It seems that he was now engaged to assist Sir James Lamont in raising Royalist recruits in Cowal and was further charged to accept some 300 of the Highlanders to be under his command. It was agreed that the Highlanders would take a brief furlough and return to Glasgow "within forty days in greater strength and numbers." Thus *Alasdair* and his men were to make their way through the west, raising loyal clansmen before returning to Glasgow by 13 October (in good time for the parliament that had been summoned by Montrose, to meet there on 20 October).

In later years, writers alleged that *Alasdair* and his men turned their back on the cause at this point and deserted the flag, so it is worth stressing that Montrose actually ordered the Highlanders to take this leave and "urged them to settle their affairs with diligence". No doubt Montrose recognised their need to see to their harvest and to the condition of their homes and families, but he also will have wished to avoid any depradations being carried out upon the properties of the lowland burgesses. It was essential to act with discipline and authority, since Montrose, as Lord-Governor, was the King's personal representative. He took the opportunity to thank *Alasdair* publicly and with some formality, in the King's name and *Alasdair* "in a formal speech" returned his thanks and "solemnly promised" to return in good time.

Meantime, rather than retain an idle body of soldiers unoccupied on the fringes of the tempting city of Glasgow, Montrose himself departed on an expedition into the Lowlands; Rev. Wishart states that this journey was undertaken on the specific orders of the King and was intended to lead on to the Tweed, where he was to link up with a body of cavalry which Charles was to despatch from England. Thus strengthened, Montrose's army would be an ample match for the Covenanting expeditionary forces under Leslie, known to be poised to return. Whilst *Alasdair* secured the west, the Gordons, a substantial and important proportion of his original force, were to make their own way back to their homelands in the north-east.

Since Edinburgh was plague-ridden and presented no threat, one imagines that this disposition of Montrose's forces was not without logic. Whilst he carried the King's commission into the Lowlands and Borders, the balance of his admittedly small army would be more mobile and less vulnerable when in the field, victuals and accommodation could be more readily secured and the men, returning as victors amongst their own kinsmen, could be wonderful recruiting agents.

It must be remembered that this was a time of near-total success: "Everything was thus succeeding to Montrose's wish. The northern parts of the kingdom were secured behind him. The road to the south lay open. Everywhere the strength of the Covenanters was broken. Their leaders, whose guilty consciences despaired of pardon, were driven from the realm." Towns and cities clamoured to prove their loyalty, the Royalist prisoners had been released, money and recruits were promised on every side. The population was released from bondage and heady with relief – it seemed that nothing was impossible.

In the event of course, matters were to take an unfortunate turn as events in England came inexorably to their own conclusion. Later, at the Restoration, it would never do to admit that the vast bulk of lowland Scots had, in truth, never been loyal to their King and it became the task of historians to find some other explanation for Montrose's waning. They needed a scapegoat, but that they chose to blame the loyal and faithful Gordons (said to have departed in a fit of pique) seems strange. That *Alasdair* has also been accused of deserting the cause seems downright incredible, but the charge was necessitated by revisionism and is explicable within the wider context of the second half of the seventeenth century. For our own purposes it is sufficient to review the simple course of events as they happened, bearing in mind that neither *Alasdair* nor *Colla* have ever been seen as other than heroic throughout the lands of the Gaels.

Defeat of Montrose at Philiphaugh

Firstly, we follow Montrose. Leaving Bothwell on 4 September and parting next day from Aboyne and most of the Gordons at Calder Castle, Montrose made his way to Galashiels, where he was met on 7 September by the Marquis of Douglas and 1000 cavalry reinforcements. Sadly, nemesis was at hand, in the form of the redoubtable General David Leslie and his army, who had crossed the border at Berwick the previous day; such was the latent support for the Covenanters that Montrose received little warning of his proximity.

On the morning of 13 September 1645, Leslie and a force of some 4000 men fell upon Montrose and his army encamped at Philiphaugh, near Selkirk. Montrose had had inadequate sentinels and was suprised, his forces were in complete confusion and many of his officers were not even in the camp. Within two hours it was all over and, although Montrose and most of his broken forces managed to run away unscathed, *Alasdair*'s seasoned Irish troops put up some resistance and only agreed to lay down their arms under a promise of quarter. At Leslie's command, and in complete abrogation of any shred of honour, they were thereupon murdered out of hand with the exception of three officers.[1]

Although Montrose and the survivors of his forces quickly regrouped at Atholl (late September 1645), there was little point in *Alasdair* re-joining him. The original Irish army which had been raised by Antrim had been largely destroyed at Philiphaugh and *Alasdair* could do more to help the King's cause by remaining in the west, raising the clans, harrying the Campbells and maintaining communication with Ireland, where there remained a strong body of potential support.

Montrose continued with a desultory campaign, and mounted an ineffectual siege of Inverness in April, only to be beaten off on 10 May 1646. The loyal Gordons also continued the struggle and under Aboyne captured Aberdeen on 14 May, little knowing that the King himself had become a prisoner in the hands of the Scottish rebel army nine days earlier. When the news of the King's capture was confirmed, Aboyne disbanded his forces and soon afterwards, on direct orders from the King, Montrose followed suit. In a short but poignant scene, the remnants of his force were stood down at Rattray, in Perthshire, on 30 July 1646 and Montrose himself retired abroad to Bergen in Norway (although not without considerable difficulty).

Notes

1 The three officers not immediately murdered at Philiphaugh were Stewart, Laghtman and O'Cahan. The latter was *Alasdair*'s loyal kinsman, Manus O'Cahan, who had commanded the left wing at Inverlochy and had figured prominently in all the victories, and who had been left to command the bulk of *Alasdair*'s force which, as has been seen, had been left to augment Montrose. Both Laghtman and O'Cahan were subsequently hanged in Edinburgh.

14.

THE REARGUARD – 1646

After Philiphaugh

In the light of Philiphaugh we can see that although Montrose fully deserves his special place in Scotland's affections as a charismatic and noble figure, his military skills were at a tactical rather than a practical level. At this important period, when all remaining hope relied upon a sustained *guerilla* campaign, he was totally eclipsed by the dogged staying-power of both Huntly and *Alasdair MacCholla*.

The original plan for the King's campaign in Scotland had envisaged Huntly raising the Gordons in the north-east, whilst Montrose was to raise an army amongst his own supporters and the whole force to be supplemented by an Irish army which was to be provided by the Earl of Antrim; even in this, Montrose had been the weak link. The original rendezvous had been planned for 1 April 1644 and Huntly rose on time, although his force was not enough to resist Argyll unassisted, but when Montrose arrived he was unable to rendezvous with Huntly, failed to raise any support and had to withdraw. It was only after the arrival of Antrim's forces under *Alasdair MacCholla*, in early July, that enough impetus could be created to overwhelm the revolutionaries.

Things were different in the aftermath of Philiphaugh, for the scattered Royalist forces could not now be re-united and each component would have to be self-reliant. Antrim's army had been destroyed – barely 120 men survived, but they were with *Alasdair* and amongst his own people, and Antrim immediately organised reinforcements and new equipment. Almost incredibly, *Alasdair* and his faithful Irishmen continued the war for almost two years in the heartlands of Argyll, and in this period raised once more the support of the loyal clans of the west – MacDonalds, MacLeans, MacDougalls and their separate septs, united now as never before. In this work, *Alasdair* was warmly supported by *Colla Ciotach* and by his own brothers.

The *guerrilla* war in the west was a fierce one, but it must be remembered that after the surrender at Philiphaugh it was not only the Irish soldiers that were murdered, but in separate incidents their wives and children also. It was normal for families to accompany their menfolk on campaign, but they took no part in the fighting and even after such a defeat as Philiphaugh would normally be left to bury their dead and make what shift for themselves that they could.

Not this time. Wishart records that

"The enemy did not pursue those who had escaped, but fell to plundering the baggage, where they made a piteous slaughter of the poor women, boys, and camp-followers, without distinction of age or sex. ... Many of those who had fallen into the hands of the country folk had been savagely murdered. Those whom even these barbarous wretches had spared in pity, were driven together, and, by command of the Covenanting chiefs, thrown headlong from a high bridge and drowned in the river below, men, women, and babes at the breast. As they struggled to the side they were beaten down with bludgeons and hurled back into the waters."

Reports of these atrocities will have reached *Alasdair* and his men towards the end of September, and were soon followed by further reports of the torture and execution of those of their comrades-in-arms that had surrendered on terms. It was inevitable that there would be reprisals, some of which provided the basis for stories which were preserved in folklore and which give an insight into the events of 1646.

Angus MacCholla and the Factor

Colla Ciotach's son (or step-son), Angus, has not retained personal prominence in the record of these momentous times, but Angus has a particular place in the folk-memory of Colonsay, his island home; the following story is quite detailed but has not always been dated precisely. It seems to the author that from internal evidence it is chronologically best suited to this period, surely after May of 1645 but most probably in the autumn, when in the light of the atrocities outlined above, Clan Donald will have thirsted for blind revenge.

Professor MacKinnon gives the story quite concisely, but without any exact date, when he begins by saying that the Duke of Argyll had taken possession of Colonsay, without any lease at all, relying merely upon strength of arms:

> "Argyll installed a factor, *Domhnall Ballach Mac Eóghain* ("Poxed or Spotted Donald McEwan"), who was a very harsh man, particularly upon the poor and on the widows and orphans. Between rent and rule, tax and tribute, there was no living left to the people. This oppressor even put a tax on the shellfish of the shore. Angus *MacCholla* and his people made an incursion onto the island *"chan 'eil iomradh có bhliadhna, ach b'ann ri linn cogadh Mhontróis"* – "the year is not recorded but it was at the time of Montrose's war" [i.e. 1643 – 1646]. He met a poor widow accompanied by her only cow, on a halter, going to pay "daimh-ursann" – "calps" [abolished by law since 1617!], a form of death-tax, to Domhnall Balloch. She told her story to Angus.
>
> "Go you home", said Angus, "I will arrange the matter with Domhnall Balloch". He went with a boy to Oransay, where the bailiff was staying. They went in. Domhnall Balloch offered snuff to Angus. *"A bheil iteag agad?"* – "Have you a feather?" asked Angus [snuff was commonly taken from a feather, rather than from the hand]. *"Chan 'eil iteag agam", fhreagair Domhnall Ballach, "nam bitheadh cha robh mi so romhad-sa an nochd"* – "I have no feather" [i.e. to fly], replied Domhnall Balloch, "or I would not be here before you now". There was no further chat between them.

Professor MacKinnon continues:

> "The church land of Oransay was a sanctuary to the blackest sinner as long as he was beyond the Sanctuary Cross that stood for many generations in the middle of the strand between Colonsay and Oransay. But the altar itself would not be enough to give shelter to Donald Balloch. The men did not put the inhuman fellow to death in Oransay. They took him across the strand, tied him to the standing stone that still stands in Lèana na h' Eaglais in Balerominmore, shot him with seven musket balls, and sent word to Argyll that if he sent the likes of Domhnall Ballach to Colonsay, they would treat him the same way."

The account continues in a reference to Islay, wherein Angus and most of his men were engaged "in a mighty campaign of pillaging and spoiling", and this would accord with the known campaign carried out throughout Argyll's dominions over a period of several months, whilst reinforcements were arriving from Ireland. As before, this campaign humiliated Argyll and divided his military and strategic resources.

Murdoch McNeill gives very much the same details, but mentions that it was the **Marquis** of Argyll that sent *Domhnall Ballach*, and that it was "sometime about 1644"; (Lord Lorne had become the 8th Earl of Argyll in 1638 and only became Marquis in 1641)..Angus visited the island and met "a widow taking her only cow as a tribute (*damh-ursann*)" to *Domhnall Ballach*.

Symington Grieve says that the islanders had become desperate "so they called to their assistance Angus MacColl Ciotach MacDonald; he was the youngest son of Coll MacGillespick, and at this time was probably not much over forty years of age." In fact, if this was the Angus that was *Colla Ciotach*'s stepson, he was older than any of *Colla*'s own sons, but his age would support a date of about 1645 for the incident; the fact that Angus was "called to their assistance" suggests that he and all of *Colla*'s family were no longer resident on Colonsay but were known to be available and minded to help. Again, this indicates the autumn of 1645 which was a period for recruitment of supporters and harrying of Argyll.

Grieve's account mentions that Angus landed at Balnahard (at the north end of Colonsay) with a number of men and came down through Kilchattan:

> "on their way they met at the north side of the golf course at Machrins a woman **who was afterwards the stepmother of Angus**, returning from the Strand. She was weeping bitterly, and Angus and his men enquired the cause. She said that Donald Balloch had sent men who had taken away her only cow as *Daimh Ursainn*. She had followed the men to the Strand, as they were taking the cow to Oronsay, but the tide was in and they were waiting for it to recede. As she had failed in her entreaties to get back her cow, she was returning home to Kilchattan broken-hearted. She had, however, warned the men that she would have vengeance for this outrage.
>
> "What he had heard stirred up more deeply than ever the wrath of Angus. Telling the woman to follow him and his men as quickly as she could, he hurried off. When he reached the ford where the burn that runs down to Port Lobh is crossed, he met a woman with a child. He asked to what clan the child belonged, and was told it was a Campbell. In his excited state he seized the child and struck off its head with his sword. The place where this happened is still named Ath-nan-corp [Corpse Ford, close to the 6th hole on the golf course]. He and his men then hurried on to the Strand, where they found the men of Donald Ballach still waiting with the cow, as the tide had not gone far enough out for them to get across. They compelled the men to return the animal to its rightful owner, who by this time had arrived upon the scene. She was full of gratitude to Angus and his men for what they had done, and left them to go on to Oronsay to settle their mission with Donald Ballach."

The story is continued as before, including the incident concerning the feather and the interesting detail that they found Donald at home, eating his dinner, "which consisted of potatoes[1] and seal's meat." His home, almost certainly, will have been the former "Prior's House", wherein Sir Alexander MacDonald of Lochalsh had been murdered in 1496. Grieve describes him being hustled, with some of his followers, across the Strand to Colonsay, after which:

"They took them to Pàirc na h'eaglais, where they tied Donald to the large cross. Then seven of the factor's own men were compelled by Angus and his associates to shoot him with pistols. It is said they buried him close to the place where he was killed. .... Angus appears to have been quite fearless of any consequences from his outrage upon the factor. He is said to have written Argyll, saying that unless he sent a good man as factor of Colonsay and Oronsay he would kill every one of them.

"Argyll sent Colin Campbell, son of Campbell of Dunstaffnage, as factor, who proved himself to be a good and prudent man and kind to the inhabitants. He was three years upon the islands."

Thus, local tradition seems very clearly to put this incident to late 1645 or so, a period when Angus was exiled from Colonsay but at liberty and a date which would also permit Colin Campbell to become well-established prior to the mighty upheavals of 1647. Loder proposes that the factor being resident upon Oransay suggests that he was the agent of William Stirling of Auchyle (i.e. Argyll's steward) rather than that of Campbell of Ardesier (second son of Sir John Campbell of Calder), to whom Colonsay had been feued by Argyll in 1640 but who had died before 1642; it will be remembered that Auchyle last appeared when bargaining over the hostages in May. Of course, it is likely that the factor will have occupied Oronsay in any case, for the obvious reasons: the best farm and most easily worked, naturally fenced and defensible against casual depreda-tion, with safe havens and the opportunity for discreet comings-and-goings.

This writer rather suspects that Donald Ballach himself was one of the MacIains of Ardnamurchan whose lands and Castle of Mingary had been seized in 1612 by Mr. Donald Campbell (later to become Sir Donald Campbell of Ardnamurchan), acting on the instructions of the 7th Earl of Argyll. It was this same Donald Campbell who led the raid on Colonsay in 1639 and it was his castle that *Alasdair* had seized for his own headquarters. A formidable figure, "fleshed in blood from his verie infancie", he will have had little difficulty in finding some pliable *gaimbin*-man from among the remnants of the shattered MacIains.

On the matter of the year of the above incident, Ronald Black has put forward the interesting and well-argued suggestion that a better date would be before 1625 in which year, Margaret, sister of Sir James MacDonald, married Ranald of Keppoch and thus became **the stepmother of Angus**, as mentioned in Grieve's account. Black therefore considers it likely that the poor widow was Margaret herself. Unfortunately, although elegant, his proposal seems unlikely, for who was the husband that she had just lost? Why was she living in Kilchattan, rather than in Kiloran with the rest of the MacDonalds, at that period of reasonable prosperity? And why was she so poor at that time, when she was described by the Franciscan missionaries as *"Margareta Domhnaill, nobilis domina ex magna familia Domhnaldorum, quae praecipua est totius Scotiae familia, antiqui-tate et potentia spectabilis."* After all, she was clearly wealthy enough to have been a desirable prize to the much-married and discerning Keppoch.

In Colonsay it is assumed that the poor widow, whoever she was, became stepmother to Angus by the simple expedient of marrying *Colla Ciotach* himself; Mary had died long ago (in 1625 or soon after) and at the time of the incident *Colla* was at liberty, and probably was with Angus when he responded to the plea for help. By now *Colla* was 76yrs of age, a man of immense reputation despite his adversity; he was surrounded by glamour and, restored to liberty, had launched himself upon a glittering final crusade, specifically directed against the tyrant Argyll – what more natural than a union between a victim and this gallant? Very possibly he may have helped to drive the cow back to Kilchattan and perhaps paused to console the lady whilst Angus and the rest of the party went off to settle the factor.

The account of the incident opens with a reference to a landing in Colonsay at Balnahard, suggesting an arrival from the direction of Mull, perhaps even Mingary. *Domhnall Ballach* was shot at the same spot as had been the leaders of Clan MacDuffie[2], and afterwards the party continued through the Sound of Islay and on to rejoin the main campaign. After he arrived in Islay *Colla Ciotach*, still the most senior surviving member of *Clann Iain Mhóir*, soon established himself as the Captain of Dunivaig and he retained the castle as his personal headquarters right to the end.

Conquest of Argyll's Estates

Alasdair's movements at this period have been largely reconstructed by Stevenson. Although he retained Mingary Castle as his headquarters, he was always on the move. With Sir James Lamont, he crossed first into Cowal then continued through Argyll, Lorne and Kintyre, harrying the Campbells and recruiting all the way; by November they had raised 2,000 men and their united effect was devastating. The beleaguered Campbells now discovered that they were the object of a co-ordinated attack, squeezed on the east and south by Lamont and *Alasdair* and now attacked on the north and west by the rest of their traditional enemies, including Clanranald, Clan Gregor and the MacLeans. By 19 October, George Campbell, the sheriff depute, was able to recognise that even if the Covenanters were to be relieved "this countrey must be anew conqueist."

By December the Royalists were able to hold a meeting, at Kilmore (near modern Oban), and felt confident to sign a bond in which they swore to devote themselves to the utter destruction of Clan Campbell. By January *Alasdair* was back in Cowal together with Lamont, and in February 1646 he was in Bute. Leaving Lamont in Cowal, *Alasdair* made his way back into the "farr Isles of Loghaber" and persuaded Clanranald to come to his aid in Islay, then spent the balance of the year in and around Kintyre and Islay, awaiting the moment when he could return to centre stage. It has been suggested that perhaps he and his supporters were indulging their private grudge against Argyll, but in early 1646 it was still intended to re-unite the army under Montrose and they were biding their time. Later in the year, *Alasdair* and his forces were on standby whilst Antrim and Montrose negotiated at a political level in France and Ireland.

Sabhal nan Cnàimh

Alasdair features in a number of traditional stories about this period, one of which concerns an abominable crime committed in Glen Iuchar, not many miles south of Oban. The story is preserved in J.F.Campbell's "West Highland Tales", Vol. II, and must presumably relate to the period immediately following the massacre of the wives and camp-followers after Philiphaugh. The incident does not appear to be in line with the character which, from various contemporary sources, Wedgwood describes as follows: "He was twenty-five years old [1644], stood six foot six in his brogues, and had already distinguished himself in the Irish fighting. A popular chieftain and a valiant warrior, Macdonald had with him his young wife and children[3] and his attendant priests. Ruthless in war, he was well-behaved in the necessary intervals, never sat down to meat without hearing a Latin grace or went into battle without first devoutly taking the Sacrament."[4]

Nonetheless, in the story of *Sabhal nan Cnàimh* (Barn of the Bones), *Alasdair* and his men are said to have approached across *Monadh Rogharain* [the moor of Raray] and come down into the valley at *Lagan Mór*, where they surprised many people of the Glen hiding in a barn. As they approached, one of *Alasdair*'s men gave a shout of warning, and was murdered for his pains, at *Alltan a' Ghille Chaoich* ("Stream of the Mad Fellow"); the piper then gave his own warning, playing "Women of the glen, it is time for you to arise", for which contribution he was run through with a sword. All the men who were in the barn escaped save one, *Iain Beag mac Iain mhic Dhomhnaill*, but *Alasdair* is said to have ordered all the fleeing women to be rounded up and put back into the barn, which was then set alight. (One woman escaped, despite being pregnant, and later gave birth to twins in the nearby wood of Fearnagan; descendants of that lady still live in Glen Iuchar).

A barn was built again on the same site and the bones of the women who had been murdered were buried there; it was the new barn that was called "*Sabhal nan Cnàimh*" and its slight remains can be seen to this day, under the tree closest to the entrance to the farm.

But they say that *Iain Beag*, from *Braigh Ghlinne*, managed to escape from the barn, with a peat-creel over his head to protect himself from the blows of *Alasdair*'s men, and rushed into a shoemaker's house where he pretended to be an apprentice until his clumsiness gave him away; "*A Iain Bhig, ged a rachadh tu an craiceann an deamhain fhéin dh'aithne'ainn thu, agus tha mi a' dol 'gad chrochadh ris an spàrr*". ("Wee John, though you would put on the skin of the devil himself, I would know you, and I am going to hang you from the rafter").

And then, *Alasdair* is said to have relented; he asked *Iain Beag* what he himself would do if the roles were reversed. "Well", said *Iain Beag*, "I would place you in a circle in the middle of my men, and I would give you your sword in your hand, and if you could make your way out through them, I would let you do it." Nothing loath, *Alasdair* gave him his chance and *Iain Beag* began to try a few feints against the men surrounding him and they, no doubt, were just toying with their victim when, quite suddenly, *Iain Beag* threw his sword, spinning, straight up into the air above the circle. The men dodged back, not knowing where the blade would fall, and *Iain Beag* sprang nimbly through the gap and made his escape. *Alasdair* was delighted at the ruse and ordered his men to hold their fire.

The amusing tale of *Iain Beag* cannot counteract the more chilling story of *Sabhal nan Cnàimh*; we do not know if *Alasdair* was there in person, but there seems little doubt that a dreadful crime was committed there by men for whose actions he was respon-sible. Perhaps it is well to consider again just what had happened after Philiphaugh, when General David Leslie ("stealthy and ferocious as a wild-cat") had let his men give full vent to the nature of their covenant with God:

> ..."there were three hundred women, that, being natives of Ireland, were the married wives of the Irish. There were many big with child, yet none of them were spared, all were cut in pieces, with such savage and inhuman cruelty, as neither Turk nor Scythian was ever heard to have done the like: For they ript up the bellies of the women with their swords; till the fruit of their wombs, some in embryo, some perfectly formed, some crawling for life, and some ready for birth, fell down upon the ground, weltering in the gory blood of their mangled mothers. Oh! impiety; oh! horrible cruelty...." ("Britain's Distemper").

We can never know the exact details of *Sabhal nan Cnàimh*; perhaps propaganda, perhaps a vicious reprisal by some of the bereaved, perhaps worse. What is known is that the tales about *Alasdair* do not normally display him as evil; a wry humour can be detected in many of them, as when *Alastair* was nearly ambushed on the shores of Loch Crinan. The attackers, "on the slopes above a place called Tilleagan", waited until *Alasdair* was between their own position and that of the rebels in Duntroon Castle, then opened fire, bullets striking the ground around his mare. *"Aha", arsa Alasdair Mac Colla, "is teth na smugaidean seo mu chasan Nic Laomain."* ("Aha", said Alastair, "these spittles are hot around Miss Lamont's feet"). So hot, in fact, that *Alasdair* was forced to ride her into the sea and eventually to swim her ashore on the Crinan side of the River Add, a remarkable feat. One wonders who Miss Lamont was, and why he chose to name his horse for her? Perhaps she was a mare that he had received from Sir James Lamont, in whose company he had left Montrose and who had been with the Royalists since Inverlochy. (Lamont had had his own commission from the King but did not dare act upon it until he was captured at Inverlochy, after which he was glad enough to be allowed to join the Royalist cause).

Colla Ciotach in Islay

Neil MacMhuirich recorded that Clanranald invested Islay in 1646, expelled what Campbell forces were there and then remained in strength. From various sources Stevenson has suggested that Argyll's own regiment (which returned to Ireland after the debacle of Inverlochy) made an assault on Islay (and possibly Kintyre) in the spring of 1646 and that it was probably in response to this that Clanranald occupied that island. Although *Colla Ciotach* had based himself at Dunivaig, he will not have had more than a defensive garrison, but his presence there is confirmed by Rev. Hill: "Coll Kittagh came forth as a veteran warrior once more, and his bravery and experience induced the Scottish royalists to place him again in charge of the important castle of Dunyveg in Isla. He held this position gallantly from 1644 until 1647, the year of his death."[5]

In a curious echo of the tale of "*A Cholla, mo rùn...*", when *Colla Ciotach* received the piper's warning to avoid Dunivaig in 1615, there is a story that either *Alasdair* or *Colla* was warned away from Duntroon Castle in 1646 in much the same fashion. This time the piper played his warning to the tune of "*Fuaim na Tuinne ri Duntreòin*":

"Fàilte dhuit, slàinte dhuit, fàilte dhuit a Dhuntreòin,

Sin iad thugad, so iad agad, bi air t' fhaicill a Dhuntreòin
Sin iad thugad, seo iad agad, tha iad agad a Dhuntreòin
Failte dhuit, slainte dhuit, etc.
Pìobaireachd as t' seòmar mhullaich fuaim na tuinne ri Dhuntreòin."

"Welcome to you, health to you, welcome to Duntroon,
There they are on you, here they are at you, be on your guard at Duntroon
There they are on you, here they are at you, they'll get you at Duntroon
Welcome to you, health to you etc.
Piping from the room high above the breaking wave against Duntroon."*

Despite the fact that the early part of this campaign has been recorded mainly by tradition, all sources confirm that the Royalists quickly established themselves as masters of the whole of Argyll's estates. Nonetheless, although under heavy pressure, various Campbell strongholds were able to resist assault and instead were subjected to siege. One such lengthy siege was at Skipness, an ancient MacDonald strength that had fallen into Campbell hands in 1502, soon after the Forfeiture of the Lordship of the Isles. This siege lasted through much of the summer of 1646, being conducted determinedly but unsuccessfully by *Gilleasbuig MacCholla*, and it was raised by August. The Captain of Skipness was away on service with Munro's regiment in Ireland (although he returned briefly to assist in the abortive raid on Islay, repulsed by Clanranald). In his absence the castle was defended by Malcolm MacNaughton of Dunderave, who held out despite "extraordinar distres" and who died soon afterwards as a result of his privations. *Gilleasbuig MacCholla* died during the siege of Skipness, and may have been killed in a skirmish, since reports that he was captured and hanged have been shewn by Stevenson to be based upon Parliamentarian propaganda and unreliable. When a siege is raised there is normally ample opportunity for the besiegers to fall away so, unless he was injured, there seems little reason to suppose that *Gilleasbuig* was really captured.

A version of these propaganda reports put it about that Argyll, in the spring of 1646, had sent a force of 1200 men to recapture Dunivaig, where they had slaughtered 140 defendants including the commander, said to be one of Alasdair's brothers. A further 1,600 men had supposedly relieved Skipness, killed *Gilleasbuig* and forced *Alasdair* to flee. In fact Argyll's force must have been much smaller and both assaults were repulsed. Skipness remained under siege throughout the summer and the attack on Dunivaig was aborted on the arrival of Clanranald.

Antrim redoubles his efforts

Whilst *Alasdair* and his army maintained the war in the west, there had been significant developments on the political and military fronts both in England and Ireland. In June of 1645, the Royalist defeat at Naseby had effectively marked an end to Charles' military campaign in England but in July, in a secret treaty with the Irish Confederates, the King had agreed to the full restoration of Catholicism in Ireland and thereby gained the hope of further reinforcements. Perversely, as the summer had progressed, his successes in Scotland had made it hard for him to agree to make that treaty public, whilst his reverses in England had encouraged the leadership in Kilkenny to think that he would have to accept their terms. After Philiphaugh it became certain that the only hope of military success lay in reinforcements from Ireland, but it was also clear that the introduction of such an army and on such terms was quite simply unthinkable. As he agonised, Charles was driven to use what help he could get from Ireland on an *ad hoc* basis.

On 27 September 1644, Charles had written to Antrim to express his thanks for sending *Alasdair* into Scotland, and had promised the restoration of all his lands; indeed, it was reported that he had even promised to reward him with the additional lands and title of the Duke of Argyll. No doubt encouraged by this, Antrim redoubled his efforts and on 26 January 1645 had been created, like Montrose, a Marquis.

In February, Antrim went personally to deliver letters from the King to his queen, who was at St.Germain in France, "in which jorney he obtained from the Spaniards two ffriggotts, with considerable number of Armes and Ammunition". Before he left France, Antrim was approached by Rinuccini, the newly-appointed papal nuncio to Ireland, who was very anxious to get to Ireland and offered to pay handsomely to be carried there aboard the frigates. Antrim, who did not wish to introduce more difficulties, absolutely refused to carry him and in fact it was not until 21 October 1645 that Rinuccini reached Ireland. (Even then, despite Antrim's efforts, Rinuccini was not too late to introduce such an element of intransigence as was enough to destroy not merely Charles' hopes but those of Ireland too).

The Queen herself thanked Antrim for baulking Rinuccini and wished him godspeed on his return to Ireland; although as it happens, Rinuccini actually saved time by making his own way to Ireland, since Antrim was engaged in a more complicated transaction than has been generally recognised and Ireland was not his immediate destination. R.A.Stradling has researched this period in "The Spanish Monarchy and Irish Mercenaries" and has produced much new and fascinating information. As he points out, King Charles, having raised a formidable army in Ireland some few years earlier had hesitated to use it in England, until eventually it had become a drain on his resources and am embarrassment to all concerned. A possible solution lay in its redeployment elsewhere, particularly in the Spanish service.

Since the 1620's Irish mercenaries had made an important contribution to the Spanish war effort and in the 1630's the traffic had increased markedly. Various individuals began to act as agents in the trade and were well rewarded. In 1640 it became clear that Catholic soldiers from Ireland would again be warmly welcomed by Spain, particularly for service in the Low Countries, and the Earl of Strafford was negotiating to send some 20,000 men for a consideration of 1,200,000 escudos. Even after Strafford was impeached, negotiations were continued, both by Ormond and by the Kilkenny Confederation; in summary, thousands of Irish soldiers had been almost routinely supplied to Spain over a period of years.

The Spanish contract

In 1645, the Earl of Antrim took advantage of this situation and seems to have used it to create an extraordinary opportunity for his cause and also for his clan. He made his way to Brussels and offered to supply 1,200 crack troops, to be collected by Spanish ships from Kintyre. His interlocutor, Castel Rodrigo, was in desperate straits and willingly agreed to pay the going rate; as it happened however, he was not in a position to supply Spanish military vessels and this caused no little delay until, in October 1645, the sum of 1,000 escudos was advanced to hire merchant vessels. The resulting contract of 6 December 1645 is described by Stradling as "abortive" but it seems that Antrim did obtain some vessels at about that time. One observer felt that Antrim's plausible nature had achieved almost too much, since he had gained the frigates ("of 20 pieces of artillery both") together with "a great quantity of arms" with which to go to Scotland and defeat the rebels, all in exchange for only the promise of soldiery for Spain... "In fine he carries away our frigates and leaves us the expectation of men."

In fact, he went with these two vessels only to Falmouth. Once there he was able to offer signal service to the monarch both by bringing fresh arms and munitions to be pressed into service in the desperate attempt to save Cornwall and by providing those same frigates for the evacuation of the Prince of Wales, who was taken by Antrim to Pendennis Castle in the Scilly Isles. "The prince made use of one of the frigates to transport his person into Scilly, and from thence to Jersey, without which convenience his highness had been exposed to great difficulties, and could hardly have escaped the hands of his enemies." – *Life of Clarendon*, quoted by Hill.

This crisis was heightened, because on 16 January 1646 the London Parliament had been informed of Charles' secret treaty with the Irish Confederates, and when in February the Confederates finally agreed to send 6000 troops to his immediate aid, it was by then too late: Chester, the port that was vital to the reception of reinforcements from Ireland, had fallen to the Parliamentary forces on 3 February. The redundant message with its promise of "immediate" aid was handed to the future Charles II as he stepped aboard Antrim's ship and into exile.

Antrim's negotiations continued in Flanders and in November 1646 a further contract was agreed, this time with Jacques le Gouvernour of Dunkirk, which was to be of particular significance to *Clan Iain Mhóir*. Stradling states "Le Gouvernour undertook to provide two so-called "flyboats" *(fluitschepen)*, the basic Dutch-built merchant vessel type, and an accompanying escort warship to pick up Antrim's army from Kintyre. ... He demanded payment in advance of one-half the total value of the contract, a matter of 18,000 florins, and in November 1646, Castel Rodrigo ordered the paymaster to meet this charge immediately..."

Antrim returns to Scotland

This sequence of events is followed by Rev. Hill, who quotes from a memorandum written by Antrim, suggesting that the Marquis had not waited for Le Gouvernour's ships but had returned to Scotland in the spring of 1646: "after some time the Marquis went from thence to Scotland (being in 1646) by his Majestie's directions, expecting the king's comeing theither; in hopes thereof, hee put his people in Armes, and kept them in a body upon his own accoumpt till his Majestis comands to laye downe Armes, as it appears by severall letters from his Majestie dated Newcastle the 15th and 19th of June, and 29th of July 1646."

Although Antrim received instructions from the King to lay down his arms in the summer of 1646 (15 and 19 June, also 29 July), at the same time as did Montrose, he did not conform immediately and in his Memorandum this is cheerfully admitted.

"After laying downe Armes in Scotland, **about the latter ende of the same yeare**, the Marquis went back to Ireland for the purpose to renew the kings service there, and to make himselfe capable to renewe the warres of Scotland, when comanded by his Majestie."

Antrim's resolve was in some contrast to that of his opposite number in Scotland where, after he had disbanded his own forces, Montrose had withdrawn via Norway to rejoin the Queen and the Prince of Wales at St. Germain. All this time, Antrim had been busily engaged in hatching plans to rescue the King from his captors; he collaborated in this with the Earl of Crawford, and the latter went to St. Germain in October 1646 to receive royal consent to the undertaking. Antrim remained in Scotland until the end of September, and united the Royalist leaders to his cause and to the renewal of the war:

> "For this object these leaders had actually pledged themselves to raise an army of 30,000 men, nearly all of which was to be made up as follows: – the marquis of Antrim, in the name of the Clandonnel, 2,000 men; MacLean, 2,000; Macranald, 1,300; MacLeod of Harris, 1,200; sir James Macdonnell, 200; the earl of Seaforth, 2,000; the lord Reay, 1,200; the countrie of Atholl and Badenoch, 3,000; clan Gregor and Farquharson, 1,200; Grant, 1,000; Clanchattan and Strathearn men, 1,000; the marquis of Huntley, 1,500; the earl of Airlie, 400; the earl of Airth, 700; MacNeill of Barra, 500; Glengarry, 500; the earl of Nithsdale, 1,000; the marquis of Montrose, 1,000; the lord of Dalkeith, 100 horse. The prince, afterwards Charles II, warmly approved, as well he might, and as appeared from his letter to the marquis of Antrim, dated St. Germains, October 26 1646." (Rev. Hill)

Having made his arrangements in Scotland, Antrim returned to Ireland in October 1646 only to discover that he would be unable to obtain the support of the Confederates for his scheme and that the ports were tightly controlled to frustrate him.

Although *Alasdair* and his men were continuing the war in the west, it was now clear that their cause was doomed; without the prospect of a general renewal of the war, Antrim knew that he did not even have the option of negotiating to disband his forces upon terms. His only hope lay in the fulfillment of the arrangements that he had made with Castel Rodrigo. It became a matter of a desperate race against time, a race to withdraw his own forces and equipment and to gain time for the clansmen to disperse before the victorious Covenanting army could be redeployed against them. It seems to be agreed that, during the course of 1646, Antrim had augmented *Alasdair*'s forces with something over 1,000 Irish reinforcements and, as the year closed, it became clear that David Leslie and his re-modelled expeditionary army would shortly return from England.

Notes

1 The first historical reference to the potato in the west of Scotland was in 1695, by Martin Martin

2 Once again, one must note that the two stories may have become confused.

3 *Alasdair*'s wife was a daughter of Hector McAllister of Loup, the respected head of a major MacDonald sept with which *Alasdair*'s family was on very close terms. Their two sons were Coll, born c. 1645 and Gillespie, born c. 1647

4 It seems that his father was a little more modern, for a grace in the English language, taken from the psalms, is noted in the margin of *Cathal MacMhuirrich*'s poem; it has been transcribed by Ronald Black [modernised spelling]:
"The eyes of all things do look up and trust in Thee, O Lord; Thou givest them their meat in due season. Thou openest thy hands, and fill with Thy blessing, every living [being]. Good Lord, Bless us, and this thy gift, which we receive from Thy large and bounteous [liberality], through Christ Jesus, O Lord and only Saviour. So be it, Amen."

5 The reference to 1644 is one of a number of suggestions that just conceivably *Colla* achieved his freedom rather earlier than his sons, but they are not convincing. There is a story that he was living peacefully in St. Kilda, but this seems to be a confusion with his visit thirty years earlier and much the same can be said for the stories of *Colla* having spent much of his life aboard his galley, haunting the shores of Islay. His prowess as a seaman was undoubted, and there is a certain maritime flavour to the (exaggerated) account of his death – "both hanged and drouned!" – but there is no evidence of an extended career as a sea-rover.

6 The words are as quoted in Ronald Black's paper for the Gaelic Society of Inverness, which paper should be consulted for a detailed examination of the background to both these tunes

7 The Campbells (later the Malcolms) retained their seat at Duntroon, although later generations built a new and magnificent mansion house, Poltalloch; in course of time this became so much of a burthen that they demolished it and returned to the Castle of Duntroon, on the north side of Loch Crinan. The old building required extensive renovations and the then head of the family, being an officer in the Royal Engineers, took charge of much of the work. His grandson, Mr. Malcolm, was good enough to assure the writer that on raising flagstones in the old kitchen the skeleton of a man was discovered, that his grandfather personally was in attendance, and that on examination the fingers of the right hand were found to have been severed.

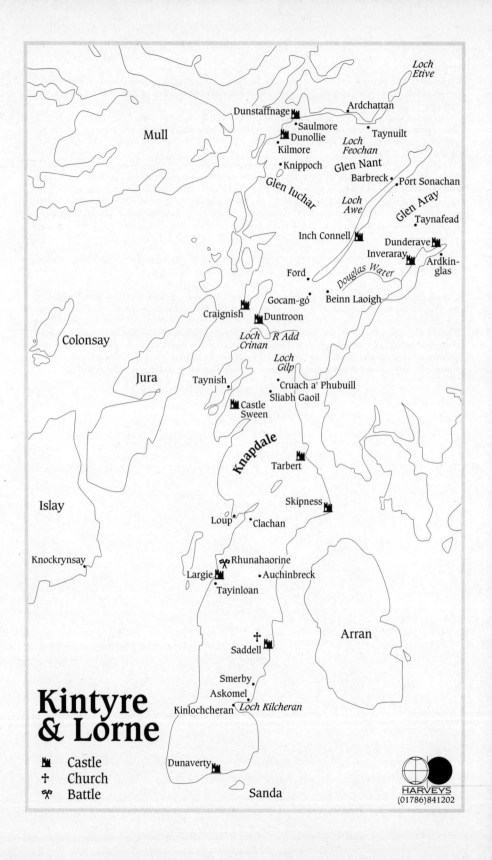

Loch
Etive

Dunstaffnage 🏰   Ardchattan

Mull   • Saulmore

🏰 Dunollie   • Taynuilt

• Kilmore   Loch
     Feochan

• Knippoch   Glen Nant

Barbreck   • Port Sonachan

Glen Iuchar   Glen Aray

Loch
Awe   • Taynafead

Inch Connell 🏰   Dunderave 🏰

Inveraray

🏰 Ardkin-
glas

• Ford   Douglas Water

Gocam-gò   • Beinn Laoigh

Craignish 🏰 • Duntroon

Colonsay

Loch   R Add
Crinan

Jura   Loch
    Gilp

Taynish •   • Cruach a' Phubuill
     Sliabh Gaoil

🏰 Castle
Sween

Knapdale

🏰 Tarbert

Islay

Skipness
🏰

Loup •   • Clachan

Knockrynsay

⚔ Rhunahaorine

Largie •   • Auchinbreck

• Tayinloan

Arran

† 🏰
Saddell

• Smerby

Askomel •
Kinlochcheran   Loch Kilcheran

Kintyre
& Lorne

🏰   Castle
†   Church
⚔   Battle

Dunaverty 🏰

Sanda

HARVEYS
(01786)841202

15

LESLIE THWARTED – 1647

The sale of the King

Like *Alasdair MacCholla*, Huntly remained loyal and determined throughout this period; indeed he actually re-opened his campaign in December 1646, when he seized Banff in conjunction with an attempt by King Charles to escape from the Covenanters on Christmas Eve. The King's plan was a failure but, having seized the town, Huntly and a garrison of some 1800 men occupied it until March 1647.

Had the King escaped, it would have been a serious embarrassment to the rebel leadership who had maintained an expeditionary army in the field for some two years without pay and without the means to be paid. In order to kill two birds with the one stone they had decided to sell their King to the English, but negotiations had been difficult. Finally, on 23 December, a figure had been agreed, yet the following day the merchandise had almost escaped! The guards were redoubled and General David Leslie took personal control of the arrangements; it will have been with no little sense of relief that he handed Charles over to the English jailors on 2 January, to be imprisoned at Holmby.

There was still unease about the price. This was eventually agreed at £200,000 in all, half to be paid cash-down and the balance when the Scots had crossed the Tweed. With both parties united in dishonour, it was hardly surprising that there was but little hint of trust. It was not until these sordid details had been resolved that the Scots rebel army withdrew from Newcastle and on 30 January 1647, as the streets re-echoed to the taunts of the inhabitants – "Judas! Judas!", the Scots rebel army finally turned for home. The regiments were to rendezvous "within 8 miles of Barwicke in Scotland" where they would be paid off. The bulk of the army was to disband on 9 and 10 February, but not without protest. Having been paid a proportion of their arrears of pay, they were ordered to give up their arms and to swear an oath of loyalty "to bee faithful to the Covenant and cause of both Kingdoms, and not to ingage with any against them".

The "New Model" army

It was reported that "At first they refused" and that some of those who were being disbanded "resolved to joyne with Kilketto, being much incensed...", but they were eventually cowed through the combined blandishments of General Leslie and "partly by the incitements of their Ministers." A hard-core was retained as the "New Model" army. "Most of these are of the Arguile party, officers and souldiers.... the new Model is fourteen hundred Horse and five thousand Foot". Under the command of Leslie, this force now embarked upon a ruthless mopping-up campaign.

By now, *Alasdair*'s fame had spread far and wide, and he featured regularly in the "Scottish" section of the broadsheets published by the Parliamentary side in London, extracts of which have already been given above. The issue of 18 February 1647 included a lot of Scottish news, and details of the Scot's withdrawal were eagerly reported by various correspondents, including news that:

"4 Cartloade of mony were brought into the Towne of Berwick Feb 7. The same day about 3 a clock in the afternoon, his Excellency Gen. Leven came into this town [Berwick], himself on horseback, with a smal retinue of his Officers and Gentlemen, and lodged here all night..... On Tuesday Feb 9 divers Regiments passed through this town, many foot, and some horse... some of the soldiers passed merrily, & cheerfully: others had rather joy, but we hope all wil march out orderly, according to expectation; though perhaps there may bee some Reliques of a disbandede Army, &c..

"Some troopes passed with their drawne swords, many Companies of foot, some with their matches cockt, and lighted, as rejoycing at that great tryumph, which God has given them and us in subduing of the enemy in England, and to the disheartning and danting of the Rebels that yet remain in Scotland, who have increased much this winter.

"Wee have news here reported by some come out of Scotland, that have beene at Edenburgh, who say that Colkittoth with his Forces, is within 30 miles of Edenburgh: the truth of the particulars, I do not certainly know, but it seemes, that either hee or some of his party, have given them an alarum about Edenburgh."

Writing from Berwick on 22 February, a more detailed report was supplied:

"concerning the proceedings of the new modelled army in Scotland, upon their Design Northwards against Kilketto and his adherents, who not long since were within thirty miles of the City of Edenburgh, plundering most of the Inhabitants thereabouts, and driving many Heads of Cattel towards the North; but were frustrated of their designe: for, upon an alarum, that Lieutenant Generall David Lesley, and Major Generall Brown, were advanced over the Tweed, and upon their march towards the North of that Kingdom, with a strong party of Horse and Dragoons, immediatly took his retreat towards the North, leaving most of the Cattell behind him.

"Sir, not long since, Major Generall Middleton fell upon a party of the Kilkettonians, as they were ranging the country, killed many of them, and took divers prisoners, and some few days after that, he fell upon two or three Garrisons, which were kept by the Irish Rebels, stormed them, and put many to the sword.

"Kilketto is supposed to be about foure thousand strong, his army consisting of one thousand Horse, and three thousand foot, most of them compleatly armed, and very expert Souldiers; yet somewhat timerous of spirit, and fearfull of maintaining the Holds, now in their possession: for, by a Messenger from those parts, it is declared unto us, that the Irish have deserted severall Garrisons, and have drawn up their whole Body towards the high Mountaines, fortifying, and planting their Ordnance, upon severall convenient Hills, cutting off several passages, and making great preparations of war, yet (its verily believed) to little purpose; for Lieutenant Generall David Lesley, lets no opportunity slip, for the putting an end and period to the distractions of that Kingdome..."[1]

Leslie marches north

In the above accounts, the situation is described with some accuracy. Turning his attention first to Huntly, Leslie quickly overcame the garrisons of the few remaining Royalist castles and any Irish troops that were discovered were slaughtered on the spot (although the common Scots soldiery were usually granted terms). Isolated and untenable "Holds" were abandoned by the Royalists, whilst resources were concentrated on the fortification of "the high Mountaines" (i.e. Kintyre peninsula). The correspondent was clearly puzzled by this, it being recognized that the war was as good as over; but neither he nor Leslie was to know that the Royalists were already engaged in an orderly withdrawal and that they had to hold Kintyre for that purpose. The excellent natural harbour of Loch Kilcheran (now Campbeltown) is accessible from virtually all points of the compass by sea, but access by land is restricted to two narrow coastal strips running the length of a very long peninsula. Even to reach that peninsula, almost 40 miles long and barely 8 miles wide, an invader has to pass through a tiny gap, at Tarbert, barely a mile wide. A handful of men could defend Kintyre against an army, and this was clearly the intention. At the same time, it must be remembered that Kintyre had especial significance as it was not merely ancestral territory of *Clan Iain Mhóir*, territory which had been re-granted by the crown twice within living memory, but had actually been re-purchased from Argyll's brother as recently as 1637.

By now it was obvious that there was no point in further resistance in mainland Scotland, and equally clear that there was no hope of any sort of honourable surrender. Having disbanded the bulk of his force, hopefully to melt away to their homes, Huntly began to make his way westward with a small body of men. He cannot have expected to join *Alasdair* in his enclave, but may have hoped to reach Ireland, perhaps with the help of the Islesmen.

Evacuation from Kintyre

By the end of April, Leslie was in a position to concentrate his own attention on the only serious opposition that remained, that of *Alasdair MacCholla* and the western clans; it was public knowledge, as has been seen, that the remaining Royalist forces had adopted a strongly defensive position in Kintyre. On 17 May, Leslie's army left Dunblane, where he had been joined by Argyll, and marched swiftly to the west; despite poor weather the insurrectionists made rapid progress and within a week had fallen upon *Alasdair*'s positions. Before leaving Edinburgh, the French agent there had tried to persuade Argyll to allow *Alasdair* to withdraw peaceably. Stevenson tells us that Argyll became enraged, and said the the only choice for him would be "as to whether they would make him shorter or longer than he was" – a reminder of the choice that was said to have been offered to Auchinbreck.

This indication of French interest reminds us of the commercial value of *Alasdair*'s army and that throughout 1646 Antrim had been very active in negotiating with Spain. The theme of Spanish interest was continued and on 9 March 1647, the French agent had been able to report that *Alasdair* had been in correspondence with members of the Scottish Parliament, offering to leave Scotland provided that he and his men could go to Spain. This overture had been rejected and instead "On 4 March an act of parliament had confirmed that Alasdair was not to be pardoned or granted any terms." (Stevenson).

Whatever the exact details may have been, it is clear that the crux of the matter lay in the fact that neither Huntly nor *Alasdair* could hope to disband their forces peacefully, as Montrose had done; even in the case of Montrose, the Covenanters had tried to double-cross him, but now they were not even under any pressure to do a deal. Huntly had little option but to try to lay a false scent, accompanied by a small lifeguard, in the hope that whilst the enemy was engaged in hunting him down, the rest of his men might manage to be re-assimilated in their own communities. In the case of *Alasdair*, the intention was to maintain a secure bridgehead and to organise the orderly evacuation of his force. We do not know exactly how advanced this evacuation had become by mid May, but we do have evidence that Antrim's negotiations had born fruit.

As Stradling has shown, at least one contract had been agreed for the uplifting of Antrim's men from Kintyre, in merchant vessels with a Spanish naval escort. It seems likely that that contract was fulfilled: "Early in 1647 a new force of nearly 700 Irishmen appeared on the musters of the army of Flanders. The figure is consistent with a hypothetical number of survivors [i.e. post-Philiphaugh] from an original 1,600 ... These twelve companies, commanded by John Murphy, were added to Patrick O'Neill's four to make up a respectable Irish *tercio* of 947 effectives."

Further withdrawals may also have been made, and of course a steady evacuation into Ireland was possible, particularly from Islay. Shipping was not a great problem for that short crossing since, for generations, the traditional mass-movement of gallowglass troops had been effected in simple craft made from wicker and covered in hides. Such craft were used just once, with a suitable tide and a fair wind, but naturally the hides could be brought back again for future use.

Colla Ciotach appointed Commander-in-Chief

That the general evacuation was at an advanced stage is indicated by the fact that on 5 May *Alasdair* had formally issued a commission to his father in the following terms:

"Commission:
Sir Alexander McDonald, Knight; Sergeant Major General of his Majesty_s forces in the Highlands of Scotland.

"I do hereby nominate, ordain and appoint my well-beloved father, Coll McDonald, to command-in-chief over the lands of Islay, and all other lands unto me belonging, within the said kingdom of Scotland, with my said father.

"Charging and commanding all and several, the inhabitants of the said several lands, to all such employments as shall concern the advancement of his Majesty_s service, when occassion shall require. As also, to man, victual, defend and keep the fort and garrison of Dunniveg, against all manner of invasion of the enemy.

"Calling to his aid and assistance Captain Daniel O_Neill, who is hereby likewise ordained, appointed and commanded for his assistance, in maintaining the fort aforesaid, to execute and exercise all manner of martial discipline, and keep all soldiers appointed for maintenance thereof in martial employment, according to the law of Armes, and to [share or disshare?] or punish any soldier, according to their desire to; being always answerable unto me for his Majesty_s forces herein, until further orders from the Lord Marquis of Antrim or me to the contrary. Given under my hand, the 5th of May 1647
Subscripter: SIR ALEXANDER McDONALD"

It seems that *Alasdair* himself was now poised for a final withdrawal from Kintyre, since it was his duty to preserve himself and his men at the service of the Marquis of Antrim and for the continuing service of the King. On the one hand, the Kilkenny Confederates had at last agreed to permit Antrim to raise a fresh army of some 5,000 men for service in Scotland; and on the other hand it was known that the English parliament had agreed to send a substantial army to reinforce Lord Inchiquin, with which to overthrow the Confederates. Either way, within the wider context of the struggle, *Alasdair* was needed in Ireland. There was no hope of holding Kintyre long-term, but there might be something to be gained by attempting to defend Islay for as long as possible, if only as a rallying point and as a conduit for communications.

Colla Ciotach was an old man, but he remained the head of *Clann Iain Mhóir* and it was only appropriate that the Royalist leadership should now pass to his shoulders. From his ancestral home, the head of a proud and ancient family conferred legitimacy upon the proceedings. Other men had no homes to go to, or had a price on their head, so they now joined Clanranald and the remnants of *Clann Iain Mhóir* to form the garrison on Islay. A tiny rearguard still defended Kintyre, their ranks significantly swelled by members of Clan Dougall from Lorne – one imagines that it was planned that this rearguard would melt away by sea as soon as the final evacuations were complete.

Leslie moves west

Leslie was not to know all this; as far as he knew, there was talk of additional reinforcements on their way from Ireland and he hurried off to try to forestall their arrival. Passing through a wasteland, burned and harried with meticulous care over the proceeding months, he was himself astonished to meet with no effective opposition and astounded to catch *Alasdair* wrong-footed. Only a skeleton force remained upon the peninsula and the speed of Leslie's advance almost overwhelmed them. As the "Book of Clanranald" states: "Sir David Leslie and Mac Cailin came to Kintyre, without any notice being obtained of the time they would come till they came to Largie, where Alaster and his men were separated asunder. Alaster's party were dispersed; Ranald Og, son of Alaster, son of Angus Uaibhreach, was taken prisoner, and was put to death at Invereray some time after that."

The above lightning sketch bears amplification. Most writers have suggested that the campaign was a swift affair and that the Royalists were out-generalled, but fortunately General Leslie's own somewhat disingenuous but revealing report survives:

"Right Honourable –

"I thought it a part of my duty to give your Lordships a full account of my proceedings since the receipt of your letter with the instructions sent me by Mr. Thomas Hendersone to Drumblaine. After I had lain there with the Army in expectation of the two months pay, and waiting whilst grass had grown up for the horses, and stayed so long that I could not with safety stay longer because of the contagion breaking out in the places about, I lifted on Monday the 17th of this instant and took my march towards Inverary, where we arrived Friday thereafter, having had very bad weather and evil way. I did confidently expect, and the whole Army looked, to have received their two months pay and provision of oats, meal and ammunition, according as it was formerly, of a long time, appointed; but, though the soldiers were very necessitous and wearied, we found none. So that, after a day_s rest, and that I had sent letters to Captain (Dirk) and others to attend with their ships and boats, and advertised the General Commissary of the soldiers necessities and discontentments, I continued my march upon the Lord_s Day, (for so the good of the service enforced me, that no time should be lost). And the next day, being the 24th, we marched with the horse near forty miles, and twenty four with the foot through the most of the day. At the close of the day, very near sunset, we had a view of the enemy, consisting of 1300 as we were informed. I charged them with a fore-troop and two more; and, though neither the time nor the horses could well serve for action, yet it pleased God to give us the advantage over them. Their whole body was dissipated, and three or four score killed upon the place; and three of their captains, "pryme leadeing men", were taken. We had only nine routers [foot soldiers] wounded; but neither the day nor the ground would suffer us to prosecute the victory. So we returned that night to the body and, the morrow thereafter, the whole Army being over-wearied, we rested upon the fields.

"In the afternoon [Wednesday 26th], I received intelligence that Alaster with his father had fled, in disorder, to the Isle of Gigha that same night we did skirmish, whereupon I forth-with commanded Col. Campbell of Inverary, with a party of 300, to go back to the castle of Swina [Castle Sween], where I understood some boats lay, and from there to go to that Isle for searching him out; but through want of boats to pursue him he had gone to Islay. And as I did formerly, with much earnestness, desire your Lordships to cause provide boats constantly to attend the army, so must now again represent to you that the want thereof is the greatest obstruction of your service; and without they be here ready at all occassions, it will be alto-gether impossible to prosecute the same. For, if the boats and shipping had been furnished us when we put the rebels out of the fields, and forced them to the sea, none would have escaped. I have used all means that lay in my power for having of boats, by sending to the Sheriff of Bute, and by writing to the Lord Chancellor for such ships and boats as were appointed to be sent from the Sheriffdom of Ayr and Renfrew; but, to this present, have not had the least assistance, either of ships or boats. And I humbly conceive that no time has been lost, nor any thing neglected, by the Army, that could possibly have been done for the destruc-tion of the rebels upon the fields.

"Alaster having deserted those that followed him, the country people did write to my Lord Marquis of Argyll and me, desiring pardon for what was past, upon assurance of submission. To the which we returned answer, that, if their intentions had been honest and real, they had taken Alaster or some part of his forces, and secured the boats that the Irish might not escape, and then we would have interposed with your Lordships to grant them favour. The next day [Thursday 27th], we advanced to the house of Loch Kilkerran, where we found four piece of cannon, some ammunition and provision; and a fort, at the mouth of the harbour, with seven piece of cannon and some ammunition, and did understand there that some Irish had gone a-shipboard for Ireland, and the rest to the castle of Dunaverty; before which I am now lying, with the intention, God willing, to do everything that may be, for the most speedy and effec-tual reducing thereof. The footmen are likewise in great want of shoes. What I have further to communicate to your Lordships, I refer to this gentleman, the bearer, the laird of [Charnetoune?], who will more particularly impart the same, according to his instructions. So I rest,

Your Lordships_ most humble servant – DAVID LESLIE
From Dunaverty in Kintyre, the last of May 1647"

We have also an eyewitness account from Sir James Turner, who accepted the post of Adjutant General in Leslie's army for this expedition:

"I was necessitated to stay for some baggage a day or two, and therafter met the army at Inverraray, Argiles chiefe house. From thence we marchd to Kintire, which is a peninsull. Both before and at the entrie to it, there were such advantages of ground, that our foot, for mountains and marshes, could never have drawne up one hundreth in a bodie, nor our horse above three in breast; which if Sir Alaster had prepossest with these thousand or 1200 brave foot which he had with him, I think he might have routed us, at least we sould not have entered Kintire bot by a miracle. Bot he was ordaind for destruction; for by a speadie march we made ourselves masters of these difficell passes, and got into a plaine countrey, where no sooner he saw our horse advance, but with little or no fighting he retird; and if the Lieutenant Generals foot had been with him to have given the enemie a salve or two, which would have disorderd him, I beleeve none of them had escaped from our horse."

Sir James Turner's account will be continued below, but first it may be as well to consider other descriptions of what took place, particularly where there seems to be conflicting detail. The Public Library at Campbeltown has a detailed account, written in 1776 and first published in "Argyllshire Monthly Magazine" in 1833; other details can be culled from traditional stories as recorded by J.F.Campbell (and from the diminishing pool of stories that remain current). The account can be taken up as Leslie approached Kintyre [i.e., Sunday afternoon], at which time Sir *Alasdair* is said to have been at the north end of Kintyre, his father being based at Kinloch Castle: "On reaching the Mill of Gochgomgo, near the south end of Lochaw, they [*Alasdair* and his men] found a few bags of meal and oats, and were about to remove the same, and to set the Mill itself on fire, when Sir Alexander received intelligence........ that General Leslie, with 2500 foot and 500 horse, was within a few miles of Inverary".

This tradition suggests that *Alasdair*'s scouts, (possibly signalling from *Beinn Laoigh*), had spotted Leslie crossing the Douglas Water, 4 miles southwest of Inverary. The "Mill of Gochgomgo" is about 2 miles south of Ford. Thus, with the enemy barely 30 miles from the Royalist defences at Tarbert, *Alasdair* found himself in a terrible position. He himself was more than 20 miles from his own front line and must follow a route which would converge with that of Leslie, at the head of Loch Gilp, so that for the final 15 miles Leslie's cavalry would be galloping at his heels.[2]

There are many accounts which refer to *Alasdair*'s alleged wild flight down through Kintyre. Being traditions preserved amongst the descendants of his deadly enemies, they do not always show him in the best light but they have the virtue of immediacy. By these accounts, *Alasdair* accepted snuff from the miller at *Gocam-gò* and in exchange spared his buildings, although his men carried off the meal. When he set his standard in the ground "*air mullach cnocan cruinn ris an abairte Gocam-gò*" ("on the top of a round hillock that they call Gocam-gò"), a penny jumped from the base of the staff. Alarmed, *Alasdair* then learned the name of the place; a moment later he saw that his standard was blowing the wrong way. The next portent was the loss of his "*leug buaidh*" or lucky charm – the place where he lost it came to be called "*Dàil na Léig*" (Meadow of the Charm). According to Professor MacKinnon, "the heart of a hero, that never turned away from an enemy, now became as the heart of a child ..."[3]

In truth, there is no question of faintheartedness, nor even of prophecies; *Alasdair* and his raiding party were in a highly exposed position, well outside their own defences and some sixty miles from their ships and embarkation point. Not surprisingly, *Alasdair* immediately headed south, and at some speed, not pausing until he reached "the Forest of Sleavegoyle" [modern *Sliabh Gaoil*, some 8 miles south of Lochgilphead]. At this point, the pursuing cavalry would be restricted to a narrow passage between the mountain and the sea; a neighbouring eminence (of greater strategic importance) is still called *Cruach a' Phubuill* ("Hill of the Tent"). Although *Alasdair* had the option of defending this pass, he chose to abandon the position; from this we might imagine that the garrison was not in readiness, but on reflection this seems unlikely. Even if the pass were to be held, there was no way in which the whole peninsula could be defended from the seaborne assault which would become inevitable, so instead we may assume that he did not consider that the brief respite to be gained was essential, and that there was still time to complete the planned evacuation. So it was that *Alasdair* headed on, past Tarbert, out of Knapdale and into Kintyre proper, where, that same Sunday night, he met up with his father, *Colla Ciotach*, and a further 300 men at "Rounachoirine" [*Rhunahaorine*, facing Gigha, some 17 miles south-west of Tarbert].[4]

Evacuation to Islay

That night, according to traditional accounts, *Alasdair* was at Largie Castle whilst Sir David Leslie was at the "inn of old Kilcalmonell"; from a study of Blaeu's contemporary map, the latter spot was at the modern village of Clachan, 7 miles from Largie. If so, it must presumably have been only the vanguard of Leslie's army that had penetrated so far, since Leslie makes it clear that his cavalry did not get a sight of the enemy until sunset on the following evening, Monday. Thus far, *Alasdair* had maintained a slight lead, even over the vanguard, and had reached the main body of his troops. It seems that everything was in readiness for those of his forces that were bound for Islay to depart by boat from Largie, following which the rest of his men could quite simply fall back to the south end of Kintyre. More boats were waiting at Kinloch, to evacuate the remaining Irish troops, and the final evacuations would be completed from the beaches at Dunaverty.

As it happened, *Alasdair*'s activities were completely misunderstood by his enemy; it was 48 hours before Leslie discovered that he had been thwarted and that there had been a substantial evacuation via Islay, presumably led by *Colla Ciotach*. Instead, he assumed that the Royalists would give battle in a conventional way; Alasdair seems to have obliged by remaining long enough for a skirmish at sunset on the Monday, but, since most of his men had already departed, he obviously avoided a set-piece – so it was assumed that he had merely being caught napping: " But before he had time to choose his ground, the van of the enemy was in sight, and preparing for an onset... Sir Alexander retreated but kept up a skirmish with the enemy, that lasted the whole day , in which he lost a number of his men."

In fact, from Leslie's own account, this skirmish took place on the Monday night and the following day, Tuesday 25 May, Leslie's men had a day of rest! It was during the course of that day that the balance of the Royalist force moved further south, down the peninsula of Kintyre.

By the time that Leslie heard of the evacuation via Gigha, the story was a couple of days old and, no doubt, already becoming garbled. Thus there was a curious story that, at the time of the battle (Monday night), *Alasdair* had been so unaware of the proximity of Leslie that he was actually drinking ale at the inn of Tayinloan, with a friend, MacIntosh of Airneal; in this story *Alasdair*, panic-stricken, sprang into the saddle of his faithful mare and galloped away, jumped across a place that seemed impossible at the waterfall of Killean (not far from Tayinloan), and got to an old boat on the shore at *Bealach a' Ghaochain*. Here he patched the boat, then killed the mare with his own sword ("If ever a mare deserved a hero's death, it's you"), and taking a bare crew set off for Islay and thence to Ireland. As for anybody else that tried to lay a hand on the gunwhale of the boat, *Alasdair* sliced off their fingers with his sword!

Such rumours as this will have constituted "intelligence" for the Covenanters and will have been quite unhelpful. Eventually, on the Wednesday, Leslie got word of the withdrawal of a Royalist force to Gigha, but possibly he was deliberately misled into believing that the whole of *Alasdair*'s army had made its escape because, instead of pressing on in pursuit of the rump, he diverted part of his force to Castle Sween in a fruitless search for non-existent boats (acting perhaps on further misleading intelligence?) before settling down to his correspondence. Reading his report, it is clear that he has realised that he wasted time at that point, since he immediately starts to make his excuses. With all this delay, it was only on the Thursday, after *Alasdair* had had two full days to himself, that Leslie resumed his leisurely way south, reaching Kilkerran that day unopposed, and at leisure to examine the ordnance that had been abandoned. On that same day he learned that it was he who had been out-generalled and that all of *Alastair*'s forces had been successfully evacuated, with the exception of some 200 Highlanders who had retreated to Dunaverty.

Leslie's revenge at Dunaverty

Leslie's humiliation was complete and, as a damage-limitation measure, the story of *Alasdair*'s wild flight was coined. Like a man possessed, like a frightened child, he had rushed down Kintyre and into the sea in such a panic that even the crack cavalry troops of the New Model Army could not keep up; he was said to have refused to stand and fight, to have abandoned the passes, to have deserted his men, to have hacked off the fingers of men who tried to enter his boat....

In fact, *Alasdair*'s withdrawal was so well co-ordinated that even now, whilst the Covenanters paused at Kinloch, their quarry, just a few miles away at Dunaverty, had a further thirty to forty boats waiting on the beach and was evacuating the final beachhead. Sadly, it seems that there were not quite enough boats to complete the withdrawal, or perhaps the boats were engaged on a final run across the north channel with the last of the Irish, when Leslie made his appearance. With no option, the remaining Scots made the best of things and huddled into the little fort. Subsequent accounts have perhaps misled us when they suggest that it was decided that 300 of the best soldiers should occupy the fort "being all the place could contain" whilst 200 should go with *Colla Ciotach* to Dunivaig in Islay; and that the balance should proceed with *Alasdair* to Ireland "and there endeavour to raise an army, as speedily as possible" for the relief of both Dunaverty and Dunivaig.

This account of the disposition is frankly misleading: the garrison for Dunivaig had made their departure days earlier and the 300 (or rather less) that had to stay at Dunaverty will have been more properly described as being "all that the boats could not contain" rather than what the castle *could* contain. Although described as "impregnable" it is hard to visualise it now as such. It is a tiny place today, but even with its original outworks in position it would have been small and somewhat vulnerable from the land; it was well suited as a watching post, could dominate the little adjoining landing beach and would provide ample warning of enemy ships moving towards Kinloch, but had no serious defensive capacity when confronted by any sort of army. It was suited for a more traditional role in which, if attacked, the garrison would light a signal beacon and hope to hold out for a few hours until reinforcements arrived, a scenario in which the hinterland would be in friendly, rather than hostile hands.

Incredibly, these two-to-three hundred Highlanders put up an heroic resistance. They are said to have been well-provisioned, and must certainly have had ample ammunition, but they had no water and the place was in no wise prepared for defence. Surrounded by some 3000 seasoned troops, the flower of the New Model army, this tiny band held out for a number of days repulsing assault after assault, inflicting heavy casualties upon their assailants. "The Royalists... might have stood out for a year against any number of men, but about the 10th of [June] the besiegers discovered that the garrison was supplied with water by means of pipes...." Once they were deprived of water, they had to surrender, but having surrendered "they were confined for five days within the walls of the fortification at the foot of the [fort]. They were then turned out, when all the beseiged were put to the sword, except one young man and a nurse with a child."

Here we should return to the eye-witness account, that of Sir James Turner:

"Alaster, like a foole, (for no sojor he was, though stout enough,) put in 300 of his best men in a house on the top of a hill, call'd Dunavertie, environd with a stone wall, where there was not a drop of water but what fell from the clouds.....We beseegd Dunavertie, which keepd out well enough, till we stormd a trench they had at the foot of the hill, wherby they commanded two stripes of water. This we did take in the assault. Fortie of them were put to the sword. We lost five or six, with Argiles Major. After this, inexorable thirst made them desire a parley. I was orderd to speake with them; neither could the Lieutenant Generall [Leslie] be movd to grant any other conditions, then that they sould yeeld on discretion or mercy; and it seemd strange to me to heare the Lieutenant Generalls nice distinction, that they sould yeeld themselvs to the kingdomes mercy, and not to his. At length they did so; and after they were comd out of the Castle, they were put to the sword, everie mothers son, except one young man, Mackoull, whose life I begd, to be sent to France with a hundreth countrey fellows whom we had smoakd out of a cave, as they doe foxes, who were given to Captaine Cambell, the Chancellors brother."

Sir James Turner now pauses for an aside, in which he gives a considered account of the massacre; it is noteworthy that he selected this episode for special attention, an episode that will never be forgotten. He states that Lieutenant General Leslie "was two days irresolute what to doe" with the captives, and goes on to state "I never heard" the Marquis of Argyll advocate their murder. During those two days, he himself spoke to

Leslie in favour of sparing them, "and he always assented to it." In the view of Turner, Leslie was finally persuaded to permit the atrocity by the urgings of Rev. John Nave, a "chaplain" appointed by the Commissioners of the covenanters' General Assembly. He went further than urging – "yea, and threatened him with the curses befell Saull for spareing the Amalekites[5], for with them his theologie taught him to compare the Dunavertie men. And I verilie beleeve that this prevaild most with David Lesley, who lookd upon Nave as the representative of the Kirk of Scotland........ Bot I reallie beleeve, advise him to that act who will, he [Leslie] hath repented it many times since, and even very soone after the doeing it."

In fact, we can more reasonably accept that this atrocity was Leslie's personal revenge for the humiliation that he had suffered. His report, written on Monday 31 May outside Dunaverty, had been carefully drafted to minimise his personal discomfiture, but it did not contain the full truth: "What I have further to communicate to your Lordships, I refer to this gentleman, the bearer, the laird of [Charnetoune?], who will more particularly impart the same, according to his instructions." The verbal report will have included the vital information that the Royalists had largely escaped and that the largest proportion, the best and most disciplined of them all, was now in Ireland under its invincible commander, *Alasdair MacCholla*. Perhaps the verbal report included an assurance that he would take horrible revenge upon the only poor victims available to him.

This pathetic story of "repentance" is also suggested in the story recorded by Bishop Guthrie: "For, while the marquis [Argyll] and he [Leslie], with Mr Nevoy [Naves] were walking over the ankles in blood, he turned about and said – "Now, Mass John, have you not, for once, got your full of blood?" More revealing than these excuses is the further persistent tradition that after thirst had forced them to surrender, the defeated garrison was further tortured by being held without water; and that some of those who begged for water were tied together in pairs and thrown off the top of the rock into the sea, to the mocking taunts of the Presbyterians. "In the year 1822, an unusually violent sea broke up a large sandbank at the foot of the cliffs, and thus revealed a very charnel house of bones, the sight of which appalled beholders, as but too significantly establishing the truth of the ghastly local traditions that still live on the Mull" – Rev. Hill.

So great was the bitterness of the Covenanters that they sought to punish even the bodies of the fallen, which were refused a Christian burial beside the neighbouring chapel, and were instead buried in that open field on the sea shore where, generations later, a stone wall was built to surround the plot. Amidst the horror of this killing field there are one or two tales of survivors, the most famous of which brings credit to Campbell of Craignish. According to the story, Archibald *Og* MacDonald of Sanda was in command of the defence of Dunivaig, and his infant son, Ranald, was brought into the fort by his nurse for protection. After the surrender it is said that the nurse, Flora McCambridge, managed to escape, carrying the naked infant in her arms. As she ran along the beach, she was seized by Captain Campbell of Craignish, but she said that the child was her own. "It has the eyes of a MacDonald" said Captain Campbell, "but no matter, it wants clothing." So saying, he cut off the tail of his own plaid with a knife and gave it to her for a covering; the nurse and her infant charge managed to find shelter in a cave and in later years the child grew to manhood and married Anne Stewart, sister of the first Earl of Bute.

Another story mentions a young man who survived:

"James Stewart of the Blackhall family, Renfrewshire – when taken out [to be done to death] he requested leave to read his Bible. Stewart of Ardvorlich, who was an officer in the beseiging army, discovering the name and lineage of his namesake, interceded for his life, which not being opposed by John Naves, by reason of his finding that James Stewart was able to read his Bible and speak the English language, being qualifications in which his unfortunate companions were sadly deficient, his life was spared."

The man saved by Sir James Turner, "young Mac Coul", was evidently one of the MacDougalls, spelled thus by the use of English phonetics. There survives a traditional account of a MacDougall who was saved, by his own quick thinking and in the following remarkable circumstances:

"Bha Mac Dhùghaill Chille Mhunna ann agus glaodh e, "A bheil aon idir ann seo a thèarainneas deagh sgoileir?" Glaodh e a rithis ann an cainnt eile, "A bheil aon idir ann seo a thèarainneas deagh sgoileir?" Agus ghlaodh e ann a còig cànainean e. Chaidh Iarla Earra-Ghàidheal far an robh e agus chuir e a chleòch thairis air, agus mar sin chaidh Mac Dhùghaill Chille Mhunna a thèarnadh le Iarla Earra-Ghàidheal." ["MacDougall of Kilmun was there and he shouted "Is there any man here at all who will save a good scholar?" He shouted again, in another language, "Is there any man here at all who will save a good scholar?" And he shouted it in five languages. The Earl of Argyll went to him and put his cloak around him, and that is the way that MacDougall of Kilmun was saved by the Earl of Argyll."

Notes

1 In a report of 1 March, the pamphleteer could essay a little humour: "The Parliament of Scotland are full of consultation concerning the payment of their new Modell which are to March against Antrim and Kolkittoe: It is reported and you may believe it that hearing the King is at **Hollmby** they would fain be at home too, though the place where the King is (if he please) is but a **By** for his **Home** to **London**."

2 Note the reference to the Mill of Gocamgo; at Alasdair's birth [Chapter 4] his nurse had said he would one day set up his standard at that spot, and that he would never be successful afterwards. There is no denying that this seems to have been the turning point for *Alasdair*.... The mill survives in the form of a green conical mound to the east of the old road from Ford to Kilmichael Glassary. It is a couple of miles from Ford and perhaps one hundred yards from the road, slightly below it and beside the burn. It is curious that such a prominent monument seems to have been overlooked by RCAHM surveyors.

3 On his flight south through Glen Glassary he had to pass the crannog in *Loch Leathan*; MacIver of Barmolloch was hiding there and fired a shot that killed the man marching beside *Alasdair*. In an earlier skirmish in the locality, *Alasdair* had lost some men, the place were they were buried became known as *"Uaigh Fir Alastair mhic Colla"* ("Grave of Alasdair MacCholla's Men").

4 This was familiar ground to *Colla Ciotach*. In July 1615 Sir James MacDonald had based himself there whilst *Colla* and his fleet had been based across the sound, on Cara. [Chapter 6]

5 After various vicissitudes, only a small remnant of the Amelekites survived, but eventually the word of the Lord was fulfilled and their name (supposedly) blotted from the earth, in their utter destruction. Saul, having been very little less than assiduous in this work of extirpation, was unworthy of Jehovah, who therefore appointed David to succeed him; Saul became jealous and depressed; when the Philistines developed a great army, Saul turned for advice not to God but to the witch at Endor. Her advice being ambiguous, Saul launched an attack on the Philistines and got beaten, after which he committed suicide. There is said to have been no more pitiable character in history than the wretched Saul, wracked by doubt and indecision, swayed by evil, tormented by his own conscience.

16.

THE END OF THE STRUGGLE

Alastair needed in Ireland

Returning to 26 May 1647, Sir James Turner states that *Alasdair*, having left 300 men at Dunaverty, went across to Islay:

> "where he playd just such ane other mad prank, leaveing his old father, commonlie called Coll Kettoch, with neere 200 men in a castle, called Dunneveg, where was no water either bot what the heavens afforded. The rest of his men he carried with him to Ireland...."

We may reasonably assume that *Alasdair* was making best use of limited resources; he had only thirty or forty boats, capable of transporting perhaps one thousand men in calm conditions. These boats may have been just one fleet, used first in its entirety to transport many men quickly to Gigha; then, whilst a small number remained there to ferry that force to Islay, the bulk of the fleet could have sailed to (modern) Campbeltown to uplift more men as they retreated down the peninsula. Having carried those men to Ireland, the evacuation will have continued as long as possible from the remaining beach-head, beside Dunaverty. It seems that, in total, about 500 men either could not or would not be evacuated and that *Colla Ciotach* chose to return to his post as commander of the Dunivaig garrison. Very probably the disposition of men at Dunaverty was inadvertent, but at Dunivaig it was definitely by design, for whilst Leslie spent several weeks in besieging Dunaverty and arranging transport to reach Islay, there was nothing to prevent the garrison there from withdrawing to Ireland or even from scattering amongst the isles.

Whatever happened, *Alasdair* himself would not now be coming back in person to relieve these garrisons. The King, under duress, had agreed to meet many of the Parliamentarians' demands, which included giving his consent to the enforcement of anti-Catholic penal laws and, worse, ratifying the policy of oppression against both the native Irish and the "Old English" Catholics in Ireland. For those who stood for freedom, the battle was lost in England and Scotland (soon to be united under Cromwell), but that same battle would continue in Ireland, perhaps for many years.

The Scots Covenanting army in Ireland, under Robert Munroe, had suffered an humiliating defeat at Benburb the previous year, when 5000 Gaelic Irish and Old English troops, under the command of Owen Roe O'Neill, had inflicted very heavy casualties. By that victory, virtually all Ireland was in the hands of the Confederates and with the exception of tiny areas of countryside around Derry, Belfast and Cork, only a few of the major towns remained outside their control. One such town was Dublin, where Ormonde was soon forced to choose to which side he should surrender. So great was the intransigence of Rinuccini, refusing any accommodation in the matter of religious tolerance, that Ormonde, in June 1647, handed over his command to the representatives of the English parliament.

This was the very point at which Leslie's arrival in Kintyre had forced *Alasdair*'s hand

and the actual news of *Alasdair*'s Catholic army having crossed into Ireland was perhaps a factor in Ormonde's decision – the news of *Alasdair*'s arrival reached Dublin on 9 June. It might even be that *Alasdair* was ordered to delay the final evacuation of Kintyre until the last possible moment just because the situation in Ireland was so sensitive.

At this poignant moment, as he sails away from Scotland for the last time, one may reflect upon the magnitude of *Alasdair*'s achievement. Having fought a long and difficult campaign against extraordinary odds, a campaign which was eventually lost not in Scotland but through shameful treachery in England, he had almost completed a measured and careful disengagement. Many of his Scottish recruits had already been permitted to slip away to their homes and most of his Irish troops had made their way to Ireland or to the Continent. General Leslie's dramatic arrival certainly brought matters to a head, but it seems certain that *Alasdair* was ready to withdraw his remaining forces at a moment's notice. It was an absolutely extraordinary accomplishment by Colonsay's greatest son – three centuries later, many of the Allied troops who had to be abandoned at Singapore would have welcomed leadership such as his.

Surrender of Dunivaig

Back in Islay, events moved inexorably to the *dénouement*. Sir James Turner continued to write up his Memoirs after the massacre at Dunaverty, starting again with events on or about 20 June 1647, by which time the Covenanters had managed to obtain some boats:

> "From Kintire [West Loch Tarbert] we went by sea to Yla [in stormy conditions, landing eventually at modern Port Ellen], and immediatlie invested Dunneveg. I must remember, by the way, that we carried bot about fourscore horses with us after we left Kintire, the rest of the troops being left in Lorne, under the command of Colonell Robert Montgomerie, since Generall Major, who blockd up the house of [Dunollie] belonging to [MacDougall] in Lorne, whose clan was, as I said, extirpated very neere at Dunavertie.
>
> "Dunnaveg, after a short resistance, for want of water, came to a parley. I am appointed to treate with one Captain Oneale and one Donald Gorum, who came out of the house on the Lieutenant Generalls word. Life was promised to them; all the officers to goe where they pleased; the sojors to be transported to France, and given to Henry Sinclaire my old Lieutenant Colonell. The articles I saw couchd in writeing and signed by both Argile and Lesley. This capitulation was faithfullie observed."

The account is laconic, but the surrender of Dunivaig on 5 July 1647 may be seen as an important national milestone, marking the fall of the King's accredited representation in Scotland; from that day to this, the country was never again to be governed in Church or State other than as a pendicle of the English parliament. The terms of the surrender have been preserved:

> "ARTICLES agreed upon between my Lord Marquis of Argyll & General Lieut. Leslie, on the one part, and Ronald McDonald, Donald O_Neill and Donald McDonald, on the other part
> "In primis, the foresaid Ronald McDonald, Daniel O_Neill and Donald McDonald oblige

themselves to perform these conditions, after set forth fully:

1. That they shall deliver up the fort of Dunniveg, with all the goods, plenishing, Arms and ammunition therein, at or before 12 of the clock, on Monday the 5th of July, 1647
2. They, and every one of them, are to swear never to carry arms, upon any pretence whatsoever, against the public or kingdom of Scotland.
3. They are to leave and quit the fort without any arms or other baggage with them, except their necessary habitment, and, if the General Lieut. shall bestow any thing else upon them, it is to be at his discretion.
4. That, as many as the General Lieut. shall make choice of within the fort, shall go along, and remain constantly, with the Army whilst the rest of the strengths be gained, or the Army leave the [field?]; who are to have assurance now, and safe conduct then.

"Upon the performance whereof, we, Archd. Marquis of Argyll & Gen. Lieut. Leslie, promise, and oblige our soldiers, to grant unto all and every one within the said fort, their lives; and to promise all the country people, or Scotch men, to pass home and enjoy their own livings peaceably.

"And shall also transport safely the whole Irisches therein to Ireland or France, provided always that the said Ronald and Donald McDonald, and one Alaster McAlaster, must pass out that kingdom of Scotland, unless it shall please the Marquis of Argyll & General Lieut. to permit them to stay.

"For witness whereof we have –
– these proceedings at Dunnyveg the 4th of July, 1647"

Turner makes reference to the garrison being short of water, and says this forced the capitulation, but it sounds unlikely. Admittedly, in 1615 the castle had suffered "three dayes batterye" by Lambert's ordnance, and it is possible that the well was damaged then.[1] However, in the following thirty years there had been ample time for Campbell of Calder to have had it repaired, and in fact *Colla Ciotach* had had Dunivaig as his own headquarters for almost two years and had known for almost a month that he and two hundred men were to make a final stand therein. Even if the well could not be repaired, there is an ample supply of excellent water nearby (enough to justify the existence of the famous Lagavullin distillery and, earlier, the eponymous "mullin" or mill); hogsheads, skins, even boats drawn up within the curtain wall could all have been used for water storage.

Leslie, in the report that he wrote that very day to accompany the Articles of Surrender, made no reference to any lack of water having assisted him in his siege; but he did explain the fact that the surrender document was signed by *Raghnall MacCholla* and two other officers, rather than by *Colla Ciotach* himself (unfortunately, the document has suffered some damage and a few lines are missing or obscure):

"5 July 1647. Right Honourable –
" [Since I wrote] last to your Lordships, Coll MacGillespick [has fallen into our hands, in curious circumstances. He came to take conversation] of us without any assurance, propounds some conditions (though not reasonable), upon the which he would deliver up the fort of Dunniveg; but I [refusing] thereto, and proposing other, reasonable ones, which were refused

by him, for the [time] parleying was left off. Upon the 29 of Jun, Coll desired to speak with the Captain of Dunstaffnage, one of his old acquaintance, without a mention of any assurance for his safe return. After some [talk], part about yielding the house, he safe in again to the fort. [He sent] out again one of his soldiers, with a letter to [Dunstaffnage, in which] he desired XXX dollars worth of aquavite for [*defective*]; the captain shall be welcome to a share of it if [he supplies it] to him. It being enquired if the soldier, unless [*defective*] give in to him or not [*defective*]....... never once mentioning a word for assurance, either to those in his company or for his own safe return, from me or any others under my command: this so fair an opportunity of seizing upon so notorious a traitor, could not in reason be any longer slipped. And, therefore, order was given that, if he should again confer after that manner any more, they should lay hands on him, which fell out the next morning [*defective*] at which time he was apprehended by Lieut. Col. Munros[?] and three more. At all these former meetings, he seemed to be so far from [requesting] to me, or any other of my officers, assurance for his safety that he relied wholly upon himself and those brought out with him, who were in number four, coming always well-armed with swords, targes, hagbuts, long guns and some side-pistols. Which, in the meantime they were drawing of him into our sconce, escape to their own fort. Three days, after the acting hereof, was no thing but hard shooting, in which we received some small loss.

"Upon Sunday the 4th July, they called for a parley and, after long debate, they agreed to the enclosed conditions; and marched forth upon the 5th of this instant, to the number of 176 able fighting men, and to carry some of them alongst with me of the country men, until the rest of the strengths be reduced, so that [is] what I did.

"I was forced there to do what was contrary to my desire, for we are still straighted by reason of the want of all things specified in my last to you. [*Defective*] having nothing, except a little powder and lead, [*defective*] no meal at all, so that I conceive we might [*defective*] if not a little fresh flesh. The want also of all manner of timber, either for fire or making any works, this island affording little or none. This being added to the strength and fortification of the place, with the want of all manner of materials to work with, the impossibility of mining for rocks, the want of [sappers] or delvers, having so few we should get at best half a mile to the fort [*defective*] all the materials, and for storming ladders to Ireland (which are still as yet not come), yet the place being scarce stormable, the house well fortified and manned, and now the summer almost passed [July 5th!], conform us to these conditions; so that wherever I have done amiss cannot be payable to me, it being none of my fault, but of their who have furnished us.

"I intend now, God willing, if I can but get a few fresh fleshes with our bread, to set forward to O'Neill; although I can be no less than eight days in transporting my number here over, for want of boats. They will have been so few, for of the first promised number, and notwithstanding of all your Lordships' orders since, there is not a boat except the [four ?] that were sent by my Lord Montgomerie come from the lowlands yet, nor the least appearance of any.

"McLean has written me, professing in his letter that, since the pacification with James Grahame, he had never taken up arms; and, although the getting of his assurance be of consequence, yet I do not intend to protect him until he deliver up all his strengths to your Lordships, [likewise] all the Irisches (which are in his bounds, they being reported fifty), and find surety for his after carriage. However [I] intend to set forward thither, notwithstanding of all difficulties, which I resolve not to pursue; (by reason, in my opinion, the often and earnest representing of the same, should make your Lordships very sensible of them).

"I resolve to make safe of Colla, in the respect of the authority which his commission, herein enclosed, gives him, until the rest of the strengths be reduced; and then, as your Lordships' desire me to do with him shall accordingly be obeyed.

"I am informed that your Lordships have sent for my Lord Marquis of Argyll, wherefore , seeing his Lordship is [answerable] unto us in these isles, I shall desire your Lordships will give contrary order, for his stay, until it please God we come to the mainland, and then your Lordships may do as ye think fit.

"I have given the Tutor of Cawdor, who is Captain in Ardkinglass' regiment, the command of this house, and the captain of my dragoons Skipness and Kilkerran (until I know your Lordships' further orders), by reason no one else will grant to stay in them.

"Further I shall not trouble your Lordships; but register again my former supplications, that you will be more mindful in providing for the forces, at least not to suffer them to starve; which is all can be said for the present by,

Your most faithful and obedient servant – DAVID LESLIE

Dunivaig in Islay 5 July 1647"

[Postscript]
"If it had not pleased God to give our ships a prize in 300 bolls meal, was we had starved ere now; and seeing that also is all spent, I know not but we may yet starve before your Lordships send us any."

Leslie's account does not mention any shortage of water but rather suggests that the negotiated surrender was a matter of mutual convenience, particularly now that the King's representative had been seized. At least the surrender should mean that the 300 of *Alasdair*'s men who were slaughtered at Dunaverty would not be joined by 200 more, the agreement to send the Dunivaig garrison to France will have been politically expedient and even General Leslie will no doubt have been glad to avoid another lengthy siege and the sickening bloodbath which would have ensued. There had been talk of an imminent invasion by 4000 Irish reinforcements, which could have been a spur to negotiations, but perhaps recent intelligence from Ireland had defused that threat.

Even now, one tiny force of Royalists held out, but of no significance: "A litle skurvie ile in the end of Yla [the little castle in Loch Gorm] was keepd by a bastard sonne of Coll Kittoch [Angus], which we left to its fortune." In due course Angus made his way over to Antrim and made his home there, where his family continued for many generations.

Colla Ciotach kidnapped
The future was now very black for *Colla Ciotach*, despite the fact that he had been formally commissioned by *Alasdair* and was now the King's senior representative in Scotland; of noble birth and lineage, he had made the mistake of underestimating the depths to which Leslie would sink and had accepted his word of honour. Remembering that *Colla* had recently spent some years in captivity at Dunstaffnage and that Dunstaffnage's son had served as an acceptable factor in Colonsay in recent years, it was hardly surprising that *Colla* was happy enough to acknowledge an old acquaintance, siege or no siege:

"... before we were masters of Dunneveg, the old man Coll, comeing foolishlie out of the house, where he was governour, **on some parole or other** [author's emphasis], to speake with his old friend the Captaine of Dunstaffage Castle, was supris'd and made prisoner, not without some staine to the Lieutenant Generalls honor." Turner.

Leslie quite simply dishonoured the parole. *Colla* was seized on 1 July and hustled away into renewed captivity; on 27 July it was ordered that he should be sent to Edinburgh, and by 7 September he had arrived there by sea, in the charge of one Captain Brown. Somehow, Argyll managed to intervene and had him sent straight back to the west, to be lodged once again in Dunstaffnage. Meanwhile, on 5 July, in flagrant breach of the "faithful" observation of the terms of surrender, *Colla's* son *Raghnall* was also handed over to Argyll for private vengeance, as was another signatory, Donald Gorm MacDonnell. Whilst these and other prisoners awaited their (predictable) fate, Leslie's operations continued:

"From Yla we boated over to Jura, a horrid ile, and a habitation fit for deere and wild beasts [actually Norse for "wild beast island"]; and so from ile to ile till we came to Mull, which is one of the best of the Hebrides. Heere Maclaine savd his lands with the losse of his reputation, if ever he was capable to have any. He gave up his strong castles to Lesley, gave his eldest sonne for hostage of his fidelitie, and, which was unchristian basenes in the lowest degree, he deliverd up fourteene very prettie Irishmen, who had bene all along faithful to him, to the Lieutenant Generall, who immediatlie causd hang them all. It was not well done to demand them from Macklaine, bot inexcusablie ill done of him to betray them.

"Heere I cannot forget one Sir Donald Cambell, a very old man, fleshd in blood from his very infancie, who with all imaginable violence presd that all the whole clan of Macklaine sould be put to the edge of the sword; nor wold he be commanded to forbeare his bloody sute by the Lieutenant Generall and the tuo Generall Majors, and with some difficultie was he commanded silence by his chiefe the Marques of Argyle."

As we leave the pages of Sir James Turner's Memoirs, it is some relief to have read his simple testimony, and to know that some such men of honour and feeling had served in the ranks of the now-victorious rebels. He was in remarkable contrast to "Sir Donald Cambell", an extraordinary individual who, as *Colla Ciotach's* contemporary, has drifted in and out of these pages. Born in 1570 the illegitimate son of Sir John Campbell of Cawdor, he originally trained for the church; and it was his father who came to our attention when he was murdered at Knipoch, on 4 February 1592, as part of a comprehensive plot to undermine the 7th Earl of Argyll. It fell to his son to avenge the murder and in so doing young Donald wormed his way into the confidence of his even younger chief, then barely 18yrs old.

A man of remarkable resource, the young Sir Donald achieved his revenge and carved out a successful career in those turbulent times; he came to be known as "Barbreck" for his estate of that name at Loch Awe and was noted both for his ambition and his utter ruthlessness. Hardly surprisingly, he became useful to Argyll and was typically employed when, in 1612, Argyll sent him to seize Mingary and the lands of the long-deluded MacIans. A few years later, Argyll gave him a lease of those lands, but he was hated to such an extent that his tenantry, through Clanranald, actually sought help against him from the Earl of Argyll.

He entered the frame again in the rebellions centred on Dunivaig in 1614/15, and was in the thick of the forces which ejected Sir James MacDonald from Kintyre. His career continued to prosper and after the 7th Earl left for Spain, Donald received further lands through the young Lord Lorne, lands such as Airds in Appin, lands in Mull and in the Small Isles and in 1628 he gained his baronetcy. He appeared again in 1639, at the head of the Campbell invasion of Colonsay, leading to the despoiling of the island, the lengthy incarceration of *Colla Ciotach* and his sons and, memorably, the installation of *Domhnall Ballach* as the hated factor. Again we met him when, in 1644, *Alasdair* and his invading army overthrew his defences and made their base in his castle of Mingary; it was Sir Donald who mounted the siege described in the journal of Rev. Weir, a siege which was hurriedly abandoned when *Alasdair* returned. He turned up again in the battle of Inverlochy, where he was amongst those captured but spared by the victors. He was at Dunaverty and Dunivaig, now he is in Mull, still clamouring for blood; at 77 years, every bit as active as had been *Colla Ciotach* himself.

As for *Colla Ciotach*, he was by now *en route* back to Dunstaffnage and his familiar prison.[2] Tradition has it that he was by no means an unwelcome guest, and that Campbell of Dunstaffnage did everything that he could to ease the situation, even going so far as to give him personal liberty on parole. By some accounts, Campbell had married Beatrix, a daughter of Sir James MacDonald, and one might imagine her to be sympathetic.

"Trial" and execution

Arrangements were made for *Colla Ciotach* to be "tried" before a court packed with Campbells, under the jurisdiction of George Campbell of Airds, brother of John Campbell of Islay and heir-to-be of old Sir Donald. It was well known that under George Campbell, Argyll's sheriff-depute, there could be only one verdict and only one sentence; but it seems extraordinary that the normally cautious Argyll, as Justice General, was prepared to countenance, indeed actually promote, the murder of the man who now held the Royal commission, yet it is certain that *Gilleasbuig Gruamach* ("Grim Archibald"), as Argyll was known because of his squint and his sinister countenance, took personal charge of Coll's fate.

The "trial" took place in late September, certainly during harvesting; *Colla's* final hours have been widely preserved in tradition – the following account is largely based on those traditional renderings, particularly that of Professor MacKinnon. The story is still current; the author has heard it on a number of occasions with the dialogue, in particular, never varying.

Although there were few crops to be harvested elsewhere that year, at Dunstaffnage Mains, a fertile peninsula under the very walls of the castle, the corn had ripened in safety and there was now an urgency to save it. Every able body was at work, and in the warm sunshine, under his parole, *Colla* worked away with his captors, following the reapers.

Somehow, Argyll is said to have got an inkling of these congenial proceedings; Dunstaffnage was at Inveraray and Argyll asked him to his face "Is Colla under restraint?" Dunstaffnage did not dare to admit the truth, but Argyll saw through him.

"*Ma gheibh mise mach nach 'eil, dìolaidh tusa air*" (If I find out that he is not, you will pay for it!). This was the signal for as wild a chase as was ever seen, a cross-country race of some 40km, for whilst Argyll sent a messenger to find out the truth and to deliver Coll's death warrant, Dunstaffnage sent his own foster-brother, MacPhilip, to try to get ahead of him.

The route taken by Argyll's man can be easily seen on Blaeu's map (as published in 1654) and it mostly follows the line of modern roads: up Glen Aray to Taynafead, then down to Port Sonachan and across Loch Awe, straight up Glen Nant to Taynuilt and along the shore of Loch Etive, about 42 kms in all. Taking another route was much longer, but using all speed and every short cut that was possible, MacPhilip got down to the shore of Dunstaffnage Bay with a slight lead, and shouted across the water at the top of his voice: "*Colla fo gheimhlean!, Colla fo gheimhlean!*" (Coll in chains! Coll in chains!).

Colla was gathering the corn into bundles, forming stooks; he heard the shout on the calm, warm air, and understood. He left the field quickly and made his way down into his cell, where he fixed the chains about his ankles with his own two hands; and it was as a firm prisoner, secured and fettered, that the Earl's messenger found him when he arrived. The sentence of death was pronounced, and with Campbell of Airds as Depute Justice there was little chance of a reprieve.

Of course, a reprieve was irrelevant, since *Colla* would not request it. To the old man, death was preferable to colourless, comfortless life. "*An robh thu aig Inbhir Lòchaidh?*" ("Were you at Inverlochy?"), *Mac Mhic Eóghain* (MacLean of Ardgour) demanded of him in the court. "*Air mo bhaisteadh, a bhodaich, is mi bha, agus rinn mi barrachd sgath 's an teugmhail na rinn thu fhéin.*" ("I was there, old man, it was my baptism, and I made much more havoc and battle than you did yourself"), he replied with contempt.[3]

Coll, who was always very partial to his snuff, then expressed it as his dying wish to be buried close to Dunstaffnage's own lair, so that they could take snuff together sometimes, when his old friend would also be stretched beneath the sod.

Colla was eventually executed on 21 September 1647, and it is said that he was hanged from the mast of his own galley. Some say that the mast was laid across an inlet behind the castle, but most people are agreed that it was erected on *Tom a' Chrochaidh* ("Hanging Hill"), the hillock beside Saulmore Farm across the bay[4]. Very possibly his body was exposed on the gibbet for some days as was common practice, but eventually it was taken down and buried. As far as we know, *Colla* had his final wish fulfilled and was buried, under the second step, at the entrance to Dunstaffnage's tomb in the beautiful chapel beside the castle.[5]

There is a slightly confusing story that Coll was buried in "the old Parish Church of Oban"; taken literally, this would mean Kilmore, near Loch Nell, some 10kms away and quite a carry for the ripe remains of a supposed public enemy. In fact, in the troubles of the recent past there had been no regular ministry in the area and most churches had fallen into disuse and disrepair. In these circumstances the church at Dunstaffnage will have become the effective "parish church" for a wide radius.

Alastair fights on, in Ireland

Other quasi-judicial murders were carried out, notably in Inverary where the victims included *Raghnall MacCholla*, veteran of *Alasdair*'s campaigns. *Gilleasbuig* had died in the siege of Skipness, but *Aonghus* had made his way over to Antrim and was eventually to be the sole survivor of *Colla*'s sons; *Alasdair* was unable to join him as he had already been ordered south, where he and his men were deployed by Rinuccini in order to boost his own support in the increasingly divided Irish factions.

In July 1647, the army of the Old English had been engaged in an abortive siege of Trim, but the following month, when their forces had swollen to include part of *Alasdair*'s army (the "Catholic Scots" of Angus MacDonald of Glengarry), it was engaged in battle at Dungan's Hill and badly beaten by the Parliamentary forces. The Kilkenny Confederation was by now in dire straits and the rest of *Alasdair MacCholla*'s forces were required in Munster, to oppose the growing Parliamentarian threat of Murrough O'Brien (alias Lord Inchiquin). As lieutenant general of the Munster army (under Lord Taaffe), *Alasdair* was appointed governor of Clonmel, strategically placed on the banks of the River Suir. Lord Taaffe was based a few miles away, at Cashel.

Taaffe himself was not a military strategist and in August he made the mistake of sending most of his army on an offensive into County Cork, the heart of Inchiquin's territory. Ignoring the offensive, Inchiquin seized the opportunity and, in September, threw his forces into the lush, defenceless acres of the Golden Vale where his men carried out terrific depredations, culminating in the sack of the Rock of Cashel and the slaughter of some 3000 terrified countryfolk, including 30 priests. Significantly, he did not go on to try his luck against *Alasdair*, but withdrew once more to his own territory.

Plots and rumours of treachery were widespread and in early November, in an attempt to clear his name, Taaffe determined to engage Inchiquin in open battle. Knowing that Inchiquin was at Mallow, Taaffe got behind him and into Kanturk, between Mallow and the town of Cork itself. Inchiquin, inevitably, turned back to meet the threat and Taaffe, having the chance to select the field of battle, assembled the Confederate forces on the crest of *Knocknanoss* ("The Bushy Hill"), a few miles to the east of Kanturk.

Curiously enough, this important site is nowadays unremarked; it is not marked on maps, there are no signposts, even the inhabitants of neighbouring villages seem to have only a hazy idea of either the location or the importance of the battle that was fought there. *Knocknanoss* itself is now a large, open hill, the crest of which is good arable land, uncluttered by fences or modern development. One can readily imagine the scene as Inchiquin and his Parliamentarians launched an assault across the shallow valley and up a steep brae. Today, we are tempted to marvel at the thought of some 5000 Irishmen throwing themselves into war on behalf of the English parliament, in pitched battle against another 8000 Irishmen who were fighting for the English king.

In fact, it was a little more complex and it is worth remembering that this crucial battle had arisen as a result of Rinuccini's intransigence. He had intervened to prevent a pro-Royalist alliance which would have united the forces of the Confederates and of Ormondee with those of Inchiquin in the Cork Plantation. Rinuccini had rejected a guarantee of religious freedom for all and, by insisting that Catholicism had to become the Established religion, had made an impossible demand. The Confederates, heavily influenced by Spanish and Roman interests, had been drawn into a battle for their King, for their religion and for their way of life, whilst their opponents had been driven to resist what had become an almost overwhelming threat to their own existence.

Now, on the evening of 12 November, with the armies encamped within sight of each other, a chivalrous notion came to Lord Taaffe, which prompted him to send a note to Inchiquin, offering an even match between 1000 men from each army, "more for recreation than with a suspition that it might breake your army". Inchiquin's response was somewhat stiff: "you have performed as much as I desire in bringing your Army hither, I shall not desire you to loose any advantage you have in numbers of men, being your offer was only made for Recreation."

The above exchange is given by David Stevenson, who recreates the battle scene in some detail; suffice to say that *Alasdair* and his men took the right wing and triumphed by means of their redoubtable Highland Charge. Inchiquin's men were overrun and routed, and *Alasdair*'s men fell to plundering the baggage train. Taaffe and his own men were on the left, rather a long and shallow slope running down to a small river; between the two flanks the hill is steep and forms a bluff which obscured communication. As it happened, Taaffe's men had been outmanoeuvred and had fallen into confusion. Not knowing this, *Alasdair* and a small party came back to reconnoitre, but were spotted by a strong party of cavalry and, being out of reach of the main body of the Royalist troops, the little party was captured.

Alastair is murdered

Beside the pleasant river is the beautiful house of Assolas, formerly a monastery (*Atha Solais* ("The Ford of the Light"), there always being a light for the aid of travellers), and the old monastery had been commandeered as the Confederate Headquarters. *Alasdair*'s captors, under "a cornet of horse" called O'Grady, hustled him away from the battle-field by another route, crossing the river at the one place that preserves his memory, still known as "The Chieftain's Ford".[6] As the party crossed the ford, *Alasdair*'s horse paused to drink and naturally he leaned forward also, thus exposing a gap in his armour. At this opportunity, one of his captors, Major Nicholas Purdon of Ballyclough, stabbed him in the back – so died Sir Alastair MacDonald of Colonsay, Knight of the Field, 13 November 1647.

There were various other accounts that circulated later, but it is agreed that *Alasdair* was murdered in cold blood and it seems likely that the cause was jealousy – that his captors had vied to claim the honour of his capture. It is said that O'Grady was outraged and that, in revenge, "the Coronet for Seven Years fought Pourdon every year but most commonly got the worse, which was more the Pity ...".

With *Alasdair* dead, the tide of battle turned again and at last it was the Confederates that were routed; 3000 or more were killed, the flight and slaughter continuing even through the following day. Rinuccini himself commented on the disaster that "This battle is rendered memorable by the ignominious flight of the Catholics and the loss of Macdonnell, who had fought thirty battles in Scotland, victorious always, in defence of religion and the King, and he would have been so now had not the Munster troops basely abandoned their brethren."

A long way from Dunivaig, *Alasdair* and his hardy Scottish soldiers had been in the thick of it, and had actually won the victory that their less experienced colleagues could not hold; it is interesting to note that at both the battles in which they were engaged, at Dungan's Hill and now at *Knocknanoss*, *Alasdair*'s Scots gained the same magnificent reputation as had his "Irisches" in his Scottish campaigns.

The author of "A Contemporary History" traced these events in detail, and was completely convinced that *Alasdair* was the victim of a deliberate plot, inveighing against the "inhuman treachery of General Taaffe". He describes the battle:

".. the right hande of the field was alotted to this Machabeyan souldier and his reddshankes, his task was to give the first onsett, which he performed on the enemie with such an undaunted courage that he caused all the armie suspense, rather wonderinge at his valerous charge, then any way able to oppose it, gained ground so farr, that in a thrice was master of the enemie ordinance.

"His proper Generall [Taaffe] obsearvinge, how he was too farr engaged, instede of relivinge or seconddinge him, oblivious of all honor and worth, comannded the rest of his armie to marche out of the field, leavinge this onelie gentleman in action against the enemie multitude." At this, one Richard Butler challenged Taaffe and "besought him with all vehemencie possible, to turne and relive that brave champion McDaniell, for allmost the field was his owne alreadie, and beinge relived, without question was theires.." Taaffe refused, upon which Butler made a striking speech, concluding ".. though alone, I will venture the battle to the extreame hazard of life, onely to share in honor for future ages, with that martiall broode [Alasdair and his redshanks].

This did not please Taaffe: "By the livinge Lord, if you would once offer to doe it, I would pistle you." Butler replied that he had better not to attempt it, or "he would bullett him, like an archtraytor, as he was", and with that went to join Alasdair on the field. At this stage, Inchiquin's right moved through the positions abandoned by Taaffes left, and wheeled round to attack Alasdair's men from the rear, who were caught by suprise "verily beleevinge those to be their owne untill experience taught them to theire losse the contrary."

"Then began the mortalitie on either side, the event doubtfull untill at lenght, the heroycke and valiant reddshankes, never yeldinge, but rather gaininge grounde, were all for the most part slaughtered, theire warrlike chieftaine behavinge himself like another Jonathas, that none durst aneere him; noe such feates was seene by our progenitors acted by an ordinarie man (unless assisted by a higher power), who could not be either killed, vanquished or taken prisonier; but of his owne accorde, seeinge the mortalitie of his men and his owne present danger, yelded upon quarter of life and arms."

As soon as the victory was assured, the victorious army moved off towards Limerick, leaving the vanquished to bury their dead. *Alasdair*'s funeral was to Clonmeen, on the opposite bank of the Blackwater, where he was buried in the family plot of Donough O'Callaghan, a member of the Confederate Supreme Council and a supporter of Rinuccini. It is possible to follow the route of the sad cortège through the little boreens, to visit the ruined chapel and somewhat jumbled graveyard; no stone preserves the name or memory, but it takes little imagination to picture the scene of lamentation as this youthful hero was laid to rest, a mere 27 years of age. It is said that a pibroch, "Mac-Allistrum's March", was played at the funeral, as it had been played before the battle, and that for two hundred years it remained current in Munster, with the human voice serving instead for the drone of the pipes.

Gilbert published one of the many epitaphs that were written:

"Alexandri Colliadae Mac Daniell, Tribuni militum (Qui velut alter Machabaeus, pro fide et patria, fortis-

sime certans, gloriosus occubuit)

Epitaphium:
Ad Nossas heros vicit, victorque perivit,
Venditus a sociis, emptus ab hoste, suis.
Infelix praxis Judae, non Martis alumni,
˙Qui patriam tradens, vendidit aere ducem.
Inversum fatum, Taffum, tunc nominis esse,
Dum laetum in tristem, verterat arte diem."

Alasdair MacCholla MacDonald, Military Commander (who just like another Maccabaeus,
for faith and native land, of great unwavering strength, lies glorious)
To (Cnoc nan) Nos the hero conquered, and perished as a victor,
Sold by his associates, purchased by his enemy.
A faithless act of Judas, no fosterchild of Mars,
Who betrayed his native country, sold the general for bronze.
Perverting fate, then, Taaffe, made famous thus,
Whilst cheerful in despair, inverts the day's success.

Coll's epitaph?

So ends the story; there is no monument to Coll or his family in Colonsay, nor in the Chapel at Dunstaffnage, not even at Dunivaig. Professor MacKinnon commented that "in the present day" [c.1900], the heroic *Colla Ciotach* deserved fame and honour in his native land, whilst in his own day he had enjoyed only fame, without reward. Although MacKinnon felt that *Colla* was not a completely innocent victim, he emphasised that his murder, in old age, was to the great disgrace of his enemies and Professor MacKinnon's final comment might make a suitable epitaph:

Chaill e a bheatha a chionn gun do chuir e
earbsa an onoir Leslie is Mhic Cailean

He lost his life because he trusted
to the honour of Leslie and Argyll

On the other hand, *Colla Ciotach* himself might not wish to share his renown with lesser men. Fortunately Ronald Black, in his study of a manuscript of *Cathal Mac Muireadhaigh*, has drawn attention to the following inscription, "superimposed in a large, coarse hand". Although there is no specimen of *Colla*'s handwriting available for comparison, Ronald Black wondered if it could have been written by him, and at least we can be confident that it was a maxim of which he would have approved:

Reid or thow Judge then Judge thy fill
******* the best and mend thy w[ill]

Pause, before you judge, then judge your fill;
Deciding for the best, strengthening your will.

Notes

1 The well can easily be seen today, in a corner of the bawn. It is partly collapsed and rubble-choked, but this may well have been deliberate damage when the castle was finally de-commissioned.

2 The prison in Dunstaffnage is in the west tower and was entered by a trapdoor; although sufficiently spartan, it did at least boast a latrine.

3 By historical accounts, *Colla* was still imprisoned at the time of Inverlochy, although many traditions have him participating in this and other battles.

4 It is worth noting that road widening has become a threat to this important site NM 83/93 892339

5 This extraordinarily fine chapel is one of the gems of pre-Reformation architecture that have survived to us in Argyll. The monument is in the care of a State body that seems more concerned with the nearby castle, where a recent visitor was assured that the attendant had never heard of *Colla Ciotach* MacDonald. The lairage at the eastern end of the chapel is, of course, a much later affair; *Colla Ciotach*'s grave would be close to the doorway in the south, surviving wall.

6 The Chieftain's Ford is no longer in use, there being a modern farm bridge some 100 yards downstream, but local people still know the spot and will point it out.

EPILOGUE

King Charles

The death warrant of King Charles I was issued on 29 January 1648:

> "Whereas Charles Stuart, King of England, is, and standeth convicted, attainted, and condemned of high treason, and other high crimes; and sentence upon Saturday last was pronounced against him by this Court, to be put to death by the severing of his head from his body; of which sentence, execution yet remaineth to be done; these are therefore to will and require you to see the said sentence executed in the open street before Whitehall, upon the morrow, being the thirtieth day of this instant month of January, between the hours of ten in the morning and five in the afternoon of the same day, with full effect. And for so doing this shall be your sufficient warrant. And these are to require all officers, soldiers and others, the good people of this nation of England, to be assisting unto you in this service. To Col. Francis Hacker, Col. Huncks, and Lieut.-Co. Phayre, and to every of them.
> Given under our hands and seals
> JOHN BRADSHAW
> THOMAS GREY
> OLIVER CROMWELL &c. &c.

The office of King was abolished by Act of Parliament on March 17 1649, and the House of Lords was abolished two days later.

Huntly

Some individuals had experienced their own troubles. Huntly was effectively on the run all through the summer of 1647; passing west through Badenoch, he continued as far as Lochaber where, in November, he was betrayed by the Camerons. Although Aboyne escaped into exile, Huntly was captured and later executed.

Montrose

The Marquis of Montrose had sought to assist the Restoration by direct action and was encouraged by Charles, who made him a Knight and Companion of the Order of the Garter on 12 January 1650. Montrose organised an invasionary force to be based upon Kirkwall in Orkney; the advance party arrived in January, having had great difficulties due to bad weather, and he arrived to join them in mid-March. After further difficulty on the crossing to the mainland, his expedition was shortlived, getting no further than the head of the Kyle of Sutherland, on the border of Sutherland and Ross-shire, where his forces were routed on 27 April 1650. Montrose had his horse shot from under him, but the bravery of a colleague enabled him to escape from the field; half-starved, he fell into the hands of MacLeod of Assynt and was delivered to Leslie. He was "tried" in his absence without benefit of defence and, on his arrival at Edinburgh, he was met by the public hangman and allowed to read his sentence to be hanged for three hours "with the book of his deeds and his Declaration to the Scots tied about his neck". As he was driven through the streets, he was surrounded by tears and prayers, to the discomfiture of the Covenanters; it was characteristic that he gave the hangman a tip: "Fellow, ther is drink monie for dryving the cairt!" Montrose was hanged, on a specially built scaffold 30 feet high, in the High Street on May 21 1650. His head and limbs were exposed at Edinburgh Tolbooth, and at Stirling, Glasgow, Perth and Aberdeen. His last words were to entreat "God Almighty have mercy on this perishing nation!" In 1661 his scattered remains were recovered and buried in St. Giles', being accorded a magnificent funeral; all his remains except for his heart... which is another story.

Argyll

> "Now Earl of Guile, and Lord For Lorn thou goes
> Leaving their Native Prince to serve his foes;
> No faith in plaids, no truth in tartan trews,
> Chameleon-like, they change a thousand hues."

The Marquis of Argyll, for all his wiles, did not survive the Restoration and the crimes on which he was arraigned included the murder of *Colla Ciotach* and his son Ranald. Chameleon-like, he had been astute enough to welcome the monarch on his initial return to Scotland in 1650 "upon whose Head, at the Solemnity of his Coronation, *anno* 1650, he put the Crown." But when Charles II suffered a reverse in England, Argyll decided to side with Cromwell... thus, at the Restoration, he may have been disappointed but can hardly have been surprised to be confronted with his crimes. Found guilty, Argyll was beheaded in May 1661 at Edinburgh, by means of the Scottish guillotine, "The Maiden". He knew how it worked, for on 20 December 1645 when the same instrument had been especially brought to St. Andrews and erected at the Market Cross, Argyll had taken an upstairs room nearby and watched discreetly from behind the curtains as Sir Robert Spottiswoode was executed. By another little irony, Argyll's head came to occupy, above the Tolbooth, the very spike that had so recently been vacated by that of Montrose.

Antrim

The Marquis of Antrim stood by his monarch in these troubled times and eventually was restored to his estates, but not without the greatest difficulty. It was held that in signing "that execrable oath of Association" at Kilkenny he had acted as a traitor; in fact, of course, the new occupants had no wish to relinquish their possession of his property, and sought to whip up support for their cause by reference to the 1641 Rising, accusing Antrim of "being one of the Irish rebels in the beginning of that war, when in the horrid massacre two hundred thousand protestants were murthered". It was a tremendous battle and brought great business to the lawyers, but eventually a "decree of innocence" was issued in August 1663. Charles II instructed Ormonde that:

"Our will and pleasure is that you Insert a Clause in the Bill of Explanation lately transmitted from our Kingdome of Irelande, whereby our Trusty and Well-beloved Cosen, Randall Marquess of Antrim, may be Declared to be an Innocent Papist, and as an Innocent Papist, bee restored unto all Lands, Tenements, and Hereditaments whatsoever whereof he, or any interest for him were lawfullie seized and possessed upon the Three and Twentieth Day of October 1641 ...."

Restored to a significant proportion of his states, he and his wife lived quietly in retirement.

Alastair's family

It was fortunate for many that Antrim was eventually restored, for he seems to have remained generous in spirit throughout all his vicissitudes, and found energy and means to assist many of his clansmen. Rev. Hill has recorded what facts are available in some detail. It seems that *Alasdair MacCholla*'s wife and two sons had been in the care of his wife's parents, Hector MacAllister of Loupe and his wife (who was a connection of Argyll); old Hector had defied Argyll and was, with his own two sons, on the way to join the garrison at Dunaverty when he was captured by Argyll and murdered, at Whinny Hill, near Campbeltown. "First hang the whelps, and then the old fox" are said to have been Argyll's instructions, whilst his kinswoman, Hector's wife, arrived too late – " she fell on her knees invoking the most fearful curses on *Gillaspick Grumach*; and the people of the district, "who to this day tell the story" [1873], never fail to add that this heart-broken woman's curses clung to Argyle until he himself was dragged to the scaffold."

Fortunately, his own two young sons went with *Alasdair* and his wife to Ireland, where they remained in the Glens of Antrim. The elder, Coll, was known as *a' mhuillinn* ("the miller"), indicating a position of some standing. He had reasonable estate and lived at Kilmore, in Glenariff, being married to one Anne Magee, originally of Island Magee. It is clear that Coll and his own son, Alexander, were under some protection from Antrim and his descendants, and that the Marquis fulfilled his trust. Alastair's second son, *Gilleasbuig Mór*, who had been but a babe in arms in 1647, later joined the army "and became a distinguished officer"; he married Anne Stewart, of Redbay, and died in 1720, after he had retired to "Glassmullin, in the parish of Layd". Their children were Catherine and Coll (the latter marrying Anne M'Donnell of Nappan). Doubtless, thus, there are many direct descendants of *Colla Ciotach* alive today, descendants of Sir Alastair MacDonald.

The family burial-place in Layde Graveyard contains a number of interesting memorials. "Here lieth the remains of Coll McDonnell of Kilmore, Glenariff, who died 25th March 1719. Son to Major General Sir. Alexr. McDonnell (MacCollcitto) by his wife, dtr. of McAllister, Laird of Laup...." "TOUT TOUTS PRET. Here lyeth the body of Captn. Archd. McDonnell, son to Alexr. McDonnell Major Genl. & Knt. of y field who departed this life Sepr. 28th 1720 aged 73...."

The rivals at Knocknanoss

Further south, Lord Inchiquin changed sides again and came to support the

Confederates; thus he found himself in company with Lord Taaffe and Richard Butler when, August 12 1652, the Act for the Settlement of Ireland specifically excluded them from "pardon for life or estate." Purdon was never punished for the murder of *Alasdair* and his roofless, ivy-clad but intact tower-house still stands nearby, a mute reminder.

Clan Donald adherents

Back in Scotland, the remnants of the MacDonalds and their adherents had a thin time of it, there being every sign of a deliberate campaign to destroy them utterly. Campbell of Dunstaffnage may well have been, as in tradition, a true friend of *Colla Ciotach*, but by his wife Beatrix MacDonald he had a daughter, Janet, of a different hue. This Janet married her second cousin, George Campbell of Airds, Tutor of Cawdor and the Depute Justice who had murdered so many innocent men. (George was eventually the heir to Sir Donald Campbell of Ardnamurchan, "Barbreck", when he died in 1652.) Janet became immortalised in an unpleasant story recorded in the Manuscript History of Craignish, a story which gives a hint of the undoubted efforts to extirpate the whole name of MacDonald:

> "[One Duncan Campbell] kept a large Birling when a young man which he traded with to the coast of Ireland and the north Isles, and kept a strong band of men aboard of her generally; and it being the practice of a wicked woman [Janet] of the Family of Dunstaffnage then in Chief Command of the Island [of Islay] – she was married to the first George of Octomore son to Calder – this wicked woman was in practice of seizing in the night all the followers of the Family of McDonald who was and is still the chief of the inhabitants [i.e. the majority] upon that Island. By this womans orders the people would be bound hand and foot and carried away in boats and Birlines in the night time and before day and left on Desart Rocks and Islands in the seas there to perish. This [Duncan] Campbell would come and relieve them and land them on the coast of Ireland and Island of [Rathlin], and its told he always had the fair wind going and coming while he was relieving them. There was another wicked woman at Dunstaffnage [Beatrice?] that had the same practice of persecuting the remains of Coll McDonalds and his son Alexanders men, wherefrom he carried two cargoes with the like success...."

Seemingly this was an account given by the children of the rescued victims; if Campbell of Dunstaffnage was any friend of Coll MacDonald his wife and daughter cannot have embarked upon their bloody sport before his death in 1652, and it seems unlikely that it will have been politic to continue after the MacDonalds' return to grace (1660). The extraordinary feature of the story is that Janet ("The Black Bitch of Dunstaffnage") was said to have been the grand-daughter of Sir James MacDonald of Dunivaig.

Clan Donald of Colonsay

In Colonsay, Argyll retained possession for some years and the tacksman in 1651 and 1652 was one Donald MacFie, but by 1653 he had been replaced by a John Campbell. Eventually, at the Restoration, *Colla Ciotach*'s loyalty and bravery was rewarded by a grateful monarch. The estate of which he had been dispossessed was restored to him by Act of Parliament in 1661, in the person of his eldest surviving heir, Sarah, (the daughter of his eldest son, *Gilleasbuig* "of the yles of Colinsay and Ornsay"). The following year, property which *Colla Ciotach* had held from the Bishop of the Isles was also restored by charter, with new title deeds being issued to Sarah by Bishop Robert Wallace.

As it happened, in 1663, following the execution of the Marquis of Argyll, the Earldom of Argyll was granted anew to his son Lord Lorn, and included the superiority of Colonsay and Oransay (in the barony of Ardnamurchan); this grant was confirmed in 1667, (although Oransay and Garvard were then restored to the barony of Balwill). When, as ninth Earl of Argyll, Archibald was himself executed for treason in 1685, his possessions reverted to the Crown but some of his followers may have failed to realise that fact, or possibly tried to take advantage of the death of Charles II on February 2 1686 to try to re-establish the old order. Whatever the reason, on 8 July 1686 Sarah had cause to complain to the Privy Council:

> "Summons at the instance of Sarah McDonald of Oronsay, Aeneas McDonald, her husband, for his interest, and Donald McDonald, Tutor of Largie, against [blank] Campbell of Craikaygg and Archibald Campbell in [blank], who with twenty men in arms, with swords, pistols and hagbuts, invaded the said Donalde McDonald while he was uplifting the rents of the lands of Oronsay conform to a commission and factory from the said Sarah MacDonald, and threatened him for meddling with the said rents; and when he produced his warrant and took instruments of protestation and proceeded to poind [distrain goods] conform to law they assaulted and beat him and his assistants and deforced them by retaking the poinded goods and gear."[1]

The new sovereign was a committed Catholic and, believing that he ruled at God's command, saw rebellion as little better than sacrilege. No doubt this small matter was handled by his secretariat, but they acted on his command. Within months the legal position was clarified, when, on 22 October, King James VII granted a renewed charter to Sarah for her lands in Oransay and Garvard, in the following terms:

> "**Charter by King James the [Seventh],** in consideration of the singular bravery and constant fidelity of the late Colonel Coill McDonnell *alias* McGilespick VcDonnell of Colonsay, and Archibald [Gillespick], his son, in the cause of the King's father, and that the said Archibald was killed in that service, while the said colonel was violently murdered for his firm adherence to the cause, and also considering that the colonel and his son were forfeited by the late usurper, and were ejected from their whole estate, because of their faithful service in joining with the late Marquis of Montrose;
>
> "**and because** the said estate, from the death of Colonel McGilespick and his son, had been dealt with by the late Marquis of Argyll and others until 22nd May [1661], when the late King and the Parliament restored to Sara McDonnell, only lawful daughter and heir of the late Colonel Coill McGilespick, her grandfather, the rights and estate of the islands of Colonsay and Oronsay, and ordained her to enter on possession, declaring that she should lawfully enjoy the same, as heir served and retoured to the said Archibald McDonnel, her father, or Colonel Coill McGilespick, her grandfather, notwithstanding the spoliation and burning and destruction of the writs of the lands, which rendered her title incomplete;

"**considering, also,** that the Isle of Oronsay belonging to the McDonnells, formerly held of the late Earl of Argyll, is now held of the Crown, and desiring also to confer a new right to the lands, the King grants to the said Sara and to the heirs-male of her body by Aeneas McDonald, her spouse, the said lands and isle of Oronsay, including Island Nirone [Eilean nan Ron, "Seal Island"], Island Giddimull, [Eilean Ghaoidmeal "Island of Stolen Rent"], Island Nenine [Eilean nan Eun "Bird Island], and island Vuag [Eilean Bhugaig "Whale-like Island"], extending to five merks of old extent, the 16s 8d lands of Garvart in Colonsay, with all pertinents, lying formerly in the shire of Tarbat and now in the shire of Argyll: To be held in feu-farm – Oronsay for £3 yearly and Garvart for 13s 4d yearly."

The sasine to this charter, dated 3 September 1687, was registered on 19 October 1687, witnessed by "John MacKay, in Beauchmeannoch, Alexander Heyman, in Bellachgerran, John MacKay, servitor to Archibald McDonald of Largie, and Alexander McCoull [MacDougall], in Glaickindunen" Thus Sarah, like Jeremiah with the Babylonians at the gate, ensures that the legal contract to her land is signed, sealed and delivered. "The Lord Almighty, the God of Israel, has said that houses, fields and vineyards will again be bought in this land."

But within months, William of Orange had received a formal invitation to invade England and on 5 November 1688 he landed, at Torbay. On 22 December, James fled to France. On 11 May 1689, William and Mary accepted the Scottish throne with a settlement "which restored Presbyterianism and put the ecclesiastical clock back to where it had stood in about 1592" (Stewart Ross). Under this regime, it did not take long for the Campbells to oust the MacDonalds of Colonsay and on 25 May 1695 Neill McNeill of Taynish, at Kilmichael Glassary, received a 19-years tack of Colonsay and Oronsay, from Charles Campbell, brother to the Earl of Argyll. After a very few years, the islands were sold outright by the 10th Earl of Argyll to Malcolm McNeill of Knapdale, March 1701 who soon afterwards, in a nice twist of fate, married Barbara, daughter of the then Campbell of Dunstaffnage.

Notes

1 It is an interesting fact that a small island beside the main anchorage in Oransay is called *Eilean Ghaoideamal* ("Island of stolen rents") and that a story concerning just such an incident is often told; (sometimes the story is that the rent was stolen and that the robber hid here until the pursuit died down; sometimes there is said to be a secret tunnel connected with the priory, through which the rent was carried off). But the name must be mere coincidence, since the map published by Blaeu in 1654 already gives that island the name of "Oilen na Gyid" and by 1686 it is recorded as "Island Giddimull".

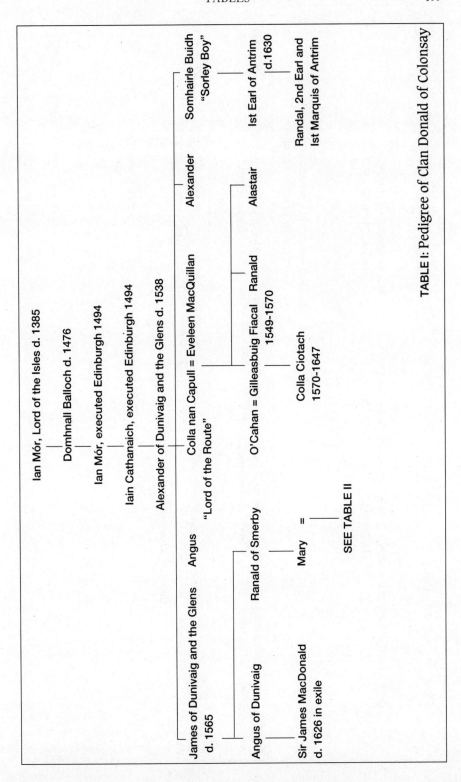

TABLE I: Pedigree of Clan Donald of Colonsay

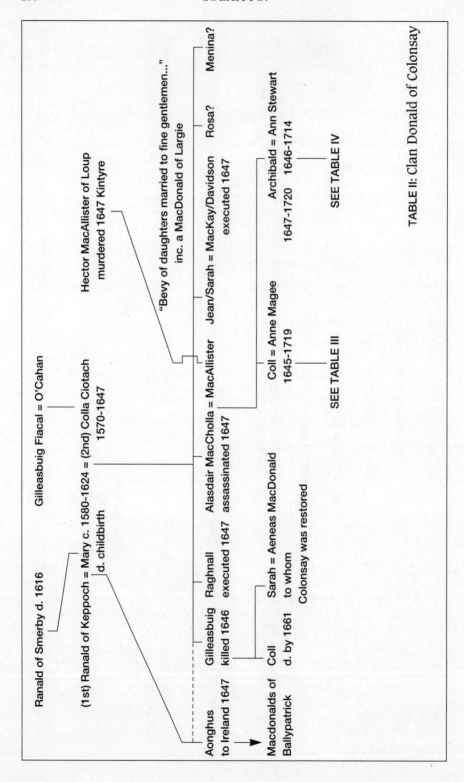

TABLE II: Clan Donald of Colonsay

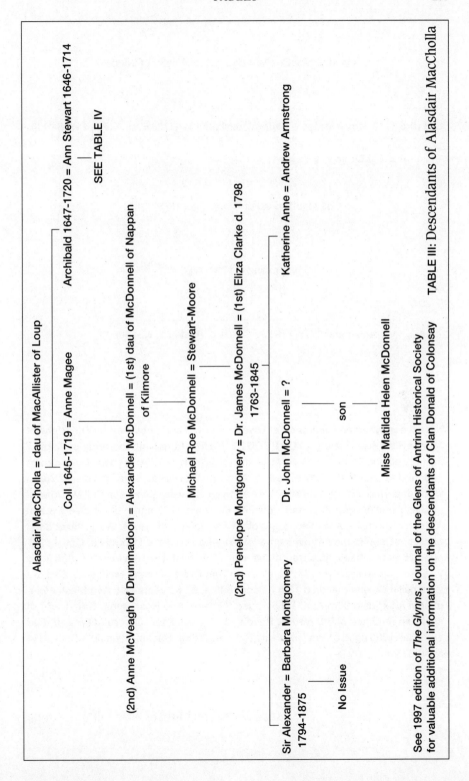

Alasdair MacCholla = dau of MacAllister of Loup

Coll 1645-1719 = Anne Magee

Archibald 1647-1720 = Ann Stewart 1646-1714

SEE TABLE IV

(2nd) Anne McVeagh of Drummadoon = Alexander McDonnell = (1st) dau of McDonnell of Nappan of Kilmore

Michael Roe McDonnell = Stewart-Moore

(2nd) Penelope Montgomery = Dr. James McDonnell = (1st) Eliza Clarke d. 1798
1763-1845

Dr. John McDonnell = ?

Katherine Anne = Andrew Armstrong

son

Miss Matilda Helen McDonnell

Sir Alexander = Barbara Montgomery
1794-1875

No Issue

See 1997 edition of *The Glynns*, Journal of the Glens of Antrim Historical Society
for valuable additional information on the descendants of Clan Donald of Colonsay

TABLE III: Descendants of Alasdair MacCholla

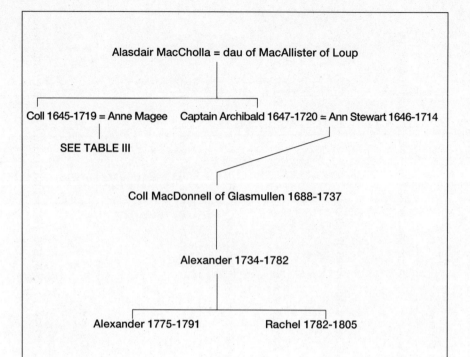

Alasdair MacCholla = dau of MacAllister of Loup

Coll 1645-1719 = Anne Magee   Captain Archibald 1647-1720 = Ann Stewart 1646-1714

SEE TABLE III

Coll MacDonnell of Glasmullen 1688-1737

Alexander 1734-1782

Alexander 1775-1791   Rachel 1782-1805

Note the gravestone inscription at Layde recorded and published by The Glens of Antrim Historical Society: "TOUT TOUTS PRET. / Here lyeth the body of Captn / Archd McDonnell son to / Alexr McDonnell Major Genl / & Knt of ye field who depart / ed this life Sepr 28th 1720 ag / ed 73. Also Ann Stewart sp / ouse to yd said Captn who / departed this life April 6th / 1714 aged 68. Likewise their / son Coll McDonnell of Glas / mullen who departed / this life 6th June 1737 aged 49 / & also his son Alexr McDonnell / who died July 26th 1782 aged / 48 years. Also Alexander / McDonnell son to the / above named Alexr who / died the 11th day of Octr / 1791 aged 16 years. Also / his sister Rachel who / departed the 19th March / 1805 aged 23 years. / Also said Alexr McDonnells dtr Ann / wife of Archd McElheran Esq of / Glasmullin Cushendall died 18th / Decr 1885 aged 61 years also Ann Black / wife of said Alexr died 30th April 1885 / aged 98 years also Rose Anne, Grand / dtr of said Ann mcElheran 2nd dtr / of Randal McDonnell Esqr Kilmore / Glenariff died 18th May 1850 aged 31 yrs / also said Randals 3rd dtr Rachel / died 30th Decr 1854 aged 33 yrs."

TABLE IV: Descendants of Alasdair MacCholla

APPENDIX 1

Details of Trial of Angus *Og* following his surrender of Dunivaig Castle.
The charges are recounted in Pitcairns "Criminal Trials" (spelling modernised here):

"July 3 – ANGUS OIG McDONALD, Allaster McAllaster, Angus McAllaster, Allaster McArliche, Johnne McCondochie, Johnne Gair McMoylane.

"Accused of the treasonable taking, keeping, and detaining of his Majesty's Castle of Dunyveg, in Islay, and resisting of the Laird of Caddell, his highness' Lieutenant and Commissioner &c.; as in THE DITTAY [indictment] following:

"FORSAMEKILL AS, they, accompanied with Coil McGillespick and others, their complices, all rebels and broken men, to the number of fifty persons or thereby, in the month of November last, most treasonably convoked themselves in arms, came forward in open and battle array to his Majesty's Castle and strength of Dunyveg, in Islay; and there by craft and policy, took in the said Castle, which they stuffed [provisioned] and furnished with muskets, hagbutts, powder, lead and other warlike furniture, for holding thereof: which treasonable practices, so enterprised by them and their complices, being made known to the Lords of His Majesty's Secret [Privy] Council; and they, for redress of the said rebels' enormities, having directed the Laird of Caddell, with companies of waged men of war, as Lieutenant of His Majesty, with an Herald [Robert Wynrahame, Albany (Islay)], and trumpeter, to charge them, in his highness' name and authority, to render the said Castle, and to recover the same forth [out of] their hands. LIKE AS, the said Lieutenant, with his forces, together with the said Herald and trumpeter, having come to the said country of Islay, to the effect foresaid, the aforenamed persons, with their rebellious associates, understanding thereof, directed forth a great number of their rebellious company against the said Herald and trumpeter and most treasonably stayed and interrupted them from coming forwards to the said Castle, for giving of the said charge; through which, for fear of their lives, they dared not come forward to the said house: Lyk as, after his Majesty's Lieutenant had planted him self with his forces round about the said Castle, and had saluted the said rebels, being therein, with nine score shot of ordnance, shot by them thereat, the said persons on panel [on trial], notwith-standing of the said Assault made by the said Lieutenant to the said Castle, most treasonably held out, kept and detained the same against him, he being clad with his Majesty's authority, as Lieutenant and Commissioner, for releasing thereof; and treasonably shot forth again [returned fire], out of the said Castle, at the said Lieutenant and his company diverse shots of muskets, and therewith slew Captain Crawford, with four other of his Majesty's faithfull servants and subjects, who were in service with the said Lieutenant, in the execution of his Commission. AND the said persons on panel, and every one of them, are art and part of the said treasonable crimes....

"VERDICT: The Assize, all in one voice, ... found, pronounced, and declared the said persons on panel, and every one of them, according to their own Depositions, and approbation thereof in judgement, to be ffylet, guilty, culpable, and convicted of art and part in the whole treason-able crimes contained in the Dittay. – SENTENCE. To be taken to the Market Cross of Edinburgh, and there to be hanged upon a gibbet, untill they be dead; and all their moveable goods to be confiscated and brought in; and all their lands, heritages, and annual rents pertaining to them, to be forfeit to his Majesty's use, &c."

APPENDIX 2

Statements concerning the defeat of Sir James MacDonald, 1615.

Detailed statements concerning the military response to Sir James MacDonald's campaign in 1615 appear in the "Register of the Council of James VI", and/or The Denmylnes MSS; the best summary is given in "The Book of Islay". These eye-witness statements are of great interest in their own right, and also form the basis for criticism levelled at Colla Ciotach by modern writers, but it will be seen from the sequence that Argyll was seeking to exculpate himself from allegations of leniency, and therefore sought to show that his negotiations with Colla Ciotach had been beneficial to the Crown. The truth was known to contemporary witnesses, and is reflected in the fact that Colla was a great and popular hero, eulogised in song and story. For convenience these statements are reproduced here with spelling and some few words or phrases modernised:

Dunyvaig, 13th October 1615.
Letter from Earl of Argyll to Secretary Binning [of the Privy Council]

"My very good Lord, as I wrote to your Lordship in my last letter from the Lodinnis [Port Ellen] in Islay that after I landed my men I made an onset on the rebels where they were encamped at Eilean Orsay in Islay, where the greatest part of the rebels' boats was apprehended. And, if it had not been that some of the tenants were near to my camp and seeing my forces row away in their boats, the moon shining, who presently made on great beacons upon the top of an high hill; the which, so soon as Sir James did see, before my men were at him by six or seven miles of sea, he went to his boat accompanied with McRannald, Sorle McJames, and some four and twenty or thirty with them, otherwise he could not have escaped.

"As they were going into their boats, some of the principal tenants of Islay desired him to have stayed, and because they had hazard all for him and knew there would be no mercy showing to them they should all die at his feet, but McRannald persuaded him to the contrary. After his going from Islay he made his first course towards Inchedaholl, an isle upon the back of Inchewin in Ireland. Sorle McJames and his company of Irishmen did leave him there, and are fled to the woods of Ireland. I have written to the commanders of these places to be careful in apprehending of them.

"Another of his boats being manned with some of the tenants in Kintyre, who never left Sir James until he was brought to such extremity, are fled from him and come to Kintyre. They affirm that Sir James his resolution is to cast him self in some great mans lap, who will intercede at his Majesty's hands for him.

"I have sent spies both to Lochaber and to the North Isles if he go there, for in my opinion he dare not adventure to stay in those parts. I am certainly informed there is not any man with him but three, saving him self. At Sir James his waygoing out of Islay all the tenants of the country stayed behind him. **Coll McGillespie having the keeping of the castle of Dunyvaig and the isle of Loch Gorme, he stayed in his strengths and followed not Sir James. Before the landing of His Majesty's cannon to the castle, Coll submitted him self and came in. He has rendered both the castle and isle to me, and has delivered Colin Campbell of Kilberrie, who was his prisoner. Likewise he has undertaken to do such service as may relieve him self.**

"I have apprehended all the principal ringleaders and such as could be tried to have gone willingly with Sir James. Some of them I am to send to the Lords Commissioners, and the rest I will execute here. **I have presently employed Coll McGillespick in service against these that are outlaws, whose success your lordship will know at my next advertisement.** McRannald's sons and Glengarrie's brother are gone to their own countries, and I have sent after them. So soon as I have ended here in Islay I intend to return back to Kintyre and to spare none that willingly joined with the rebel Sir James, for the greatest part of them are in Kintyre and Arran. So soon as I can try what part of His Majesty's dominions Sir James has taken him to, your lordship shall be assured I shall not be long in pursuing him. I shall likewise, God willing, take such an order with those that has followed him as His Majesty shall not need to doubt of good obedience in their parts in time coming. My lord, the extremity of the weather and distance of the place has been the cause that I have been so long in advertising of your lordship of my proceedings. So for the present I rest, Your lordship's assured friend [ARGYLL]

Barnbougall, Monday 16th October
Reply from Secretary Binning to the Earl of Argyll [*This reply is very critical in tone: the Earl having failed to produce any ringleaders had better be ready with an explanation; and his letter being late means that it contains no new information. The final sentence is very sharp.*]

"My most honourable good lord – I received this night your lordship's letter of the 13 of this month from Dunyvaig making mention of Coles [Colla Ciotach's] incoming to your lordship and Sir James' escape with all these that ever I had named principle men in his company, but I hope your lordship will have care so far as can be to make a good account of them to his Majesty

"Your lordships letters have come here with good speed, being written upon the 13 at Dunyvaig, but a packet sent from this to Court upon the 12 of this instant contained advertisement from my Lord Chancellor to Court of all that your lordship's letter of the 13 has now brought to me, which I shall signify to Court with all convenient diligence, expecting better news by your lordship's next advertisement, which I pray God to send. At the next meeting of the Council I think there will be a great number of the Commissioners, to whom all your lordships proceedings shall be communicated.

I think your lordship will do wisely to avise what course is most fit to be taken with his Majesty's ships, for, if your lordship have no necessary use of them, their stay in these seas idly can avail nothing, but may put his Majesty to great charges and bring danger to the ships, which God forbid. Always, so long as your lordship has necessary use of them, his Majesty and the Council will undoubtedly allow that your lordship retain them and employ them in any needful service.

"...... So, beseeching God to grant your Lordship the honour and happiness to cut off the roots and heads of the Isles rebellion, and expecting that hereafter your lordship's followers or neighbours shall not prevent [i.e. presage] your lordship in the report of your proceedings, I rest, your lordship's most ready friend to do your service [BINNING]

Dunyvaig, 20th October 1615
Letter from Archibald Campbell to Secretary Binning
[*Evidently stung by Binning's letter, Argyll does not reply personally – but does review his excuses, and promises some executions.*]

"My very honourable good lord, – your lordship's letters of of the 4 and 5 of October from Edinburgh and Barnbougall came here to my lord upon the 18 of this instant. The cause of their delay so long by the way and that your lordship has not more frequent advertisement sent from this is the extremity of the winds and the currents that runs so strongly in this seas, which makes it almost impassable between this isle and the main[land]. My lords' letters herein enclosed will sufficiently inform your lordship of the success of his Majesty's service. **Those that are already execute are not of the number that Coll McGillespik has apprehended.** My lord intends tomorow, if wind and weather serve, to go to Kintyre, and has left a roll of certain persons with Caddle, who are to be taken order with, and to that effect has given him commission. So that, on my credit to your lordship, there is nothing left undone in Islay that concerns the well of his Majesty's service or can do good to Caddle, whereof I doubt not he will acquaint your lordship him self.

"The greatest number of the rebels are in Kintyre. They are watched so that they cannot escape. I hope my lord shall no sooner come to Kintyre but your lordship shall hear of due execution. I can hear no certainty if McRannald be gone to his own country, or if he be gone to shift a barque or a ship to carry him away, but it is certain that he has parted company with Sir James, as I wrote to your lordship before My lord has sent both to Lochaber and Glengarry's bounds to see what may be done against the rebels. Your lordship may easily consider how difficult a thing it is to find out such a number of renegades who draws themselves to lurk in divers corners of the kingdom, yet I hope in God, although it be pains to the Earl of Argyll and to those that follow him, his Majesty shall have a sufficient account made before long of these villains.

"As concerning the rest of the Islanders I will write nothing at this time, but I hope the exact performance of this service shall make them a little more tractable than they have been heretofore. I believe, seeing the service is come to such perfection, that my lord expects not any more pay from the Treasurer, unless it be for a very few number and a short time. When your lordship hears the particular, I doubt not but your lordship will find it very reasonable. I think it expedient that in your first letter to my lord your lordship write that, seeing there is not six of the rebels together, it is thought expedient that there be no more pay sent until your lordship know from my lord what number [is] requested. For the present I will not trouble your lordship with remembrance of any particular any more, neither doubt I of your lordship's favour, if it be my good hap to deserve it, as God knows I am most desirous, and shall ever remain, Your lordship's to serve you [Archibald Campbell].

"[P.S.] At my lord's coming to Kintyre he intends to dismiss the *Charles* and the barque [the *Cran*] wherein the ordnances are, seeing they are chargeable to his Majesty, and is to keep Captain Wood with the ordnance until your lordship has an account of the service and that his Majesty conclude what further is to be done in these parts."

c. 20th October 1615
Secretary Binning to Archibald Campbell
[*This letter crossing the one above, Binning is still unhappy that he is getting all his news from third parties and underlines the disappointing nature of Argyll's success.*]

"Loving friend – I received your letters of the 15 of this month from Dunyvaig, but no news in them, because upon the 12 day I heard the substance of all that your letters bears, which that same 12 day was written to Court by my Lord Chancellor.

"I am glad that my lord is master of these strengths, **and sorry that all the principal men are escaped, except Coll, who has gotten conditions;** but I hope that my lord's diligence, wisdom and good luck shall overtake them and rid his Majesty and the country of their encumbrance, for, if it should fall otherwise forth, as God forbid, **you know what constructions men would make of the great preparation made by sea and land, at so great charges to his Majesty, without any effect but the wreck of the poor beggarly tenants of Islay and Kintyre.** For, since Sir James and his son, with McRannald and his son, and Glengarry's son, and McSorle, are all escaped, and Coll pardoned, **I know not what ringleaders these are whom ye write ye are to bring in.**

"Always, it is good that their forces are scattered without harm or danger, yet **so long as the heads are all to the fore, the rebellion will never be thought quenched.** Wherefore I know my lord will have such care as agreeth with his honour and his Majesty's expectation.

"I have no certainty of the Depute Treasurer's dates, but I hope that he will be here about Hallowmass, and will assuredly perform his promise, yours being observed, which I heartily wish. So, remembering my loving commendations to your brother Colin, and **praying you to prevent**

your curious neighbours in the advertisements of my lord's proceedings, which I wish may be prosperous, I rest, your very loving friend at power, [BINNING]."

Dunyvaig, 29th October 1615
Letter from Earl of Argyll to Secretary Binning
[*The scarcely subtle tone of Binning's letter produced an immediate and personal response from Argyll; and a marked change of tone. In this reply he elaborates on the good service that Colla Ciotach is supposed to have performed, and specifically states that "this day", 29th October, Colla has handed over McDuffie (although in his later, official report Argyll makes it clear that McFie had really given himself into custody, just as soon as Colla Ciotach had agreed surrender terms). Argyll is clearly becoming desperate to restore his own position, as will be seen in his postscript.*]

"My very good Lord – As I wrote to your Lordship in my last letters from Dunyvaig the xiii day of this instant that Coll McIlespick before the landing of his Majesty's cannon had given up the castle of Dunyvaig and isle of Loch Gorme, had delivered Colin Campbell of Kilberrie, and was gone about to do further service for himself, so **this day** he has returned to me, and has brought with him nineteen of the chief and principal that were with Sir James. **One of them had the commandment of forty men; his name is McDuffie**. I purpose to present some of them before your lordship, that your lordship may be the more certified of Sir James' proceedings since his last rebellion; the rest of them [I] intend to cause execute here.

"My Lords, the cause of my stay so long here is waiting until I hear what Sir James intends to do. At the writing of my last letters unto your lordships I understood not which way he was gone out of Inchedaholl, an isle on the back side of Ireland, to the which he went whenas he was forced out of this isle; but I am now surely informed that he is parted with McRannald and landed in a place called Rowvallin in Ireland, near where the late Lord Tyrconnell's lady dwells, for she is his father's sister. His intention is, as I understand, to go to the Deputy and to deliver himself in his hands. So, how soon as I have done what I intend, God willing, in Kintyre, I will make your lordships certified of the whole estate of the service, wherewith I hope his Majesty shall be well pleased and my friends sufficiently satisfied, for I purpose, God willing, so to conclude it as there shall be no place left for any ever to attempt the like in these parts. Leaving to trouble your Lordships any further for this present, I rest, Your lordship's assured friend [ARGYLL].

" [P.S.] After the writing hereof, I am informed that Sir James McKoneill bought four horses on the coast of Ireland, and one gentleman, called McKarie, has followed him; and as I believe, he can hardly escape. This day I have caused execute nine of the principals and leaders of the rebels, whose names I have herewith sent to your lordship. **I hoip now dayly to be busie in execution whill his Hienes rebellis be brocht to ruine**."

Aboard H.M.S. *Cran* , Loch Kilberran in Kintyre, 22nd November 1615
Letter from Captain Wood to Secretary Binning
[*This testimonial to his good and faithful service will have been a very welcome help to the rather rattled Earl of Argyll*]

"Right honourable and my very good lord, – I received your letter of the 16 of October and thinks myself very much bound [obliged] for your honourable favour. My lord of Argyll has been very careful and has settled things in Islay, and the greatest he found there adherent with the rebels he has caused execute; others of them he has brought here to Kintyre, and has possessed Sir John Campbell peaceably in the two strengths which the rebels did hold in Islay. The castle of Armorthy is to be delivered to his lordship's servant, and the keepers to present themselves to their lordships service. Sir James McConneill is discovered, and my lord knows where he is, and for the apprehending of him has sent ten sufficient men either to attack him or kill him. He has wrought all means possible to effect the same, as your lordship shall know in my next letter.

"There is here a great number in Kintyre, which has been associate with the rebels, and for that cause I have desired his lordship to keep aboard his Majesty's ships to such time that his men repair from onsetts where he has appointed them, at which time he will take order with them. The rebels has spoiled mightily the land, that the poor tenants is almost undone. I se it will be near the end of November before my lord make an end here, wherefore, because it is the dead of winter, I mean to remain in some good harbour in Eyde, where his Majesty's ships may be in safety, except I receive warrant from your lordship and the rest of the Council to the contrary, – I will be so sparing to burthen the country of Scotland as possibly I can.

"My lord of Argyll told me he would write to the Council to know if I shall leave the munition here which is not spent, which I could not do, as I told his lordship, without special warrant from his Majesty, in respect I received it by warrant from him and has indented for the same in the Tower what I must be accountable. All other proceedings concerning me your lordship shall have intelligence. Thus I humbly take my leave, giving thanks for all your honourable favours, and shall ever remain, your lordship's servant [WOOD]."

Edinburgh, 24th November 1615.
Sederunt – Chancellor; Secretary; Treasurer Depute; Clerk of Register; Advocate; Medop.
[*In this report, given on behalf of Argyll, Archibald Campbell is suitably imprecise as to the date on which McFie came into custody, but does maintain Argyll's earlier story that it was Colla Ciotach that handed him over.*]

"The which day in presence of the Lords Privy Council appeared personally Archibald Campbell on behalf of Archibald, Earl of Argyll, His Majesty's Lieutenant over the Isles of this kingdom, and gave in in writing the report hereunder of the said Earl's proceedings in the execution of his Majesty's commission of lieutenantry granted unto him against the traitor [Sir James] McDonald; of the which report the tenor follows:

"Immediately after that the Earl of Argyll had received his Majesty's commission of lieutenantry over the Isles he addressed himself with all convenient diligence to Duntroon, where the greatest part of his forces did meet him. And, being surely informed that the traitor Sir James McConeill [MacDonald] and his accomplices, to the number of seven or eight hundred men, were for that present in Kintyre and of full intention there to remain untill they were by a greater power forced out of it, his Lordship resolved to make an attack without any delay both on their vessels and on the rebels themselves, and therefore commanded the Laird of Caddell [Calder], who had the command of the forces of Lorne, to make his attack on their vessels where he could hear them to be, either in Isle of Gigha, the Isle of Cara, or on the mainland of Kintyre.

"Likewise his Lordship gave command to the Laird of Auchinbreck and to some special of Auchinbreck's friends to march overland to the Tarbert with his Lordship's forces of Argyll. My Lord himself, being accompanied with the men of Coull [Cowal], went by sea to the Tarbert on the other side of the mainland. My Lord went from Duntroon on the day of September, and was that night in the Tarbert, where Auchinbreck with the men of Argyll did meet him that same night. Coll McIllespik [Colla Ciotach], having Coline Campbell of Kilberrie set out to him, come with fifty men the aforesaid night to Loch Tarbert, where he captured the said Coline and some four of five with him, whom he made his prisoners.

"Early the next morning, Coll McIllespick being on his way back again towards the Isle of Cara, – where he had left McRannald [Keppoch] and his sons and Sorle McJames [Somhairle MacDonnell], who were appointed to remain in Cara for keeping [protecting] of the rebels' vessels, – he, being on his way as is said, perceived my Lord of Argyll's forces of Lorne sailing towards Gigha; and some of them, having gone in behind Gigha, made an attack on the rebels who were in Cara, but were prevented [forestalled] by some of the Laird of Largie's servants, who perceived my Lord of Argyll's forces going towards the isle where the rebels were, and set on [lit] great beacons to warn them, – the aforesaid isle not being distant from land above two or three miles of sea. Yet, before the rebels could get away in their boats, there were some of McRannald's men captured and slain.

"Coll McIllespik, as is said, being on his way to the Isle of Cara, was warned by a servant of the Laird of Largie that my Lord of Argyll's forces had chased McRannald and those that were with him out of the Isle of Cara, and had established themselves there; so he immediately was forced to land in Kintyre. Some of my Lord of Argyll's men, having foregathered with him in his landing[place], killed a fifteen or sixteen of his men, and took his four vessels from him.

"My Lord of Argyll the aforesaid day sent his forces of Cowal and Argyll within twelve miles to the place where Sir James McConeill and his accomplices were; but he, being warned that my Lord of Argyll's forces were coming by sea and land upon him , fled away to the Isle of Rathlin, where he remained two nights, and thereafter went to Islay. My Lord of Argyll being notified thereof, and hearing that his Majesty's ships were arrived at the Isle of McAcharmick, his Lordship, with his forces of Lorne, and some of the men of Argyll who had their vessels on that side of the mainland [(made?)] towards his Majesty's ships, where he was stormbound for three days, thereafter went to the Loddrumes [the anchorage for modern Port Ellen] in Islay, a harbour convenient for his Majesty's ships to abide in, and good for landing of his Lordship's forces out of the danger of the enemy. Having stayed there for two days for refreshing his men, and until he should hear where the rebels were and in what order, immediately being notified that Sir James with his accomplices were in the Rhinns of Islay and in a little isle near by called Eilean Orsa, my Lord made an attack upon them by sea; wherein his Lordship's men were prevented [forestalled] by some who set on [lit] beacons in the Oa of Islay, whereby Sir James was warned that my Lord's forces were coming on him.

"So, as Sir James McRannald and his sons and Sorle McJames flies away that night to Inchedachole [Instrahull], an isle off the coast of Ireland, **Coll McGillespick, having the keeping of the Castle of Dunyvaig and the Isle of Lochgorme, rendered them both to the Earl of Argyll, and Colin of Kilberry, whom he had taken captive, and apprehended McPhie, one of the principals who followed Sir James, and delivered him to the Earl of Argyll**. And I have presented him this day before your Lordships, with other five Sir James' accomplices. After that the Castle of Dunyvaig and fort of Lochgurme were taken, my Lord apprehended fifteen of the principal men of Islay who were leaders of the poor ones to follow Sir James; whom he caused to be execute there.

And, having delivered the aforesaid Castle of Dunyvaig and fortalice of Lochgurme to the Laird of Caddell, his Lordship come from Islay in his Majesty's ships and arrived in Loch Kilkerrane [Campbeltown] on the 16th day of October last. His Lordship no sooner come there than that there came one of Sir James' followers who went with him to Ireland, and undertook to bring some of my Lord's servants to the place where he left Sir James; and, if he were not to be found there, he was sure to find him in the town of Galloway [Galway?] in Ireland in Valentine Blak's house or Robert Blak's house there, who are alleged to be receivers of Jesuits. My Lord, being this surely informed of Sir James' proceedings, has directed thirty of his men in two expeditions to Ireland after him. As to Sorle McJames and the two and twenty that he had with him, they are in The Route and Glens of Ireland [Antrim]. It is alleged that the sub-officers there has given them promise of protection for two months.

As to McRannald and his sons, they are fled to Lochaber, and my Lord's forces are in pursuit of them there. As to Glengarry's son, he is received in his father's bounds, and my Lord has some of his servants after him. At my Lord's coming to Kintyre out of Islay he apprehended some of the principals there who had followed Sir James, and those who made warning to the rebels of the Earl of Argyll's forces coming to Cara. Likewise his Lordship dismissed Captain Wood, Captain Merrick, with his Majesty's ships, and the bark wherein his Majesty's cannon and munition was, on the tenth day of November inst."

AS ALSO the said Archibald Campbell gave in the articles following, whereunto he craved the said Lords advise and answer: Of the which articles and answers the tenor follows:

QUESTION

First, to enquire if their Lordships think it not a sufficient exoneration of the Earl of Argyll [in his Commission] that Sorle McJames is in Ireland and has two months respite as is alleged.

ANSWER

The Lords think that the Lieutenant has done his duty and should be exonerated of Sorle McJames, if he be in Ireland, as is alleged, seeing his lordship's commission gives him not power to pursue Sorle McJames in Ireland.

QUESTION

Secondly, to crave their Lordships' opinion if their Lordships thinks it not sufficient, if McRannald's sons may not be apprehended by my Lord of Argyll's efforts before my lord's coming to the Commissioners, that my lord prove in whose bounds they have had actual residence.

ANSWER

If MacRannald and his sons cannot be had before the Lieutenant's coming here, if the Lieutenant will verify and prove where and by whom they are received [harboured], and within whose bounds they have their actual residence, he does his duty in that point.

QUESTION

Thirdly, to enquire their Lordships if Glengarry will not be obliged [to answer] for his son, it being clearly proven that he has actual residence in his father's bounds.

ANSWER

Glengarry will be obliged to answer for his son, it being proven that he is received and has his actual residence within Glengarry's bounds.

QUESTION

Fourthly, to assure their Lordships that my Lord of Argyll finds the whole country people of Kintyre, Islay, Colonsay, Jura, and Gigha guilty in being in company and bearing weapons and mustering with Sir James McConeill at such times as he apppointed, and in giving meat, drink and lodgement to him [and] his followers; and for the most part they never left Sir James, neither in Kintyre nor Islay, untill he was constrained to leave them. Yet, my Lord of Argyll finding the number so great, and that they allege it was just through fear that they went with him or showed him any favour, therefore my Lord has only put to the acknowledgement [notice] of an assize such as had command of companies with him, who might have done service on Sir James and his followers and have left them at their pleasure, and forbears the rest until he know the Commissioners' pleasure, – although the extremity of the law would take all their lives.

ANSWER

The Lords are of the Lieutenant's opinion concerning this article; but they will first acquaint the King's Majesty therewith, and have his Majesty's will and pleasure concerning it, afore they give any advice therein to the Lieutenant.

QUESTION

Fifthly, to assure their Lordships that the Castle of Dunyvaig and Isle of Lochgorme being surrendered to the Earl of Argyll, he has delivered them to the Laird of Caddell, and desires the Council's allowance to the same.

ANSWER
At the coming of the Lieutenant and of the Laird of Caddell here this article shall receive an answer.

QUESTION
To assure their Lordships that he who has undertaken to bring my Lord's servants to the place where Sir James McConeill has residence in Ireland assures my Lord, if Sir James were out of that place where he hoped to find him, he would surely be in the town of Galloway in Ireland, lodged either in Valentine Blak's house or in Robert Blak's house, for they dwell in that town and has a certain sum of money paid them yearly for receiving of Jesuits, and Sir James had his mind made that by their means he should be transported out of the country.

ANSWER
The Lords will write to the Lord Deputy of Ireland concerning this article."

Letter from the King, Newmarket, 12th December 1615.

"Right trusty and well-beloved cousin and councillor, and right trusty and well-beloved councillors, we greet you well. – We have received the relation of the Earl of Argyll's proceedings in our service in the Isles, and do well allow of the answers given by you to every several article thereof. As for the article which you thought fit to be referred unto us, we so far agree with your opinion therein as we think the course which our Lieutenant has taken with the inhabitants of Kintyre, Islay, &c. most convenient to be followed until these countries be fully settled; but, because these people are not to be trusted, we leave to you to devise the way how all means of further rebellion may be taken from them.

   "And, forasmuche as we understand that our said Lieutenant has dismissed our pinnace and the hoy which carried our ordnance, and retained our ship and our said ordnance, we have thought good earnestly to require you (considering that we already lost one ship in that kingdom) to cause special care to be taken that this other, with all our said ordnance, be carefully attended and safely returned so soon as the season of the year will permit. And, lastly, whereas it is reported that the traitor McDonald and certain of his associates are in Ireland, as we doubt not but that before this time you have, according to your promise, written to our Deputy to have a special care of his apprehension, so we desire you with all convenient expedition to advise us of his answer, to the intent that we know how far to urge him in that point. So fare you well. Given at Newmarket, the 12 of December 1615. Sic suprascribitur James R."

Edinburgh, 21st December 1615.
Personal appearance of Earl of Argyll before the Privy Council.
[*This is the final and official report; by now Argyll is confident that he has redeemed his position and therefore gives the plain facts without embellishment. In this report he makes it quite clear that "the fortis wer na sooner randerit bot McFie ... desirit protectioun.... to do his Majestie service". Thus McFie gave himself up on or before 12 October, whereas Argyll, under pressure to excuse his leniency to Colla Ciotach, had claimed in a letter to Binning that McFie was rounded-up by Colla and handed over on 29 October.*]

"The which day, in presence of the Lords of Secret Council, appeared personally Archibald, Earl of Argyll, his Majesty's Lieutenant over the Isles of this kingdom, and gave in writing the report underwritten of his proceedings in the execution of his Majesty's commission of Lieutenantry granted to him against the traitor McDonald: of the which report the tenor follows: -

"As soon as I received your Lordships commandments, I addressed myself with all convenient diligence to Duntroon, where I had occasion to bring my army near together within four miles distant by land; where my vessels lay in safety, the one upon the west, the other upon the east, of that continent [Kintyre peninsula].

"The first thing I intended was to proclaim his Majesty's clemency to such as alleged themselves to be retained by the rebels by force, having no place of retreat; to whom I gave the time prescribed in his Majesty's letters.

"While this was in doing, I did try the place where Sir James did camp and where his vessels lay, whose number I did find to be nine hundred and seventy, his vessels drawn up upon the coast within a quarter of a mile to his camp and most part in Laray. Whereof I being certified, I directed two of his Majesty's companies there under pay, – viz: 'Johnne McDougall of Ragray and Mr. Donald Campbell, Sir Johnne Campbell of Caddell, the lairdis of Lochinnell and McCoull' (sic), to the number of seven or eight hundred men, by sea; to whom I gave special instructions to go directly where Sir James' vessels lay, and if it were possible to them, to suprise them by night; failing whereof, to encamp themselves on a point of land called the point of Ardrisaig, where they were to attend my coming by the east side of the land accompanied by two others of his Majesty's companies under the conduct of 'Capitaine Boiswell, with Robert Campbell, Capitaine of Dwnone, and Coline Campbell of Kilmichell, – the lairdis of Ardkinglas, Lamond, McLauchlane' [sic], being with myself to the number of seven or eight hundred men.

"In the night (with the foresaid companies) I came to the Tarbert within ten miles to Sir James' camp, who at that time being uncertain of my coming had directed Ronnald McRonnald, his uncle, to the number of three or four hundred men, to stop the passage upon that quarter. Coll McGillespik [*Colla Ciotach*] was also sent by him to the Tarbert with threescore in number and three boats; who, finding Coline Campbell of Kilberrie, accompanied with three or four in number being separated from the camp, took him prisoner, and conveyed him back in their boats; whom I pursued [not?] notwithstanding of my cousin's [Kilberry's] imprisonment, fearing it had been "ane trayne" [a ruse]; but remitted it to the care of those that I appointed to go by the west coast, because of necessity Coll was to pass that way.

"Coll with his prisoner directed his course toward the Isle of Gigha; who passing by the coast of the Laird of Largie's lands, a fellow called McSorlegeir [sic] spoke to him and told him his enemies were in the Isle of Gigha. Yet he, not believing that it could be possible, went on directly his course till such time as he heard and saw his enemies. Then he turned with all diligence toward the coast of Kintyre; to which place he was hotly followed, his vessels taken, and some of his folk killed.

"At this time, such as went to pursue Ronnald McJames and McRonnald of Lochaber in the Isles of Gigha and Cara were disappointed of their enterprise by the treasonable lighting of beacons and fires by the Laird of Largie's people, as his own statement at more length reveals. Yet, notwithstanding, McRannald was chased by Mr. Donald Campbell and Lochinnell to the south end of Kintyre, where he escaped very narrowly with the loss of his vessels and some of his men.

"Ronnald McJames with the rest of the men of Islay were chased by the Laird of Calder within shot of the house of Dunyvaig. In the meantime Sir James, perceiving his men to be so disordered, forsook his camp and took to flight himself.

"At this time I directed the Laird of Ardkinglas with the number of four hundred men to assist those that were in the pursuit of Sir James McConeill, with special direction to them to follow him to Islay if he had left Kintyre. All that night they did camp in his camp, where they were certainly informed that he was gone to the Isle of Rathlin upon the coast of Ireland; upon which information I with them went to the coast of Jura, and there encamped together; at which time we met with his Majesty's ships, and there we understood by our spies that he was come back from Rathlin to Islay, and had encamped himself near to a little island called Isle Orsay, being accompanied with five hundred men. As soon as I understood of his coming to Islay, I addressed myself in his Majesty's ships to a harbour called the Lodomeis [i.e. Port Ellen], where I did secure the landing of my whole people till they were strongly encamped.

"Sir James, then perceiving himself not able to resist by force nor yet possible to fly towards the north, which was then his principal intention, did send a messenger to me desiring assurance for four days, promising betwix and that time absolutely to render himself in his Majesty's mercy. To which assurance I yielded conditionally, providing he would surrender the two forts he kept within the space of 24 hours; otherwise I would esteem his offer to be of no other end but to await a south wind to escape. **He** finding himself caught between two extremities, **did urge Coll McGillespick to surrender the two aforesaid forts** with the prisoners to relieve them out of their necessity; **which Coll altogether refused.**

"Whilst this answer was in coming, I was preparing my self to make an attack that night by sea upon his vessels, which was the only means by which he might escape. Having received his answer that he could not surrender them on the one part, and being notified secretly by Coll that he was willing to surrender them to me, that same night that I was first made acquaint herewith I directed Sir Johnne Campbell of Calder, Capitaine Boiswell with his Majesty's companies, and others, to the number of a thousand men, either to suprise him in his camp or suprise his vessels. But, the way between the two camps being a great deal shorter [i.e. in terms of time] by land than by sea, he was acquainted with their coming, so that in this extremity he was constrained very hardly to escape by sudden flight, with McRonnald, Sir James McSorley's son, all being to the number of forty persons, to an island called Inchdaholl. **The rest of his companies were forced to take the hills in the night. McFee's boat was taken;** which serves as a ship boat to his Majesty's ships.

"On the morrow after, **Coll McGillespik made offer of the two forts and two prisoners for the safety of his own life and some few others; which I did accept**, in respect of the unseasonable weather, the extreme sickness of the most part of the soldiers, and the great scarceness of provisions, without any hope of supply.

"The forts were no sooner surrendered but McFie, [at] present prisoner in Edinburgh, and Johnne McEane Voir, desired protection while they were about to do his Majesty service, wherein they desired no limitation but enduring the merit of their service and my pleasure; which I suspended during my abode in the country. But, howsoon I was to repair towards your Lordships, I dared not adventure to leave such remarkable ringleaders behind me without an assurance of their loyalty to his Majesty. In consideration whereof I have presented them to your Lordships. There was also ten of the specials that followed Sir James hanged in Islay at that time.

"The two foresaid forts were delivered to Sir Johnne Campbell of Calder, the island being thus void of all rebels. Sir James McConeill, having retired to Ireland with his company foresaid, finding the inconvenient of so great a troop, did send back to Scotland McRonnald of Lochaber and his sons, with some of the McAllasteris and McKyis in Kintyre; of which number your Lordships has one McKy here prisoner. I directed to Lochaber in search of McRannald. In pursuit of this I left Islay, and came to Kintyre, where I directed out some of my companies to seek them; but they, hearing of my coming, fled away and are secretly in some obstinate place.

"This I did in the space of three months, his Majesty's ships being dismissed according to my former adverteismentis [reports].

"And, whereas Capitaine Boiswell, who had the charge of a company in this service, has very worthily, carefully, and painfully behaved himself in this service, therefore I crave of your Lordships that the gentleman may be recommended by your Lordships to his Majesty's favourable consideration."

"THE present state of his Majesty's service within the bounds of my commission:
    The principal author of the rebellion, Sir James McConeill, with his natural son, and one called

Sorle McDonald, are in one company [i.e. together] in Ireland.

Sir James McSorley's son, with the suspected son of the late old Angus McConeill McCloyd, with some few others, are in the woods of Ireland [i.e. Glens of Antrim]. None of the other rebels are within Kintyre, nor Islay, nor the Isles within my commission; neither is McRannald within any part of the Sheriffdom of Argyll and Tarbert.

The rest of the Islanders presumes themselves to be good subjects, seeing they appear together before your Lordships as oft as they are cited; so that, the one part being unabled to rebel, and the other so willing to obey, in my opinion there is no danger of rebellion in these places. But this I remit to your Lordships' wisdom.

"After the submission and reading of the above report, the said Earl made two verbal propositions, about which he craved the Council's answer, advice, and opinion: the first concerning those who disobeyed his Majesty's proclamation and came not to assist him in his Majesty's service, and such others as came and remained not during the time of the proclamation, but departed and passed home without licence; and his desire was to be resolved what course should be taken with them. And the second concerning the non-payment making to him of his pay and allowance for the month of November and half of this month of December; wherein he alleged he was heavily prejudiced [i.e. injured], seeing he had men in service and under pay all this time.

"Concerning the first article and answer thereunto, he was instructed to submit a catalogue and roll of all the persons, and of their rank and quality, who disobeyed the said proclamation in not coming to the service and in departing and passing home without licence, to the effect the Council, after due consideration of the said catalogue and of the rank and quality of the persons, may resolve whether it be more expedient to call them criminally before the Justice in the Tolbooth in Edinburgh, or to give commission for their trial to some unsuspected [impartial] judges and in some convenient place for the ease both of the parties and assessors.

"And, concerning the second article of the third month's pay, it was answered that in the beginning of November last the Commissioners whom his Majesty trusted with the directions and despatches concerning that service had by warrant and direction from his Majesty discharged all further pay to be made in that errand, – whereof the said Earl received timeous notice by a missive letter written from the Commisssioners to him to this effect; and that now they could not alter their first conclusion in that point.

"Thereafter the Earl was demanded what order he had taken with all those who had joined with the traitor McDonald in this service, whom by his report he gave up to be in number nine hundred and seventy persons, and what surety was taken off them for their future obedience. To this he answered that the number foresaid consisted of diverse ranks of people, – to wit, of North Isles men, of Irishmen, and of those of the South Isles; and of them, he said, some were fled to Ireland, others to the North Isles outwith the bounds of his commission; and of those of Kintyre and Islay, he said that he himself would be answerable for those within Kintyre and other Isles pertaining to himself, and he doubted it not but Caddell would make the like answer for Islay; but he altogether refused to undertake to be answerable for the obedience of Islay in time coming, protesting nevertheless that he and his forces should ever be ready to join with Caddell in his defence if so it fell out that Caddell were of new distressed and troubled. And, if it were the Council's pleasure that those of Islay should now be brought here to their punishment, he was willing to exhibit them.

"This answer being heard, he was ordered to submit a roll of all those who were with Sir James at the intaking [capture] of Dunyvaig, to the effect the Lords, upon consideration of the roll and of the rank and quality of the persons, may advise upon the next expedient for their future obedience."

APPENDIX 3

A comparison of the varying treatments accorded to *Colla Ciotach*'s negotiated surrender in 1615 and the associated "capture" of MacDuffie:

HILL (1873):"He now held it [Dunivaig] until Argyle was fain to grant him and his garrison the right of marching out, which they did, when no further fighting was of any avail. Coll then returned to Colonsay, where he had large landed property, and enjoyed a high social position."

Significantly, this account pre-dates Gregory and contains no suggestion of dishonourable conduct.

GREGORY (1881): "Sir James, finding himself now much straightened, urged Coll MacGillespick, who at this time had the command of both the forts, to give them up to Argyle; but this Coll flatly refused to do. .... [after the flight of Sir James] Coll MacGillespick surrendered the two forts and his prisoners, upon assurance of his own life and the lives of some few of his followers. .... Coll .... became an active partisan against his former associates, and crowned his treachery by apprehending and delivering to Argyle Macfie of Colonsay, one of the principal leaders of the rebels, and eighteen others."

This account by Gregory is based upon a misleading interim report by Argyll's secretary, rather than upon the definitive report. Most other writers are later than Gregory and their versions appear to echo him:

MACKINNON (1903): *"Dh' fhosgail e dorsan Dhún Naomhaig is Locha Guirm do 'n Iarla is chaidh e a mach gu dealasach a shealg cheannairceach. Ann an úine ghoirid ghlac e Mac-a-Phí Cholbhasa is áireamh de dhaoine inbheach eile ..."* [He opened the gates of Dunivaig and Loch Gorm to the Earl and went out zealously rebel-hunting. In a short time he captured MacDuffie of Colonsay and a number of other important men...]

This seems to be simple repetition of Gregory's account, but it suggests that it was credible to an educated native of Colonsay; one, however, who was very much dependent upon such influential people as the modern but still powerful Lords of Colonsay, Kintyre and Islay. MacKinnon lived and flourished in Campbell country!

GRIEVE (1923): "... it appears that Coll Ciotach MacGillespic became a traitor. He made terms with the Campbells by which he saved his own life and those of a few of his followers, upon his agreeing to surrender the castle of Dunnyveg and the fort of Loch Gorme. He also apprehended and delivered to Argyll, Macfie of Colonsay, and eighteen others, Macfie being described as one of the principal leaders of the rebels. ... Macfie and another leader called John MacIan Vor now made the best terms they could for themselves. It was agreed upon their doing His Majesty service against the remaining rebels, they were to have a temporary assurance of their lives."

Grieve seems to have accepted Gregory's criticism of Coll, but without giving the matter any independent consideration.

LODER (1935): "Coll, as soon as he saw the game was up, made approaches to Argyll. He was promised a pardon if he surrendered Dunnyveg and Loch Gorm, and helped to round up the remaining rebels. To these terms he agreed, purchasing his life at the expense of his friends."

The criticism is gratuitous, and of course completely unfounded. Matters of friendship do not take precedence in affairs of military diplomacy and this simplistic allegation simply ignores the plain facts as given in Argyll's own testimony. Faced with certain defeat, only a mindless commander would expose his forces to annihilation, whereas Coll certainly obtained terms for his men and may well have been responsible for Argyll's clemency to others.

BLACK (1973): "Sir James [from Orsay!] now started negotiating for a truce, and Argyll asked him to surrender Dunnyveg and Lochgorm as proof of his good faith, but Colla refused to comply. The reason was simple – he wanted to save his own skin, and was conducting private negotiations with Argyll."

This seems hard. Sir James had been in charge of the mainland force, had been utterly defeated and had had to retreat to Ireland. *Colla Ciotach* had had to take command in his absence and clearly any negotiations would have to be conducted with him, the man in actual possession of the castles and the hostages, and in command of the military forces. Sir James was by now perched on a defenceless rock, in peril of his life and in no position to negotiate with anyone. In any event, Coll will have remembered the fate of Angus *Og*, hanged barely five months earlier, and who had agreed to surrender unconditionally.

D.J.MACDONALD (1978): "Sir James was forced to abandon all hope of successful resistance. He therefore sought a truce with Argyll who agreed providing the strongholds of Dunnyveg and Lochgorme were surrendered within 24 hours. This Coll Ciotach refused to do.... Coll surrendered his strongholds on terms which secured his own safety and that of a few of his followers but left the rest exposed to the implacable vengeance of their enemies and the summary justice of the King's Lieutenant."

Not strictly true, since King James had specifically forbidden "summary justice" when he ordered that "such of the rebels as might be taken alive were to be tried by a jury" (Gregory); any summary executions were carried out illegally and in defiance of the King's instructions, being the result of the pressure that Secretary Binning had brought to bear on Argyll. As has been seen, *Colla Ciotach* secured safe-conduct for himself and his garrisons, i.e. those men who had remained at their posts and under his command, and there is no suggestion that any men under his command were executed. Of course, he was not in a position to protect those people who had been outside of his forts, and who had been forced to "take the hills" when Sir James and his close companions abandoned them.

APPENDIX 4

A list of Colonsay inhabitants "converted to the True Faith" by Patrick Hegarty O.F.M., submitted to his superiors in 1625. The list seems to include the results of more than one visit to the island, so that some duplicated names may represent the one individual attending the Sacraments on different occasions. A married woman would not necessarily have the same "surname" as her husband. Bearing in mind the system of patronymics and nicknames in operation on Colonsay in the present day – Donald Gibbie, Duncan Sandy, Para Mór, etc. e.g. "Daniel Alexandri" could simply be "Domhnall Alasdair". The following list has been arranged alphabetically to highlight duplications and family names. The original list (published by Cathaldus Giblin, Dublin 1964) is probably in sequential order and it includes many other names, the inhabitants of neighbouring islands. The Latin names do not all have obvious modern English or Gaelic equivalents; those that have been suggested (many by Alastair Scouller) reflect the families that are known to have been associated with Colonsay. Some local placenames have been given which preserve their memory:

Adami	Catarina	[MacAdam? (*Mac Adamh*)]	[Catriona]
Aimreid	Daniel		[Domhnall]
Alexandri	Aeneas, nobilis	[MacAllister (*Mac Alasdair*)]	[Aonghus]
	Daniel		
	Donatus		[Donnchadh]
	Eneas		
	Gillatius		[Gilleasbuig]
	Godfredus, baptizatus		
	Joannes		[Eogharn or Iain]
	Joannes, nobilis		
	Nola		
Aodha	Nellanus, baptizatus		[Niall]
	[MacKay (*Mac Aoidh*) – see "Kay" below]		
Bachluin	Mora		[Mór]
Badin	Daniel		
Bagod	Daniel		
Beotadh	Margareta, baptizata		[Màighread]
	Nola, baptizata		
Biatadh	Edmundus, baptizatus		[Beath, Beaton, MacBeth (*Mac Bheatha*) cf. "*Sgeir Nic Bheathain*"]
	Jacobus, baptizata (*sic*)		[Seumas]
Biocara	Catarina	[MacVicar? (*Mac Bhiocair*)]	
	Catarina		
	Daniel		
Braitain	Aeneas	[Galbraith? cf. "*Roc Iain Mhic Bhreatannich*"]	
	Anna, quae, etiam cum fuisset possessa, Dei auxilio est liberata		

Brehuin	Christophorus	
	Maria	
Brehuyn	Cecilia	
	Mora	
	Nola	
	Nola, baptizata	
Breithuin	Maria	[Brown? (*Mac a' Bruithainn*); or MacBrayne? or Galbraith?]
Brotbacon	Menina	
Buacadh	Joannes, baptizatus	
Buatadh	Daniel, baptizatus	
	Mora, baptizata	[Buie? (*Buidh*)]
Camloyd	Aeneas	[Campbell]
Cartain	Catharina	
Chaaltuir	Dorothe	[Could this be Calder? (*Caladair*) or MacArthur']
Chaiou	Maria	[MacKay (*Mac Aoidh*) – see "Kay" below]
Chaoig	Daniel	[Mac Thaoig (son of Teague)]
Chaoin	Caterina	[O'Cahan]
	Christina	[Cairistiona]
	Elizabeth, nobilis	[Ealasaid]
	Nola, baptizata	
	Sile	[Sile]
Chatain	Gillatius	[Hattan? (*Mac Gille Chatain*) cf. "*Cille Chatan*"]
Cheachad	Gormlea	[McCaughey? (*MacEochaidh*) or Mac Eachuinn]]
Cheacharne	Eneas	Gillatius
Cheachorn	Nola	
Cheochain	Nola	[MacEachern (*Mac Eachairn*)]
Chemus	Thomas	[Mac Shenomais]
Cheoin	Antonius, nobilis dinasta	[O'Cahan? or MacIain? cf. "*Bogha Mhic Iain*", "*Dreis Nic Ceothain*", "*Clach Mhic Ceothain*", "*Eilean Mhoir Nighean Eoin*", "*Glaic Dhughaill 'ic Eoghainn*"]
	Cecilia	
	Christina, nobilis domina	
	Christina	
	Gillatius	
	Margareta	
	Maria	
	Mora	
Chorruidh	Moria	

Chorur	Christina	[Curry (*Mac Mhuirrich*)]	
Chreachearn	Catherina	[MacEachern (*Mac Eachairn*)]	
Chuacarrinn	Dorothea		
Churluidh	Leonardus	[Mac Shomhairle]	
Cinocoil	Moria	[Nicholson? see Cniocoil below]	
Cleontinus	Cormacus	[MacLeod]	[Cormac]
Clari	Petronella		
Clerici	Mora		
Clery	Christophorus	[Clark (*Mac a' Chleirich*) cf. "*Pàirc Iain Chleirich*"]	
	Donatus		
	Gillatius		
	Maria		
	Milerus, baptizatus		[Aon Muilear]
Closthuyr	Joannes, baptizatus		
Cneill	Barbara		
	Benedicta		
	Catarina		
	Columba		[Calum]
	Columba, nobilis		
	Daniel		
	Daniel		
	Daniel		
	Gillatius		
	Maria		
	Maurus		
	Mora		
	Mora		
	Nellanus		
	Nellanus		
	Nola		
Cnell	Nellanus, baptizatus		
	[MacNeill (*Mac Niall*) cf. "*Sguid Dhomhnuill 'ic Neill Oig*"]		
Cniocoil	Daniel	[Nicholson? (*Mac Niocail*)]	
Cnocoig	Aphrica		[Eifrig]
Columbae	Christina	[McCalman (*Mac Caluim*) or Malcolm cf. Poltalloch]	
Comhalston	Catarina		
Cranog	Emerus		[Iomhair]
Cremin	Mora	[MacCrimmon? cf. "*Carraig nic Cruimein*", "*Sguid nic Craomain*"]	

Cuboig   Nellanus
cf. *"Bogha Chubaig"*, *"Caolas Chubaig"*

Domhnaill   Alexander [Alasdair MacCholla?]
                      Gillatius [Gillespic MacCholla?]
                      Margareta, nobilis domina ex magna familia Domhnaldorum, quae prae-
                      cipua est totius Scotiae familia, antiquitate et potentia spectabilis [sister of
                      Sir James MacDonald]
                      Margareta, nobilis
                      Maria, nobilis [Coll's wife]
                      Nola [one of the "bevy of fine daughters"?]
                      Nola, nobilis matrona
                      Nola, nobilis
                      Eneas [Angus, Coll's stepson]
                      Rosa [another daughter?]
Domhuil   Maria, nobilis [Coll's wife again, or possibly Malcolm MacDuffie's widow?]
Domnall   Menina, nobilis [another daughter?] [MacDonald, Coll's immediate family]

Donchod   Joannes   [MacConnochie – *MacDhomchaidh* (son of Duncan)]

Dorach   Nellanus   [Darroch, important local family. cf *"Carraig nan
                                         Darach"*, *"Tigh Iain Darraich"*, *"Roc Beag Neill Daraich"*
                                         – see also Gillariabha, below]

Dubhhuy   Maria (n.b. Malcolm's widow was "Marie McDonald")
Dubhuy   Cecilia (possibly "Katherine McPhie"?)
                      Daniel (possibly "Donald Oig McPhie"?)
                      Nellanus   [MacDuffie a.k.a. Duffy (*Mac Dubhshith*) cf. "Buaile
                                         Mhic a'Phi", *"Carraig Mhic a'Phie"*, *"Leab' Fhalaich
                                         Mhic a'Phi"*]

Duibuill   Eugenius   [MacDougall (*Mac Dughail*)]   [Eoghan]

Emir   Joannes   [MacIver – (*MacIomhair*)]
Enemain   Reginalda

Fergata   Anna, baptizata
Fergusa   Columba
Fergusa   Daniel   [Ferguson? (*MacFhearghais*) cf. *"Carn Fhearghuis"*]

Fiacri   Christina   [MacVicar (*Mac a'Phiocaid*)]
Foil   Patritius   [Padhraig]

Giliosa   Mora (?)
Gilliosa   Mora
Gilloiosa   Daniel
Giolloiosa   Daniel   [Gilles or MacLeish (Gill' Iosa, "Servant of Jesus") cf.
                                         "Goirtean Ghill' Iosa"]

Gillabride   Maria   [MacBride (*Mac Gille Bhride*, "Servant of Bridget")]
                      Reginalda

Gillachristi	Calicia	
Gillachristia	Aphrica	
	Christia	
Gillachristius	Christophorus	
	Gillatius	
	Nellanus	
Giollachristia	Catarina	[Gilchrist or Ogilvie (*Gille Chriosd*, "Servant of Christ")]
Gillaglas	Nola	[Grey? or Douglas? (*Dubhghlas*)]
Gillariabha	Catharina	[Darroch (*Mac Ghille Riabhaich*, a Jura form) cf. "*Eilean Mhic a' Riabhaich*"]
Giollabarba	Eva	
Giolladuibh	Nola	[Black (*Mac Ghille Dhuibh*)]
Giollagann	Menina	
Giollaintail	Catarina, baptizata	
Giollamaihin	Aeneas	[*Mac Gille Mathain* (Matheson)]
Giollamcoclin	Anna	[*Mac Gille Mhic Lachlain* (MacLachlan)]
Giollamesti	Aéneas (?)	[could this have become "Amos"? – an old Colonsay family name]
Giollamhoilin	Columba	[Miller, MacMillan, MacMullen also anglicized "Bell"
Giollamuilin	Daniel	(*Mac Ghille Mhaolain*)]
Giollamuyl	Daniel	
	Nola	
Giollarua	Richardus	[Gilroy, MacIlroy (*Mac Ghille Ruaidh*) cf. "*Caolas Mhic a' Ruaidh*", "*Eilean Mhic a' Ruaidh*"]
Giollaseachhnaidh	Christina	
	Daniel	
Giollaseanuidh	Joannes	[Shaw (*Mac Ghille Seathanaich*), a Jura form of MacDuffie]
Giollasoroche	Thomas	
Gabann	Daniel	
Goban	Christophorus	
	Maria	
	Mora, baptizata	
	Nola, baptizata	
Gobann	Columba	
	Donatus	
	Milerus	
	Patritius	
	Reginalda	
Gubagam	Daniel	[McGovern, Smith (*Mac a' Ghobhainn*) cf. "*Cnoc Mor Ghart a' Gobhann*", "*Traigh a' Gobhann*"]
	Moria	

Goffra	Eugenius	
Gollomtoil	Maurus	
Grady	Minima	
Groill	Maria	
Guaert	Joannes	[McQuarrie? (*Mac Guaire*)]
Hedain	Joannes	
Hering	Maria (c.f. "*Port Iain Hert*"?)	
Huiginn	Margareta	
Huroh	Nola	
Kay	Alexander	[MacKay, Magee (*Mac Aoidh*). The MacKays of the
	Aphrica, nobilis	Rinns of Islay are an old and respected family, tradi-
	Aphrica, baptizata	tional lieutenants to the MacDonalds; "Hugh
	Catarina, nobilis	MacKay's Grave" on Orsay is a remarkable
	Catarina	mortuary-house in Irish style]
	Catherina	
	Constantinus	
	Daniel	
	Daniel	
	Daniel, nobilis	
	Dorothea	
	Gillatius, brother of Daniel	
	Joannes	
	Joannes	
	Joannes	
	Margareta	
	Maria	
	Mora	
	Mora	
	Mora	
	Nola	
Kenlatyar	Maria	[*Ceann Laidir* – a nickname?]
Leoin	Aphrica	[Nic Gill Eoin]
Linn	Columba	
Loiniudh	Ricardus	
Logart	Anna	
Mathei	Aphrica	
Mertuin	Gillatius	[Martin (*Martain*); important local family. cf. "*Eilean*
		Mhartain"; "*Aoineadh Mhic Mhuirtean*"]
Moruod	Gellatius	
Muiraod	Moria	
Muireadh	Catarina, baptizata	[Currie (*Mac Mhuirich*); important local family. cf.
	Christina	"*Baile Mhuirich*", "*Calum Caol Mac Mhuirich*", "*Beinn*
	Christina	*Mhuirich*", "*Lon Neill 'ic Mhurich*"]
	Daniel, baptizatus	

	Daniel	
	Joannes	
	Ludovicus	
	Margareta	
	Margareta	
	Maria	
	Maurus	
	Mora	
	Mora	
	Moria	
Muiren	Mora	
Muirin	Catarin	
Muiriodha	Catarina	
Muriadh	Edmundus, baptizatus	
Muriod	Columba	
	Mora	
Muyruad	Catharina	
Murtadh	Christophorus	
Muilin	Dorothea	[Miller, MacMillan, MacMullen, locally anglicized Bell
Muylin	Columba	(*Mac Mhaolain*)]
	Donatus	
	Gillasius	
	Hugo	
Patricii	Joannes	[Iain Phàdraig?]
Persin	Maria (?)	[MacPherson?]
Roinuidh	Donatus, baptizatus	
Ronog	Mora, baptizata	
Sagoire	Aphrica	[Nic an t-Sogairt? (MacTaggart)]
Saoir	Daniel	[MacIntyre (*Mac an t'Saoir*) cf. "*Fang an t' Saoir*"]
	Donatus	
	Fiecrus	
Segaint	Maria	
Senog	Catarina	
Sparan	Duballus (N.B. a McDuffie forename)	
		[MacSporran (*Mac Sporain*)] [Dubhgall]
Stochuir	Daniel	
	Maria	
Syndagain	Catarina	
Thomae	Elizabetha	
Tuail	Daniel	
Vosdin	Columba	
	Joannes	
	Margareta	

APPENDIX 5

The Latin translation of a testimonial provided to the Franciscan missionaries by *Colla Ciotach*; the Gaelic original has not survived but this was verified to be a faithful translation:

"Ego, Collatius Kiotach Macdonell, dominus de Coluossa et Orbusa, fidem facio venerandum patrem fratrem Cornelium Wardaeum, ordinis minorum de observantia, nec non ex parte Congregationis de Propoganda Fide in Scotia missionarum, extitisse ter per vices in hac nostra insula, eumque una cum patre Patritio Hegerty et Patre Jacobo Oneill simul hic afflictae patriae oppitulantibus, omnes fere incolas ad sacrosanctum Christi dogma assequendum convertisse. Testor porro omnia quae habentur in hisce duabus aliis litteris testimonialibus per aliquot Scotos approbatis, partim in Ilia 17 Martii scriptis anno Domini 1629, partim in Coluossa 25 Martii eiusdem anni, esse vera, nihilque superfluum inesse, quod not sapiat ipsam veritatem aequoque conforme sit.

"Denique hoc ipso anno 1629 nullum cuius praesidio et protectioni se committat praefatus pater Cornelius Wardaeus (adeo enim saevit haereticorum et ministrorum in hunc praesertim virulentia, nisi ego et me, et bono in eo tuendo periculis exponerem) cognoscat. Unde et indelebiles mihi acquisiverim iniurias, immo haereticis ipsi insidiantibus armisque in eum prope irruentibus non sine meo damno abduxi.

"In cuius rei fidem his subscripsi in insula Coluossa, Aprilis 1, 1629

"Coill Macgillespick, qui supra, dominus de Coluossa. Ego, Daniel Mhac Mhuireadhuigh, idem testor"

APPENDIX 6

The Journal of Rev. John Weir was given in Chapter 12 but additional material is given here with thanks to the Trustees of the National Library of Scotland.

The text refers to the following individuals:

Mr. John Weir, a Covenanting minister, Mistress Weir (née Janet Cunningham), his wife, and their expected child

Mr. James Hamilton, minister of Dumfries, who undertook the completion of the document; Mr. David Watson, minister in Ulster and father-in-law to Mr.. J. Hamilton, and Mr. Thomas Johnston, a preacher in Ulster

Also, three lay persons: William Hamilton, merchant from Glasgow; William Irving, merchant from Dumfries; Archibald Bruce, from Lanarkshire

Substance of some pages found with John Weir minister of Dalserf, and ye Lord's prisoner at Mingary castle at ye tyme of his death 16 Octbr 1644

The Lord's ends in our suffering:

1. To hyd pryd from our eyes Job 33. 17
2. To make us sensible of the Lord's trial
3. To cause us feel with others in their particular trials
4. To make us stand in the gape (especially for this part of the land)
5. That we might vow against al known Evills of commission or ommission
6. To mak us sensible of our deliveri from Eternal bondage
7. To prepare us for further sufferings
8. To fit us for more employment
9. To wean us from the world
10. To be a scoole for us
11. To conform us to our head [i.e. Christ]
12. For trial
13. For exercise
14. To put us in mind of the sufferings of our head, Christ Jesus

Our perils and threatned fears at sea from ye 3 of july to ye 15 of july

1. Present stabbing
2. Drowning
3. Of being sent to the king, [kilkdam], dublin or wexford
4. Perils of battels at sea
5. The frequent passions of the seamen
6. The fruits of their frequent drunkeness
7. The peril of taking our bibles from us

Our Sufferings at Sea

1. All wer robbed at sea of money & cloathes, writes, books & horse
2. our servants were separated from us
3. The seamen's continual blasphemie, [reiking rebukes], constant boastings, threatnings
4. we wer continuali searched
5. we wer slaved by al in dyet, lodging etc
6. our room was everi night mor & mor straitned & bedclothes removed from us

7. distemper of our bodies & minds
8. our clothes wer never changed
9. restraint of joynt worship
10. restraint of al compani especiali such as spoke plain
11. restraint of paper, ink & pen
12. some of us wer buffeted and abused
13. no liberti to writ to friends
14. base & sluttish meat, as the worst of salt samond, salt bacon, peas, litle bread, and that sometimes mouldi, and that after al had done, unclean bear, and sometimes water to drink, and
sometimes straitned therein
15. at night allmost choaked for want of air, being thrust under deck.

mercies at sea

1. Deliveri from all the fore-named perils & fears
2. we had no storme at sea
3. we had some favour of the captain & of some other gentlemen that visited us
4. respect was givn to the gentlewoman, and to us for hir caus
5. we had convenienci of mutual prayer in al thir sea conflicts or persuits sometimes tuo or
three together on the over list
6. it was a merci that Colkittoys was a prisoner before us
7. we had all reasonable good health; yea even the aged & the gentilwoman (with child)
8. our deliverance from that ship, after which she had not 48 hours rest from tempest or sore
assaults
9. we found frequent & strengthening manifestation of the love of God, in the use of the means
& secret ejaculations & sweitnings of our suffering
10. we wer conformed to our dyet, rayment & lodging with a very contented sweitness

Sufferings at land in Mingarie castle where we entred

15 July 1644
1. at our our entry in the evening to a grim & nastie lodging
2. we lay on boards a while, & with our cloathes on a month, without ani night-cloathes til the
16 of august
3. we had small provision of ferns, after of straw to ly on and very scarce of room
4. we were scarce of clothes & had our linens to shift us
5. we had continual scarciti of bread til the 19 of august, sometimes none, offtimes it could not
be discerned of what grain it was
6. our flesh for the most part was without salt, oft without bread, for sometimes il boyled, cold,
in ane scarce, being starved milk kows long kept after killing, and after boyling putrified & stinking
7. from the 25 of july til the 19 of august, seven of us had scarce the dyet of two men
8. our dyet was stil uncertain sometimes once, & sometimes twyce a day
9. our drink was always water & sometimes scarce of that, sometimes rotten and stinking, &
afteruard muddied & full of sand
10. from the 19 of august til the 7 of october, we received nothing from the castle but 12 Scots
pynts of rye
11. we had great want of fyre, save sometimes to make meat, & for most part no candle
12. our doors were kept sometimes by sentries, sometimes by day & always by night they wer
locked, & we were kept within doors for the most part til 19 of august, after quilk we were sometimes checked for going on the wals
13. we wer restrayned of pen, ink & paper, & writing for most part
14. we wer restrayned of al compani for the most part a long tyme
15. we wer forced to bear mani reproofs, lykewise blasphemies & oaths

16. we had some dystempers, sometimes in bodie, sometimes in mynd
17. we wer restrayned of joynt singing of psalms
18. they had & used mass, crucifixes, crossings & beads in our sight & hearing
19. we were sometimes interrupted in our joynt worship
20. there was much sickness among the souldyer, in the last som dyed
21. amongst ourselves one was with child and one veri seik
22. we sustained common hazards in the castle in the siege from 7 aug til 5 oct
23. we had little intelligence from the publick or friends
24. we wer long desired of relief & debard to wryt for it til 26 july
25. we wer weighted with our restraint from our charges
26. and with our conception of the greif of mani in our behalf

Mercies at land

1. we were al togidder in one room the best chamber in the castle and most fit for worship (joyntli or severali) neir the hall, [*bultrie?*] & entrie to the castle
2. we found a wonderful pertinensi in al the scriptures red by us privatlei or publicklie
3. our minds wer maid plyable to our dyet & estate
4. our hearts wer fired against il tydings, that wer oft reported
5. soon after greater difficulties, some comforts arose; as will appear by this diurnal and we trust our memories shall never forget
6. Mistress Weir, Wm. Hamilton, Wm. Irving & Archibald Bruce wer set at liberti in al tym most necassarie & fit for them
7. after they went from us we wer convenientlei served by divers soldiers and women in the hous
8. after Sir Donald Cambel's camp was removed, fyre, water, bread, flesh wer abundantlei givne us with much good wil for a long time

Mr. Weir had also noted the matr of everi sabath exercise as follows:

21 july psal 13 & 14	1 Sep psal 62 & 63	He had also pickt out texts
28 july psal 22 from vs..7	8 Sep psal 70 & 71 til vs.14	which he purposed to
to the end	15 Sep psal 75, 77 til vs.12	handle at his returne
4 aug psal 31 from vs..15 to the end	22 Sep psal 81	Ros 13 vs 9 to 15
11 aug psal 37 vs..12 to the end	29 Sep psal 88 thus far he	Am: 4 vs 12 & 13
18 aug psal 45	had noted, thereafter	Am: vs 5 & 7 to 10
25 aug psal 51 vs 12 to the end	5 Oct psal 91 & 92	Mic 4 vs 11, 12, 13
and psal 52	13 Oct psal 97 & 98	Mic 6 vs 5, 7, 8
	Zach 3 vs 8 to end	Nah 1 vs 7, 8, 9, 11
	Zach 1 vs 10 to end	Levati 1 vs 12 to end
	Zach 2 vs 5 to end	Habak 3 vs 15 to end
	Zach 3 vs 15	Zep 2 vs 8 to 12
	Zach 4 vs 6, 7, 8	
	Zach Chap.7 al	Zach 10 vs. 5 to end
	Zach 9 vs 9 to end	Zach 11 vs 10 to the end
		Zach 12 al chap.
		Zach 13 al

Having writen out such observances as wer writn by Mr. John Weir in his imprisonment that I found with him at his death, & having continued the diurnals til the day of his burial I have thought fit to give some observance anent his death also.

Al that knew him from a child of ten years or therbi, might easily have discerned in him a perpetual preparation for death by his grave & holi behaviour but when our Lord saw his tym of departure approach he set him apart in a marvelous manr to make himself redi for eterniti. For since according to the apontment of the General Assembli, held at Edr. 1643, he went to Irelande & spent 3 months in painful preaching of the gospel viz, al april may & jun 1644, almost everi day he laboured in spreading the covenant of God with Mr Wm. Adair, minr at Ayr, who togider persuaded the people to swear the said covenant in Carrickfergus, Antrim, Coleraine, Derry, Raphoe & Enniskillen and in all the countrie churches which lay about them, the Lord working mightili with them. In the tym of his travel in Ireland he helped to give the comission at Derry with Mr. Wm. Adair, at Newton in the countie of Down with Mr. John (R)uachal and at Killiblagh with Mr. James Hamilton. In these two places he gave the communion upon the last 2 sabaths of his being in Ireland, God seeing it meit to make him take ane double meal because the journey was grate before him & he was to get in prophesy of that food in the mountain of the Lord.

Upon the 2oth [*sic*] day of July, which was the last day of wherein he was in Ireland he preached at Donachidie on Heb. 12 the 21 first verses the mater of which sermon did much refresh him in al his sufferings afterward. Upon the sam 2 of july as he was returnimg from Ireland, with his wyf, Mr. James Hamilton, minsr at Dumfries, Mr. David Watson, father-in-law to the said Mr. James, with Mr. Thomas Johnson (preacher) & mani others passengers wer takn prisoners at sea by ane Wexford frigot called the Harp, wherein was Alaster Mcdonald, the general-major to Antrim's forces, coming along with 3 shyps full of soldiers to invaid Scotland. The said Alaster determined to keip the said prisoners til he could get his father Col mckgillespie alias Colkittagh & his 2 sons, brethren to the sd Alaster, releved for them, wherefore he took 7 of them to prisoners aboard the frigot, leaving the rest in the prize where these 7 wer takn, viz Mr. David Watson, Mr.John Weir & his wyf, Mr. Jas. Hamilton, Wm. Hamilton of Glasgow, Wm Irving of Drumfries, & Arcd Bruce ane dweller besid Hamilton. 4 of [the] 7 wer kept prisoners in the said frigot til the 15 day of july at night, and got not liberti joyntli to exercise worship togider, but everi one did as best might apart, only they had now & then conferences of what they red, for their bibles was spared to them by the good providence of God, and also when the frigot was pursuing ani bark or boats the prisoners being al closed under decks & alone took opportuniti to pray togider.

Upon the said 15 july the said prisoners wer caried from the said frigot to castle Meagrie, & wer al put in one chamber togider. Everi day thence the said Mr. Weir & Mr. James Hamilton did both of them expone ane psalm or ane part of a psalm, the one praying before the other the said exposition, which they did in the hearing of those other fellow prisoners which wer above named so long as they wer togider which was til the 23 of Septr in which tym they had proceided in exponing til the 81 psalm. One weik thereafter, Mr. Watson, Mr. Weir & Mr. James Hamilton being kept prisoners & none being with them in the room, did al of them expone twyce daly til the 30 Septr & proceided to psalm 89. Upon the 30 Septr, three Irish men & ane Irish woman wer made to lodge with them in that sam chamber that they could not ordinari open prayer performed togider, but as they [*obscure line*]...............could catch oportuniti did read & not[e] forward on the psalms til psal 93, upon the 7 october Mr.. Weir grew so weak that he could not joyn ani mor in noting or expounding the psalms. From the beginning of his imprisonment so long as he had ani health, he read privili the Scripture from the book of Ezra til the end of the New Testament, al except the psalms which he reserved for exposition with his fellow prisoners; he did also usuali sing a part of the psalms by himself & proceeded from the beginning til the 69 psal,; he did communicate the substance of his private reading as he saw occasion to some one or other of his fellow prisoners, especiali with Mr. James Hamilton conferring on the hard places, and declaring his most remarkable observances. In al which his notings & observance both private and with his whole fellow prisoners he uttered always veri much wisdom , zeal & piety, graviti in great varietie. So that I trust al his fellow prisoners shall always with great joy & fruitfulness remember on him; at least they have al cause to do so & wil be veri inexcusable if they did not. Wherefor you may say he had ane ful half year's preparation for death before his removal

2. And there wer some presages of death in him. As when he would be praying most earnestlei for libertie out of prison, he would corect himself & add "yet Lord keep us from making ane heavn or a God of our libertie" and at divers tymes he prayed to God that his eyes might never see Alaster Macdonald again, in the tearmes wherein we did see that he meant a prevailing man, & so it fel out to him.

3 When Wm. Hamilton, Wm Irving, & Arch. Bruce wer relieved he said to Mr. David Watson & Mr. James Hamilton, who only them remained with him now that the younger & weaker chris-tians are removed, "let us lay our accompt it along & for trial".

4. When the three Irish men & Irish woman wer put to lodge in one room with us he said "this is a forerunner of a veri great change", & indeed so it was for within eight days thereafter Sir Donald Cambel's camp removed from the sieg and about ten dayes after that Mr. Weir himself died.

5.When after the siedg was removed he got libertie to walk abroad for his health upon the 7 of october, (after he had first walked abroad), he said "it will be ane brave change for to goe from Mingary to Heaven".

6.Upon the 9 of october, after his walk, he told Mr. James Hamilton "alay upon the grass a litle while, I find the grave wil be ane sueit bed to me, it smells sueit". Upon the 10 of october he kept his bed & never rose after, he got ane cool that 10 of october at night, & seemed to mend kindly three dayes, but upon the 13 october he fell in the fever again & never mended but died 16 october 1644 about ten a clock at night, the day being the ful fyftent weik of his captivitie.

His sickness was very heavy upon him, & made his bodie lumpish & his mind seem much weighed; often he said "I said my bed shall comfort me, the night shal eas my complaint, then Thou scarest me with dreams & terrifiest me with visions". Yet, fearing that his heaviness should be scandalous to his proffession & sufferings, he declared to his fellow prisoners that in al his feavers he had ever been so, & that he was 9 weiks seik in his last feaver, when he had al things neir to him that wer necessari and which he desired; (but, said he to them) "Doubt not the of my calling, I thank God I am sur He is mine & I am His; I wanted not these 4 years that white stone & the new name [*ref. to Zechariah 3 vs 9*]; yea the Lord hath sometime so far revealed Himself unto me that I have been forced to say "Lord, withdraw thy face, I cannot be able to bear it any mor.""" "I am making conscience", sayed he, "to doe as is said, "Delight thyself in the Lord & He shal give the the desires of your heart""; also had manie sore groans for the publick state of this kingdom, which he conceived to be in great straits because our liberation was delayed, & said "Israel lost mani thousands both when they lost the arck & got it again – 1 Sam. , 4 & 6 Chap. I fear it shal be so with Scotland at this tyme."

He said often in his imprisonment that God would bring ane refined peic [piece] of work out of al these troubles in Scotland, & veri often repeated the words Psal 31 v. 14 "I trusted in thee, O Lord: I said, Thou art my God, my tymes are in thy hand." Being asked which he would say, concerning his wyfe, parents & parish, he said "I have laid the burden of them upon the Lord & am eased", as concerning them; privili, the day before his death som Irish wer bragging of Alaster's victories at Perth & Aberdeen, he prayed Mr. James Hamilton neither to believe al that they said, nor to be moved withal. He often called to his two fellow prisoners that they should bear him up to God in their prayers.

Upon the 15 October, about 10 o'clock at night, he heard som musket shot and asking what it meant it was told him that Alaster Mkdonald was returned & that the shots wer a vollie for his welcome; he cald for a drink &, as it was held to his head, his head fell down upon his breast with a groan, but he was not able to drink.

When Mr. James Hamilton asked if he should pray for him first, he saw the tym of his removal approach; he answered, "For God's sake doe, there was never more neid, & pray on at once", meaning that he & Mr. Watson should pray one after another.

After Mr. Hamilton had prayed, he said "Thank God, I have found som eas", & desired to rest, & after a litle space he gave 3 short sighs & yielded up the ghost being of age 34 years.

"Precious in the sight of the Lord is the death of His saints"psal 116 v. 15

"The righteous perisheth, & no man layeth it to heart: & merciful men ar takn away, none considering that the righteous is takn away from the evil to come" Isaiah 57 vs 1

"The tym is come that judgement might begin at the house of God: & if it first begin with us, where shal the end be of them that obey not the gospel? and if the righteous scarcli be saved, where shal the unrighteous & sinners appear?" 1 Pet 4 vs. 17 & 18

"Yet mark the perfect & behold the upright, for the end of that man is peace" psal 37 vs. 37

CIVIL WAR CHRONOLOGY

1642

July	First fatality in Civil War, Manchester.
	Argyll effective ruler in Scotland, supports Parliament in England.
	Owen Roe O'Neill returns to Ireland from Spanish Netherlands.
Aug 13	Ormonde writes to warn King Charles that his Irish Council is of doubtful loyalty.
Aug 22	King Charles raises his Standard, at Nottingham, declares Commons traitors.
Autumn:	Irish Catholic Confederacy set up in Kilkenny and established as Royalist Parliament with claims to independence from England but under the Crown.
October:	Antrim escapes from captivity of Scots at Carrickfergus, flies to Oxford; received by Queen Henrietta Maria.
Oct 23	King Charles vs. Essex (for Parliament), at Edgehill, 12000 a-side. Inconclusive result but Royalist victory on points.
Nov 12	Prince Rupert vs. Denzil Holles at Brentford. Roundhead defeat, but Royalists later repulsed.
Dec 5	Royalist troops seize Marlborough and disrupt vital route for cloth trade.
Dec 8	Riots in London when Parliament introduces new general tax to pay for war.
Dec 13	Parliament seizes Winchester, ejects Royalists.

1643

Spring:	Uneasy pause – King Charles in Oxford, involved in apparent Treaty negotiations with Parliament; really each side manoeuvering for a decisive military advantage.
	Irish Parliament in Dublin ordered by Charles to eject London Parliament's commissioners.
	Scottish commissioners received by King Charles at Oxford but forbidden to go to London; these commissioners refuse their King the help of the Covenanters in the Civil War unless they are promised that the Church of England will be wholly reformed along the lines of the Scottish Presbyterian model.
Apr 7	Negotiation between Charles and the Covenanters abandoned.
Apr 15	Negotiations between Charles and Parliament abandoned.
Apr 23	Charles officially instructs Ormonde to make a truce with the "rebel" Irish; and privately adds instruction that, as soon as truce is made, Ormonde should enlist as many men as possible, Irish or English, for service on the King's behalf in England.
May:	Antrim (escaped from Scottish Covenanters' captivity at Dunluce) joins the Queen, at York; offers to arrange truce in Ireland and to raise 20,000 men for service against the Scottish Covenanters. Montrose consulted but refuses to act without explicit authority from King Charles.
	On his way to consult with the Kilkenny Confederates, Antrim captured for second time by Scottish army (at Newcastle, Co. Down), and his plans to raise an Irish force to invade both Scotland and England are revealed. Plot includes involvement by Huntly and his son, Montrose, Airlie, Nithsdale and Sir Donald Gorm MacDonald of Sleat.
June	Parliament suffers reverses. King Charles gains North of England. Queen moves from York to join the King at Oxford.

July	Ormonde ordered by King Charles to arrest four Roundhead members of the Dublin Council, to assure its loyalty.
July 13	Parliament's Western Army suffers severe defeat at Devizes.
July 14	Queen enters Oxford with Charles
July 28	Prince Rupert and Prince Maurice overwhelm Bristol. Meanwhile, Argyll proposes formal alliance between Scots Covenanters and English Parliament, as response to the plans of Antrim and the Queen, betrayed by some of his captured servants. Argyll makes Montrose an offer of high office in the proposed new army; Montrose makes no definite reply, then flies to King and reveals Argyll's treachery.
August	Heroic defence of Gloucester rallies Parliamentarian spirits.
	Alliance between Scottish Convention of Estates and English Commissioners – 21,000 Covenanters to march into England, against their King.
Sep 5	Essex relieves Gloucester and Royalists withdraw. King Charles nonetheless consolidates gains in the West and urges Ormonde to expedite his truce with the Irish.
Sep 15	Ormonde signs truce with Confederate Irish.
Sep 25	Members of both Houses of Parliament sign the Solemn League and Covenant at St. Margaret's, Westminster. Lord Leven agrees to be commander-in-chief of new Scottish expeditionary army and Argyll loans £12,000 to the rebel cause – but maintains the fiction that he is acting in the interests of the King.
October	Lord Taafe offers 4000 Irish troops to the King, who join him via Bristol and Chester; (In 1647, Taafe is to be *Alasdair MacCholla*'s commander, in his final Irish campaign). Confederate Irish vote £30,000 aid to King Charles. Taafe seeks permission to destroy the army of the Covenanting Scots in Ulster.
	Antrim escapes for second time from Scottish army in Ireland, now flies to Kilkenny.
	Cromwell's well-trained cavalry wins a significant victory at Winceby.
November:	*Alasdair* and Ranald *MacCholla* embark on second expedition against Covenanting forces in Scotland, once again concentrated against Argyll (possibly at Antrim's behest, perhaps to impress Kilkenny Convention).
Nov.24:	News of the incursion reaches Edinburgh ... *Alasdair* reported to have landed with 300 men, "all papists", and two priests. Argyll empowered to organize resistance (appointed "King's Lieutenant" to oppose the King's own loyal forces!).
Nov. 26:	*Alastair MacCholla* attacks the merchantman *"Paul"* in Colonsay.
Dec. 6	Argyll commissions James Campbell of Ardkinglass to act for him in the "defence".
	Winter approaches with falling morale on both sides of English civil war and no sign of an early or conclusive finish to the conflict.
Dec. 8	Death of Pym, Parliament's evil genius. Is succeeded in Parliament by St. John, but both Cromwell and Sir Harry Vane adopt a part of his mantle, in malignancy and craft.
	Royalist advance into Sussex, seizing Arundel. King Charles finally rejects the suspect counsels of the Hamiltons in Scotland and embraces those of Montrose, Ogilvie and Aboyne.
	Antrim joins King Charles in Oxford, from Kilkenny; announces himself to have been created General-in-Chief of the Irish forces. Is now encouraged by King Charles himself to organize an alliance between his own Irish forces and the Royalist forces that Montrose hopes to raise in Scotland.

1644

Year opens in uneasy attempts by Scots Covenanters and English Parliamentarians to become comfortable in the same bed. Scottish army launched under the command of Lord Leven with David Leslie as cavalry general. Argyll joins as Colonel of his own regiment, still pretending to act in the best interests of the King, and moves into England with the army.

	Arundel recaptured by Parliament.
Jan 20:	Antrim receives commission from the King. He is to have 10,000 Irishmen sent for the King's service in England, and take charge of 2,000 Irishmen to invade Argyll's estates; in this invasion he is to co-operate with Montrose and, *inter alia*, he is to seek to persuade the Scottish army in Ireland to return to their allegiance.
Jan 22	King Charles opens rival Parliament, at Oxford (100 members of the Commons attend, with 30 Peers). Scottish Covenanting army condemned as foreign invaders and Montrose repudiates them as his "traitrous countrymen".
Jan 23	Royalist reverse at Nantwich.
Jan 28:	Charles having agreed details of plans to distract Scottish Covenanters army, Montrose signs accord with Antrim. The former to raise Royalists in England and Scotland, whilst Antrim is to return to Ireland to collect 2,000 men, to be sent to the aid of Montrose in Scotland. Meantime, 10,000 further Irish troops to continue to be sent direct to England, to the aid of Charles himself. Ormonde now formally appointed Lord Lieutenant of Ireland.
	Murrough O'Brien (a renegade Irishman better known under his English title of Lord Inchiquin) now arrives at Oxford. A known supporter of Parliamentarian aggression, he expects to be confirmed as President of Munster and is refused; he returns to Ireland "as full of anger as his buttons will endure", confirmed in his enmity to the Confederate Irish.
Feb	Scottish Army, invading England under contract to the Parliamentarians (who agree to pay all their expenses), are more or less immobile, being engaged in laying siege to Newcastle.
	Kilkenny Confederate parliament approves Antrim's plans to launch invasion into Scotland against the King's rebels; delay in determining suitable port of embarkation.
Mar 21	Stunning Royalist victory in England, at Newark.
Mar 25:	Report that 800 of *Alasdair MacCholla*'s invasion force are assembled at Portumna, Co. Galway, under "Colla Kittagh's son". Ormonde hesitates to permit main force to assemble under arms in northern counties of Ireland.
Mar 29	Significant Parliamentarian gain, at Alresford
	Further Royalist reverses in South Wales and (at hands of Scots Covenanters) in North of England, through March and April. Scottish and English rebels lay siege to York by late April; first Oxford Parliament suspended.
April 1:	Planned date for Antrim and Montrose to launch their united assault on rebel forces in Scotland passes without avail. *Alasdair MacCholla*'s forces continue to harry Argyll territories as he prepares to accept command of the main invasion force. Late in the month, he obtains authority to use Waterford or Wexford as his port of embarkation for men and munitions.
April	Montrose crosses into Scotland with 1300 men but fails to join up with other forces from Aberdeen at Stirling as planned, retreats to Carlisle, where he harries Covenanting forces. Meanwhile, under pressure from Argyll (who has been forced to return from England), Royalist force under Huntly, at Aberdeen, dissolves.
May 16	Prince Rupert sets out to the relief of York, but King Charles makes military errors at Oxford. Rupert has successes in following three weeks and captures a

number of towns, including Liverpool. King Charles also recovers ground in later June.

May 16: Antrim contacts Ormonde to complain of delay and of the cost in maintaining 2000 fighting men in readiness. Refers also to *Alasdair MacCholla*'s men being in possession of Rathlin and requiring supplies.

Late May: Military reverse for Royalist cause in Scotland when Ardkinglas corners and annihilates a significant proportion of *Alasdair MacCholla*'s expeditionary force, which had withdrawn to Rathlin Island. A hundred men that escape to Islay and Jura are pursued and executed, chastening the inhabitants.

June 24: *Alasdair MacCholla* sails from Passage and Ballahack, near Waterford, with 1600 men aboard 3 merchant ships and the frigate "Harp", but hits storm and is driven back. Sails again on 27 June.

June 28: Argyll reports to the Scottish Estates that all "rebells" (i.e. *Alasdair MacCholla*'s expeditionary force) were dead or captured, save some 13 individuals in flight.

Jul 1 In daring manoeuvre, Rupert relieves York, but is defeated next day by Cromwell, at Marston Moor.

Jul 3: *Alasdair MacCholla* and his force on passage – captures a ferry off Antrim coast.

Jul 4: At anchor, Sound of Islay.

Jul 5: At anchor off Duart, in Mull.

Jul 6: Captures two merchant-men in Sound of Mull.

Jul 7: Small force lands on mainland shore, to attack Kinlochaline Castle.

July 8 **Alasdair MacCholla lands at Ardnamurchan with 1100 men, attacks Mingary.**

Jul 14 The Queen flees, to France. Mingary Castle falls to *Alasdair MacCholla*. *Alasdair* leads his force onwards, into the heart of Scotland.

Jul 16 York falls to Parliamentarians.

Late August Montrose joins up with *Alasdair MacCholla*, at Blair Atholl and raises Royal Standard – about 2000 men by now, with followers.
On to Tibbermore and victory over 6700 Covenanters; Montrose enters Perth.

Aug/Sep Royalist consolidation in the West Country, although weak elsewhere.
Scottish Covenanters and English Parliamentarians lacking harmony.
In Ireland, Inchiquin nails his colours firmly to Cromwell's mast, giving him valuable ports of Youghal, Cork and Kinsale.

Aug 31 Essex crushed at Fowey and slips away.

Sep 13 Montrose reaches Aberdeen, which defies him; whereupon he attacks, defeats and sacks the city.

Oct 19 Newcastle falls to Scottish Covenanters under Leslie.

December As year closes, Montrose enjoys further success at Fyvie Castle and elsewhere. Mild weather encourages him to agree to a lengthy and devastating incursion into the Campbell territories – swoops on Inveraray, via Loch Awe; Argyll flees by sea, abandoning his lands and his clansmen in a major humiliation.
Plague rages in Edinburgh.
King Charles, in optimistic mood, reviews his troops at Oxford.

1645

January Montrose withdraws from Kintyre via Loch Awe and Loch Etive to Loch Leven.

Feb 2 Battle of Inverlochy; 3500 men, under Campbell of Auchinbreck vs. 2600 under Montrose and *Alasdair MacCholla*. Argyll watches from the safety of his galley. 1500 Campbells killed, all others routed – Argyll flees once more.

Feb 19 King Charles hears of the stupendous success at Inverlochy.

Feb 22 Desultory peace negotiations between Charles and Parliamentarians allowed to

	abort once more.
	Parliamentarians establish New Model army on national footing; all captured Irish prisoners henceforward ruthlessly executed by Roundheads.
	Royalists lose Shrewsbury. Royalists divided by intrigue, heightened by establishment of second, satellite, court for young Prince of Wales, in Bristol.
April 4	Montrose loots Dundee with impunity, then withdraws.
	Irish Confederates seize Duncannon.
	Antrim arrives in Brussels to negotiate relief of *Alasdair's* forces.
May 9	Battle of Auldearn – "a very absolute victory" for Montrose.
c May 29	*Colla Ciotach* and his sons released from captivity in exchange of hostage.
May 31	Royalists seize and plunder Leicester in one of a series of successful spring offensives.
June 14	Battle of Naseby marks effective defeat of all King Charles' forces in England. Royal correspondence of previous two years captured and subsequently published by Parliament as "The King's Cabinet Opened".
	Royalist rump gathers at Hereford, still dreams of help from Ormonde in Ireland.
	Victory for Montrose at Alford.
July 10	Royalist defeat at Langport, near Bridgewater – which is itself surrendered to Parliamentarians a few days later. There follows the fall of Carlisle, Ponfret, Scarborough...
	King Charles recognizes his position is desperate, but his resolve remains unshaken. Considers going to Scotland. As he moves towards northern Welsh Marches, further fruitless appeals are sent to Ormonde. Irish Confederates will not settle for mere toleration of Catholicism and insist upon full restoration of their religion in Ireland. King Charles gives his agreement in a secret treaty, but Confederates wish for public consent.
	At Lichfield, King Charles hears of Montrose's success at Alford, in which the Covenanters were crushed. Scottish divines appoint a day of penitential Fasting.
Aug 16	**Battle of Kilsyth**; another stunning victory for Montrose. Argyll (again) amongst the first to flee. Montrose now effectively unopposed in Scotland, the cities sue for peace.
Aug 18	Montrose receives King's commission (via Spottiswoode) as Lieutenant Governor of Scotland and enters Glasgow in triumph. *Alasdair MacCholla* knighted.
Aug 21	Bristol besieged by Parliamentarian forces.
Aug 24	King Charles hears news of victory at Kilsyth.
Sep 5	Montrose commences his march south, but without *Alasdair MacCholla*.
Sep 10	Prince Rupert, in extremis, surrenders Bristol on terms and withdraws to Oxford; King Charles, from Raglan, Wales, has him arrested and then banished.
Sep 13	**Battle of Philiphaugh**. Montrose, fighting for almost the first time without *Alasdair MacCholla*, is defeated by Leslie and his forces almost utterly destroyed.
Sep 23	King Charles at Chester, his last significant seaport; is harried onwards; by early October is in Newark. Further losses, even Winchester and Basing House.
	Spain advances 1000 escudos for hire of merchantmen to relieve *Alastair MacCholla*.
Nov 3	King Charles, having lost almost all, leaves Newark.
Nov 5	King Charles reaches Oxford and joins the remnant of his court.
1646	
Jan 16	Parliament learns of King Charles' secret draft treaty with Confederate Irish.

Feb 3	Chester, the vital port for the landing of Irish troops, falls to Roundheads.
February	Too late, Irish Confederates agree to send 6000 troops immediately to aid the king.
Mar 13	Final surrender of Royalists in the West of England.
April	By now, Scots Covenanters and English Parliamentarians on very poor terms. The King resolves to surrender himself to the Scots Covenanting army, which is maintaining a siege at Newark; but they refuse to accept him other than under abject and humiliating terms.
Apr 26	King Charles disappears from Oxford.
May 5	King Charles reappears, when he surrenders himself to the Scots at Newark, under Leslie. Is immediately carried 200 miles northwards, to Newcastle and henceforwards subjected to ceaseless psychological torture by the fanatical Covenanting ministers. Refuses demands to order Montrose to submit, knowing that he is under sentence of death.
	Montrose and *Alasdair MacCholla* fight on, the latter in Arran, Bute and Kintyre.
May 19	King Charles agrees to order Montrose to lay down his arms, with a safe-conduct into exile abroad.
	Argyll joins the King's captors at Newcastle.
	Monro, at Benburb. Hugely significant to Irish and Catholic hopes.
June	King Charles is forced to order Ormonde to cease negotiations with Confederate Irish, and to renew command to Montrose to lay down his arms.
	In late June, Argyll is received courteously at Westminster, to negotiate joint Scots/English terms to deal with the King, in light of the new developments in Ireland which threaten their stolen property and imposed religion.
June 25	Argyll's speech to the English Lords, in which he abandons Scotland's national identity – "one language, in one island, under one king, one in religion, yea, one in covenant."
July	Montrose disbands his forces, at the King's command.
July 30	King Charles absolutely refuses the joint demands of Scots Covenanters and English Roundheads, as brokered by Argyll – will not devolve his royal powers over the military forces, and above all will not sign the Covenant.
July 31	A motion in Parliament to send 6 regiments to Ireland, to the aid of Inchiquin, is narrowly defeated.
Sep 18	Owen Roe O'Neill enters Kilkenny in league with Papal Nuncio – Ormonde's hopes are finally dashed. Confederate Irish Government re-drawn, the native-Irish and Noman-Irish Lords are overthrown. All are now striving for an Irish, Catholic independent state under the Crown.
	Argyll and his henchmen come to understand that King Charles will not sign their Covenant under any circumstances; that they cannot bring him back to Scotland, where his loyal subjects would rally to his cause; that they cannot release him for the same reason; and that they cannot retain him in in England as a captive in their own hands. So they decide to sell him for ransom.
	Only Huntly and *Alasdair MacCholla* fight on in the Royalist cause in Scotland, the latter with the possible hope of reinforcements from his clansmen in Ireland.
November:	Spanish authorities order urgent despatch of two merchantmen and a naval escort to uplift *Alasdair*'s men from Kintyre.
Dec 23:	Financial negotiations complete, the Scots agree to a price for the King but next day nearly lose the cash when King Charles attempts to escape. The guard is re-doubled and General David Leslie personally obstructs any avenue of escape.

1647

Jan 2   Scots Covenanters hand over their King to the English, for imprisonment at Holmby.

Jan 30   Having secured their cash, the Scots pull out, to cries of "Judas" from the inhabitants of Newcastle.

Still *Alasdair MacCholla* fights on, in Kintyre.... 700 of *Alasdair*'s men seem to have been rescued in the early months of the year, since they appear in Spanish muster lists by Spring 1647, but *Alasdair* himself did not withdraw from Scotland until the end of May and Dunivaig was not surrendered until 5 July.

SELECTED BIBLIOGRAPHY

Since this book was written in Colonsay, maximum use was made of sources which are available locally, either in the author's own library or that of Miss Georgina Hobhouse, Scalasaig. The following list of such sources is not exhaustive, but includes many favourites – the dates refer to the edition which was consulted. Some of these works were used for background purposes only, but are listed in the absence of specific references throughout the text.

Bede, Cuthbert, *Argyll's Highlands or Mac Cailein Mor and the Lords of Lorne* (Glasgow 1902)

Brady, O'Dowd & Walker (Eds.), *Ulster, An Illustrated History* (London 1989)

Brett, S.Reed, *The Stuart Century 1603–1714* (London 1964)

Brown, Archibald, *Memorials of Argyleshire* (Greenock 1889)

Buchan, John, *The Marquis of Montrose* (London 1913)

Budge, Donald, *Jura, An Island of Argyll* (Glasgow 1960)

Burke, Hugh, *Assolas*, (An unpublished note for visitors n.d.)

Cameron, Joy, *Prisons and Punishment in Scotland from the Middle Ages to the Present* (Edinburgh 1983)

Campbell of Airds, Alastair, *The Life and Troubled Times of Sir Donald Campbell of Ardnamurchan* (Society of West Highland & Island Historical Research c.1990)

Campbell, J.F., *Popular Tales of the West Highlands* (Paisley & London 1890)

Campbell, J.L., *Canna, The Story of a Hebridean Island* (Edinburgh 1994)

Campbell, Robert, *The Life of the most Illustrious Prince, John, Duke of Argyll and Greenwich* (London 1745)

Clifford, Brendan *The Battles of Knocknanoss and Knockbrack, A speech given to the Dunhallow Heritage Centre on 21st November 1990* (Cork 1991)

Connellan, Owen, *The Annals of Ireland, Translated from the Original Irish of the Four Masters* (Dublin 1846)

Dallat, Cahal (editor) *The Glynns*, Journal of the Glens of Antrim Historical Society Vols 11–25

Deoir, Ian, *Blar Traigh Ghruinneaird* (Edinburgh 1950)

Dewar, John, *The Dewar Manuscripts. Vol 1: Scottish West Highland Folktales* (Glasgow 1964)

Donaldson, Gordon, *Scotland, Volume 3. James V – James VII* (Edinburgh 1990)

Drummond, James, *Sculptured Monuments in Iona & the West Highlands* (Edinburgh 1881)

Ecclestone, Eric, *Sir Walter Raleigh* (Harmondsworth 1941)

Edwards, R.D., *An Atlas of Irish History* (London 1973)

Gardiner, Samuel R., *The Constitutional Documents of the Puritan Revolution 1625–1660* (Oxford 1958)

Giblin, Cathaldus, *Irish Franciscan Mission to Scotland 1619–1646* (Dublin 1964)

Gordon, Patrick, *A Short Abridgement of Britane's Distemper* (Spalding Club 1844)

Grant, I.F., *In the Tracks of Montrose* (London 1931)

Gregory, Donald, *The History of the Western Highlands and Isles of Scotland from A.D. 80 to A.D. 1625* (London 1881)

Grieve, Symington, *The Book of Colonsay and Oronsay* (2 vols., Edinburgh 1923)

Hibbert, Christopher, *The Virgin Queen, The personal History of Elizabeth I* (London 1990)

Hill, George, *An Historical Account of the MacDonnells of Antrim* (Belfast 1873)

Hill, J. Michael, *Celtic Warfare 1595 – 1763* (Edinburgh 1986)

Hill, J. Michael, *Fire and Sword, Sorley Boy MacDonnel and the Rise of Clan Ian Mor, 1538–1590* (London 1993)

Linklater, Eric *Scots of the Swedish Service* in an introduction to *Scots in Sweden* by Berg and

Lagercrantz. Pub by the Nordiska Museet, Swedish Institute (Stockholm 1962). (Thanks to *An Ceathramh* for the loan.)

Loder, John de Vere, *Colonsay and Oronsay in the Isles of Argyll* (Edinburgh 1935)

Macdonald, Charles, *Moidart; or, Among the Clanranalds* (Edinburgh 1989)

Macdonald of Castleton, Donald [Donald J. MacDonald], *Clan Donald* (Loanhead 1978)

McDonnell, John, *The Ulster Civil War of 1641 and its Consequences, with the History of the Irish Brigade under Montrose in 1644–46* (Dublin 1879) N.B. *"This Sketch in vindication of the calumniated Ulster Irish in the war of 1641 is Dedicated in the Memory of Major-General Sir Alexander McDonnell, Knight of the Field, and his Heroic Fellow-Soldiers of the Montrose Irish Brigade"* – written by a direct descendant who had become "an uncompromising Protestant" and been received into the Establishment.

MacGregor, Alexander, *The Feuds of the Clans* (Stirling 1907)

MacInnes, Allan, *Charles I and the Making of the Covenanting Movement 1625–1641* (Edinburgh 1991)

Mackechnie, John, *The Dewar Manuscripts Volume One* (Glasgow 1963)

Mackenzie, A.M. (Ed), *Orain Iain Luim, Songs of John Macdonald, Bard of Keppoch* (Scottish Gaelic Text Soc. 1964)

Mackenzie, John, *Sar-Obair nam Bard Gaelach: or, The Beauties of Gaelic Poetry* (Edinburgh 1904)

Mackenzie, W.C., *The Highlands and Isles of Scotland, A Historical Survey* (Edinburgh 1937)

Mackinnon, Lachlan, *Prose Writings of Donald MacKinnon 1839–1914* (Edinburgh 1956)

Maclean, Donald *The Counter-Reformation in Scotland 1560–1930* (London 1931)

McNeill, F.C.A., *Oransay and Its Monastery; Iona's Rival* (Glasgow, n.d.)

McNeill, Murdoch, *Colonsay, One of the Hebrides* (Edinburgh 1910)

M'Sparran, Archibald, *The Irish Legend of M'Donnell and the Norman De Borgos* (Glasgow n.d.)

Moncreiffe, Iain, *The Highland Clans* (London 1973)

Monro, Donald, *Description of The Western Isles of Scotland called Hybrides* (Glasgow 1818)

Munro, Neil, *John Splendid. The Tale of a Poor Gentleman and the Little Wars of Lorn* (Edin. 1948)

O'Faolain, Sean, *The Great O'Neill, A Biography of Hugh O'Neill Earl of Tyrone, 1550–1616* (Cork 1992)

Pennant, Thomas, *A Tour in Scotland and Voyage to the Hebrides* (Chester 1772)

Power, Patrick C., *History of South Tipperary* (Cork 1989)

Reid, Stuart, *The Campaigns of Montrose. A Military History of the Civil War in Scotland 1639 to 1646* (Edinburgh 1990)

Ritchie, A & E., *Iona, Past and Present* (Edinburgh 1947)

Robinson, Philip, *The Plantation of Ulster, British Settlement in an Irish Landscape 1600–1670* (Belfast 1994)

Ross, Stewart, *The Stewart Dynasty* (Nairn 1993)

R.C.A.H.M.(Scotland), *Argyll, an Inventory of the Monuments, Volume 5* (1984)

Sanderson, Margaret, *Mary Stewart's People: Life in Mary Stewart's Scotland* (Edinburgh 1987)

Sanderson, William, *A Compleat History of the Lives and Reigns of Mary Queen of Scotland and her son and Successor James the Sixth, King of Scotland and (After Queen Elizabeth) King of Great Britain. France and Ireland, The First (of ever blessed memory)* (London 1656)

Smith, G.G., *The Book of Islay; Documents Illustrating the History of the Island* (Privately Printed 1895)

Smout T.C., *A History of the Scottish People 1560–1830* (London 1985)

Steer & Bannerman, *Late Medieval Monumental Sculpture in the West Highlands* (Edinburgh 1977)

Stevenson, David, *Alasdair MacColla and the Highland Problem in the 17th Century* (Edinburgh 1980)

Stevenson, David, *The Covenanters. The National Covenant and Scotland* (Edinburgh 1988)

Stone, Jeffrey, *Illustrated Maps of Scotland, from Blaeu's Atlas Novus of the 17th Century* (London 1991)

Stradling, R.A., *The Spanish Monarchy and Irish Mercenaries. The Wild Geese in Spain 1618–68* (Dublin 1994)

Watson, William J., *Bardachd Ghaidhlig; specimens of Gaelic poetry 1550–1900* (Stirling 1932)

Wedgwood, C.V., *The King's Peace 1637–1641* (London 1983)

Wedgwood, C.V., *The King's War 1641–1647* (London 1983)

Wedgwood, C.V., *The Trial of Charles I* (London 1983)

Whyte, I & K, *The Changing Scottish Landscape 1500–1800* (London 1991)

Wishart, George, *Memoirs of James, Marquis of Montrose 1639–1650* (London 1893)

Wood, Ian S. (ed.) *Scotland and Ulster* (Edinburgh 1994)

Youngson, Peter (ed.),*Stories of Jura collected by Rev. Charles Robertson, "Robertson fada"* (Kirriemuir c.1987)

Additional material

The librarians of Trinity College,Dublin, The British Library and The National Library (Edinburgh), were most helpful in providing access to the following material. In some cases photocopies were supplied and, since Colonsay is rather remote, the courtesy was much appreciated.

Black, Ronald, *A Manuscript of Cathal MacMuireadhaigh* ("Celtica", x, 1973)

Calendar of State Papers relating to Ireland

Campbell A., *The Manuscript History of Craignish* ("Miscellany" iv SHS 1926)

Gilbert, J.T., *A Contemporary History of affairs in Ireland from 1641 to 1652* (Dublin 1879–1880)

Macdonald A.J. & A.M. (eds.), *The Macdonald Collection of Gaelic Poetry* (Inverness 1911)

McNeill C. (Ed), *The Tanner Letters* (IMC 1943)

Matheson, A. (ed), *Traditions of Alasdair MacColla,* (TGSG v 1958)

Pitcairn, Robert *Criminal Trials in Scotland*

Register of the Privy Council of Scotland

Spalding, J. *Memorials of the Trubles in Scotland* (Spalding Club 1851)

Turner, Sir James, *Memoirs of His Own Life and Times* (Bannatyne Club 1829)

Watson, W.J. (ed) *Unpublished Gaelic Poetry iii* (Scottish Gaelic Studie ii 1927)

Lambert's report is to be found in the Register of the Great Seal of Scotland.
Leslie's report is in the Scottish Record Office.
Rev. Weir's journal is in the National Library of Scotland – Woodrow Mss, Quatro xxix ff 63–8

Campbeltown Library kindly provided *Account of Massacre of Dunaverty*, a traditional account first published in the Argyllshire Monthly Magazine.